EMPEROR, PREFECTS, AND KINGS

Emperor, Prefects, & Kings

The Roman West, 395-565

P.S. Barnwell

The University of North Carolina Press

Chapel Hill and London

First published in the
United States in 1992 by
The University of Carolina Press

Library of Congress Cataloging-in-Publication-Data

Barnwell, P.S.
   Emperor, prefects, and kings : the Roman West. 395-565 / P.S.
Barnwell.
     p.   cm.
   Includes bibliographical references and index.
   ISBN 0-8078-2071-7 (cloth) : alk. paper)
   1. Rome—Politics and government—284-476.   2. Italy—Politics and
government—476-1268.   I. Title.
JC89.B36   1992
320.937′6—dc20   92-16720
                                               CIP

Photoset in North Wales by
Derek Doyle & Associates, Mold, Clwyd.
Printed in Great Britain by
Redwood Press Ltd, Melksham

Contents

Preface

This book had its origin as part of a doctoral dissertation prepared at the University of Leeds. It is a pleasure to record my gratitude to that institution, and to many of its members, for having provided the most congenial of work-places: I owe a particular debt to the staff of the Brotherton Library for their helpfulness, courtesy and friendliness.

Dr I.N. Wood was a demanding supervisor, always ready to entertain discussion, but never to force his conclusions upon me: without his enthusiasm, both while I was a student and subsequently, this book would not have existed. Advice and criticism were provided by Professor G.R.J. Jones; his encouragement, together with that of Dr C.R.E. Cubitt, Dr J.M. Hill and Mr R.K. Morris, have meant a great deal. Away from Leeds, the book has benefited greatly from Dr J.L. Nelson's challenging criticism of its earlier incarnation, and her support for the project has been an important factor in bringing it to fruition. Although other people's comments have improved the book and saved me from a number of errors, the views expressed are my sole responsibility, as are any remaining infelicities.

I am grateful to Mr A.T. Adams for drawing the maps which appear at the end of the volume.

Finally, but by no means least, I owe my parents more than can be expressed. In many ways, both practical and less tangible, they have been supportive and encouraging over a period of many years: without them, I would never have been in a position to start research, still less to complete a book.

P.S.B.

Introduction

The subject of this book is the administrative structure of the western half of the Roman Empire in the fifth century, and that of the 'barbarian' kingdoms which came to be established in the territory of the Empire during the course of that century. My purpose is to examine the extent to which 'barbarian' government was influenced by its Roman predecessor. The period chosen commences with the 'definitive' splitting of the Empire on the death of Emperor Theodosius I in 395, and its end lies in the sixth century, at approximately the time of the death of Emperor Justinian and the subsequent abandonment of serious attempts to re-conquer the west from the 'barbarians' who had occupied it in the intervening period.

Although much research has been undertaken on both late-Roman administration and the governmental structures of individual 'barbarian' kingdoms, the fifth century has often been seen in the shadow of the fourth. Implicit in much of the literature is a feeling that the fifth century saw the disintegration (in the face of 'barbarian' hostility) of an ordered Roman governmental system, the elements of which can be seen in the fourth century, and its replacement by a series of more or less disorganised 'Germanic' administrations. In the present book, by contrast, an attempt has been made to arrive at an understanding of the fifth-century western Empire on its own terms – to see what logic underlay its functioning without considering the way in which it differed from its fourth-century predecessor. Once the character of fifth-century Roman government has been elucidated, and the problems in reconstructing it have been appreciated, the question of 'barbarian' administration is examined and is set against the specifically fifth-century Roman background.

A second, though related, feature of this book concerns its methodology. Faced with the scarcity of source material for much of the period,[1] previous authors have tended to place equal weight on each type of source, regardless of its individual purpose, and to try to obtain answers to the same questions from all the surviving writings of the age. In addition, in order to render the problems posed by the paucity of evidence for the fifth-century imperial administration less intractable, the writings of Cassiodorus (produced in the sixth century) have often been used to amplify understanding of the previous era. The

1

rationale behind this is that they relate to the most obviously 'Roman' of the 'barbarian' kingdoms, and that whatever remained of Roman traditions in the sixth century must reflect the period before the 'barbarians' arrived. In this book, however, reading back from later sources has to a large extent been deliberately avoided. Although this approach renders discussion of the fifth-century imperial administration more difficult, it is believed that it results in a new understanding both of that governmental system and of its 'barbarian' successor. In addition, the method adopted enables some of the sources themselves to be examined in a fresh light, and, as a by-product of the enquiry, some new suggestions are made as to their character. Indeed, it is stressed throughout the book that an understanding of the nature of each individual document – of the reasons why it contains the information it does, and omits other data – is a vital pre-requisite to its use: without that background, it is not possible to arrive at an appreciation of the kinds of question each may be expected to answer, and what conclusions to draw from the answers (or lack of them) it gives. Although this method may at first appear to limit the range of topics which can be discussed, it is believed that the result of its application is to permit of greater clarity concerning the issues which can be addressed.

With one exception, all the available types of source material – the written word (including epigraphy), numismatics, and (where appropriate) archaeological evidence – have been used. The exception is material written in the Greek language. One reason for this is that, although Greek narrative histories were produced in the fifth century, and might be thought to fill a gap left by the Latin sources, their authors had little real interest in the western half of the Empire.[2] Even in cases in which the west did receive attention, Greek authors were writing at a distance from the events they described and, since communications between the two halves of the Empire were becoming increasingly poor from as early as the time of Stilicho, the information conveyed in works composed in the east may not always be accurate in terms of detail. The problem was appreciated by some of the Greek writers, such as Eunapius, themselves:

> During the time of Eutropius the Eunuch, it was impossible to include in a history an accurate account of events in the west, for the length and duration of the sea-voyage made the reports late and useless because they were out of date, as if they had fallen into some chronic and long-drawn-out illness. If any officials or soldiers had access to information on political activity they related it as they wished, biased by friendships or hostility or a desire to please someone. And if you brought together three or four of them with conflicting versions as witnesses, there would be a great argument which would proceed from passionate and heated interjections into a pitched battle. They would say, 'Where

did you get this from?', 'When did Stilicho see you?', 'Would you have seen the event?', so that it was quite a task to sort out the tangle. From the merchants there was no reasonable information, since they either told many lies or sold what they wished to profit from.[3]

A few Greek authors were rather better placed to gain information concerning the west: perhaps the best-known example is that of Olympiodorus, whose sources lay amongst the supporters of Stilicho.[4] Even in those instances, however, there were misunderstandings and problems in translating official titles. For example, Gregory of Tours, in one of the passages of his *Decem libri historiarum* which is based on the work of the fifth-century historian Renatus Frigiredus, describes Aetius as having held the office of *cura palatii* at the time of the attempted usurpation of the western imperial throne by John.[5] A Greek author, Philostorgius, however, believed that Aetius was a *hupostratêgos*, or low-ranking military commander.[6] The potential for this kind of confusion was clearly appreciated by at least some contemporaries, because Avitus of Vienne on one occasion advised the Burgundian king, Sigismund, to write to the eastern emperor in Latin rather than in Greek, in the hope that this would reduce the risk of misunderstanding arising between the two rulers.[7]

In view of the problems posed by the Greek sources, such documents have not been used extensively in the following pages, and references to them are confined to places where they support or confirm evidence gleaned from Latin material. A brief exploratory survey of the Greek writings has been carried out, and has not produced any evidence which would contradict the arguments presented here. At a later date, when the eastern documents have been analysed on their own terms and in relation to the eastern Empire, it may be possible to arrive at a better understanding of their potential contribution to the administrative history of the fifth-century west.

In order to keep the references in the notes within bounds, not all the relevant secondary literature has always been cited, but an attempt has been made to list other important works in the bibliography. In particular, the notes do not include references to many of the well-known major histories of the fifth and sixth centuries, or to the prosopographical works relating to the period: this should not be taken to mean that they have not been consulted with profit. Within the notes themselves, the rescripts contained in the Theodosian and Justinianic Codes are cited in chronological order.

PART I

The Emperor and the Imperial Court

The government of the later western Empire consisted of a number of overlapping elements. At the centre of the administration was the person of the emperor, together with his courtiers – his *comites* or 'companions' – who formed the basis of the central government. Then there were the provincial administrators, ranging from the governors of individual provinces to the much more powerful praetorian and urban prefects who were responsible for government in large groups of provinces: such governors were not members of the imperial court during their terms of office in the provinces, but could be associated with it, as *comites* of the emperor, at other stages of their careers.[1] There were also local governmental officials, based in the *ciuitates* and other local administrative units of the Empire, but they seldom, if ever, aspired to membership of the imperial court during their tenure of local office, and are not the subject of the present study. Finally, there was the Senate. By the fifth century, this body had lost almost all its formal executive functions and was, in reality, little more than a self-supporting, and often self-interested, body of aristocrats. Some senators might, however, be involved directly in the government either as *comites* of the emperor, or as provincial administrators, and the collective opinion or advice of senators was still sought on occasion. Although the Senate had little formal power left, the co-operation of its members, who were large land-owners and influential patrons, considerably eased the task of implementing government policy: that the opposition of the Senate was something to be avoided is graphically illustrated by the events of 476, when the refusal of its members to give the Germanic federates a share of the wealth of Italy unleashed the events which led to the establishment of Odoacer as the ruler of the Italian peninsula. On account of the lack of formal collective executive functions in the fifth-century western Empire, however, the Senate as a body will not be discussed in the pages which follow, but it must be borne in mind that many of the men who held the governmental offices which provide the subject of this work were members of that traditional, and quintessentially Roman, aristocratic body.[2]

5

The main foci of attention in the pages which follow are those elements of the imperial administrative system which were centred on the emperor's court, and those which concerned the governance of the provinces at a level above the purely local. Rather than treating these two elements together, the scheme adopted here divides them so that the former is examined in Part I, and the latter in the first chapter of Part II, which traces the evolution of provincial administration from the 'definitive' splitting of the Empire in 395 into the sixth century. The sources for both elements of fifth-century 'Roman' government are, however, treated together in Part I in order to avoid the unnecessary duplication which would otherwise be engendered by the fact that, in many cases, the same documents reflect both spheres of activity.

1

The Sources

Before any detailed examination of the administrative structure of the western Empire in the fifth century can be undertaken, it is vital that the nature of the sources should be appreciated: without that background, it is impossible to determine the precise questions it is prudent to ask of the documents which have survived from the period, or what type of answers to expect from them, and an unnecessarily confused picture could emerge.

Almost all the written documents of the fifth century which have any bearing on imperial administration, except for imperial law collections, were produced outside Italy, and certainly not in circumstances closely associated with the imperial court. The evidence furnished by the 'narrative' histories – the chronicles published in T. Mommsen's three volumes of *chronica minora* – is, in addition, vitiated by the conflicting and often artificial chronologies of such documents[1] and by the brevity of the entries dictated by the chronicle form.[2] Further, the inspiration for these works was primarily ecclesiastical in that they form continuations of the great world chronicle of St Jerome. Such men as Hydatius, writing in Galicia, Victor, in Africa, the authors of the Gallic Chronicles, writing in *Gallia Narbonensis*,[3] and even Prosper Tiro, in Rome, were much more concerned with the Church, with natural wonders, and with the broad course of events interpreted in a theological, or even eschatological, fashion than with the workings of secular administration. This is equally true for the government at Ravenna, Constantinople and even in the regions in which the authors lived and wrote: as R.A. Markus has shown, a writer such as Prosper Tiro viewed 'historical narratives' as being among those things which could draw men's minds to the contemplation of God.[4] Despite such problems, these documents are the nearest the fifth century approaches to narrative material, and they contain much information on secular matters which would otherwise be lost,[5] being more helpful for the subject of the present enquiry than are their elder brothers as ecclesiastical texts, the full-scale theological works of Augustine, Orosius and Salvian, whose *Weltanschauung* they share. The writings

7

of these latter were also produced outside Italy, and, although in part dealing with the relationship between the heavenly and earthly kingdoms, their approach is *via* the broad sweep of human endeavour and morality: the details of earthly government are not their concern. Very occasionally, reference is made to a specific incident, and some enlightenment may be afforded, but even in such passages it is greater for questions of morality and social attitudes.

Of more, though still very patchy, assistance for the present subject are some of the letter-collections of the period. The letters of Augustine and Pope Leo I are, as would be expected, primarily of ecclesiastical interest, though they do contain passing references to governmental officials with whom their authors came into contact. More can be gleaned from the secular letters, in particular those of Sidonius Apollinaris and Quintus Aurelius Symmachus. The letters of the former, even those produced during their author's tenure of the city prefecture (*c.* 468), are fundamentally social and literary documents, as are his poems, and only contain fragments of useful information. This is also true of the vast majority of Quintus Aurelius Symmachus' letters: like the theological works, these documents are of more use for an examination of the social and cultural world of the late-fourth and early-fifth centuries than for an enquiry into the functioning of the imperial court and other administrative *fora* of the Empire. Part of the collection of Quintus Aurelius Symmachus' letters is, however, of much greater relevance, for book X contains the official letters sent by their author during his own tenure of the city prefecture, in 384: as will be apparent when the position of the city prefect is discussed in Chapter 5, these documents are such a mine of information that they cannot be ignored even though strictly they fall outside the chronological scope of the present study. Equally important is a short set of letters relating to Quintus Aurelius Symmachus' nephew, Symmachus (the younger), when he, in his turn, was prefect of Rome, in 418-419: regrettably, this collection only relates to the events surrounding the contested papal election of that year and Symmachus' role in maintaining order within the City, but it is, nevertheless, of great importance.

The one major set of documents which is directly concerned with government, and is, indeed, a product of the administration, is the *Codex Theodosianus*. The imperial law of Rome was communicated by the emperor to his officials by means of a series of edicts or rescripts, often issued in response to a specific case of request for enlightenment. Such rescripts were usually addressed to individual officials and were posted up in prominent places, usually wherever the emperor happened to be at the time, though sometimes elsewhere also: by this means, rescripts gave general application to laws issued in response to specific cases.[6] Analysis of the documents contained within the Code is, therefore, of primary importance in establishing in what spheres of activity the officials addressed were engaged. None the less, there is one shortcoming of this tool: the majority of the Code's documents, and not only those issued in the fifth century or in the western Empire, are addressed to those officials whose duties took them away from the imperial court for a high proportion of the time. Thus, for example, there are approximately two hundred and eight documents in the collection produced in the western half of the Empire after AD 394 which are addressed to the praetorian prefects, sixty-nine to the proconsuls of Africa, and forty-nine to the city prefects, who were situated nearer to the court. As regards laws addressed specifically to *court* officials, the highest number is twenty-six for the *comes rerum priuatarum*, with half that number for the *comes sacrarum largitionum*; the masters of the offices only received seven, and the *comites domesticorum* a mere two. This bias in favour of those officials who operated outside the palace is understandable, since those with easy and regular access to the emperor will have had much less need than those who operated at a distance from him for his will to be expressed in the formal written form of a rescript. The effect of this is of the greatest importance, for it means that there is much less information on the court officials than could be desired: the balance of data is tipped towards the provinces, and in the same direction, therefore, as that provided by the chronicles. In addition to that bias in the Code, there is another, equally important one, in favour of the top rank of officials. The reason for this is that subordinate officials would usually appeal to their immediate superiors for advice, rather than directly to the emperor, thus making the issuing of rescripts to them by the emperors a rare occurrence. These limitations do not mean that the *Codex Theodosianus* is of no practical assistance: it remains the largest single source for fifth-century administration, and the type of information contained within it is of a different nature from that found elsewhere, as it is primarily concerned with law and the government. It is essential to recognise, however, that it does not contain answers to all questions, and that the questions to which answers can be expected from it are to some extent governed by the nature of the document.

Another major source which is a product of the administration itself is the proceedings of the 411 Council of Carthage. This is a significant text in that it is almost the only place in which the lower levels of the administration can be seen in operation, but it is, once again, a document produced in the provinces and in connection with the Church: light is not, therefore, cast on the workings of the imperial court. The existence and importance of the lesser officials seen in action in these proceedings is underlined by the *Notitia Dignitatum* – apparently a handbook of all the officials, both of high and of low status, in the imperial and provincial administration. While the *Notitia* lists such officials and illustrates their spheres of jurisdiction, it is no more than a list, and presents a schematic picture which may not always accurately reflect the more complex and shifting patterns of everyday government. In addition, although the portion of this document which relates to the western Empire may have been compiled *c.* 425, it is probable that its author used information which was out of date and not strictly relevant to contemporary administration.[7] The *Notitia* does not appear to have been an official document and may, perhaps, have been produced by someone with an antiquarian interest, thus rendering it less helpful for the present enquiry than might at first appear.

There are two further types of source which must be briefly examined. First, there is a small body of useful material in some of the hagiographical literature produced in the early middle ages. Most such material is, however, removed in time from the fifth century, is once again Church-orientated, and was in the main produced outside Italy itself: these factors limit its role in elucidating fifth-century Roman administration to a supportive one and to very restricted cases. One major later document which may be of more assistance, is Gregory of Tours' *Decem libri historiarum*, which contains passages based upon the lost work of Renatus Frigiredus, though the total length of such passages is very short.

Secondly, there is a body of information preserved in the official inscriptions which survive from the fifth century, especially at Rome. Most of these documents are commemorative, whether they take the form of epitaphs, dedications, or commemorations of specific events such as the restoration of buildings. Save in the case of the last category, they do not illustrate anything of an official's actual functions. What inscriptions do, almost uniquely, permit, however, is the reconstruction of the progress of men's careers, on account of the fact that it is not uncommon for all the positions a man had held, both past and present, to be recorded in them. A single example of the relevant form of inscription, found on the base of an honorific statue, will illustrate the point:

> To Flavius Olbius Auxentius Drauco, *uir clarissimus* and *illuster*, a man of patrician family, who discharged the duties of the Senate with ready devotion; *comes* of the first order and vicar of the city of Rome; *comes* of the sacred consistory; prefect of the city of Rome ...[8]

The use to which material such as this can be put will be seen at the beginning of Chapter 5.

2

The Emperor

The limitations imposed by the nature of the sources become immediately apparent in an examination of the position and function of the western emperors, an important prelude to any discussion of the mechanics of imperial government. The logical place to start would seem to be the Theodosian Code, because it contains the only major body of evidence produced directly by the emperors and their administration. However, the Code does not permit much advance beyond an ability to make the simple statement that the emperor's function, as seen through it, was to make law, either in the form of edicts (that is, in matters in which he himself took the initiative), or in the form of rescripts (in response to specific requests for enlightenment and clarification, mostly on procedural matters, from the judicial and governmental officials of the Empire). Although it is not always easy to distinguish between the two types of document, it is likely, since the vast majority of the material contained in the Code is in the form of letters from the emperors to specific individuals, that the latter − rescripts − was the more common. There is only one direct external reference to the emperors' function as law-givers: in the panegyric Sidonius Apollinaris wrote on Avitus, it is indicated that whereas Avitus as praetorian prefect had administered the law, now, as emperor, he would have to make law.[1] It seems clear, however, despite this single brief statement, that law-making was a very important function, for the Code and its associated Novels contain some four hundred and twenty-two laws issued by fifth-century western emperors, with new documents still being produced into the reign of Anthemius in the late 460s.

Other sources are much less helpful. It is apparent from Sidonius Apollinaris' panegyric in honour of Anthemius that the emperor could be supposed to be something of a military leader, as the author expresses the hope that Anthemius would overcome the Vandal king, Geiseric.[2] Anthemius did not, however, personally participate in such a campaign, and the impression may be gained that the emperor's role was more as a figure-head who should direct wars from a distance, without endangering himself, and who should derive credit from military success without risking having his reputation damaged by failure. This idea gains additional strength from the fact that there are only three references in the fifth century to a western emperor taking the field in person, one implied by Sidonius Apollinaris, and the other two, in Hydatius' Chronicle and the *Chronicle of Saragossa*, more definite, recording that Majorian campaigned against the Vandals in Spain, *c.* 460.[3] This is all the more significant because military campaigns and battles are widely reported in the chronicles, and it is unlikely that an imperial presence would go unremarked, especially as the leaders of the armies are almost always named. The reference to Majorian's campaign is almost the sole occasion on which an emperor is mentioned in the chronicles other than in relation to the succession, thus giving the impression that the emperors did not have a very high active profile in the provinces, where most such documents were produced.

The contrast between the importance of the emperor as a law-giver and the apparently low level of imperial activity revealed by the chronicles becomes more striking when the relative amount of space such documents devote to imperial women in the west is observed. The significance of women for the succession is clear: Galla Placidia was married against her will to Constantius in order to enhance his position as emperor by giving him a dynastic claim to the throne;[4] she was later sent back to the west as *augusta* to hold the regency for the young Valentinian III.[5] Later, Theodosius II married his daughter, Eudoxia, to Valentinian III, in order to link the position of the two rulers more closely by making the dynastic bond between them stronger.[6] Subsequently, when Maximus seized the imperial crown, he forced this same Eudoxia to marry him in the hope that he would thereby gain a more legitimate title to rule.[7] Perhaps even more telling is the case of Valentinian III's half-sister, Honoria, who, after an affair with Eugenius, a *procurator*, was expelled from Italy. Cassiodorus, writing later, thought that the reason for this was that she had attempted to persuade the Huns to invade Italy: her exile is more likely to have been brought about by a fear that if she produced children, they would stand to be heirs to the western throne and would, therefore, be potential rivals to any children Valentinian himself might have had.[8]

It was not only in this relatively passive sense that fifth-century western imperial women were important, because they could dispense patronage and engage in political intrigue. Galla Placidia, for example, was responsible for recalling Boniface from Africa and for setting up the situation in which he could oppose Aetius in open battle.[9] It is also alleged that, after the murder of Valentinian III, the widowed Eudoxia called in Geiseric, King of the Vandals (to whose son her daughter,

Eudocia, had earlier been betrothed) to save her from the usurpation of Maximus.[10] Further, it is significant that the *Chronicle of 511* records that, after her marriage to Valentinian III, 'Eudoxia received the kingdom at Ravenna',[11] as if this were a significant fact, while Bishop Germanus of Auxerre was (as his biographer, Constantius, knew) clearly aware of the position and power of Galla Placidia in her position as regent for Valentinian III, since it was to her that this Gallic bishop presented his petition on behalf of the Alans.[12]

Such records of activity on the part of imperial women do not reach the level of those known for the eastern Empire,[13] but are, none the less, in marked contrast to the lack of evidence, save in the making of law, for activity on the part of the emperors. This lack of perceived action is often interpreted as a sign of the decadence of the Empire, and the emperors themselves are characterised almost as 'empereurs fainéants' in the same way as the later Merovingian kings are described as 'rois fainéants'. To view emperors in this way, however, is to pre-judge the question as to how contemporary society expected emperors to behave: it is, therefore, suggested that a fresh examination of the issue is necessary, and that the discussion should be based on what the sources reveal both of the attitudes of the men whose actions they describe, and of the attitudes of their authors to their subjects.

When the type of information concerning emperors which the chroniclers do record is analysed, it becomes apparent that one of the most important subjects, in their eyes, was the question of the imperial succession. There is a fairly large volume of material in the chronicles concerning the succession, and some of it shows that their authors were, at least on occasion, clearly aware of the detailed circumstances surrounding the creation of new emperors. For example, Hydatius notes that:

> On the order of Emperor Leo, Anthemius, the brother of Procopius, accompanied by Marcellinus and other chosen *comites*, and with a considerable army, set out from Constantinople, according to the will of God, for Italy.[14]

Equally striking is the fact that Prosper Tiro and Hydatius were clearly aware that Valentinian III was at first only *caesar*, and was not elevated to the position of *augustus* until later: this shows that the distinction was both understood and perceived to be of some significance.[15]

The importance of emperors may be underlined by the fact that 'rebels', of whom there were many in the fifth century, regularly continued to seek to create or exploit emperors right up to the 470s. To take only a few examples: the early fifth-century risings of Constantine

III and of Jovinus were both primarily supported by members of the provincial aristocracies, and are better seen as expressions of the frustration of certain sections of the provincial community at the apparent inability of emperors based in Rome to deal adequately with the problems of the Gallic prefecture after the breaching of the Rhine frontier *c.* 406. It is true that even after the suppression of Jovinus by Honorius' master of the soldiers, Constantius, northern Gaul still did not immediately return fully to the 'legitimate' imperial fold, but it is significant that during that period the aristocracy based at Trier appears to have supported the puppet emperor Attalus by minting coins in his name.[16] This provides eloquent testimony to the fact that at least in the early fifth century it was individual emperors, or the kind of Empire some of them personified, who were opposed, rather than the concept of Empire itself.

Similar patterns can be seen later in the century. When Majorian and Ricimer removed Aetius they created a new emperor in the person of Majorian himself;[17] when Majorian, in his turn, was murdered by Ricimer, a new emperor, Severus, was immediately made.[18] Indeed, it is only with the demise of Severus that a period without a western emperor was initiated. Too much should not be read into even this, for little is known of the precise circumstances of, or events which succeeded, Severus' death: it is not even absolutely certain whether Severus died of natural causes or was murdered by Ricimer.[19] Furthermore, once Leo had sent Anthemius to take up the western crown, there was a resumption of fighting over the imperial title in the west for about ten years, during which there was no reported attempt to dispense with western emperors altogether.[20] It is against this background that the factional manoeuvrings in Gaul during the same period have to be seen. The obscure *coniuratio Marcelliniana*, of the years following the deposition of Avitus in *c.* 456, was probably no more than an attempt to find a new Gallic leader to replace Avitus.[21] The apparent complicity of the aristocracy of Lyons in the Burgundian expansion into their territory at the same time is likely to have been an expression of similar opposition to Majorian.[22] In turn, Aegidius' later secession to northern Gaul was most certainly a result of the deposition of the emperor (Majorian) who had promoted him to the position of master of the soldiers in Gaul.[23] What these, and other, events in fact betoken is not a series of revolutionary attempts to overthrow the position of the emperor, but, rather, a series of rebellions against the individuals who held that position.[24] This clearly demonstrates the vitality of the idea of Empire, not only in the eyes of the aristocrats who participated in the events outlined, but also in those of the chroniclers who recorded them. If the position of emperor had been unimportant, it would not have mattered who had held the title or by whom emperors were nominated or created: in short, no one would have thought it worth fighting over the issue or recording it.

Despite the fact that emperors were considered of importance, it has already been noted that they do not appear to have engaged in one particular, high-profile, form of activity – military leadership. This cannot simply be taken to mean that they were militarily incompetent: three of the last seven western emperors had held high military positions before assuming the purple – Majorian as *comes domesticorum*,[25] Anthemius as master of the soldiers,[26] and Julius Nepos as master of the soldiers in Dalmatia.[27] This, together with the lack of criticism in the sources (even in the early-fifth century when they are more plentiful) that emperors did not participate in military campaigns, leads to the suspicion that such activity was not seen as being an imperial duty. Although the literature of the tetrarchic period places great stress on the military nature of the imperial office,[28] it is important not to assume that the same values were prevalent in the fifth century. In fact, M. Reydellet has shown that as far as at least one contemporary writer, Sidonius Apollinaris, was concerned, the emperor was primarily an aristocratic figure – a dispenser of patronage and offices.[29] Such a change of attitudes is not, perhaps, surprising, given that the consequences of emperors being actively engaged in military campaigns had been felt in the fourth century, particularly with the problems caused by the defeat of Julian at the hands of the Persians and, more especially, the death of Valens at Adrianople in 378. In the years immediately following the latter disaster, it is not possible to discern any 'policy' with regard to emperors leading military campaigns, for the circumstances of Theodosius I's reign meant that he had little option but to take the field himself on occasion, while the fact that Honorius was still only a boy when he became western emperor in 395 meant that he could not be expected to lead the army in person. However, it is possible that the lessons of 378 had been learnt because the *missorium* of Theodosius shows the emperor dressed in civilian costume, not in armour, and, during the succeeding Theodosian era, emperors were not depicted on coins as military figures:[30] it may also be significant that neither Honorius (when he came of age), nor Arcadius in the east, ever assumed the role of military leader.

If, then, the emperor was not supposed to be a military leader, what was his function, and how important was it? Attention has already been drawn to Sidonius Apollinaris' views on the matter, and it has been demonstrated that even in the late 460s emperors were active in the making and interpretation of imperial law. It is not surprising that the chronicles do not note this legislative activity: they are annalistic in form and predominantly provincial in provenance, and legislation rarely produced the type of event of immediately-perceived import which their authors were likely to record, especially when it was enacted in distant Italy. It is important that this should not lead to a minimisation of the significance of law-making, particularly given the precise nature of imperial law, which made the emperor the ultimate source of appeal in specific matters.

It may be possible to refine the picture of the emperor as law-maker and patron, and to ask whether he was perceived as being of the same importance in this respect throughout the west. One way of looking at this is to analyse the numbers of rescripts sent to each part of the western Empire, since the result should reflect the areas in which the highest resident officials most frequently appealed to the emperors for assistance in solving their problems. There is unlikely to be significant regional bias in the documents preserved in the Theodosian Code, as there is no real evidence that its compilers used more material from one area of the western Empire than from another. Indeed, it has been suggested that, for the forty years prior to its publication in 438, the Code is likely to be fairly complete except for the years after 432: in addition, the Novels issued by the western (though not all the eastern) emperors are almost certainly all recorded.[31] In order to ensure as strict a comparability as possible between the various regions of the west in the following analysis, it is only the rescripts issued to the highest provincial officials which can be taken into account, because all the lower office-holders would first appeal to their immediate superiors rather than going straight to the emperors themselves. The officials concerned are, therefore, the proconsul of Africa, the praetorian prefects, and the city prefect.

To start with Africa: it is clear that the emperor was considered of great importance in that province, because sixty-nine rescripts were addressed to its proconsuls after 394. This flow of documents is all the more impressive when it is realised that it ceases in 429, after the Vandals became active in the area, rather than continuing until the 460s as in the case of the rescripts addressed to the praetorian and city prefects. The cessation in 429 is also significant because it is very abrupt, there being no sign of a tailing off before that date, thus perhaps indicating the impact of the arrival of the Vandals even before the take-over of Carthage, the proconsular headquarters, *c*. 440.[32] It might be assumed that, after the last of the rescripts, the position of the emperor was perceived to be of much less importance in the area than formerly. It would not, however, be true to say that the Empire meant nothing further to the government of the provinces of Africa and Byzacena, even after *c*. 440, because Geiseric would scarcely have responded to Eudoxia's call for assistance against the usurper Maximus *c*. 455 had he not thought that he could benefit from it himself, nor would he have been so keen for Eudocia to marry his son, Huneric, unless he had thought that an alliance with the imperial dynasty would in some way enhance his status or legitimise his power.

Similar motivation may also be seen in Geiseric's further attempts to have Olybrius, the husband of Eudocia's sister, Placidia, made emperor.[33] What may have happened is not so much a total collapse of imperial authority in Africa as a change in the type of importance attached to the position of the emperor in Africa – a move away from his being the ultimate source of justice in a practical sense, to his being a more distant, perhaps hegemonic, authority, a figure-head who could in some way legitimise or protect the power of local rulers.

The position in Gaul may not have been very different, though the process began there at least a decade earlier, with the eventual settlement of the Visigoths in the province of Aquitanica II. King Atauulf of the Visigoths may have thought that his marriage to Galla Placidia would somehow give him greater authority to rule part of the Empire.[34] Although neither any system of rescripts between either the Visigothic or Burgundian kings and the emperors, nor any similar means of communication is known, it is not impossible that kings could occasionally have sought the advice or assistance of emperors, and it may be significant that the *Uita Lupicini* depicts Chilperic I of the Burgundians very much as a Roman official.[35] In addition, emperors must have been thought to be of some importance, because the Visigoths became involved in the factionalism of the Gallo-Roman aristocracy when they tried to influence the imperial succession by assisting the Gallo-Roman supporters of Avitus.[36] The Burgundians became similarly involved, both when they opposed Majorian,[37] and when later (under Gundobad, a representative of Ricimer's kin-group) they assisted Glycerius to become emperor.[38] This change in type of imperial authority was not restricted to areas of the 'barbarian' settlement: even for those areas of Gaul which remained directly subject to the emperors, remarkably few surviving rescripts were issued to the Gallic prefects after *c.* 410,[39] indicating that even in such a thoroughly 'Roman' area as Provence, the heartland of the prefecture, the emperor was no longer, in the fifth century, regularly used as the ultimate source of justice. It is striking that, of the two hundred and eight rescripts in the Theodosian Code sent by western emperors to praetorian prefects after 394, only eighteen, or less than a tenth, were sent to the Gallic prefects.

The other one hundred and ninety rescripts in this category were all sent to the praetorian prefects based in Italy, and there are another forty-nine addressed to the city prefects. This large number of documents sets Italy apart from the rest of the west in continuing, even up to *c.* 468, to use the emperor directly as the head of the government in a practical sense. The important thing for the provinces was to have an emperor who would lend support, often only symbolic, to the authority of the local rulers. In a very significant series of passages, written in the last year of the fourth century, Claudian depicts Honorius (through his regent, Stilicho), as having established kings to rule over pacified 'barbarian' peoples (the Sueves and the Chauci – a Frankish group) in the Rhineland, some of whom supplied military aid to the Empire: moreover, he gave them laws.[40] This clearly establishes the importance of the emperor as a legitimising authority for 'barbarian kings', at least at the beginning of the period under examination. While the giving of laws is unlikely to refer to the establishment of a rescript system between the leaders of the 'barbarians' and the emperor (since no rescripts or any hints of them survive), it could be related to the transmission of Roman provincial law: the full significance of this will become apparent in Part II.

Later, in the middle of the fifth century, Sidonius Apollinaris could praise Majorian for being able to draw on the services of a vast number of 'barbarian' peoples in opposing Geiseric – Bastarnae, Sueves, Pannonians, Neurans, Huns, Getes, Dacians, Bellonoti, Rugians, Burgundians, Visigoths, Alites, Bisalts, Ostrogoths, Procrustians, Sarmatians and Moschans:[41] even allowing for the resurrection of a number of obsolete tribal names, and a large dose of poetic licence in the passage, which comes from a panegyric, it seems clear that as late as the 450s the western emperor had a degree of real influence, if not power, in the provinces. The change from the fourth century is also shown by the different ways in which the ceremony of imperial *aduentus* was illustrated under the tetrarchy and in the Theodosian era: in the former period, *aduentus* was depicted as being at a particular time and place, while by the end of the fourth century a more abstract and 'universal' image was employed in order to convey a 'truth' or theory about the governance of the Empire.[42] This type of understanding of the authority of the emperor in the provinces helps to explain the fact, already noted, that in the predominantly provincial chronicles the emperors are only discussed in detail in relation to the succession, and rarely in terms of any specific activity.

In Italy, the historic centre of the Empire, progress towards the full realisation of the new interpretation of the emperor's position was slower. It was not until the removal of the last emperor in c. 476 that Italy joined the trend set in other areas of the west and became a province of the new, less tightly-knit, imperial structure, rather than its centre: after that time, its rulers sought association with, and legitimisation from, the remaining, eastern, emperor in the same way as did those of other western provinces. For as long as an emperor was resident in Italy, it was difficult for him to be perceived as the detached figure-head he was for more distant parts of the west, and he remained the effective head of the administration of the peninsula. It is the way in which the central imperial administration, which was based in Italy, worked for the last eighty years of its existence that is the subject of the rest of Part I, and which forms the background for the subsequent analysis of the changes in provincial administration during the fifth and early sixth centuries, and, finally, of the way in which the government of Italy was transformed in the period after the departure of the last emperor.

3

The Imperial Court

The management of the imperial court

In order to assist him in his more active role as head of the administration of Italy, the emperor employed a number of officials who made up his imperial court. Following the discussion of the position of the emperor himself, it seems logical to commence an investigation of the fifth-century western court with an examination of the position of some of the officials who were closest to the person of the emperor, and yet who are amongst the most obscure – the *cubicularii*. It is characteristic of the sources that documents concerning men who worked within the imperial bedchamber should be rare: it has already been suggested that the nature of the sources is such as to provide less information the nearer to the emperor the courtiers lived and worked. Hence, not a single rescript addressed to the head, or *praepositus*, of the *sacrum cubiculum* survives; and such an official is only once mentioned in a fifth-century document of western origin, when the city prefect was informed that the *praepositus sacri cubiculi* was to have equal rank with the masters of the soldiers, the praetorian prefects, and the holder of his own office.[1] This reference is, however, of the greatest significance, for it clearly demonstrates that, despite his elusiveness in the documents, the head of the bedchamber was a man of the very highest importance. Something of the potential power of this figure, who must have had almost unrivalled access to the emperor's ear, may be seen in the fact that Heraclius, variously styled as *praepositus* and *spado*, allegedly had such great influence over Valentinian III that he persuaded him to murder Aetius.[2] This is enough to indicate that western *praepositi* may have been as influential in imperial politics as their eastern counterparts, the Byzantine eunuchs. The only other reference to a courtier of this type comes in the *Uita Germani*, in which it is recorded that Acolus, 'head of the royal bedchamber', was in office when St Germanus visited the imperial court, that a servant of his was the subject of a miracle performed by the Saint, and that he embalmed Germanus' body after the Saint's death.[3] This type of information is typical of that found incidentally in the hagiographical sources, and does not add to the sum of knowledge concerning the offices to which reference is made. In view of the paucity of data concerning the head of the bedchamber, it is particularly unfortunate that the relevant sections of the *Notitia Dignitatum* have been lost.[4]

As regards the *cubicularii* who worked under the *praepositus*, there is even less material. The only reference to a *cubicularius* as such is on a gravestone in Rome which is so uninformative that it is not clear whether the individual concerned was attached to the imperial court at all, or whether he belonged to some other great household.[5] It is conceivable that the lesser officials of the domestic organisation – for example, the *cura palatii*, the *decurio sacri palatii*, and the *castrensis sacri palatii* – may have been in some way connected with the bedchamber, but practically nothing is known of such positions save that they are mentioned in the sources.[6] It is also possible that the emperor's bodyguards, the *spatharii*, should be seen as having been members of the bedchamber,[7] but since the only time they are mentioned in the Latin sources for the west is when some of their number assisted Valentinian III to murder Aetius,[8] this cannot be proved.

If knowledge of the officials of the bedchamber suffers on account of their proximity to the person of the emperor so too, though in a rather different way, does an appreciation of the duties of the *comes domesticorum*. The narrative sources reveal that men bearing this title could and did operate in the provinces, and that, when they did so, their function was as military leaders. Hence, for example, Castinus is depicted as having led an army against the Franks while bearing the title of *comes domesticorum*,[9] and St Augustine refers to Boniface as 'comes of the *domestici* and of Africa' while he was leading a great army.[10] Confirmation of a military role comes from the fact that Castinus is also known to have been referred to as a *dux* and as 'magister militum':[11] Boniface too became a master of the soldiers,[12] and Majorian was a *comes domesticorum* and then briefly master of the soldiers before becoming emperor.[13] This military setting is finally underlined by the appearance in the Theodosian Code of a rescript addressed to Maurianus, 'comes domesticorum and agent of the master of the soldiers'.[14] From these preliminary indications, it might reasonably be supposed that the *comes domesticorum* was primarily a high-ranking army leader. As will be seen, such an impression would not be strictly accurate.

The *domestici* of whom the *comes domesticorum* was the chief are hardly ever glimpsed in the sources for the fifth-century western Empire. The *Notitia Dignitatum* simply states that those under the authority of the *comes domesticorum* are the *domestici equites* and the *domestici pedites*, together with their subordinates.[15] This would seem to imply that these men were soldiers, an impression confirmed by an imperial rescript concerning *domestici* who became *praepositi* of the imperial standards.[16] These cannot have been the same as the *domestici* of the provincial governors or other high-ranking officials, since the military *domestici* were of high rank themselves, the *praepositi* of the standards being equal to the esteemed *ex-consulares*.[17] In fact, it is likely that the *domestici* who were subject to the *comes domesticorum* should properly be described as *protectores domestici*, men of such high standing that they automatically became senators when they retired.[18] Such officials were imperial palace guards and, therefore, members of the imperial household – perhaps, it has been suggested, young men undergoing military officer training, who would later pass out from the court with high military commands.[19] However this may be, *protectores domestici* can only be seen in action once in the course of the Roman fifth century, when, in the proceedings of the 411 Council of Carthage, it is recorded that three of their number were present during the Council's sessions.[20] In exactly what capacity these men were acting is unclear, but it may not be unreasonable to see them as part of the imperial contingent, sent to ensure that order was preserved.

If it is right to envisage the *protectores domestici* as being subject to the *comes domesticorum*, and as being primarily palace guards, then it is, at first sight, rather surprising that the only references to actions by *comites domesticorum* refer to provincial theatres of operation. When the types of source which record the activities of such men are taken into account, this apparent paradox becomes easily explicable: predominantly provincial chronicles and letters are inherently more likely to describe military campaigns, especially those in their own areas, than the *minutiae* of palace administration in distant Italy. The real clue as to the location of the main activities of the *comites domesticorum* comes from the fact that only two rescripts were issued to such men in the fifth-century west:[21] as men close to the person of the emperor did not need to receive instructions or advice in written form, this may be taken to indicate that the palace was indeed the place in which *comites domesticorum* normally operated. If this interpretation be correct, the extra-palatine activities of such men have to be seen as being exceptional. It is, perhaps, reasonable to suppose that any experienced military leader, such as the head of the palace guards must have been, could be called upon in times of crisis or manpower shortage to lead armies. It is certainly true that Castinus' Frankish campaign of *c.* 420 came at a time of great tension, when the western Empire was militarily stretched. Boniface's activities in Africa are also exceptional because, at the time when Augustine mentioned him, he was in rebellion against Valentinian III's government. It is also conceivable that Africa, as a particularly important province, might, in times of crisis, have been afforded the extra protection of a contingent of troops particularly well connected to the palace.

Problems of a very similar nature, though of even greater scale, beset the examination of the position of the *comes stabuli*. The title itself suggests that such a man was connected with the imperial stables and, therefore, with the cavalry. This would seem to be confirmed by the fact that a rescript addressed to the praetorian prefects and the *comes sacrarum largitionum* states that *comites stabuli* were to receive a cash commutation of the African horse tax.[22] It is not difficult to see how a *comes stabuli* could come to be involved in a military campaign such as that against the Visigothic king, Euric (this was, incidentally, apparently the last fully-operational imperial army to be active in Gaul).[23] Apart from these meagre indications, the sources are silent concerning the *comes stabuli*, and that, together with the fact that not a single rescript appears to have been issued to such a man in the west after 394, seems to indicate that the *comes stabuli* was another 'invisible' official who normally operated within the imperial court itself.

The function of one type of high-ranking official whose duties lay at the heart of the imperial court, the master of the offices (*magister officiorum*), is rather less obscure, though even in this case the evidence cannot be said to approach the extensive. It is apparent that the master of the offices was involved in a certain amount of provincial administration, since it is in relation to that sphere of activity that almost all the references to such officials are to be found. Hence, for example, the seven western rescripts addressed to masters of the offices after 394 reveal that such men were in charge of the *agentes in rebus* who were largely connected with the provinces: the concern with *agentes* is explicitly stated in a rescript from the reign of Constantius,[24] and is elsewhere underlined by the fact that the masters of the offices were told to supervise promotions within that service,[25] were instructed to ensure that criminals were not amongst its employees,[26] and were to see that *agentes* were not deployed by anyone without the express permission of the emperor.[27] Similar evidence comes from the *Notitia Dignitatum*, which states that the whole of the *schola* of the *agentes in rebus* was subject to the master of the offices, and that the deputies of its members in the *scrinia* were in his charge, as were the *cancellarii*, and various kinds of armourer. Further, the master of the offices had *curiosi* (spies) in all the provinces, and supervised the *cursus publicus*.[28] The effect of jurisdiction over such a wide range of officials was to make the master of the offices responsible for much of the permanent staff of the provincial administration, especially given that, as in the fourth century, the chiefs of the *officia* of all the major magistracies are likely to have been *agentes*:[29] it is in this context of their responsibility for a large number of officials in the provincial administration that the addressing of rescripts to the masters of the offices on such matters as the prohibition of the employment of heretics in imperial service,[30] the regulation of the *scriniarii*,[31] and the notification of an amnesty for the supporters of a usurper (Attalus or Jovinus),[32] should be seen.

It would, however, be premature to assume that simply because he was involved in the management of a large number of the central administration's agents in the provinces, the master of the offices was primarily a figure of provincial government and operated at a distance from the imperial palace. It has already been seen that the *comes domesticorum* operated within the palace, even though most of the surviving evidence concerning his position refers to the extra-palatine activities of holders of the office, and the same is broadly true with regard to the position of the master of the offices. The first clue that this was the case comes from the fact that very few rescripts – only seven – appear to have been sent to holders of the position in the west after 394. On this occasion it is possible to confirm that the small number of rescripts is likely to reflect an official's proximity to the person of the emperor, since in one of his poems, Rutilius Namatianus recalls that, when he was master of the offices, he ruled the palace and the armourers.[33] Nothing more is said, however, so that it is impossible to ascertain what his exact functions in palace management were.

The discussion of the position of the master of the offices has emphasised the importance (and, at the same time, the limitations) of chance references in literary sources which do not have the same bias as the documents produced by the administration itself. Another feature of the nature of the documentation is underlined by the surviving information concerning the *agentes in rebus* who were subject to the master of the offices. Most of the fifth-century western references show no more than *agentes* carrying letters between senior officials and men placed high in the ecclesiastical hierarchy;[34] the only other mention of *agentes* comes when three of their number were sent to Africa *c.* 407 in order to enforce anti-Donatist laws.[35] Such a paucity of data is predictable, since men such as these – that, is, not in the top rank of civil officials of the Empire – will not have required to receive imperial rescripts, as their appeals would first have been to their more immediate superiors, often, perhaps, to the master of the offices: if an appeal reached the master of the offices and if he, in turn, needed further advice, he would have been able to communicate directly with the emperor, thus obviating the need for rescripts instructing him as to how *agentes* should act. If *agentes* were too low down the hierarchy to appear in imperial documents, their individual actions were also not significant enough to have been noted in the literary and theological sources.

The imperial writing office

In the preceding section, it has been suggested that the types of source material available for a discussion of the management of the imperial court tend to make apparent the extra-palatine activities of the officials concerned, while leaving concealed their more routine duties within the court itself. Another sphere of imperial administration in which the nature of the sources demands a cautious approach is that of the imperial writing office. Perhaps the most obvious point concerning the writing office is that, although there is very little evidence concerning its mode of operation, the very existence of the fifth-century rescripts is testimony to its productivity and importance. As the head of the writing office was, presumably, usually involved in the production of rescripts, it would be surprising if there were in existence any number of such documents addressed to him. In fact, only one rescript was sent to the chief of the office, the quaestor, in the fifth-century west.[36]

It is clear from that one rescript that the quaestor was a member of the imperial court – a *comes* – and that he supervised all appointments to the 'lesser register' (*minus laterculus*). Similar general information comes from the *Notitia Dignitatum*, which records that the quaestor was in charge of the various *scrinia* of the court, and was responsible for dictating laws and dealing with petitions.[37] Such a list of tasks confirms that the quaestor was in charge of the writing office and was involved in the production of rescripts: it also implies that its incumbent was possessed of a high degree of education and literacy, an impression which may be confirmed by Sidonius Apollinaris' description of Victor, quaestor in the court of Anthemius, as 'learned'.[38]

As was the case in the discussion of the position of the master of the offices, more·is learnt of the actual activities of quaestors from literary writings (this time predominantly those of Sidonius Apollinaris) than from any other single type of source. For example, the function of the quaestor as the author of rescripts is emphasised by two independent poetic descriptions of such men as the mouth-pieces of the emperor.[39] Other passages concerning quaestors refer to activities outside the palace, as when Licinianus, quaestor of Julius Nepos, was sent to Gaul to negotiate peace between the Arverni and the Visigoths c. 474-475.[40] He was later sent to Gaul again, bearing the codicils of the patriciate to Ecdicius,[41] though on this occasion it is not clear whether he was still in office as quaestor. Such references as these do not mean that their author, Sidonius Apollinaris, misunderstood the type of official involved, nor are they to be seen as some form of aberration. Although the activities involved took the quaestor away from the palace, the embassy to the Visigoths would certainly have required a highly trusted official: a quaestor, as a *comes*, and as the member of the court most used to handling petitions and drafting responses to them, might well have been seen as a sensible choice for such a delicate mission.[42] In addition, it has already been argued that court-based officials, such as the *comes domesticorum*, were sometimes sent out into the provinces to deal with exceptional situations.

That the main sphere of activity of the quaestor was within the court is emphasised by the kinds of subordinate official he controlled – two each of *magistri epistolarum*,[43] *magistri memoriae*,[44] and *primicerii notariorum*.[45] Little is revealed of the functions of the lesser officials, save that the *Notitia Dignitatum* states that the *magistri memoriae*, *epistolarum*, and *libellorum*, all of whom were subject to the quaestor, were in some way responsible for the handling of petitions and imperial correspondence – almost a statement of the obvious given their titles.[46] The only other revealing remark also comes in the *Notitia Dignitatum*, where it is recorded that the *primicerius notariorum* was in charge of the 'civil list':[47] the information contained in the *Notitia* is, however, not rooted in the fifth century. It is a measure of the importance of this antiquarian document for enlightenment concerning lesser officials that its silence concerning the office of referendary (which emerged in the east *c*. 427[48]) makes it impossible to be certain whether that office was ever adopted by western emperors, even though it does appear later in some of the 'barbarian' kingdoms.

On the whole, it is clear that the functions of most of the lesser officials of the writing office are almost as obscure as those of the subordinates of the master of the offices or, indeed, of the head of the bedchamber, and the reasons for the lack of evidence are likely to be the same. In the case of the writing office, however, more is known of one category of men, the *tribuni et notarii* – the imperial notaries, apparently constituted under this precise title in the fourth century.[49] Some of the references to men of this title are, inevitably, uninformative as to their role in the administration. It is, for example, recorded that Petronius Maximus had been a *tribunus et notarius* before he became emperor,[50] as, possibly, had Gaudentius before he was *uicarius septem prouinciarum* (a high-ranking figure in the provincial administration of Gaul),[51] but nothing is said of their functions. More helpful is a reference by Sidonius Apollinaris to one of his correspondents, Consentius, as having been educated in rhetoric before becoming *tribunus et notarius* to Valentinian III,[52] perhaps an indication that such a training was of practical assistance in performing the duties of such a post. This impression is strengthened by the fact that Marcellinus, a *tribunus et notarius* about whom a great deal, relatively speaking, is known, was responsible for the management of the Council of Carthage in 411.[53] The position of Marcellinus as organiser of the proceedings was clearly one of the greatest importance, and has little direct connection with the duty of writing imperial decisions, still less with the task of recording the proceedings of the Council, a task which was presumably performed by the two scribes whose presence is noted in the attendance list at the start of the proceedings.[54] Marcellinus' status is underlined by the fact that Orosius records him as having assisted in the restoration of Catholicism in Africa and as having been murdered on that account.[55] It is not difficult to see how a *tribunus et notarius* might become involved in high-level activity of this type, since such an official would, in the course of his more normal duties, become familiar with the thoughts of the emperor and had to be trustworthy: competent and trusted men might reasonably have been seen as useful imperial agents (as they had been in the mid-fourth century) even in spheres tangential to their normal official duties.[56] Similar reasoning may be used to explain how *tribuni et notarii* could become involved in other particularly sensitive missions, as when Aphrodisius was sent by Honorius to assist the city prefect, the younger Symmachus, to restore order in Rome during the contested papal election of *c.* 419.[57]

In addition to the references specifically to *tribuni et notarii*, there are occasions on which men simply described as *tribuni* – tribunes – are mentioned. It is not clear whether such were military men with the rank of tribune, or *tribuni et notarii*, but that the latter is possible is illustrated by the case of the Marcellinus involved in the Council of Carthage: he appears in the official record, the proceedings of the Council, with his full and correct title of *tribunus et notarius*, but when Orosius, an author not connected with the government and, probably, not particularly interested in the niceties of secular titles, mentions him it is simply as 'tribune'. Similar imprecision may be suspected in the case of Hysechius, who was sent by Emperor Avitus to Theoderic II to announce the former's successful accession to the imperial throne:[58] the author on this occasion is Hydatius who, like Orosius, was not necessarily interested in precise titles and could well have contented himself with the general term 'tribune'. Further, in view of the case of Aphrodisius, it is not impossible that Severianus, who was also sent to assist Symmachus in Rome, was, too, a *tribunus et notarius*, though on this occasion the document involved is an official letter.[59] More debatable cases are those of one Petrus, who sought assistance from Sidonius Apollinaris in presenting petitions to Bishop Auspicius of Toul,[60] and of one Eleusianus, a tribune stationed at Timgad, who sent a letter to St Augustine concerning a petition from the inhabitants of that town:[61] these men could have been notaries stationed in the provinces, especially since they are only seen when dealing with documents, but the case remains open. Even less clear is the position of men such as Barnabus, a tribune who was alleged to have murdered Bishop Patroclus of Arles on the orders of the master of the soldiers,

Felix,[62] and of the 'man of tribunican authority' whose child was healed by St Germanus at St Albans.[63] It is not possible to know what was the real position of men such as these since 'tribune' was a military rank,[64] which had been applied to imperial notaries by extension: it is, however, just conceivable that the man at St Albans could have been a notary, as he is mentioned as having been active some time after the withdrawal of Roman troops from Britain.

The emperor's financial officials

Although there is rather more material in the Theodosian Code concerning the highest-ranking of the court's financial officials, information relating to the ways in which such men operated is still far from plentiful. Perhaps the most important of the financial officials was the *comes sacrarum largitionum*, the title of whose office clearly indicates involvement with the imperial treasury. This impression is confirmed by the *Notitia Dignitatum*, which shows that the *comes sacrarum largitionum* controlled many officials who were concerned with money and taxation – the *rationales summarum*, *praepositi thesaurorum*, and *procuratores monetarum* – while his office staff included men with titles similarly linked to monetary affairs – *primicerii scriniorum canonum*, *numerorum*, *auri*, *ab argento* and *a pecuniis*.[65] The schematic picture presented by the *Notitia* is supplemented by the Theodosian Code, which provides specific examples of the kinds of business with which the *comes sacrarum largitionum* was involved. Hence, for example, the Code reveals that provincial governors were to pay the taxes they had collected to the *comes sacrarum largitionum* three times a year,[66] and that this official was to receive the cash-commutation of the tax payable in military clothing;[67] he also, under the terms of a Novel of Theodosius, received a third of the property of those who died intestate.[68] The *comes sacrarum largitionum* could allow towns to keep up to a third of the *uectegalia* they owed, in order that they might maintain their walls and public buildings,[69] though his more usual function was to maximise the income to the imperial treasury from towns, as illustrated by a Novel of Valentinian III instructing such an official to ensure that all commercial transactions were conducted in towns, where they could be taxed.[70] While it is clear from these examples that the *comes sacrarum largitionum* was an important figure in the collecting of imperial revenues, there is almost no evidence concerning expenditure, save that the holder of the office controlled the gold supply (and, presumably, the minting of coin),[71] and that he was to provide imperial officials with ceremonial dress to designate their rank[72] – this was probably delegated to the *uestiarii* recorded in the *Notitia Dignitatum* as being under his authority.

Although the *comes sacrarum largitionum* was to a large extent ultimately responsible for the collection of taxes, there is little information as to the manner in which revenues reached him. The *Notitia Dignitatum* records that he had a large office staff – both in the provinces and in the form of a central *officium* – and this is confirmed by two rescripts which give the total number of his office staff as five hundred and forty-six.[73] Further, the *comes sacrarum largitionum* had a certain amount of jurisdiction over provincial governors and decurions: this was removed by Valentinian III in 440, but was restored two years later.[74] Earlier, it had been made clear that it was the direct responsibility of the holder of this office to ensure that imperial agents who were in the provinces without authorisation were punished: the law presumably only refers to agents of the *largitiones*.[75] Those local officials must have collected the revenues into local treasuries, where they were kept or whence they were forwarded to a central treasury.[76] With a staff of over five hundred men, *rationales* and *praepositi thesaurorum* spread throughout the provinces, six *procuratores monetarum*, and a number of agents in the main cities of the western Empire,[77] it is likely that the subordinates of the *comes sacrarum largitionum* could easily get out of hand if not properly supervised: the head of the *largitiones* was clearly a powerful figure.

The only lesser official who appears in the Theodosian Code is the *comes largitionalium per Africam*, who was one step down the hierarchy from the *comes sacrarum largitionum* himself, and was the latter's main agent in Africa. Until 399, the African official had collected taxes through *palatini* – that is, by means of the staff of the *largitiones* – but from that date he had to leave the collection to officials of the praetorian prefect,[78] and the *comes sacrarum largitionum* was to ensure that anyone claiming to be acting on his behalf in Africa was punished.[79] Although the lack of references to subordinate officials in the Theodosian Code conforms to a pattern observed in preceding sections, the foregoing discussion of the position of the *comes sacrarum largitionum* has made use of a number of rescripts, many of which were addressed to holders of that office: in fact, the Theodosian Code contains some fourteen such documents issued in the west after 394, to which Justinian's Code adds another four. If, as has earlier been suggested, the *comes sacrarum largitionum* was a courtier (as is implied by the use of the word *comes* in the title) and, therefore, had fairly easy access to the person of the emperor, it may be thought strange that he should have needed to receive more rescripts than his colleagues the *comes domesticorum*, the master of the offices, and the other high-ranking figures previously discussed. The solution to this apparent contradiction may lie in the fact that because the activities of the *comes sacrarum largitionum* involved a sphere – taxation – in which there was much potential for abuse which would directly affect a large number of provincials, imperial decisions concerning the administration of taxation were made public by means of rescripts, even though the *comes sacrarum largitionum* himself might well have received the answers to his appeals in person: officials such as the chief of the palace guards or the head of the imperial staff were involved in more internal spheres of government which did not demand the safeguard of publicity in the same way. This does not mean that the earlier suggestion that the offices whose incumbents worked near to the emperor can be identified by the lack of rescripts addressed to them is invalidated, because the *comes sacrarum largitionum* still received very few such documents compared to the great provincial officials, as will be seen in Chapter 5.

Although the *comes sacrarum largitionum* was mainly concerned with the financial administration, he was not solely involved in that sphere of activity, any more than the *comes domesticorum* was purely concerned with the palace guards or the quaestor with the drafting of imperial documents. For example, the Theodosian Code reveals two cases in which *comites sacrarum largitionum* were commanded to act in non-financial affairs – the first being connected with the Church and clerics,[80] and the second with an amnesty for the officials of the unsuccessful usurper Eugenius in 395.[81] Furthermore, it is precisely in this category of non-financial activities that the one informative reference to a *comes sacrarum largitionum* in the non-legal material is found, when Sidonius Apollinaris records that the holder of that office in *c*. 468, Flavius Ansellus, was made responsible for guarding the allegedly treacherous Gallic praetorian prefect Arvandus.[82] It would be possible to see the involvement of a *comes sacrarum largitionum* in this affair as being connected with the policy of confiscating the goods of traitors, and, therefore, with the imperial revenues: however, it could also be argued that the employment of such an official to guard a high-ranking prisoner in unusual circumstances more plausibly shows that he could be expected to undertake special commissions outside the normal range of his duties – perhaps when he was the nearest high-ranking person to the scene of an incident who did not have any other pressing engagements at the time.

There is one sphere of the financial administration in which the *comes sacrarum largitionum* was involved which has not yet been mentioned, and which could be thought to fall into the category of special commissions – that of the administration of imperial estates, usually seen as being the preserve of another high-level courtier, the *comes rerum priuatarum*. It has been suggested that the *comes sacrarum largitionum* was the 'state treasurer', and that the *comes rerum priuatarum* was, as his title implies, in charge of the emperor's private affairs or was 'manager and treasurer of the government and crown properties'.[83] As early as 398, however, a rescript was issued instructing the then *comes sacrarum largitionum* to supervise the restoration of decayed buildings belonging to the imperial patrimony.[84] Furthermore, in 366 and 399 orders were issued to the effect that the *comes sacrarum largitionum* was ultimately responsible for the collection of rents from imperial lands, yet in 405 it was the *comes rerum priuatarum* who was notified that such dues were to be collected more promptly.[85] This might seem to imply that the *comes rerum priuatarum* was in some way subordinate to the *comes sacrarum largitionum*, but that is unlikely, because a Novel of Theodosius to an eastern praetorian prefect describes an instance in which the *comes sacrarum largitionum* acted in place of ('ad uicem') the *comes rerum priuatarum*, the opposite of what would be expected had the former been the superior of the latter.[86]

Despite this, it is still reasonable to assume that the primary concern of the *comes rerum priuatarum* lay with the administration of the imperial estates, and it is in this context that the rescript of 405 concerning the prompt collection of rents should be seen. Other, similar, documents point in the same direction: two rescripts addressed to such officials prohibited the making of further grants from imperial lands lest the estates became over-depleted;[87] and a third rescript states that nothing was to be dispensed from the imperial *aerarium*, or private treasury, without the authorisation of the emperor.[88] In addition, the *comes rerum priuatarum* had responsibility for decayed patrimonial buildings,[89] as did the *comes sacrarum largitionum*.

With regard to the mechanics of the administration of the imperial estates, very little is known, save that the *Notitia Dignitatum* informs us that there were various *rationales, praepositi* and procurators in the provinces in the same way as the *comes sacrarum largitionum* had provincial officials,[90] and that, although the staff of the *comes rerum priuatarum* was smaller than that of his colleague,[91] its members enjoyed the same privileges as those of the larger financial *officium*.[92] Nor was this the only similarity between the positions of the two courtiers, because the ways in which the subordinates of the *comes rerum priuatarum* were employed were broadly parallel to those found in the provincial arm of the *largitiones*. Perhaps the best example of this comes from the fact that, although a rescript issued at the end of the fourth century ordered that the *palatini* of the *comes rerum priuatarium* should collect the revenues from the imperial estates rather than the *iudices ordinarii*,[93] it was decreed a few years later that provincial governors could be called in to render the collection of such dues easier:[94] significantly, the second measure dates to 400, precisely the time at which tax collection in Africa was taken out of the hands of the *comes sacrarum largitionum* and given to the praetorian prefect. Further similarity of treatment may be seen in the fact that the measure of Valentinian III in 440 which deprived the *comes sacrarum largitionum* of jurisdiction over provincial governors and decurions also applied to the *comes rerum priuatarum*, as did its repeal in 442.[95] Finally, the *comes rerum priuatarum* obtained a third of the property of those who died intestate, as did the *comes sacrarum largitionum*.[96]

Given the similarities between the position of the *comes sacrarum largitionum* and that of the *comes rerum priuatarum*, it is not unreasonable that the former could, as noted above, stand in for the latter, and it is legitimate to wonder whether the distinction between the 'state treasurer' and the 'manager of the government and crown properties' was ever anything more than schematic, especially given the fact that it had always been difficult to distinguish between the public and private wealth of the emperor.[97] It may be just as likely that there were two courtiers, or *comites* of the emperor, one with a title officially connected with the the the *res priuata*, and the other officially attached to the *largitiones*, who between them managed the imperial finances without much regard to the demarcation between their positions, at least as far as everyday transactions were concerned. Such a hypothesis may be strengthened by the fact that the *comes rerum priuatarum* not only received rescripts concerning the imperial estates, but also a number connected with such matters as tax arrears,[98] the cash commutation of the provision of recruits to the army,[99] tax equali-sation,[100] and the census;[101] further rescripts treated of pagans and heretics, as well as of certain privileges of the Church.[102]

Some of the financial matters just outlined, and especially the recruiting tax, could equally well have come under the jurisdiction of the praetorian prefect as that of the financial *comites*. This gives the impression that the *comites* could be called upon to act in any financial matter, at least upon occasion, perhaps when one of them was simply the nearest available treasury official when a given situation arose. Further to this argument, it is interesting to observe that one Sebastian, a man described as 'comes primi ordinis' and whose specific office (if any) is unknown, received several rescripts concerning tax equalisation.[103] Had this Sebastian been a *comes sacrarum largitionum* or a *comes rerum priuatarum*, it would be very unlikely that his proper title would not have been recorded in the Theodosian Code, because the rescripts collected in the Code were official documents (as was the Code itself), which ought to be fairly precise in such matters. In view of this, it is possible to suggest that Sebastian was simply a high-ranking *comes* of the emperor (perhaps with some financial experience) who was called upon to assist in specific cases, in the same way as the *comes sacrarum largitionum* and the *comes rerum priuatarum* could be asked to act outside their normal competences.

The *comes*

All the high-ranking officials of the imperial administration whose positions have been discussed in the preceding sections either always have the word *comes* as part of their titles (as in the case of the *comes domesticorum*, the *comes sacrarum largitionum*, and the *comes rerum priuatarum*), or strictly speaking should do (as in the case of the *comes et quaestor sacri palatii* and the *comes et magister officiorum*): the only possible exception to this is the *praepositus sacri cubiculi*. The significance of this use of the word *comes* is that the men described were palace officials or courtiers of the emperor. It has been noted that the holders of the offices so far examined received very few rescripts from the emperors, and it has been argued that this was largely a product of their proximity to the imperial presence. In Chapter 5 it will be seen that officials active in provincial government both received many more rescripts than even the *comes rerum priuatarum* (to whom more were addressed than to any of the other imperial agents so far mentioned), and were not described as *comites*: it is argued that the attribution of the quality of *comes* to an official is often an indication that he was a member of the central, imperial, government, rather than of the provincial administration which worked at a distance from the court and emperor.

There are titles other than those already discussed which include the word *comes*, but which do not denote specific offices: a *comes primi ordinis* was encountered earlier, and there are also *comites consistorii*. A Novel of Valentinian III and an inscription imply that there is a difference between these two titles,[104] but fourth-century evidence seems to indicate that they were for practical purposes the same, and that their holders were the closest advisers of the emperor.[105] In the fifth century, so little evidence is available that any form of precision is impossible.[106]

There is also a technical military sense in which the term *comes* can be used. The evidence of the fourth century shows that a *comes* of this kind (strictly, a *comes rei militaris*) was in charge of a unit of the field army:[107] the origin of this must be that, as the field army was at one time usually based with or near the person of the emperor, its commanders could be said to be his 'companions', in a way in which the commanders of the more distant frontier armies, the *duces*, were not. That such a specifically military significance could still be intended at the very end of the fourth century is illustrated by a rescript of 400 which refers to the responsibility of *comites* and *duces* for the direction of military service,[108] and by another rescript from almost the same time which refers to the provision of senior office staff for *comites* by the masters of the soldiers:[109] in 397, there is official evidence, also contained in the Theodosian Code, for the full title of *comes rei militaris.*[110]

Another source in which the word *comes* can be seen to have a specifically military connotation is the *Notitia Dignitatum*. This document mentions *comites prouinciarum* in Tingitania, at Strasbourg, and in Italy, who were in charge of a given area and whose responsibility was clearly military: it is likely that these men were *comites rei militaris* stationed in the provinces, for their subordinates were also provided by the masters of the soldiers.[111] It is not only in the pages of the out-of-date *Notitia Dignitatum* that *comites prouinciarum* are to be found, for a rescript concerning the commutation of the military tax payable in horses into a money payment addresses Gaudentius of Africa by the title,[112] while the Chronicle of Hydatius shows Asterius, 'comes Hispaniarum', leading a campaign against the Vandals.[113] Similarly, it may be significant that St Augustine refers to Boniface as 'domesticorum et Africae comes constitutus' leading a great army, especially since Boniface had already led an army against the Moors as *tribunus* (possibly here designating a military rank) and later became a master of the soldiers: it is conceivable, though, that on this occasion it was, as suggested earlier, the title of *comes domesticorum* which gave Boniface his military competence.[114] Seen against the background just outlined, it is not unlikely that Heraclius, described as 'Africae comes', was, even before his rebellion of *c.* 413, a military leader,[115] but the chronicles and theological works are, on the whole, silent concerning the governmental functions of men such as this: although Heraclius is several times described as 'comes Africae', he is only mentioned in the contexts of his rebellion against Honorius, and of his death.[116] A similar situation exists with regard to the other named *comites Africae* – John is only mentioned on the occasion of his murder;[117] Bathanarius is referred to in *De ciuitate Dei*, but all that is learnt is that he was a man of sufficient consequence for Bishop Severus of Milveum to have dined at his house.[118] In another province, Mansuetus of Spain was sent on an embassy to the Sueves.[119] Although this last was not a task specifically connected with the army, it is not difficult to see how an official with military competence could come to be involved. The same is true in the few other cases, seen through rescripts, in which *comites prouinciarum* acted outside the military sphere, as when Bathanarius was notified of measures concerning the confiscation of the goods of a rebel,[120] or Heraclianus was informed of measures against the Donatists.[121] Even if specifically military intervention were not envisaged, all the cases in which *comites prouinciarum* acted outside the military sphere were somewhat exceptional, and it is not unreasonable to suppose that a *comes prouinciae* might, if he happened to be in the vicinity, have been called upon to intervene despite his precise title, in the same way as has earlier been suggested for other officials.

Even if it is possible to be confident that the *comites prouinciarum* were primarily military leaders, their exact status is less certain, as is the strength of their links with the central imperial court in the fifth century: were they, for example, sent out into the provinces for a fixed term and then recalled, or did they exist only on an *ad hoc* basis, being placed in charge of special forces in order to combat specific situations?[122] Owing to the scanty nature of the sources, it is not possible to answer these questions, even in the case of Africa, where the evidence is rather fuller than elsewhere. The African evidence should, in any case, be approached with caution because an exceptional situation existed in that province for much of the fifth century owing to the presence of supporters of the Donatist heresy, which was of concern not only to the imperial administration but also to the churchmen who were the authors of most of the extant sources. It may be that the only reason the existence of a comparatively large number of *comites Africae* is known is because the ecclesiastics, who wrote the documents in which such officials are recorded, had a vested interest in the suppression of the heresy and, as a result, recorded the actions of the government against the Donatists, even though they normally had no specific interest in the imperial administration.

Another type of *comes* which is sometimes believed to have operated in the provinces is the *comes ciuitatis* who (as will be seen in Part II) formed an important element of royal administration in the 'barbarian' kingdoms. The specific title of *comes ciuitatis*, however, appears only once in an indisputably fifth-century document referring to an area directly controlled by the western emperor – a letter of Sidonius Apollinaris, which refers to such an official (Eustace) at Marseilles.[123] The question arises as to what this man's function was: was he a city governor in the sense that later *comites ciuitatum* were? Was he a *comes* in charge of a field army based at Marseilles, a city on the frontier with Euric's Visigothic kingdom? Was he stationed at Marseilles permanently, or temporarily? It is impossible to answer these questions with any more certainty than those concerning the *comites prouinciarum*. Indeed, in the case of *comites ciuitatum* the situation is more complex because, despite what has sometimes been suggested, there is no other conclusive evidence for the existence of such officials in the Empire before the fall of Romulus Augustulus. It has been thought that Arbogast was *comes ciuitatis* at Trier,[124] but this cannot be proved. Arbogast received a letter from Auspicius of Toul in which he is described as 'comes', and is clearly thought of as ruling the city.[125] This does not, however, make Arbogast a *comes ciuitatis* as such, and the fact that the heading of the letter describes him as 'comes Treueriorum' is no evidence, because the title could be a later addition,[126] and in any case does not employ a phrase as explicit as, say, 'comes ciuitatis Treueriorum'. Even if these objections were swept aside, little more would be understood of the functions of *comites ciuitatum*, because Trier was another frontier city and, therefore, in an exceptional position which might have merited the installation, on either a temporary or a permanent basis, of a *comes*, either of a military kind or as a special representative of the emperor.

A third instance – that of Attalus, who may have had authority in Autun[127] – is sometimes put forward as indicating the presence of *comites ciuitatum* in the Empire. In reality, the evidence is even more tenuous than for Eustace and Arbogast: Attalus is nowhere described as a *comes*,[128] and there is even doubt as to whether Autun was still directly under imperial control at the time, or whether it was subject to the Burgundians.[129]

On the scanty evidence presented in the last two paragraphs, it seems unreasonable to conclude that the third quarter of the fifth century saw the creation, in those parts of the western Empire still directly subject to imperial authority, of *comites ciuitatum* as the normal governors of cities, or even as a new institution.[130] Hesitancy in accepting such an innovation may, perhaps, be encouraged by the additional fact that *comites ciuitatum* only appeared in the east at a much later date.[131] It may be wiser to take a cautious approach and to see the one case of Marseilles (possibly supplemented by that of Trier) in terms of an imperial courtier being sent to a city to carry out a specific commission in exceptional circumstances.[132] This is not to deny that the case of Marseilles, in particular, may have been the basis for the later development of the formal position of the *comes ciuitatis*, but it is probably better to see it as the beginning of an evolutionary process, rather than as the final point: further suggestions as to the origins of this kind of official will be made in Part II.

It is possible to see all references to *comites* where there is no further qualification of the title such as *prouinciae* or *Africae* in the same light as that of Eustace. For example, Aetius' grandfather, Gaudentius, is called 'comes' in a report of his death, but there is no indication that he was necessarily a military man – he could have been an official of the court discharging any duty, military or otherwise, in Gaul when he was murdered.[133] Similarly, the one fifth-century western rescript addressed to a *comes* with no further qualification concerns the organisation of an extra-ordinary tax in order to supply new recruits for the army,[134] but there is no indication that the *comes* concerned was really a *comes rei militaris*, and it is equally possible that, since it was a supplementary tax which was involved and, therefore, required special organisation, any member of the imperial court might have been commissioned to oversee the work. A different sort of ambiguity may be seen in the case of Agrippinus, whom Hydatius describes as 'Gallic *comes*'.[135] It might, at first sight, be thought that Agrippinus was a *comes rei militaris*, especially since he was responsible for leading military opposition to Aegidius. The later *Uita Aniani*, however, describes Agrippinus as 'master of the soldiers', a position to which it is possible that Avitus may have appointed him.[136] If this were really the case, it would be more likely that Hydatius' 'comes' related to Agrippinus' position as master of the soldiers which made him a member of Avitus' court, rather than as a *comes rei militaris*.

In a case which serves to strengthen the last suggestion, Nepotianus is described by Hydatius as 'master of the soldiers' in *c.* 459, and yet, a year later, appears in the same work as 'comes':[137] if *comes* has to refer to a local official (*comes rei militaris*) this would indicate a demotion. Similarly, Stilicho is referred to in *c.* 408 as 'comes',[138] even though he is known, from earlier inscriptional evidence, already to have been master of the soldiers, *comes domesticorum* and *comes stabuli*.[139] Indeed, in this case it is possible to go further, for, in the period from *c.* 398 to *c.* 407, Stilicho received four rescripts which addressed him as '*comes* and master of the soldiers',[140] and two which simply describe him as 'master of the soldiers'.[141] It is absolutely clear from this that the *comes* part of the title meant nothing specifically military, but indicated simply that Stilicho was a member of the imperial court: for contemporaries the latter fact could be taken for granted. Indeed, in instances in which there is no specific evidence, not just in terms of the duties performed by officials described as *comites* but also in terms of title, it is quite impossible to determine whether such men were permanently military *comites* or were simply courtiers carrying out special commissions. Hence, although Asterius is described on a consular diptych as 'uir clarissimus et inluster', 'comes', 'ex-magister militum' and 'consul ordinarius',[142] he cannot ever be shown to have been a *comes* in the military sense, and the other sources in which he appears only describe him as a consul or as a master of the soldiers.[143] In other cases, the precise word chosen to describe a man's position may have had more to do with the impression the author wished to create, as in the case of Constantius, who is described as 'comes' in two rescript-style letters to the younger Symmachus, and in relation to his marriage to Galla Placidia, sister of Emperor Valentinian III[144] – that is, on occasions on which it was desirable to stress his proximity to the emperor. The only other occasion on which the term is used of him is in Orosius' description of the campaign against the usurpers Constantine III, Jovinus and Sebastianus:[145] here, however, the other sources for the same events describe him as 'dux',[146] and it may well be that their authors, in contrast to Orosius, were deliberately more concerned to stress his position as a military commander than his position as a close associate of the emperor.

The *dux*

A rather similar situation exists with regard to a second type of official, the *dux*. According to the *Notitia Dignitatum*, *duces* were in charge of the army in provinces on the frontiers of the Empire – Pannonia II and Savia, Valeria, Pannonia I, Raetia, Maxima Sequanorum, and Belgica II.[147] In some ways, therefore, *duces* were related to the *comites rei militaris* who were in charge of military affairs in other provinces, and, in the fourth century, the parallel is clear from the fact that field armies were led by *comites* and frontier armies by *duces*.[148] In the fifth century the picture is not quite so clear, since the only real evidence for *duces* being stationed in frontier provinces comes in a rescript from Honorius to the praetorian prefect, Monaxius, which records the responsibility of *duces* for sending wild beasts to the court from the frontier areas for court entertainments,[149] and in a Novel of Valentinian III reminding the 'dux prouinciae' of Mauritania Sitifensis that he was responsible for regulating the activities of armed bands within the area where he held his command.[150]

Whether or not they were based specifically in frontier provinces, it is clear that *duces* were still, in the fifth century, military leaders of some sort,[151] and that they could be expected to spend large sums of their own money on the administration of the army:[152] the precise significance of the term *dux* is not, however, always easy to see. The problem arises from the fact that the major source of evidence for events in the provinces (particularly those of immediately-perceived importance such as military affairs) is the chronicles, whose authors were not especially concerned with the niceties of official terminology and may have used words in a more flexible way for literary effect. Perhaps the clearest example is the *Chronicle of 511*'s description of Anthemius' *duces* operating against Euric in southern Gaul:

> Antimiolus was sent by his father, Emperor Anthemius, to Arles, with Thorisarius, Everdingus and Hermianus, *comes* [or *comites*] *stabuli*: King Euric met them on the far side of the Rhone and, having killed the *duces*, laid everything waste.[153]

It is far from clear from Mommsen's edition whether Thorisarius, Everdingus and Hermianus were all *comites stabuli*, or whether only Hermianus was, but presumably they are all three subsumed, in the second half of the sentence, under the word 'ducibus'. This leads to the conclusion that *dux* here simply means 'leader', because the official title of at least Hermianus was *comes stabuli*, and not *dux*.

Once it is realised that the chroniclers could use the word *dux* in a completely non-technical sense, to mean simply 'leader',[154] it becomes an open question whether any of the *duces* mentioned in their works were permanently based in frontier provinces or were specifically in charge of frontier armies. Prosper Tiro records that Felix waged war on Boniface with three named *duces*:[155] it is possible that all three men were *duces* in a technical sense, but it is at least as likely that they were simply the leaders of the campaign. Prosper also records that the usurper Constantine III was overcome and captured 'by Constantius and Ulphula, *duces* of Honorius',[156] a phrase echoed by Hydatius, who only mentions Constantius and calls him 'dux of Honorius'.[157] Were these men the leaders of frontier armies, or were they simply leaders of the forces of Honorius on that occasion? A similar problem is posed by references by Hydatius to *duces* of Honorius suppressing the rebellion of Jovinus and Sebastian at Narbonne.[158]

Another way of exposing and exploring the problem is to look at the careers of some of the men described as *duces*. The easiest example to follow is that of Aetius, a large proportion of whose activities are reported in a single source, the Chronicle of Hydatius. Leaving aside the problems of absolute chronology, this one source gives the following pattern for Aetius' career if it is assumed that the word *dux* must always have been used in a technical sense: *comes* (§92); *dux utriusque militiae* (§95); *dux* (§96); *dux utriusque militiae*, made patrician (§103); *dux* (§108); *dux et magister militiae* (§110); *dux* (§§112, 150 and 154); *dux et patricius* (§160). Other sources refer to him as 'dux' right up to the end of his career, *c.* 454,[159] even though a Novel of Valentinian III dated 445 (an official document, likely to reflect his true position) addresses him as 'comes et magister utriusque militum et patricius'.[160] The first point which should be made is that the title 'dux utriusque militiae' is not found anywhere outside Hydatius, either in relation to Aetius himself or anyone else. The meaning, however, is clear enough – Aetius was master of the soldiers, a title conferred upon him, according to Prosper, at about the time to which Hydatius §95 refers (*c.* 430).[161] What Hydatius does, therefore, is to employ the word *dux* in a completely non-technical sense to mean 'leader' – the master of the soldiers was the leader of the armed forces: Hydatius is not alone in this usage, for one of Claudian's poems is entitled, 'On James, master of the cavalry', but the text only refers to James as 'dux'.[162] Indeed, this general sense of the term must be what Hydatius intended whenever he used the word to describe Aetius's position: the only alternative is that Aetius was three times made master of the soldiers and thrice demoted to the position of *dux* (leader of a frontier army), a proposition bordering on the absurd.

It is not necessary to believe that Hydatius and the other chroniclers were simply ignorant of the Roman hierarchy and hence used vague terminology, or that they had succumbed to some form of 'barbarisation' and no longer comprehended the definitions of simple words, for within Hydatius' account there is a certain logic. On all the occasions on which Aetius was actually in charge of an army in the field, the word *dux* is used. Sometimes, perhaps in order to stress the high rank of the man, the idea of the mastership of the soldiers is combined with this, and once, on his death, the title of patrician is combined with it – the logic in the last case perhaps being that Aetius would be specifically remembered for his war-leadership (rather than for the more detached administrative duties of the master of the soldiers) and for his high position of honour as a patrician. Other chroniclers, perhaps viewing events in a slightly different perspective, describe Aetius as 'patricius' when discussing his involvement at the Catalaunian Fields.[163] There is a variety of reasons why they might have done this – they may have wished to emphasise the high esteem in which Aetius was held by the emperor; or the fact that, despite his rank, Aetius still engaged in battle; or (by indicating that the Hunnic threat was so great as to call for the involvement of such a high-ranking person) the scale of the 'Roman' army's achievement.

Further to the observations made so far, it is significant that the same non-technical usage of the word *dux* is applied to men who were not connected with the imperial government at all. For example, Alaric I is often described as 'dux' during his campaigns in Italy after Stilicho's death, even though he is normally thought of as being a king (*rex*).[164] Perhaps more interesting is the case of another Goth, Radagasius. In Prosper's Chronicle, he appears alongside Alaric as a *dux*,[165] but in two other chronicles he is described as 'rex' while being in charge of the Gothic army in Italy:[166] there is no way of knowing precisely what his position, or his relationship with Alaric, was. Finally, the non-technical usage of the term *dux* is illustrated by Constantius of Lyons' description of St Germanus as 'dux' of the army which won the 'Alleluia' victory:[167] Germanus was clearly not a *dux* in any official sense, but was simply the leader of the missions to Britain and a leading figure in the opposition to the Pelagians.[168]

In view of the variations of terminology within and between sources, it is almost impossible to tell when *dux* is being used in a technical way to designate the commander of a frontier army. The only occasions on which certainty is possible are when the title is used in rescripts which, as official documents produced by the administration itself, are more likely to employ correct titles. In fact, the few rescripts which refer to *duces* (which have been mentioned earlier), do explicitly state that the men whom they describe in this way were operating in the frontier provinces. All it is safe to say concerning the *duces* of the other sources is that they are always seen operating in a military context as the leaders of armies.[169] The use of the word *dux* is, therefore, broadly parallel to that of the term *comes* which, as argued above, can have a technical meaning, but is often used more informally to designate courtiers.

The master of the soldiers

If there is often uncertainty as to the military significance of the word *comes*, and as to whether *duces* were simply the leaders of armies or were the permanent commanders of frontier armies, no such confusion surrounds the specifically military role of the master of the soldiers. Holders of this title clearly occupied the chief positions in the army, and it is in precisely this context that most of the evidence concerning the activities of men bearing it are found. It has already been seen that officials known to have been masters of the soldiers could still be described as *duces* (even, in one source, *duces utriusque militum*), and that they could be involved in military campaigns. This sphere of activity is also attested for men designated by the proper title of master of the soldiers. For example, Castinus waged war on the Vandals as *magister militum*,[170] as did Vitus,[171] while Stilicho led the campaign against Gildo as master of the soldiers,[172] and Aetius is recorded as having campaigned against the Goths at Narbonne while being described as '*dux* and master of the soldiers'.[173] Finally, Aegidius fought against the Visigoths as master of the soldiers in Gaul, and certainly took part in other campaigns after Majorian had made him Gallic master, c. 457.[174]

Leading armies in the field was not the sole, nor perhaps the main, function of masters of the soldiers, but it receives attention in the sources because of their bias towards events, such as battles, which were of immediately-perceived significance. In fact, the master of the soldiers was more than a *dux* (in the widest possible sense) writ large. An examination of the *Notitia Dignitatum* (albeit an anachronistic source), reveals that the entire armed forces of the western Empire, except the palace guards and imperial bodyguards, were subject to the jurisdiction of either the master of the infantry (*magister peditum*) or the master of the cavalry (*magister equitum*), or the master of the cavalry in Gaul.[175] Later, the positions of master of the infantry and master of the cavalry could be combined in the hands of one man, known as the master of both branches of the soldiers (*magister utriusque militum*). Of the two original kinds of master of the soldiers, the *magister equitum* was simply in charge of the cavalry divisions, while the *magister peditum* not only had jurisdiction over the infantry, but also over all the military *comites* and the *duces* (in the technical sense), and over the legions and auxiliaries. Further, it was the responsibility of the holder of the power of the mastership to supply the *principes* and *numerarii* of the staff of the military *comites* and of the *duces* of frontier armies.[176]

Firmer evidence of the administrative duties of the masters of the soldiers in the fifth century comes from the rescripts received by such men. The rescripts often use the title *comes et magister militum*, making the point that these men were, even if not always specifically referred to as such, members of the imperial court rather than of the provincial administration. The subjects covered by the rescripts, of which (since the master of the soldiers was a courtier) there are not many, include the recruiting and levying of armies;[177] deserters;[178] military tax collection;[179] regulations concerning the sons of veterans;[180] the appropriation of public land by soldiers for their private use;[181] promotion within the army;[182] officers' supplies;[183] and the *officium* of the *comes Africae*, the staff of which was supplied by the masters of the soldiers:[184] a last rescript records that the master of the soldiers Segisvult was to organise coastal defences in *c.* 400.[185]

The evidence so far presented clearly marks the masters of the soldiers as the overall commanders of the army. Such men could also, occasionally, act in other spheres of imperial administration. It is not difficult to see how such influential men could come to be involved in diplomatic missions, as when Nepotianus, master of the soldiers, was instrumental in sending peace embassies to the Sueves,[186] or when Eparchius Avitus, apparently himself master of the soldiers, was sent by Emperor Maximus as an envoy to the Visigothic court at Toulouse:[187] it is pertinent to recall that other court officials, such as the *comes stabuli* and the quaestor, were sent on similar missions. In terms of more purely civil administration, there is, despite the impression sometimes given, no evidence from the west after 395 that the masters of the soldiers normally had any jurisdiction.[188] The only two rescripts addressed to holders of the office are, significantly, addressed to men described as 'comes et magister utriusque militum et patricius'.[189] The duties outlined in these documents can better be seen as special commissions of the type which any courtier could be called upon to perform, than as indications of any permanent encroachment of the authority of the master of the soldiers into the civilian area. In other words, it was perhaps the 'comes' part of the title which was important on these occasions, rather than the 'magister militum' part which was included in official documents such as rescripts.

Even without formal civilian power, the masters of the soldiers, especially those in charge of both the cavalry and the infantry, were immensely powerful individuals: control of the army gave them a ready power base should they choose to abuse their position. That masters of the soldiers did seek to further their own interests in the fifth century is a commonplace, but it is worth briefly discussing some of the main features of the story. First, even early in the century masters of the soldiers abused their position, as when Constantius, *magister militum*, allegedly influenced an episcopal election at Arles in *c.* 412 so that his friend Patroclus might become bishop.[190] This case was the subject of further abuse of high office, when Felix, master of the soldiers a few years later, had Patroclus assassinated, presumably for similar factional reasons.[191] Between these two events, there was a much more serious departure from the normal exercising of a high magistracy, when Castinus, 'who commanded the army as master of the soldiers', used his position to swing the support of the west behind the usurper John on the death of Honorius.[192] This more clearly foreshadows the events of the third quarter of the fifth century when Aegidius seceded to northern Gaul and refused to recognise Anthemius as Emperor.[193] On a wider scale, Ricimer abused his military power to bring down Emperors Avitus,[194] Majorian,[195] possibly Severus,[196] and Anthemius,[197] and, for a time, managed to do without an emperor in the west at all. It is significant that although Ricimer was almost certainly a master of the soldiers during the entire period from *c.* 457 to *c.* 472, the chroniclers almost always describe him as 'patricius' in relation to all except the first of the depositions (that of Avitus): this suggests that it was not necessarily Ricimer's position as master of the soldiers that was seen as the determining factor in his actions. In addition, it is clear that Ricimer's purpose was not to become an emperor himself, but to have an emperor who would not oppose his own kin-group's interests: it is certainly in relation to this that his removal of Avitus[198] should be seen, because Avitus was powerless to oppose Theoderic II's campaign against the Sueves, to whom Ricimer was related. Later, after Ricimer's death, the interests of the kin-group were briefly looked after by the Burgundian, Gundobad, to whom Ricimer had been related by marriage,[199] and who was influential in imperial circles under Glycerius.

Two points may be made in relation to the events outlined in the last paragraph. First, although the masters of the soldiers concerned undoubtedly abused their power to further their own ends, and seriously disrupted the course of imperial administration in the west, they did not, until after the death of Severus, try to dispense with the position of the emperor, nor did they ever try to become emperors themselves. All royal courts are subject to factionalism, and officials who can command the loyalty of armed forces are in a strong position to engage in it. There was, in addition, nothing new in factionalism in the imperial court in the fifth century,[200] and the fact that as late as its third quarter courtiers were still prepared to participate in court intrigues shows that the emperor and the Empire were still seen to be worth influencing. The people chosen as emperors may have been weak, but the position of emperor was not, at least until a succession of puppets had brought it into disrepute: by over-influencing the people they made emperors, courtiers of the mid-fifth century destroyed the power of the very men they thought they needed in order to further their own interests.

The second point to be noted is that it was not only masters of the soldiers who abused their power in this way. Orestes, who is only known to have been a patrician, behaved in a similar way to Ricimer,[201] who was a patrician as well as a master of the soldiers, and was often described as such (rather than as 'master of the soldiers') in relation to his factional scheming. More significant, perhaps, is the fact that it was Odoacer, not a master of the soldiers, but an official with control over another body of armed men – a *comes domesticorum*[202] – who finally dispensed with an emperor in the west.

The patrician

A position which has often been confused with that of master of the soldiers is that of patrician. At its most extreme, the argument has been put that in the fifth-century western Empire the title of *patricius* was almost identical with that of *magister utriusque militum*.[203] Although T.D. Barnes and A. Demandt, among others, have demonstrated that the patriciate was an honorary position, which was granted as a reward to those who had given outstanding service to the Empire,[204] a degree of confusion still surrounds the issue. Hence – to take only one more recent example – it has been suggested that, while the patriciate started as an honorific title under Constantine, it had, by the fifth century, become a high-ranking magistracy.[205] In view of the continuing lack of unanimity among recent commentators, the question is here re-examined against the background of what has already been suggested concerning the nature of other parts of fifth-century imperial administration.

If it is to be accepted that the title of patrician denoted a magistracy with a specific set of powers, it should be possible to find some indication of the ways in which the actions of men described as patricians differed from those of other men who did not bear such a title, or from those of the same men before they received the title. When clarification is sought from the chronicles, it must be remembered that their authors were not necessarily concerned to record the full and official titles of the men whose deeds they describe: it has already been seen how usage of the word *dux* could vary according to the specific emphasis each chronicler wished to give each particular event. In addition, almost all the information the chronicles do supply concerning patricians relates to the problems they caused by their involvement in high-profile faction politics, rather than to their legitimate spheres of activity. Often the chronicle references do no more than emphasise the status of the individuals concerned. Perhaps the clearest case again comes from the career of Aetius as seen through the eyes of the chroniclers. Under the year *c.* 434, Hydatius records that Aetius was made patrician,[206] but he does not always thereafter accord him the title, preferring, on most occasions, the word *dux*: this is true even when other chroniclers prefer *patricius*, as in the accounts of the battle of the Catalaunian Plains contained in the work of Prosper Tiro and in the *Chronicle of 511*.[207] One later occasion on which Hydatius (in common with Prosper, the *Fasti Uindobonensis Posteriores*, Cassiodorus, and Victor of Tunnuna) does use the word *patricius* is in relation to Aetius' murder:[208] presumably Hydatius thought it more important on this occasion to stress Aetius' rank and high position in the court, than his military exploits. With regard to other men, an official document, a Novel of Valentinian III, shows that Petronius Maximus was a patrician before he became emperor,[209] but the chronicle references to him only relate to his seizure of the throne, rather than elucidating his legitimate activities.[210] Finally, although after *c.* 457 Ricimer was both a master of the soldiers and a patrician, the chroniclers usually describe him simply as 'patricius', and in relation to faction politics.[211] The last case may help to explain how the positions of master of the soldiers and patrician have become confused in some modern interpretations, and serves to underline the problems inherent in using the evidence of the chronicles.

In order to pursue the investigation as to the ways in which the actions of patricians were distinctive, the rescripts must be considered next. As official documents produced by the administration itself, rescripts ought to be consistent in their usage of the title. There are, however, immediately-apparent difficulties, because, although a few rescripts were addressed to men described as patricians, the title is only twice found standing on its own. One of the two documents concerned was sent to Petronius Maximus (at a time before he became emperor) and concerns the trials of murderers;[212] the other was sent to Aetius, and is on the subject of the protection of men from enslavement.[213] These two cases are simply not enough upon which to build any form of hypothesis concerning the specific duties of patricians, and are probably best seen as further examples of the way in which high-ranking officials might, whatever their actual offices, be charged with governmental business of any kind. In addition, the rescript addressed to Aetius is, unusually, inexact in its form of address since Aetius was also master of the soldiers at the time: in cases of this kind it was more normal for the patriciate to be noted alongside the other titles held by the addressee, in such combinations as *comes et patricius*,[214] *comes et magister utriusque militum et patricius*,[215] and *praefectus praetorio et patricius*.[216] In those instances in which the word *comes* appears, it is once again likely that the situation is one in which courtiers could be charged with special tasks on an *ad hoc* basis. Even the fact that there is no other evidence that fifth-century western masters of the soldiers had civil jurisdiction does not prove that it was Aetius' position as patrician, rather than as a courtier (*comes*) which enabled him to receive the rescript. Finally, as rescripts which refer to 'praetorian prefects and patricians' do not differ in subject from those issued to other praetorian prefects (see Chapter 5), it is, in that case also, impossible to prove that it was on account of a man's position as a patrician that the specific commissions involved were assigned to him. It is significant that both a master of the soldiers (a court official) and a praetorian prefect (an extra-palatine figure of the provincial administration) could bear the title of 'patrician', because this provides final proof that the positions of patrician and master of the soldiers were not synonymous in the fifth-century west. While it cannot be denied that several masters of the soldiers were patricians, not all were, and those who could be described as patricians do not even constitute the majority of men referred to in that way.[217]

Given that it is impossible, alike from the evidence of the chronicles and from that of the rescripts, to define a specific sphere of activity in which patricians were active on account of their being patricians, and given that two officials as different as a master of the soldiers and a praetorian prefect could be described as patricians, it is legitimate to question whether the patriciate was an office at all, or whether it had a more general significance akin to that of the word *comes*. A further cause for suspicion is that there could be several patricians in existence at any one time:[218] except in the cases of the masters of the soldiers and, possibly, of the *comites stabuli*, only one court official at a time could bear each of the other titles so far encountered – there was, for example, only one master of the offices or *comes sacrarum largitionum*. Finally, if the patriciate was a formal office, then some officials held more than one office at a time: pluralism is not found in relation to other administrative positions, and caution should be exercised before seeing it in this case. Bearing these points in mind, it is perhaps significant that Prosper Tiro, a contemporary author, twice describes the position of patrician as an honour ('dignitas'),[219] and that Sidonius Apollinaris refers to it as the 'patricius apex',[220] which could also be interpreted to mean that it was an honorific title. Further, in relation to the conferment of the title on his own brother-in-law, Ecdicius, Sidonius Apollinaris specifically states that it was an honour and a reward for services rendered,[221] and it is in this sense that the same author's own patriciate, dating from after his tenure of the city prefecture, *c.* 468, should be seen.[222]

Before finally concluding that the patriciate was no more than an honorific title, however, a number of pieces of evidence which could point in another direction should be examined. To begin with, there are three related references: first, 'Constantius, as patrician, had his own *cancellarius*';[223] second, an inscription of *c.* 450 refers to a '*scriniarius* of the illustrious patrician seat';[224] third, the son of Volusianus (city prefect *c.* 417-418) was in charge of the *cancellarii* of the patrician Segisvult.[225] It could be argued that the ability of patricians to employ *cancellarii* and *scriniarii* is indicative of their having a specific set of functions which required that they should have such a staff, but this is not the only possible interpretation of the evidence. Patricians were active imperial agents, even if they did not hold an office with a specific set of duties,[226] and it would not be unreasonable for such men to have been provided with a small office staff to assist them in carrying out the special commissions with which they were entrusted.

The only other evidence that patricians may have exercised a specific set of powers comes in three further brief passages. In the first, Hydatius states that when, after Honorius' death, Galla Placidia and Valentinian III were sent to the west to oppose the usurpation of John and to establish a 'legitimate' western government, Felix was made patrician and master of the soldiers.[227] The implication of this could be that the title of patrician was supposed to confer a certain additional set of powers upon the holder, in the same way as did that of master of the soldiers, but it is equally possible that it could simply have served to underline Felix's authority and to give him added prestige. The second reference comes in Sidonius Apollinaris' panegyric on Anthemius, in which the Emperor is said to have held the positions of master of the soldiers and consul, together with the 'potestas patricii';[228] in addition, and finally, Litorius is said to have held the 'potestas' of the patriciate.[229] Given, however, that both Litorius and Anthemius had already borne titles denoting powerful positions,[230] it is not unreasonable to be sceptical as to the precise nature of the 'power' described, particularly in the case of Anthemius, where the reference to him comes from a panegyric which sought to flatter its subject. *Potestas* need not, in any case, be connected with a specific office, and could have more to do with 'authority' than with 'power' as such.

The evidence discussed in the preceding paragraph is not enough to outweigh that cited earlier, and does nothing to undermine the view that the patriciate was a rank or dignity rather than an office with specific duties attached to it. This does not mean that the title was completely empty, or that its holders were not important figures in the imperial administration. All the known fifth-century western patricians were men who held, or had held, high office, and who were of political and administrative importance: the title of *patricius* was a recognition of their value to the imperial administration, and gave its holders special prestige and authority. The granting of the status did not mean that the recipient had ended his career in government, because many patricians still held more formal offices: in addition, even patricians who did not hold another office could be asked to carry out commissions specially assigned to them, particularly tasks requiring persons of high rank, integrity and proven ability, such as those of an ambassadorial nature discussed by R.W. Mathisen.[231]

4

Conclusion

The purpose of the preceding chapters has been to assess the evidence for the importance of the western imperial court in the last eighty years of its existence, and to arrive at an understanding of the way in which it operated. Problems have been encountered with the nature of the sources, for neither the chronicles nor, for different reasons, the rescripts contained in the Theodosian Code, reveal as much of imperial activity or of the court as might be hoped. It has been argued that the chronicles are not works of administrative or 'constitutional' history, and should not be treated as such: they are literary and ecclesiastical works, concerned with morality and church history rather than with the administrative *minutiae* of a distant imperial court: such subjects were best illustrated by events of immediately-perceived importance, such as battles and wonders. The other literary works – poems and letters – also had quite legitimate concerns other than the administrative arrangements of the age in which they were produced, in the same way as modern poems and social correspondence have. These features of the 'unofficial' documentation are of crucial importance, and although such sources are not particularly revealing concerning the subject of this enquiry, they cannot on those grounds be dismissed as the product of a 'barbarian' age in which there was no coherent thought or writing. Indeed, it is a function of the sophistication of the authors of the sources that they deliberately selected material appropriate to their needs: the lack of evidence concerning the government merely demonstrates both the authors' lack of specific interest in this particular subject, and their skill in using other material more central to their interests. Evidence for similar sophistication and rational thinking also comes from the documents which were produced by the government itself, and it has been demonstrated that the rescripts are less enlightening the nearer to the person of the emperor, the centre of the Empire, an official operated. This is partly on account of the fact that officials close to the emperor could deal with him direct, without the intervention of written instruments, and partly because decisions which only affected the management of the court itself rarely needed to be publicised.

Despite these problems, and although they very seldom refer to the emperor or his court directly, both the rescripts and the chronicles take his existence for granted: the former were issued by the emperor himself, and the chroniclers took an active interest in the succession. Furthermore, the chronicles abound in references to faction politics which were centred around the person of the emperor: it was not only within the imperial court itself that factionalism was of importance, since provincial aristocrats became involved in factional man-oeuvrings and sometimes even enlisted the support of 'barbarian' kings. On other occasions, such kings participated in the same machinations on their own account, perhaps in order to try to obtain imperial sanction for their rule. Hence, although a fifth-century western emperor was no longer seen as a military leader, and was not anything like as closely involved in the government of the Empire as his predecessors had been, he was still perceived as being of great importance, both in the provinces and in Italy. He was the ultimate source of patronage for 'Roman' and 'barbarian' alike, and was the safeguard of the law – even though he did not issue rescripts to the new rulers of the western provinces, he could still be depicted, at least at the beginning of the period under examination, as giving laws to 'barbarians'. The disengagement of the emperor from active government was a gradual process, the pace of which was uneven and was dictated by 'barbarian' pressure: Britain, Africa and parts of Spain and Gaul lost their direct imperial administration in the first three-quarters of the fifth century; Italy followed suit in the last quarter of the century.

For as long as there was an emperor in the west, some provincial areas, together with Italy itself, continued to be administered directly. In order to assist him in this task, the emperor employed a number of officials, many of whom were based in the court. Despite the fact that, by virtue of the nature of the sources, there is little direct information concerning many of these court-based officials, it is possible to gain an impression as to the way in which the court operated. The most significant single point to emerge from the enquiry into the administrative workings of the court is that a courtier's title was not necessarily the key to an understanding of his activities at all times: although courtiers certainly held 'offices' which indicated their normal spheres of activity, such offices did not preclude activity in other areas. The administrative structure which was centred upon the court was not, therefore, bureaucratic, but depended upon a group of courtiers, or 'companions' (*comites*) of the emperor, who could, no matter what their specific titles, be called upon to carry out the emperor's will in almost any way. It might be thought that this imprecision in the definition of the competence of the holders of court offices is a result of the fairly small quantity and poor quality of the evidence, rather than of the reality of the fifth-century court, but it will become clear in the next chapter that the same is also true of the provincial administration, concerning which there is a larger body of evidence. That there was an *ad hoc* element in the administrative system cannot be doubted, but it may be exaggerated by the nature of the sources which tend to show the exceptional activities of courtiers rather than their more routine duties in the palace. In such circumstances it would be all too easy to dismiss the court as lacking any form of organisation and the imperial administration as constantly on the verge of collapse. To do that, however, would be to see the events of the first three-quarters of the fifth century against the background of *c.* 476: more importantly, it would also be to fail to grasp the sophistication of the sources, and the implications of their complexity for the interpretation of the information they can provide.

PART II
Provincial Administration

For the last seventy years of its existence, the imperial court lay at the centre of an Empire whose western provinces were undergoing a radical transformation in response to the unprecedented pressure brought to bear by the 'barbarians'. At the beginning of the fifth century, the western provinces (Map I) were administered by governors who were set in a hierarchical structure ranging from the rulers of individual provinces, through vicars (who ruled groups of provinces, or dioceses) to prefects (who ruled larger areas, or prefectures). By the middle of the century, that system had been replaced over large areas by a new one in which the highest authorities were the kings of 'barbarian' peoples, and the more local officials were supplied by members of the new royal courts.

The transformation of the provinces forms a major part of the process usually characterised as the 'fall of the western Empire'. In view of this, studies of late-Roman and 'barbarian' administration have tended to examine the Roman system of provincial administration alongside the Roman imperial court, and to treat the 'barbarian' system as a separate issue. Although there is a certain logic in such a division, it reflects a view that the 'barbarians' were opposed to the Roman world, and serves to underline the differences between Roman and 'barbarian' government. Since it is now generally accepted that the 'barbarians' were interested in assimilating Roman culture across a wide spectrum, a different framework for the discussion of their administrative systems is desirable. Given that (as will be argued in Chapter 5) Roman provincial governors, of all levels, were not members of the imperial court during their tenure of office in the provinces, it does not seem unreasonable to detach discussion of their position from that of the court. Such an uncoupling enables the examination of the great magistracies to be set alongside that of the 'barbarian' kings who were also not members of the imperial court.

In recent years, an added stimulus to the quest for continuity in provincial government has come from the renewed debate surrounding the nature of the arrangements by which the 'barbarians' were settled within the frontiers of the western Empire in the fifth century. Despite initial scepticism,[1] W. Goffart's suggestion[2] that the settlement was essentially a fiscal measure, rather one than involving the wholesale expropriation of Roman landowners by the newcomers, has gained ground.[3] In particular, J. Durliat has made a case that the basis of the settlement lay in the Roman tax system.[4] Under the arrangements now proposed, the two thirds of tax revenue which had formerly been equally divided between the maintenance of the army and of the imperial court were diverted to support the new federate army and the royal courts of the 'barbarian' kings, and were administered locally, with no intervention from the centre of the Empire; the remaining third of tax revenue continued to be used for purely local purposes. The implication of this is that the 'barbarian' kings operated an adapted version of the Roman fiscal system. Even if this new suggestion is not ultimately accepted (and there are many aspects of it which require further investigation), the traditional interpretation of the settlements as involving the physical partitioning of land, has always been seen in the context of imperial arrangements for military quartering and, therefore, equally had its roots in Roman traditions. In either case, accordingly, it is desirable to elucidate the extent to which other aspects of 'barbarian' administration grew out of Roman traditions. It is this which forms the basis of the ensuing chapters: the Roman administration of the prefects is examined first, then the royal government of the 'barbarian' kings in those areas of the western provinces for which there is a reasonable body of evidence.

5

The 'Roman' System of Provincial Administration

The highest-ranking officials of the provincial administration of the empire were the praetorian prefects, whose jurisdiction covered large groupings of provinces, and the city prefects, whose sphere of operation was more specific. Neither of these types of official is ever described as *comes*, a point which serves to underline the fact that the holders of such offices were involved in provincial rather than central government, and operated at a distance from the imperial court: it also serves as a reminder that the great prefectures were descended from a senatorial system of government which was considerably older than the imperial system which had replaced it.

The fact that provincial governors (of whatever rank) were not members of the imperial court during their tenure of office in the provincial administration does not mean that they were never involved in the court. In fact, many of the top-ranking provincial officials – the praetorian and city prefects – had held positions within the court at earlier stages of their lives. It is in the reconstruction of the careers of these men that the data provided by the inscriptions become most significant for, as was illustrated at the start of Part I, inscriptions often record, in chronological order, the full careers of the men they commemorate. A good example of the relevant type of inscription comes from Sisteron in the south of France and records a donation by a former praetorian prefect of Gaul, Dardanus: in addition to recording the gift, it tells its reader that Dardanus had earlier been a governor of the province of Viennensis, a *magister scrinii libellorum*, and a quaestor, as well as a Gallic prefect.[1] Similarly, another inscription from elsewhere reveals that after a court career culminating with the position of *consul intra consistorium*, Anicius Acilius Glabrio Faustus was city prefect three times and then praetorian prefect of Italy, Illyricum and Africa.[2] As a final example, a third inscription, this time concerning Flavius Junius Quartus Palladius, shows that its subject was a praetorian prefect for six years, after a court career which

53

involved time as a *tribunus et notarius* and culminated in the holding
of the office of *comes sacrarum largitionum*.[3]

The second major source of information of this type is the
Theodosian Code since, when the addressees of the rescripts it
contains are analysed, their movements within the top layer of the
administration can sometimes be seen. Hence, for example, Proculus
was *comes rerum priuatarum* in 422, and the following year received a
second rescript which shows that he had become a praetorian prefect.[4]
Precisely the same promotion (and in the same two years) can be seen
for Venantius,[5] while Hadrianus held two positions in the court, as
comes sacrarum largitionum and master of the offices, before becoming
praetorian prefect.[6] There are many other examples of this type of
movement from the court out into the highest positions of the
provincial administration and, significantly, none the other way. The
numbers involved are too great for this simply to be a matter of
coincidence, and it may be assumed that it was a deliberate policy for
the greatest provincial rulers to have served time at court before being
sent out to what were very powerful positions away from the close
supervision of the emperor:[7] the object of such a policy, hinted at in
Claudian's panegyric of Flavius Manlius Theodorus, would be to
attempt to ensure the ability and loyalty of the men who held such
posts.[8]

The city prefect

By the same token that the officials who operated nearest to the person
of the emperor received very few rescripts from their rulers, so the fact
that city and praetorian prefects were provincial administrators,
working at a distance from the imperial court, is illustrated by their
receipt of a large number of rescripts. Not only does the volume of
rescripts demonstrate the distance between the emperor and the
prefects, but an examination of the subject matter of the documents
reveals the immense range of the prefects' jurisdictions. Hence, for
example, in the case of the city prefect, rescripts on the following
subjects were issued in the west after 394: the African corn supply and
the provisioning of Rome;[9] the water supply;[10] the repair of buildings
in Rome;[11] the prefecture's office staff, and those in imperial service;[12]
decurions and compulsory state service;[13] rules concerning the rank of
those in imperial service;[14] the corporations of Rome;[15] ships and
shipmasters;[16] military recruiting;[17] regulations concerning the type
of dress permitted to Romans;[18] traitors, overmighty subjects, and the
supporters of the same;[19] heretics;[20] the imperial postal system (*cursus
publicus*);[21] senatorial taxation;[22] inheritance law;[23] judicial affairs.[24]

Owing to the nature of the rescript system, in which emperors issued
replies (*responsa*) to specific requests for assistance from their officials,

it is possible to state with some degree of certainty that the city prefects were, at one time or another, genuinely involved in almost every sphere of administration listed above: otherwise, there would have been no call for the rescripts to have been issued. Thanks to the survival of a large number of letters written by a city prefect, Quintus Aurelius Symmachus (who held office in 384-385), asking for the advice of emperors and informing them of certain events, it is possible further to demonstrate the wide range of such men's responsibilities. The documents concerned, Symmachus' *Relationes*, cover such subjects as supplies of corn and oil for the City;[25] the repair of buildings;[26] the staff of the prefecture;[27] the guilds of Rome;[28] taxation (including that of the Senate);[29] wills;[30] legal procedures and specific court cases;[31] the Senatorial *ordo*, and the transmission of Senatorial resolutions to the emperor;[32] games, entertainments and imperial donations.[33]

The fact that there is a considerable overlap between this list, relating to a single year, and the earlier one, which concerns the whole period from 395 to 476, may be taken to confirm the wide-ranging competence of city prefects during the last century of the western empire's existence. Sources of other types record the same range, though in a more fragmentary fashion. Hence, for example, Sidonius Apollinaris refers to his own responsibility for the distribution of food while he was city prefect, c. 468,[34] while inscriptional evidence reveals that Lampadius, city prefect under Arcadius, Honorius and Theodosius (II), was instrumental in drawing up a list of inns (*corpus tabernariorum*) in Rome.[35] A responsibility for the erection and repair of buildings and statues in the City is demonstrated by numerous inscriptions from Rome,[36] as well as by an edict of Valentinian III to the people of Rome which concerned both the restoration of the walls and gates of the City by the prefect, and the duty of that official to ensure that lands taxed for the purpose of maintaining defences, aqueducts and public transport were exempt from military taxation.[37] Yet further evidence shows that the city prefect was a leading member of the Senate,[38] though there is no direct fifth-century evidence from before c. 476 that he was the head of that organisation, the *princeps senatus*.[39]

One of the chief functions of the city prefects seems to have lain in the sphere of law enforcement. The rescripts indicate this when they record that appeals from the African provinces were to be heard by the prefect in the period after the full establishment of the Vandal kingdom based at Carthage,[40] and the consequent loss of the position of proconsul of Africa.[41] Similar implications lie in documents informing the prefects of the removal from circulation of certain of the works of the jurists which caused confusion,[42] and in an edict to the citizens of Rome confirming that the prefect was to ensure that civil cases were heard in civil, and not military, courts.[43] In addition, some of the inscriptions reveal that there was no appeal from the court of the city prefect as he judged 'in place of the emperor' (*uice sacra*).[44] Finally, it may be noted that law enforcement was not restricted to abstractions and court cases since, on the death of Pope Zosimus (*c.* 418), the younger Symmachus, as city prefect, and his officials had to maintain order in the City and control riots in a manner more reminiscent of a chief of police than of a chief justice.[45]

The sum of all the spheres of activity in which city prefects can be seen to have operated marks such officials as the chief officers of the emperor within the area of their jurisdiction; the fact that they judged *uice sacra* made them semi-autonomous. The only limitations on their power seem to have been that they had no direct responsibility in military matters, and that they were still ultimately subject to the emperors and submitted to them problems which they could not themselves solve. Athough the Theodosian Code records nothing like all the communications from the emperors to the prefects (or, indeed, to any other officials), it is likely that it was very rare for the central imperial court to take the initiative in actions within the geographical area subject to the city prefects. This is amply demonstrated by the surviving correspondence between the younger Symmachus and the emperor during the contested papal election of *c.* 418-419. The responsibility for maintaining order and securing a peaceful outcome to the proceedings was entirely that of the prefect, and only when he was unable to cope did the emperor intervene: even at that point, the imperial response was limited to sending letters of exhortation and a palace official to lend greater weight to the prefect's action.

In order to assist in the fulfilment of his wide-ranging and vice-imperial functions, the city prefect must have had a sizeable staff. According to the *Notitia Dignitatum*, there was indeed a large office staff:[46] the fact that most of its members are not attested in other sources is a reflection of the nature and paucity of the evidence which is only likely to note spectacular, unusual or particularly significant events, commonly those involving the prefect himself rather than his subordinates. Sometimes, however, it is possible to see lesser officials in action, as when, during the disturbances of *c.* 419, the younger Symmachus employed both the leading men (*proceres*) of his staff[47] and, more specifically, his *primiscrinius*,[48] in his attempts to resolve the conflict between the two candidates for the Papacy, Boniface and Eulalius. Even in this instance, though, the circumstances are exceptional, and it is unlikely that dealing with rebellious bishops and their supporters was a routine feature of the work of the prefect's staff. It is unfortunate that members of the prefectural staff are never seen in operation in more normal circumstances, but their importance in the provision of effective administration is quite clear from a complaint made by Quintus Aurelius Symmachus that he was being obstructed by an official appointed by the imperial court. It is unlikely that there is anything unusual in the fact that a subordinate official of the city prefect was appointed by the court, since it was shown in Chapter 3 that much of the permanent staff of the provincial administration was subject to the master of the offices. What is more interesting is that an official appointed in this way should have been seen by a prefect as obstructive, especially given the fact that the same prefect did not feel able to enforce his authority over that of the master of the offices in a legal case:[49] it seems that the power of the great provincial governors was weakened by the presence of court agents.

In addition to the office staff, there were other officials subordinate to the city prefect. Despite the fact that several of the lesser offices are listed in the *Notitia Dignitatum*,[50] and that a number of them feature in the *Uariae* of Cassiodorus in relation to the sixth-century Ostrogothic kingdom,[51] only one of them, the *praefectus annonae*, is attested in the fifth century before *c.* 476. The reasons for this paucity of information are the same as were noted for the lesser officials of the imperial court – namely, that subordinates do not often act in ways which are sufficiently important to have been recorded in the non-official sources, and that they did not receive rescripts from the emperors precisely because they were subordinates whose first appeal was to their immediate superior. This point is neatly borne out by the case of the *praefectus annonae*, for, although a few rescripts were sent to such men in the fifth century, all but one were addressed jointly to the city prefect and the *praefectus annonae*. Those rescripts also reveal, not surprisingly in view of his title, that the main concern of the *praefectus annonae* was with the provisioning of Rome: five of the six rescripts addressed to the prefects concern the Roman corn tax and corn supply,[52] and the sixth the bakers' guild.[53] Rescripts addressed to other officials indicate that the concern of the *praefectus annonae* with the corn supply led to a degree of responsibility for shipping from Africa (the main source of grain),[54] and for the investigation of shipmasters' claims for losses at sea.[55] Other types of source confirm this picture: letters of Quintus Aurelius Symmachus refer to the *praefectus annonae* as being responsible for the Roman food supply and for the provision of oil for the city;[56] a letter of Sidonius Apollinaris mentions an occasion on which the author himself, as city prefect, supervised the distribution by a *praefectus annonae* of five ship-loads of wheat and honey from Brindisi.[57] It is striking that these last references, the only ones to come from non-official documents, are both found in the works of men who held the city prefecture: the fact that neither Quintus Aurelius Symmachus nor Sidonius Apollinaris mentions any of the other officials whose activities they supervised, together with the existence of the few rescripts addressed to *praefecti annonae*, may be taken as an indication of the unique importance of the men responsible for supplying the City. Sidonius Apollinaris' reference is particularly significant since it comes from 468, after the time at which Africa had been taken over by the Vandals, and after the Vandal attack on Rome of c. 455, both of which events must have severely curtailed the grain trade: it may be doubted whether, after the loss of Africa, the position of *praefectus annonae* did not lose some of its importance.

The praetorian prefects

Returning to the top level of the provincial administration, perhaps the greatest position was that of the praetorian prefect of Italy (apart from the area subject to the city prefect), Illyricum and Africa; a second praetorian prefect headed the government of the Gauls (see Map I).[58] Neither prefect was a member of the imperial court while he held provincial office. In the following discussion, the position of the two prefects will be dealt with separately, and, to avoid both lengthy titles and confusion, the prefect in charge of Italy, Illyricum and Africa will be described simply as the 'praetorian prefect', his colleague in Gaul as the 'Gallic prefect'.

A greater body of material exists concerning the praetorian prefects than any other single type of official. Praetorian prefects, as the city prefects, received a very large number of rescripts from the emperors – there are approximately one hundred and ninety in the Theodosian Code which date from after 394: they were not court officials, and are never styled as *comites*.[59] With a single exception, all the evidence concerning such men comes from the Code. This is not altogether surprising, for the chronicles, which were mostly produced outside Italy, would not necessarily be expected to record their activities, especially since most of the prefects' actions were unspectacular and did not have an immediately-perceived impact upon the population. The one exception is of no real significance, and may be disposed of at once. Several chronicles record that the praetorian prefect, Boethius, was murdered at the same time as Aetius. The fact is not noted on account of any intrinsic importance it may have had, but simply because it was part of the much more significant event (in the eyes of the chroniclers) of the murder of Aetius, which unleashed the events leading to the downfall of Valentinian III. The name of Boethius is noted in passing, and nothing is revealed concerning his function within the government save his title: even that is only recorded as 'praefectus', rather than the full 'praefectus praetorio', in two of the sources.[60]

The main source of material concerning praetorian prefects, the rescripts, reveals that, as in the case of the city prefects, the range of subjects on which they received advice was vast. An approximate list of subject headings is as follows: *agentes in rebus*;[61] public buildings;[62] the Church and its privileges;[63] the clergy and those in holy orders;[64] *coloni*;[65] the competence of provincial governors;[66] compulsory imperial service;[67] the public postal system (*cursus publicus*);[68] debts and debtors;[69] decurions;[70] deserters from the army;[71] imperial domains and their officials;[72] freedmen;[73] grants and leases of land, and petitions for land;[74] holidays and Church festivals;[75] inheritance law;[76] Jews;[77] law enforcement, the statute of limitations, and trials;[78] the law of marriage and divorce;[79] the minting of coin;[80] office staff, other officials of the prefecture, and those in imperial service;[81] pagans and heretics;[82] the employment of palace officials (*palatini*);[83] prisoners of war;[84] prisons;[85] the quartering of troops;[86] the rank of those in imperial service;[87] rations for animals used in imperial service;[88] rebels, traitors, and their supporters;[89] recruiting for the army;[90] repairs to roads;[91] the Roman food and water supply;[92] the Roman guilds;[93] ships and shipmasters;[94] taxation, including tax privileges and remissions.[95] And the list is not exhaustive.

The clear implication of this long list, which covers almost every aspect of civilian life, is that the praetorian prefect was the highest authority in the provinces under the emperor. This will have made his position one of the greatest power, since although the large number of rescripts shows that he regularly consulted the emperor, it is highly unlikely that routine, unexceptional, business ever went higher than the prefect himself. There is no real way of assessing the volume of such affairs, particularly since virtually nothing is known of the procedural law of the provinces, but, given the number of rescripts, it may be assumed that it was immense. In addition, there is nothing to suggest that the situation had changed from the time of Constantine, when the praetorian prefect was granted the power to judge in place of the emperor (*uice sacra*):[96] although there is no positive evidence for the continued existence of such a power in the fifth-century west, the city prefect retained it, and that makes it almost inconceivable that the praetorian prefect did not. The authority to judge *uice sacra* will have made the praetorian prefect semi-autonomous, for it was, presumably, only he who could decide whether a case brought before him should be referred to the emperor. In addition, there is nothing to suggest that praetorian prefects were not still able to issue edicts which could have the force of law,[97] though the main function of the Gallic prefects, at least, was with the administration of the law rather than with its creation which was, as noted in Chapter 2, an imperial prerogative.[98]

The only major sphere in which praetorian prefects do not appear to have had any competence is that of military affairs. The nearest to this that can be detected is a concern to ensure that recruitment to the army was carried out properly, and that military service was not evaded: too much should not, however, be read into this, since recruitment is an area in which civil and military jurisdictions overlap. Were praetorian prefects to have had general military competence as well as civilian, they would almost certainly have been uncontrollable, especially since they operated at a distance from the imperial court. Such a situation had existed before the time of Constantine, and the resulting position of the prefect has been described by A.H.M. Jones as that of a 'kind of grand vizier, the emperor's second in command'.[99] Constantine had seen the dangers inherent in that arrangement, and had removed military power from the praetorian prefects, creating the court office of master of the soldiers instead.[100] Henceforth, the civil administration of the provinces was the responsibility of the praetorian and city prefects, who were not members of the court, and military affairs were attended to by the masters of the soldiers, who were: all three types of official had equal rank.[101] It was this situation which prevailed in the fifth century – in Italy itself until *c.* 476.

The position in Gaul is more difficult to assess. The most striking feature of the evidence is that Gallic prefects received many fewer rescripts than their Italian counterparts after 394 – only nineteen, or about a tenth of the number sent to the praetorian prefects in Italy. Other sources, notably those written in Gaul itself, are more helpful than those for the Italian prefecture, but often reveal only the names of such officials, and are uninformative concerning their role in the administration of the empire. Hence, for example, the name of Auxiliaris is known, but all that is learnt of him is that his wife was cured by St Germanus;[102] there is a similar lack of evidence concerning the governmental functions of Exuperantius,[103] Felix,[104] Marcellus,[105] Paeonius[106] and Decimus Rusticus.[107]

When the Gallic prefects are seen acting in an official capacity, the range of activity in which they were engaged is, at first sight, not very different from that noted for the praetorian prefects. Tonantius Ferrandus, for example, negotiated the end of King Thorismund's siege of Arles, *c.* 451; he was also responsible for a reduction in taxation, and prosecuted the alleged traitor Arvandus (a former Gallic prefect).[108] The future Emperor Avitus, as Gallic prefect, was described as administering the law,[109] and another prefect, Agricola, was in charge of the main provincial gathering in Gaul, the *conuentus septem prouinciarum*.[110] The rescripts confirm the picture of wide-ranging civil jurisdiction: the same Agricola received such a document concerning the Pelagian heresy,[111] while Vincentius was sent rescripts on the subjects of *coloni*,[112] compulsory imperial service,[113] the public postal system (*cursus publicus*),[114] recruitment[115] and taxation.[116] His successors, Andromachus, Dardanus and Amatius, also received rescripts on a similar range of topics – taxation,[117] local government[118] and the Church,[119] respectively.

Before concluding that the Gallic prefect fulfilled a function identical with that of the praetorian prefect, account must be taken of several further features raised by the evidence of the rescripts. First, there exists a small number of rescripts addressed to Gallic prefects which concern military affairs, and they do not only deal with the issue of recruitment which, as suggested earlier, is at the junction of civil and military jurisdiction. As early as 398, the Gallic prefect Vincentius received instructions concerning the maintenance of garrisons on the Spanish frontier;[120] he also received a rescript concerning the problem of centurions who deserted, and a third such document involves the quartering of troops.[121] The second and third cases could be seen as treating of further areas of jurisdiction which are on the margin of civil and military authority, and it may be that the existence of this small number of rescripts concerning military affairs does no more than highlight the pressures on the administration of the empire in general during the years of tension between the two imperial courts in the early years of Stilicho's regency – it will be recalled that court officials were, no matter what their titles, able to intervene in any sphere of activity as occasion demanded. However, the fact that two of the surviving nineteen rescripts issued to Gallic prefects are concerned with military affairs other than recruitment and deserters, may be more significant, especially as there are no comparable documents among the very large number of rescripts issued to Italian prefects.

A second point which arises from the analysis of the rescripts is that of their very small numbers. It might be thought that this indicates an Italian bias in the sources used for the compilation of the Theodosian Code, but that is inherently unlikely, since it was presumably the comprehensive imperial archives of the west which were used, rather than the partial and scattered provincial archives. In addition, since the additional documents preserved in the Justinianic *Corpus* do not correct the balance, the smaller number of Gallic rescripts may be taken to reflect the true situation.

An alternative explanation for the decline in the number of rescripts could be that it reflects the diminishing area subject to the Gallic prefects during the course of the fifth century, the opposing factions into which the Gallic aristocracy had split in the mid-fifth century, and the establishment of the 'barbarian' kingdoms within Gaul. Attractive though this might at first seem, it does not withstand careful scrutiny because the real drop in the number of rescripts was completed within the opening years of the century: only two were issued after 402,[122] some four years before the breaching of the Rhine frontier, and even longer before the large-scale and permanent establishment of 'barbarians' in Gaul. What is needed, therefore, is an explanation with its roots in the previous century.

During the fourth century, one of the main imperial residences in the west had been Trier and, especially under Gratian and Valentinian

I, Gallic aristocrats had been able easily to participate in the administration of the empire. In the 390s, however, Trier was abandoned in favour of the north-Italian residences of Milan and Ravenna. One consequence of this was that the Gallic aristocracy lost its ready access to the court, and many of its members felt less closely bound to the empire, with the further result that, during the fifth century, there was a tendency for them to withdraw from imperial government: a corollary to this may be that the Gallic aristocracy sought greater control over its own affairs and wished to find solutions to its own problems. One symptom of this desire for greater self-sufficiency may be found in the support of a number of Gallic aristocrats for the usurpation of Constantine III and the rebellion of Jovinus. Another, longer lasting, symptom could be that the Gallic prefects, whose discretion to act on their own initiative was probably similar to that of their Italian counterparts, simply ceased to refer matters to the emperors, but chose to arrive at decisions by other means. One such means may well have been supplied by the establishment, by *c.* 417 at the latest, of the Gallic assembly (*conuentus septem prouinciarum*):[123] even though the assembly only met in formal session once a year, the prefects could presumably seek advice from its members on a more informal basis as required.

However this may be, the cessation of the flow of rescripts quite clearly does not herald the imminent demise of the office of Gallic prefect. Although almost nothing is revealed about the later prefects from official documents, the names of several are known, the last from as late as the 470s.[124] What is equally significant, though, is that all the post-406 prefects of whom anything is known were members of the native aristocracy, rather than men from outside the diocese as had often been the case previously.[125] This is as good a sign as any of the desire of the ruling classes of Gaul to be free from centrally-imposed officials and constraints: it is a feature of indigenous society which has implications for the development of Gaul in the era of 'barbarian' settlement and beyond.

The vicars of the prefects

In order to assist them in the vast administrative task they faced, whether in Italy or in Gaul, the praetorian prefects had deputies – vicars (*uicarii*). The type of vicar about whom most is recorded is the vicar of the city of Rome who, according to the *Notitia Dignitatum*, was in charge of the governors of the provinces in the suburbicarian diocese, and had an office staff broadly similar to that of the city prefects.[126] One might expect from the title of the vicar of the city of Rome that this official was the vicar of the city prefect, but the evidence of the *Notitia Dignitatum* is against this, as is evidence from the fourth century. Diocletian had created a vicar of the city, who, although based at Rome, was in fact the deputy of the praetorian prefect: there was another vicar, the vicar of the city prefecture, but that position was abolished in 357,[127] and is not attested in the fifth century.

Despite this relatively clear picture from the fourth century, it will be recalled that the *Notitia Dignitatum* is an antiquarian document and may not reflect the reality of the fifth century. Indeed, there is some evidence from the later period which points in the direction of the vicars of the city being the deputies of the city prefects. Hence, for example, during the disturbances surrounding the papal election of *c.* 419, the younger Symmachus, as city prefect, was assisted by his vicar (unnamed) in maintaining order in Rome, and there is nothing to indicate that the official was answerable to the praetorian prefect rather than to Symmachus himself.[128] In another case, a rescript issued by Honorius commanded the *praefectus annonae* and the vicar of the city jointly to investigate claims made by shipmasters concerning losses at sea:[129] such co-operation between an official known to have been subject to the city prefect and the vicar is easier to envisage if it is assumed that the vicar was subject to the city prefect than if he was subject to the praetorian prefect. In a case involving a similar matter, Varus, as vicar of the city, published a law, *c.* 398, concerning the food supply.[130] Finally, the involvement of the vicar with the supplying of Rome is, perhaps, underlined by an inscription which records that Flavius Nicius Theodulfus restored buildings at Ostia, Rome's port, during his term of office as vicar of the city.[131]

Other fifth-century evidence is entirely unhelpful. A vicar of the city was present at the meeting of the Senate in 438 which accepted the Theodosian Code,[132] and Benignus, as vicar, received three rescripts, one concerning a tax settlement, one the shepherds of Valeria and Picenum, and the third compulsory imperial service.[133] Rescripts on subjects such as those outlined could have been issued equally well to vicars of the praetorian prefects as to those of the city prefects, and it must remain an open question as to which of the two prefects was the superior of the vicar of the city of Rome.

The vicar of the city was not the only vicar found in the western empire in the fifth century, and there can be no doubt that the other vicars were subject to the praetorian prefects. According to the *Notitia Dignitatum*, there was a vicar for each of the dioceses of the west – Britain, the Gauls, Spain and Africa.[134] It is interesting, given the uncertainty over the precise position of the vicar of the city, that although a vicar of Italy is listed in the table of contents to the western part of *Notitia*,[135] such a position does not appear in the text, whereas that of the vicar of Rome does. Even more tantalising is the fact that at least one inscription records the existence of a vicar of Italy, but cannot, of its very nature, give any clues as to the implications of the title.[136]

There is not a great deal of evidence concerning the activities of the vicars: this is not surprising, given that they were, by definition, the deputies of higher officials and, as argued in Part I, lesser governmental agents are rarely seen in the sources. Even when non-official documents mention vicars, they often reveal no more than the names of such men and the areas in which they held authority. Hence, for example, a letter of Sidonius Apollinaris indicates that Gaudentius was 'vicar of the seven provinces in Gaul', but no more.[137] Similarly, the poetic works of Namatianus show that one Victorianus was vicar in Britain for a time, but reveal nothing of his governmental role save that he was indeed subject to the praetorian prefect in Gaul.[138] Even less helpful is the evidence of inscriptions: that which refers to Nicomachus Flavianus, for instance, simply records that he was vicar of Africa for a time.[139]

The only non-official document which is more helpful is the *Notitia Dignitatum*, which shows that vicars formed an intermediate tier of administration between the praetorian prefects and the governors of the provinces over which they had control.[140] Such a position will have involved the vicars in wide-ranging administrative duties, probably broadly similar to those undertaken by the praetorian prefects, and the few rescripts which were addressed directly to the vicars reflect this.[141] It is usually assumed that the vicars, like praetorian prefects, had civil jurisdiction only, military authority being in the hands of the *comites prouinciarum* discussed in Chapter 3.[142] It is of interest, therefore, that one rescript concerns military affairs, instructing Gaudentius, vicar of Africa, to ensure that neither civilians nor Roman soldiers tried to take over frontier fortifications assigned to the 'gentiles' (= 'barbarians') for defence.[143] The total number of rescripts involved is, however, too small for the full implications of this to be assessed, especially as the case is one in which the civil and military spheres meet. Perhaps more interesting is the fact that on the only occasion on which a vicar is seen in action, Hydatius records that Maurocellus, a vicar in Spain, assisted the *comes Hispaniarum*, Asterius, in a campaign against the Sueves.[144] The precise significance of this is impossible to assess, but it is interesting to note that a potential erosion of the demarcation between civil and military authority is manifested in the case of the vicar of Spain, who was subject to the Gallic prefect: it has already been observed that Gallic prefects seem to have had some military competence which their Italian counterparts appear to have lacked. On the other hand, it is at least as likely that in *c.* 419, when the particular campaign against the Sueves took place, the empire was so stretched as to make it impossible to observe the niceties of demarcations between spheres of jurisdiction: if

Maurocellus was in the area and able to lead an army, he may simply have become involved for no better reason than that he was the only person available at the time.

Even without regular military competence, the vicars will have had as large a volume of administrative business (relative to the geographical areas they controlled) as the praetorian prefects, and this seems to be reflected by the fact that the *Notitia Dignitatum* states that they had large office staffs. It is unfortunate, but not surprising, that those lesser officials are practically invisible, but there is no reason to doubt that they existed, at least in the early part of the century, for some of their number were present at the 411 Council of Carthage.[145]

Provincial governors

When yet another step is taken down the ladder of provincial administration, to the level of the governors of individual provinces, there is even less evidence than for the vicars. This is to be expected, since provincial governors would, in the first instance, appeal to the vicars or the praetorian prefects for guidance: only rarely would the petition of a governor reach the emperor directly or require a direct response from him. There is one outstanding exception to this picture – that of the proconsul of Africa – which may be dealt with first.

The Theodosian Code preserves approximately sixty-nine rescripts addressed to the proconsuls of the province (as opposed to the diocese) of Africa in the fifth century: this is the largest number for any official apart from the praetorian prefect. The probable reason for this is not difficult to discern – the vital economic importance of Africa to Rome makes it reasonable for it to have been governed in an exceptional way. The precise form this special treatment took was for the governor to be of proconsular rank and to be endowed with the power to judge in place of the emperor (*uice sacra*).[146] In other words, the administration of the province of Africa was, effectively, lifted out from the jurisdiction of the vicar of the African diocese and of the praetorian prefect, and handed over to another vice-imperial figure. It follows that if such an official needed advice, or required to refer any business to another, higher, authority, he could only have recourse to the emperor, who would respond with rescripts. Given this situation, it is not surprising to find that a fairly comprehensive list of subjects is covered by the rescripts, at least in terms of civil administration.[147] Predictably, other sources do not reflect this wide sphere of activity, only providing scraps of information. A letter of Quintus Aurelius Symmachus refers to the involvement of the proconsul in the provisioning of Rome,[148] but two inscriptions do no more than commemorate public building works carried out by such men.[149] Otherwise, it is only in the letters of St

Augustine, and in the proceedings of the 411 Council of Carthage, that anything is seen of proconsuls and their officials, and in those documents it is their involvement with the Church which is reflected, rather than their role in the government of the province.[150] Indeed, so little is known of proconsuls that it is not possible to reconstruct their careers to see whether they conformed to the pattern of ex-courtiers being given the highest positions in the provincial administration, though there is no reason to suppose that this was not the case. The lack of evidence should not mask the great power and importance which these officials must have possessed.

The governors of the other western provinces were not in such a favoured position. According to the *Notitia Dignitatum*, such men fell into three categories – *consulares*, *correctores* and *praesides* – but it is impossible to say whether there was any meaningful distinction between them in the fifth century: certainly, the office staffs of all three were of identical composition.[151] The position of the governors appears to have been quite junior, for inscriptions reveal that governorships were held early in a man's career,[152] and it is quite likely that such positions were sometimes bought.[153] Inscriptions do not, however, reveal anything of the activities in which governors were engaged; nor, despite their provincial bias, do the chronicles, whose authors were more interested in dramatic events than in administrative decisions of a type which will have concerned the governors. The sole source of information on those administrative duties is a very small number of rescripts which were sent to governors, and they reveal involvement in the usual spheres of civil government: appeals;[154] compulsory service;[155] marriage law;[156] laws concerning the land of absentee landowners;[157] taxation.[158] Two further rescripts, addressed to praetorian prefects, confirm the role of governors in tax collection,[159] and show that they had some responsibility for imperial palaces within the areas subject to their jurisdiction.[160]

It is clear that provincial governors must have employed a sizeable staff in order to carry out their duties, but very little is known about any of its members, with the exception of those known as *domestici* and *cancellarii*. In origin, it is likely that, as their name suggests, the *domestici* (who are not to be confused with the emperor's *domestici* or *protectores domestici*[161]) formed the household staff of their employers,[162] and it may be for this reason that the *Notitia Dignitatum* makes no reference to them. It was not only provincial governors who employed *domestici*, for *c.* 395, at a time when he did not hold any government office, Quintus Aurelius Symmachus had a *domesticus* who delivered a letter for him,[163] and, at about the same time, a rescript refers to *domestici* who were household servants:[164] there are also references to *domestici*, who may simply have been servants, on tombstones.[165]

There is a more developed, or technical, usage of the word *domesticus*, which makes an appearance in the rescripts, such as that preserved in Justinian's *Corpus iuris ciuilis* which describes *consiliarii* (advisers) and *cancellarii* as holding 'officia domesticorum'.[166] Such men were obliged to remain in the provinces for fifty days after their return to private life: this provision may have been formulated in an attempt to give the provincials time to prosecute *domestici* for misdeeds committed during their term of office, a point more explicitly made in a second rescript which mentions the prosecution of 'domestici iudicorum' for the maladministration of public affairs.[167] Later, in a rescript sent to an eastern praetorian prefect, Asclepiodotus, a further attempt was made to render *domestici* and *cancellarii* accountable, since it was indicated that they should be nominated by the provincials themselves and should remain in the provinces for a full three years after the termination of their period of office.[168]

The implication of such measures as these is that some *domestici* were more than household servants, and were possessed of a considerable degree of power. It is not difficult to see how such a situation could have come about, since a governor (or any other official) might easily ask his servants to carry out tasks in public administration, probably at first on an *ad hoc* basis. There need be nothing surprising in this, since it is little more than another manifestation of the principle that members of the imperial household, or court (*comites*), could, even if they held a specific office, be employed in almost any sphere of administration if occasion demanded. As the custom of using *domestici* became more common it may well also have become 'institutionalised', so that the nature of *domestici* will have changed: instead of being simply domestic staff, they will have become, effectively, minor state officials; they may also have acted as the advisers and confidants of their employers.[169]

The close contact that must have existed between the *domestici* and their employer will have created considerable scope for corruption, since there could be very little external check on the activities of *domestici* until the consequences of their actions became known. This is perhaps the most likely background for the attempts to oblige *domestici* to remain in the provinces after their appointments came to an end, and for the efforts to break the closeness of the relationship between the governors and their *domestici* by ruling that the latter should be nominated by the provincials themselves. Without such controls, provincial governors who, given the scale of the empire, must have been possessed of a fair degree of autonomy, could all the more easily have treated their provinces as small 'kingdoms' for their own profit and, in effect, the *domestici* who were not simply household servants, could have become the 'companions' of their employers in the same way as the *comites* were of the emperor.

Conclusions

The essence of the system of provincial administration discussed in this chapter is that the civil aspects of the government were carried out at a distance from the imperial court by officials who were not members of the court during their period of office in the provinces. The highest officials of the provincial administration were the prefects, who were semi-autonomous, beneath whom were the vicars and the provincial governors, each responsible for a smaller area, but also enjoying varying degrees of freedom of action. All officials, no matter what their rank, were competent throughout the sphere of civil administration. The fact that the contemporary documentation only reveals much concerning the highest-ranking officials is a function of the nature of the sources, and, since some of those are governmental, of the administrative system itself: it cannot be taken as an indication that the lower-ranking officials were not active or important, and certainly should not be seen as part of a process of collapse of the system. Rather, the absence of a large volume of evidence could be seen as an indication that the system was functioning as it should, with little reference direct to the emperor by the lesser officials.

This does not mean that the system of government in the provinces was unaffected by the pressures to which the Empire was subjected in the late fourth and fifth centuries. The uncertainty of the Rhine frontier was a significant factor in the decision to abandon Trier as an important imperial residence in the late fourth century, and also led, not long afterwards, to the removal of the seat of the Gallic prefecture to safer territory further inside the Empire. A combination of the effects of the departure of the imperial court from Gaul, the continued and widespread military threat from the 'barbarians' throughout the Empire, and tensions between the eastern and western imperial courts in the years after the death of Theodosius I, made at least the Gallic aristocracy increasingly inward-looking, and prone to become more self-reliant than in the past. Despite this tendency towards self-sufficiency in routine matters, the Gallo-Roman aristocracy cannot be considered to have been anti-imperial, for, as was argued in Chapter 2, its members maintained a lively interest in the question of the imperial succession, and actively engaged in the factional manoeuvrings surrounding who should be in charge of the western Empire.

Gaul as a whole is the best-documented area of the western Empire outside Italy, but not all parts of Gaul are equally well served by surviving documentation, and it does not follow that changes similar to those in the better-documented areas were not also happening elsewhere in the Gallic prefecture – in Britain, Spain, and Gaul north of the Loire.[170] In the case of Britain, it is known that the 'barbarian' threat on the Continent necessitated the removal of the Roman military presence in the early years of the fifth century. What is considerably less clear is the extent to which that removal saw the immediate collapse of the 'Roman' administration: if the evidence of Gildas is to be believed, however, it is likely that, for a time at least, the Romano-British population, though cast on its own resources, thought it was still sufficiently part of the Empire to call upon imperial forces in opposing the 'barbarians' who threatened the former Roman Britain.[171]

In Spain, where there is rather more documentation, the arrival of the Vandals, Alans and Sueves in the early years of the fifth century must inevitably have caused major problems for the established administrative system, both in areas directly settled by the 'barbarians' and elsewhere. After the departure of the Vandals for Africa, a large part of the Iberian peninsula again came under 'Roman' control, the most notable exception being Galicia which remained in the non-Roman and probably non-federate hands of the Sueves until the last quarter of the sixth century.[172] In almost all areas of Spain, 'Roman' and 'barbarian' alike, there were still some local Hispano-Roman leaders throughout the fifth century. Hence, for example, Didymus and Verenianus, Spanish relatives of the emperor, organised a private army against Constans in 409;[173] one Basilius organised the *bacaudae* in Tarraconensis in 449;[174] Ospinio and Ascanius betrayed Chaves and its bishop, the chronicler Hydatius, to the Sueves in 460;[175] Lusidius handed Lisbon over to the Sueves in 469;[176] and one Peter resisted the Gothic takeover of Tortosa as late as 506.[177] Another local Roman leader may have been Terentianus, 'uir clarissimus', who, in, or shortly after, 483, travelled to Rome from Tarraconensis and carried home a letter from Pope Felix III,[178] while at least one of Sidonius Apollinaris' letters is addressed to a Spaniard.[179] In addition, Roman armies continued to campaign in Spain until 460, when the last such army to operate there was led by the emperor, Majorian, himself.[180] Against this background, it is *prima facie* likely that, despite the increasing need for the Spanish provinces to be self-reliant, something of the 'Roman' administrative system remained, at least at a local level, and there are tentative indications that this was indeed the case even in the Galician area subject to lasting settlement by the non-federate Sueves.[181] Roman traditions also formed the basis for much of the apparatus of Visigothic government in the late sixth and seventh centuries: even though the Visigoths were settled in south-west Gaul on federate terms, and will have absorbed a number of 'Roman' institutions there, it is highly unlikely that they could have imposed a 'Roman'-based system on Spain in the sixth century had the elements of that system not still been in place, still less had the native population abandoned that same system a century earlier.

After the murder of Majorian by Ricimer, part of Gaul north of the

Loire was controlled by Majorian's Gallic master of the soldiers, Aegidius, who, according to the late-sixth-century *Decem libri historiarum* of Gregory of Tours, became ruler – 'king' – of some of the Franks in the area for a time.[182] The same source relates that Aegidius was succeeded by his son, Syagrius, called 'king of the Romans'.[183] Whatever the exact meaning of the term 'king' in this context, and whatever the extent of the territory subject to Aegidius and Syagrius, the important point is that Romans, albeit disaffected Romans, were in a position of power in northern Gaul.[184] Another, even more obscure Roman leader in the same area is the *comes* Paul, a military leader;[185] while in Armorica, in 417, order was for a time maintained by Exuperantius (probably on his own initiative, as he does not appear to have held any administrative or military office at the time).[186] Where Romans were in charge, it is not unreasonable to suppose that 'Roman' governmental traditions were continued at a local level. There was probably little significant difference between the non-federated areas of southern and northern Gaul, in administrative terms, until parts of the north fell under the control of the 'rebels' Aegidius and his son – both regions were governed by traditional 'Roman' mechanisms, with decreasing direct reference to the emperor. In other, rather better-documented areas of the Gallic prefecture, the fifth century saw the creation of new administrative arrangements with the settlement of 'barbarians' ruled by their own chiefs, or kings, as federates of the Empire: as will be seen in the next four chapters, there was no complete break with the imperial past even in the regions which acquired new rulers.

6

The Kingdom of the Visigoths, *c.* 418-568

The king

The first part of the western Empire to experience federate settlement of the fifth-century western kind, was south-west Gaul, the region given to the Visigoths by Constantius *c.* 418. The Goths were no strangers to the Empire by that time, having already lived within its frontiers, as federates of a different type, for more than three decades. The story of the settlement of the Goths within the Empire in 382, and of their subsequent migrations through the Balkans and Italy has been told in a masterly way by H. Wolfram, and it is not pertinent to rehearse it here. All that needs to be said is that such direct contact with the Empire and its way of life for a generation before the settlement in Aquitaine must have had an impact upon the way in which the Visigoths behaved, saw themselves, and were perceived by members of the Roman aristocracy.

A convenient illustration of this point with which to commence detailed discussion comes from the statement by Orosius that even before the conclusion of the agreement of federation which gave the Visigoths the province of Aquitanica II in *c.* 418, a leader of the Goths, Atauulf, came to be of the opinion that the destiny of his people was to promote the interests of the Roman Empire.[1] This could, of course, be nothing more than the wishful thinking of a Roman author, seeking, perhaps with hindsight, to make the best of the unpalatable situation in which the presence of the Goths within the western Empire appeared to have become a permanent feature of the Roman world. Other events, however, tell against such an argument, for it is known that Atauulf made Galla Placidia, the sister of Emperor Honorius, his wife, and he may even have nurtured the hope that, since Honorius was childless, his own children by Galla Placidia would inherit the imperial throne.[2] However that may be, it is unlikely that the presence of so 'Roman' a person as the sister of the emperor in Atauulf's court would not have influenced both the organisation of the court and the

71

policy of the king in what was the first relatively settled period the Visigoths had experienced for some time. Further to this, it is pertinent to note that so distant a source as the Greek Olympiodorus lays stress on the *romanitas* of Ataulf in his description of the king's wedding at Narbonne:

> There Placidia, dressed in royal raiment, sat in a hall decorated in the Roman manner, and by her side sat Ataulf, wearing a Roman general's cloak and other Roman clothing.[3]

This passage, especially when taken in conjunction with Orosius' comments, makes it quite clear that the Visigothic king saw himself as being in the service of the Empire, at least in a military sense. It may be that Ataulf was exceptional, and that his aspirations were not those of his courtiers and successors. Nevertheless, it was not Ataulf, but his successor but one, Walia, who accepted the Roman terms of federation in south-west Gaul, after which Olympiodorus considered the Gothic kingship to be an *archê* – that is, a Roman magistracy.[4]

H. Wolfram has drawn attention to the fact that later in the fifth century, members of the Gallo-Roman aristocracy were prepared to refer to the king as 'dominus noster', and to accord him regnal years in the tradition of vice-imperial magistracies.[5] A similarly 'Roman' picture is to be found in Sidonius Apollinaris' detailed description of Theoderic II's daily routine. After early-morning religious observance,

> the administrative duties of his kingdom take up the rest of the morning. The *comes armiger* stands by the king's seat; a crowd of guards dressed in skins is admitted so that it be nearby, but is excluded from the royal presence itself lest it cause a disturbance; and so the guards keep up a murmur of conversation by the doors, outside the curtains, but within the barriers. Meanwhile, deputations from various peoples are introduced, and the king listens to many things but replies to few: if he intends to consider anything, he postpones a reply; if he wishes to expedite matters, he replies at once. The second hour comes: he rises from the seat in order to spend some time inspecting his treasures or his stables.

For the next part of the day, the king hunted or gambled, and during that time a petitioner could try to present his case if a favourable moment arose and if the king was in a good humour. Later, there was another formal opportunity for the presentation of petitions, after which came dinner which was, though complete with entertainments, like that of a private household, except on special occasions.[6]

This description is of the utmost significance, since not only does it emphasise the *ciuilitas* of Theoderic's rule,[7] but it places the king so clearly within the tradition of Roman aristocratic office-holding that, were it not known to apply to a Visigoth, it might almost be mistaken for a description of some great Roman nobleman's day with its blend of private and public life. To illustrate the point further, it may be observed that Sidonius Apollinaris' description portrays Theoderic in much the same terms as earlier authors, including Suetonius (whose work was known to him),[8] depicted the routine of emperors. Perhaps the clearest parallel is with Dio Cassius' comments on Severus:

> The following is the manner of life that Severus followed in time of peace. He was sure to be doing something before dawn, and afterwards he would take a walk, telling and hearing of the interests of the Empire. Then he would hold court, unless there were some great festival. Moreover, he used to do this most excellently, for he allowed the litigants plenty of time and he gave us, his advisers, full liberty to speak. He used to hear cases until noon; then he would ride, so far as his strength permitted, and afterwards take some kind of gymnastic exercise and a bath. He then ate a plentiful luncheon, either by himself, or with his sons. Next, he generally took a nap. Then he rose, attended to his remaining duties, and afterwards, while walking about, engaged in discussion in both Greek and Latin. Then, towards evening, he would bathe again and dine with his associates; for he very rarely invited any guest to dinner, and only on days when it was quite unavoidable did he arrange expensive banquets.[9]

It is not, however, reasonable to suggest that Sidonius Apollinaris was totally bound by earlier stereotypes, nor that he was merely engaging in wishful thinking, since there is some, admittedly fragmentary, evidence to support at least a few of his observations. Hence, for example, Ennodius' depiction of St Epiphanius' presentation of a petition concerning prisoners of war to Euric gives the impression that the incident took place in the presence of a high-ranking Roman governor: this is true even down to the detail of the Gallo-Roman orator, Leo (a *consiliarius* or adviser), who seems to have been requested to raise the matter with the king and to find an opportune moment to make use of his rhetorical skills.[10] No doubt the circumstances were similar when Bishop Bibianus went to the royal court at Toulouse, as the representative of his community, in order to petition for a reduction in the amount of tribute payable.[11]

The parallel between the types of activity in which the early Visigothic kings engaged and those which occupied 'Roman' officials with vice-imperial authority, can be taken a stage further. It is interesting that in Sidonius Apollinaris' portrait of Theoderic, the king is depicted as sitting on a *sella*, rather than on a *thronus*. This may be significant, because although *sella* can simply mean 'seat' or 'stool', and could be loosely translated into English as 'throne', it does also have a specific connotation with the chair of a magistrate. There is no indication that any Visigothic king before the late sixth century sat on a *thronus*, and, indeed, Isidore specifically reports that Leovigild was the first king to use one.[12] The implication of this seems to be that until Leovigild's time kings saw themselves as Roman magistrates, not as the equivalents of emperors: this perhaps demonstrates the veracity of Olympiodorus' observations, and it may be that Sidonius Apollinaris was reflecting something of the same attitude. The impression of kings being the heirs of Roman governors is reinforced by the fact that one of their principal residences – Bordeaux – was a former provincial capital.[13] It is not in fact inconceivable that even a loyalist such as Sidonius Apollinaris himself saw the kings in 'Roman' terms, as the 'treacherous' Gallic prefect, Arvandus, may have done when he plotted to hand 'Roman' Gaul over to the Visigothic and Burgundian kings rather than allow it to be ruled by the 'Greek' emperor, Anthemius.[14] Further, it is just possible that the area administered by the Visigoths may have remained an active part of the diocese of *septem prouinciae* after the settlement, and have sent representatives to the Gallic council.[15]

Much of this is necessarily rather tentative, but there is other evidence which points in the same direction, for it has been suggested, most recently by R. Collins, that the provision of law codes by both Theoderic I and Euric can be seen as a continuation of the practice of Roman praetorian prefects issuing edicts.[16] It is significant that Euric's law book is called an 'edictum', and makes no explicit claim to be *lex* in the sense of imperial or rescript law.

However that precise point may be, and it is little more than speculation, it has for a long time been thought possible that the actual content of Euric's code is not Germanic, but Roman, and that it is really a Roman edict which happened to be promulgated by a 'barbarian' king.[17] This argument has again been taken further by R. Collins, who has pointed to the similarity of content between Euric's code and the seventh-century Byzantine *Farmer's Law*, which can plausibly be seen as a written version of Roman provincial law.[18] More recently still, I. Wood has found evidence that many of the practices concerning the settlement of disputes in the 'barbarian' kingdoms are in fact Roman, and even that some of them, such as trial by oath, which have long been thought to have been 'Germanic', can be paralleled in the Roman tradition.[19] When it is recalled that Honorius, with the assistance of Stilicho, is depicted as having presided over the giving of laws to 'barbarian' peoples in the Rhineland in the 390s, it will be clear that contemporaries cannot have thought there was anything inherently improbable in Germanic peoples administering Roman law. It is only a small step from that to those same 'barbarians' codifying Roman law.

Against this line of reasoning, it has been objected that Euric's code cannot be of a similar nature to a praetorian edict because it is on a much larger scale than any known document of that type.[20] It could also be objected that some of the content has non-Roman features, such as the passages which refer to *comites ciuitatum* and Gothic *saiones*.[21] Such arguments are not conclusive, because praetorian prefects only issued supplements to the general body of provincial law, whereas Theoderic and Euric were, for the first time, gathering together the whole body of praetorian/provincial law and writing it down in one place. This does not mean that their legislative activity was of a fundamentally different nature from that of the praetorian prefects, any more than the compilation of the Theodosian Code necessarily radically altered the nature of imperial law-giving. Indeed, the move to collect Roman provincial law together could have been partly derived from the Theodosian initiative, and could be seen as an indication that the Visigothic kings saw themselves as in the forefront of the development of provincial administration. Equally, part of the impetus to have a written body of law may have come from the fact that although the Goths may have been familiar with many Roman customs from their time on the frontiers of the Empire and from their long wanderings through its territory, they might well not have been familiar with the entire body of the provincial law their rulers now had to administer.[22]

With regard to the second potential objection – that Euric's code contains references to non-'Roman' officials and even, perhaps, customs – that is not surprising, for certain details of the law could quite reasonably have been altered to suit the circumstances of the time. In fact, the same type of amendment would have had to be made were the Code to have been Germanic, since it includes references to *comites ciuitatum*, a kind of official wholly inappropriate to the Gothic situation before *c.* 418. The process can be clearly demonstrated by reference to the other monument to early Visigothic legal development, the Breviary of Alaric, or *Lex Romana Uisigothorum*, enacted by Alaric II. This book is not of the same nature as Euric's, in that it is a collection of Roman imperial and juristic law. Here, in a work which is undeniably Roman in content and inspiration, alterations were made to the earlier material in order to make it more relevant to the circumstances of the Gothic kingdom. The changes take two forms – complete omission of material of no relevance, and alterations to the wording of individual provisions in the Code. The clearest example of the former process can be seen in the failure to reproduce any of the sixth book of the Theodosian Code, which deals with the imperial court (and was not of direct concern to 'barbarians' based in the provinces, particularly after the removal of the last western emperor), and of all but one rescript from the seventh book which treats of the army (which was now 'Gothic', not 'Roman').[23] The latter process is also transparent on account of the fact that the original wording of the rescripts was preserved and then interpreted, or adapted, below. Hence, for example, 'agentes in rebus' is explained as 'those who attend the dignity of our [the royal] presence'.[24] In the same way as it is inconceivable that the *Lex Romana Uisigothorum* should be described as fundamentally 'Germanic' on account of this type of adaptation, so there is no cause to see Euric's code as being Germanic simply because it contains some non-Roman material. The very fact that even after the disappearance of the last western emperor in *c.* 476, the Visigothic kings thought that imperial law was worth preserving, and had the *Lex Romana Uisigothorum* drawn up, demonstrates that they saw it as being of some practical use, even if only as a set of precedents or formulae, or as a means of boosting the prestige of the king.[25] Such an interpretation of the purpose of the *Lex Romana Uisigothorum* also suggests that its earlier provincial counterpart, Euric's code, may have been composed in a like manner for similar reasons.

The only major feature of the depictions of Visigothic kings by Olympiodorus and Sidonius Apollinaris which could be seen as running counter to the idea that the kings saw themselves, and were seen as, successors to the high-ranking 'Roman' governors, is to be found in the references to Atauulf's military apparel, and the armed personnel of Theoderic's court. As was noted in Chapters 3 and 5, late fourth- and early fifth-century 'Roman' practice was to try to keep civil and military jurisdiction in separate hands. There was, however, nothing in earlier Roman tradition to prevent the unification of both types of power in the hands of one official – indeed, it has already been argued that the changed circumstances of the fifth century may have led, even before the Visigoths were permanently settled in south-west Gaul, to the Gallic prefects, civilian officials, intervening in military affairs. In the same way that federation, although new, was an extension of the historic principle of dividing the 'barbarians' against themselves, so the new position of the federate kings grew out of the canon of Roman tradition.

If Visigothic kings administered the area under their control within the framework of 'Roman' provincial administration, so too their military activity came from the same mould. Most strikingly, the pages of Hydatius' Chronicle are full of references to military activity on the part of the Goths, often fighting alongside imperial forces. Most of the campaigns were in the Spanish diocese, and the majority were against other 'barbarians', particularly the Sueves;[26] other targets included the Vandals and groups described as *bacaudae*.[27] Hydatius' Chronicle is the only contemporary source, apart from the very fragmentary *Chronicle of Saragossa*, to come from the Iberian peninsula and is not surprisingly the only document to mention most of the Spanish campaigns. One later work, the *Getica* of Jordanes, refers to Walia, the leader who accepted federate status, as handing over his Spanish conquests to the emperor,[28] perhaps demonstrating that the Goths were not entirely out of control, at least in the early years of their settlement.[29] Despite their silence concerning the Iberian peninsula, other contemporary documents do show the Goths fighting in concert with the Empire in Gaul, particularly in the campaign of 451 against the Huns.[30]

It would be untrue, however, to pretend that Goths and 'Romans' were always in agreement in Gaul, because there are several occasions on which it is clear that the Visigoths fought against 'Roman' Gaul in attempts to increase the area subject to their rule. It has been suggested that some of these campaigns, notably those in the vicinity of Arles, the seat of the Gallic prefecture, were intended to ensure that the Romans continued to appreciate and pay for Visigothic support.[31] There are, though, two other ways of looking at some of these events, which place them even more firmly within a late-Roman framework. First, many of the areas of conflict lay within the diocese of *septem prouinciae*: Arles;[32] Narbonne, a provincial capital;[33] and, later, Auvergne (Map I).[34] It is possible, therefore, that, especially under Euric, the Visigoths may have been trying to spread their authority throughout the diocese in the same way that, in the sixth century, after the transfer of the kingdom to Spain, Theudis tried to extend his authority to the whole of the Spanish diocese, by campaigning in Mauritania Tingitania.[35] Even if the urge to control greater areas than those initially settled in Gaul and Spain was motivated by nothing other than a desire for greater power, it may be significant that attempts to realise such ambitions took place within the 'Roman' framework of diocesan regions.

The second way of looking at Visigothic campaigns is that some of them were undertaken in support of one imperial faction and against another. This is particularly true of one major campaign in Gaul outside the diocese – Frideric's expedition against Aegidius in the 460s. On that occasion, the Visigoths were acting in support of Ricimer and his creature, Severus, against the partisans of Majorian's faction, Aegidius and the Franks.[36] This military action was in fact a later manifestation of the same kind of factional activity which had earlier led Theoderic II to promote Avitus as emperor.[37] On that ocasion, as in the 460s, the Gothic kings may have been motivated by the expectation that an emperor who was beholden to them would allow them to extend their power – perhaps within the diocese, if not elsewhere. Similar reasoning probably also led Theoderic to support the *coniuratio Marcelliniana*, as well as to participate in the anti-Anthemian moves of Arvandus.[38] Even were such concrete benefits as new territory not part of Theoderic's calculation, he must have believed that an emperor, particularly an emperor under an obligation to him, could materially benefit his people or his own title to rule, otherwise he would scarcely have thought it worth intervening in imperial politics in such a way. Preferring one emperor to another is very different from seeking to dispense with emperors altogether.

The court

If the aspirations of King Atauulf and his successors led the Visigothic kings to behave in ways derived from Roman traditions, they can only have been encouraged and assisted by the presence of a large number of Gallo-Roman aristocrats in the area they administered. It is a well-established fact that although the settlement of the Visigoths in south-west Gaul undoubtedly caused a certain amount of physical dislocation, especially to the aristocracy, it did not entail a full-scale change of administrative personnel. Indeed, it has even been suggested that members of the senatorial class may have seen the establishment of the 'barbarian' kingdoms as providing the opportunity to increase their own power and influence, without their having to travel to a distant imperial court or the the city of Rome:[39] such men may have encouraged the kings' participation in imperial faction politics. It is not, therefore, surprising that contemporary sources show that Gallo-Romans, such as Leo, Namatius and Vincentius, continued to hold posts in governmental service, becoming subject to the kings,[40] while Gregory of Tours, writing much later, relates that a number of 'senators' fought with Alaric II at the battle of Vouillé in *c.* 507.[41] Not only will the presence of 'Romans' in the Gothic court have assisted the kings to understand Roman traditions and laws, but the fact of their presence may have served to reassure contemporary observers in Gaul that the 'barbarians' did not lie wholly outside the pale of the Empire.

It is unfortunate, but, given the nature of the chronicles and literary sources, predictable, that the official titles of such Gallo-Romans in Gothic service are often unknown. Hence, for example, a letter of Sidonius Apollinaris reveals that Namatius was in charge of Euric's fleet which operated in *c.* 478 against raiders described as 'Saxones' on the Atlantic seaboard,[42] but his title and precise position are unknown to us. The real significance of this case, though, lies in the fact that a Gallo-Roman was entrusted with the conducting of an important military operation: had there been widespread tension between the Gallo-Romans and the Goths, such a task would never have been entrusted to one of the former.

In two other cases there is slightly more information concerning administrative positions. Another Gallo-Roman, Victorius, is known to have been involved in Euric's Auvergne campaign: he is described by Sidonius Apollinaris as 'comes', and by the later Gregory of Tours as 'dux'.[43] As a servant of Euric at a time when that king was at war with

'Roman' Auvergne, Victorius is unlikely to have been described by Sidonius Apollinaris as a *comes* of the emperor, and the term must, therefore, refer to his relationship with Euric. It is interesting that, although the comments of both authors relate primarily to non-governmental and moral affairs,[44] Gregory of Tours describes Victorius as 'dux', a word usually associated with military leadership. The one official function Victorius is known to have fulfilled is that he was in charge of the 'seven cities' of the Auvergne. This position might well have involved a military command, because Auvergne was a newly conquered area on the frontier of the Visigothic kingdom, and it would be possible to see Victorius as a successor to the late-Roman *dux prouinciae*, commanding a frontier army: in the relatively small area ruled by Euric, that would not necessarily prevent him from being a *comes*, or courtier, at the same time. Alternatively, it is equally possible that Victorius was a courtier who was sent simply to administer the area – as such he could easily have been described as a 'leader' (*dux*), especially by an author writing a century after the events he was recounting. Perhaps one of the most interesting features to come out of the discussion of the rather shadowy Victorius is that the range of vocabulary used by Gregory of Tours at the end of the sixth century presents similar problems to that of the contemporary sources.

Only slightly more certainty is possible in the case of Vincentius, another Gallo-Roman in Visigothic service. In recording a campaign in Tarraconensis in the early 470s, the *Chronicle of 511* describes Vincentius as leader ('dux') of the army, and later refers to him as 'quasi master of the soldiers' ('quasi magister militum').[45] After the area had been conquered by the Visigoths, Vincentius remained in the area and a letter of Pope Hilarus refers to him as 'dux prouinciae'.[46] This time, military involvement is quite clear, and, as Tarraconensis was a frontier province, Euric may well have chosen to keep a *dux limitis prouinciae* in the area. Although there is no direct evidence that Vincentius had civil as well as military jurisdiction,[47] it would be rash to envisage a situation in which the demarcation between the civil and military spheres was so firm that such an official could not have carried out commissions in the civil administration at least on occasion: this is particularly the case since 'Roman' officials could, no matter what their formal title, intervene in almost any sphere of the administration as occasion demanded, or on the orders of the emperor.

It was not only Gallo-Romans who served Gothic kings or are described as *duces* and *comites*. In a later case, and one which also serves to underline the military competence of such men, Theudisclus, a Goth, is described as 'dux' when, in *c.* 531, he led a campaign under King Theudis against Frankish incursions into Tarraconensis.[48] In a more interesting case, Suneric, a leader of Theoderic II's campaign of *c.*

459 against the Galician Suevic kingdom, is described by Hydatius as 'dux'; the same author then goes on to refer to him as 'comes' both in relation to an embassy to the Sueves and with regard to the launching of a further military campaign in the following year.[49] Given what has been seen of Hydatius' use of words regarding a 'Roman' official such as Aetius, it would seem very likely that Suneric was a courtier of the Visigothic king, who could, when leading an army, be described as 'dux' or 'leader'. Indeed, it is particularly interesting that Suneric appears in a military context as both a *dux* and a *comes*, for, on the second occasion, he was operating with Nepotianus, the imperial master of the soldiers – a court position – and it may have been Hydatius' purpose to underline the parallel status of Suneric as a member of the royal court, rather than his specific function as the leader of an army.

There are other references to *comites*, but they do not assist in arriving at an appreciation of the meaning of the term in the Visigothic context. Gauterit led a campaign in Pamplona while described as 'comes', but the single chronicle entry concerning him is so brief that there is no possibility of understanding why the word *comes* was preferred to *dux*.[50] Even less helpful in the present context is the record concerning Veila, about whom all that is known is that he was killed at Barcelona.[51] The only other significant reference to *comites* as such comes in the preface to the *Lex Romana Uisigothorum*, where it is stated that two such men were involved in the production of the law book: it would, however, be surprising if anyone other than courtiers had been entrusted with such an important task.[52]

Perhaps of greater interest are references to specific types of *comes*, and particularly to a *comes ciuitatis*. This last title appears for the first time in Euric's law code,[53] and is, as was argued in Part I, not explicitly attested in the 'Roman' parts of the Empire. The function of such an official at this date cannot be determined with any degree of certainty, but, since the law in which he first appears concerns inheritance, it could be related to civil or legal administration. It is unfortunate that this is the only mention of the title in the Visigothic material before the reign of Leovigild (569-586), beyond the finishing point of the present book. The meagre information yielded by the earlier sources begs the question as to how such an position came into being. Any response to this must involve a large amount of hypothesis, but it seems worth making a suggestion. As the Visigothic kings came to control new areas, they may have felt the need to place court officials of proven trustworthiness and ability in charge of local administration. In this respect, they could, on a smaller scale, have been imitating the imperial practice of using ex-court officials as high-ranking provincial governors. Alternatively, since *comites ciuitatum* could also be described as 'judges of the cities' ('iudices ciuitatum')[54] – presumably derived from the title of the earlier *iudex ordinarius* or governor – it may be that they were simply local governors who, unlike their 'Roman' counterparts, remained members of the court during their period of office. A situation such as that just outlined would not have been unreasonable given the relatively small area ruled by the kings, and it would have been logical to base such men in the cities, the main centres of population and of the earlier institutions of local government.

One other specific type of *comes* makes a passing appearance in the period before the reign of Leovigild: at a very early date, Sidonius Apollinaris attests the presence of a *comes armiger* at the court of Theoderic II in Toulouse.[55] Although such a title is not of Roman origin, it may, perhaps, be seen as a Germanicisation of the imperial *spatharius*, or bodyguard.[56] That some form of borrowing from the Roman tradition did occur may be confirmed by the fact that Alaric II's treasury is specifically described in the *Lex Romana Uisigothorum* as his 'thesaurus'.[57] Here, however, the borrowing appears not to be from the central, imperial, court, but from the provincial administration, for it was the provincial treasuries of the *comes sacrarum largitionum*, rather than that in the palace, which were known as *thesauri* – they were managed by *comites* or *praepositi thesaurorum*.[58]

What is most striking from the scant data concerning the royal court during the first century and a half of the Visigothic kingdoms in the western Empire is the apparent adaptation of Roman titles and traditions to fit the new circumstances of federation. It could be argued that Hydatius and Sidonius Apollinaris, the authors of the two sources which yield the largest bodies of evidence, were Gallo-Romans and would, therefore, have used 'Roman' terms to describe Visigothic officials, because they were only familiar with such vocabulary. Such a suggestion cannot realistically be sustained, for three reasons. First, not all the sources are 'Roman' in the sense that the writings of Hydatius and Sidonius Apollinaris are – the *Lex Romana Uisigothorum* and Euric's law code, however much they reflect of late Roman law, were official documents produced by the Visigothic court. Second, some of the same titles persisted, with similar usages, throughout the entire history of the Visigothic kindgoms, until the fall of the kingdom of Toledo to the Muslims in 711.[59] Finally, it is significant that the Gallo-Roman Sidonius Apollinaris uses the non-'Roman' title of *comes armiger* and may, therefore, have been clearly aware of the differences, as well as of the similarities, betwen the Visigothic terminology and that of the 'Roman' administration.

7

The Kingdom of the Burgundians

The second area of Gaul subject to federate settlement of the type accorded to the Visigoths for which some quantity of evidence survives is the eastern region, Sapaudia, granted to the Burgundians c. 443.[1] The Burgundians were not newcomers to the Empire at that date, for, as early as c. 413, they had occupied an area of the Rhineland,[2] but so little is known of their institutions in the following thirty years that their move further south can be taken as a convenient starting point for the ensuing discussion.

That the Burgundians, at least after the settlement in Sapaudia, saw themselves, and were seen by others, as part of the Empire, is not only clear from the acceptance of federation, but is additionally demonstrated by the fact that the members of the ruling dynasty held titles directly linking them to the imperial hierarchy. Hence, for example, Gundioc was a master of the soldiers,[3] as was his brother, Chilperic I, who was also described as 'patricius Galliae' or, sometimes, simply 'patrician';[4] Gundioc's son, Gundobad, was made patrician by Olybrius, c. 472.[5] This tradition continued even after the removal of the last western emperor in c. 476, for Gundobad was later described as a 'procer' of the eastern emperor, Anastasius,[6] and his son, Sigismund, was made patrician.[7] The reasons for these titles, at least before c. 476, become clear when the relationships between the Burgundian rulers and some of the fifth-century western emperors are examined. After Ricimer had had Majorian murdered, and while he was trying to establish Severus as emperor, a number of Majorian's supporters opposed him. One of the rebels was Aegidius, whom Majorian had appointed as master of the soldiers for Gaul, and it was largely thanks to the intervention of the Visigothic Theoderic II and the Burgundian Gundioc that Aegidius was prevented from marching on Italy. As a reward for this, Ricimer seems to have seen to it that Gundioc, his brother-in-law, received Aegidius' former position, while Theoderic II seems to have gained control over Narbonne.[8] Some years later, c. 472, after Ricimer's death, Gundioc's son, Gundobad (who was Ricimer's nephew), seems to have been made patrician by Emperor

Olybrius, the last of Ricimer's creatures.[9] After Olybrius' own death later the same year, Gundobad 'persuaded' Glycerius to assume the purple.[10] As part of the same manoeuvrings, Chilperic I, another of Gundobad's uncles, was made master of the soldiers in Gaul, probably based at Lyons:[11] he is also described as a patrician.[12]

The complex events very briefly outlined above do more than explain how Burgundian leaders came to bear 'Roman' titles, for they also reveal the Burgundians to have participated very actively in imperial faction politics at the highest level. In the same way as the Visigothic Theoderic II had promoted Avitus as emperor, presumably in the hope of material benefit, the Burgundians must have thought the position of emperor worth fighting about. A further illustration of similar concerns may be found in the military campaigns in which the Burgundians are known to have assisted the 'Romans'. The lack of contemporary narrative sources means that there are few references to military activity on the part of the Burgundians, but it is clear that they participated in a campaign against the Suevic kingdom in distant Galicia,[13] and in the *c.* 452 campaign against the Huns.[14] In addition, the intervention against Aegidius, mentioned earlier, could be seen as pro-imperial activity since it was executed in support of one emperor against the followers of another, rather than being directed against the concept of an emperor. Similar motives may lie behind the Burgundians' annexation of Lyons after the deposition of the Gallic emperor, Avitus, since this seems to have occurred with the support of a number of Gallic senators (probably members of the obscure Marcellinian conspiracy), who had supported Avitus and were, at least initially, opposed to the new emperor, Majorian.[15] The Burgundians also became involved in Roman faction politics when Arvandus, the Roman opposed to Emperor Anthemius, sought to hand over territory both to them and to the Visigoths.[16]

More evidence of a subordinate relationship of Burgundian kings to the emperors may be adduced from a passage in a letter of Sidonius Apollinaris which describes Chilperic I as 'our "tetrarch" '.[17] The passage in which this phrase occurs is clearly of literary form and, although it was once thought that it implied a division of the Burgundian kingdom between Gundioc's four sons (Gundobad, Godegisel, Godomer and Chilperic II), there is no concrete evidence for such a division, or, indeed, for a division of the kingdom at any other time, and it is better seen as describing Gundioc's brother, Chilperic I.[18] Further, the word 'tetrarch' does not necessitate a four-fold division, or, indeed, any division at all, for as early as the late first century BC, it could simply refer to a minor ruler under Roman control.[19] Viewed in this way, it is quite possible that Sidonius Apollinaris was trying, in a highly literary way, to do no more than reflect the fact that Chilperic owed at least some of his authority in the area to the emperor – it has already been observed that he held 'imperial' titles.

Perhaps even more indicative of the relationship between the Burgundian kings and the emperors is evidence from after the deposition of Romulus Augustulus, c. 476, for that was a time at which the Burgundians, in common with other 'barbarians' in the west, could have chosen to break free from the Empire had they been inherently opposed to it or felt that their ambitions were curtailed by it. The most telling phrases are contained in a letter written by Avitus to Emperor Anastasius on behalf of Sigismund shortly after the latter's accession to the Burgundian kingdom. The king is made to state that 'my people is your people, and it pleases me more to serve you than to preside over it', and goes on to say that 'our homeland is of your world'. Not only this, but 'when we seem to rule our race, we believe ourselves to be nothing other than your soldier'.[20] In this document, Avitus must be reflecting, albeit in a rhetorical way, what was perceived to be the relationship between the king and the emperor. If this had not been the case, he would have been trying to deceive three people – himself, Sigismund (who might have felt that his authority was being debased by such expressions), and the emperor (for whom the flattery would have been too transparent had it not been based in truth). Such is not the way to conduct diplomatic relations between rulers. This does not mean that Sigismund was necessarily an 'official of the empire' in the way that his father and grandfather had been, but is more likely to imply that he recognised that the emperor had a hegemonic claim over the land or people that he ruled. In another letter Avitus wrote to the emperor on Sigismund's behalf at about the same time, the king was made to describe his late father, Gundobad, as 'most devoted and most faithful' to the emperor, and as his 'leading man'; further, he offered the emperor his own loyalty and service in place of that of his father, to whose position he had succeeded.[21] It may also be significant that the passage refers to the emperor's 'respublica' or 'commonwealth', rather than to his *imperium* or 'empire', perhaps indicating a new type of relationship between the centre of the Empire and the western provinces. However that may be, the evidence adduced concerning Sigismund is particularly important since it comes from after c. 476, and belongs to a period when greater emphasis came to be placed upon *royal* authority as the title to rule not only over the Burgundian people, but also over the Roman population within the kingdom.[22] From the same period there is other evidence, in the form of royal coinage, demonstrative of the subordinate position the Burgundian kings saw themselves as occupying. The reverse of the coins does not carry a portrait of the king, but only the king's monogram, while the obverse was copied from the current eastern imperial types which bore the image of Anastasius: this implies a degree of imperial hegemony over the Burgundian kings.[23]

The same kind of acceptance of Roman traditions is further reflected in Burgundian legislative activity. The *Book of Constitutions* (*Liber constitutionum*), whether written in its present form by Gundobad, or, as seems more likely, by Sigismund,[24] is very similar in content to both Euric's Visigothic Code and what little is known of Roman provincial law. In fact, there is fairly good evidence for the co-operation of a Roman, Syagrius, in the compilation of the Burgundian code – for he is described by Sidonius Apollinaris as the 'new Solon of the Burgundians'[25] – suggesting that the code is likely to have been substantially 'Roman' in content. Further, it is inherently more likely that the similarity between Euric's and Sigismund's codes should be explained in terms of a common origin in late-Roman provincial law than of an *urgermanische* tradition whose very existence can only be hypothetical. Such a common origin in Roman tradition can, of course, be proved for the Burgundian equivalent of the *Lex Romana Uisigothorum*, the *Lex Romana Burgundionum*, a collection of Roman imperial law, or rescripts, made, as was the Visigothic *Lex*, after the removal of the last western emperor.

The Burgundian evidence enables the argument to be developed further than the Visigothic (prior to the reign of Levogild), since it shows that the law was not static, but could be added to and altered as circumstances demanded. Hence, for example, laws, or amendments to existing laws, were first promulgated on a number of occasions – 3 September 501, 28 May 502, 27 June 513, and 1 March 515.[26] Further, even after the general law-giving of 29 March 517, new laws were still added, for a provision concerning the making of gifts was promulgated on 10 June the same year.[27] The reasons for the alterations are often recorded, sometimes in general terms, indicating the lack of efficacy of earlier laws on the same subject,[28] and sometimes more specifically, as when one Athila had unlawfully tried to disinherit his son, an action which led to the strengthening of the inheritance law.[29]

Not only can it be demonstrated that the law was constantly developed, but something of the mechanism by which laws were made can also be understood. The 'first constitution' of the Burgundian code states that any cases arising which were not covered by the existing laws were to be referred to the king, so that he could decide what alterations and additions should be made both to the law itself, and to the procedures for its administration, so that the matter could be speedily resolved.[30] Not only is there this theoretical statement concerning the making of new laws, but there is a concrete example from 516 when Bishop Gemellus of Vaison brought Sigismund's attention to the need for a law on the subject of foundlings: a new law was duly made, and the Bishop's initiative is recorded in its text.[31] Another law, *Liber constitutionum* LII, sets out the procedures involved in more detail. The initial case involved a widow, Aunegild, who betrothed herself, in accordance with the law, to one of the king's *spatarii*, named Fredegisclus, but then committed adultery with another man, Baltamodus. The case was not adequately covered by existing laws, and was, accordingly, referred to the king, who set the amount of compensation to be paid to the injured party, Fredegisclus. The details of the case were then published so that the 'specific case should have a general application' – as a precedent to be followed should similar cases arise in the future.[32] Such a view of the function of law made in this way is expanded upon elsewhere, for another constitution states that a general definition should be set out relative to every case so that the *comites* and *praepositi*, having been adequately instructed in the law, should understand more clearly how cases should be judged.[33] This is precisely the same principle as that which governed the issuing of imperial rescripts and their subsequent publication (see Chapter 1).

Such an explanation of the function of royal law is of prime importance in two ways. First, it is clear that the law was not intended to give detailed instructions concerning every type of case: it was, rather, to establish the general principles to be adopted. The task of the judges was to apply the principles as best they could, taking into account the individual circumstances of each case brought before them. In other words, royal law was didactic and formulaic.[34] The second point arising from the nature of the law as described above is that the way in which it was created is very similar to that by which imperial rescript law, as described in Chapter 2, was made. This means that, even after the initial redaction of law for everyday purposes, modelled upon Roman provincial law, and the publication of a small collection of imperial rescripts (the *Lex Romana Burgundionum*), kings, even though becoming judges of last resort, continued to operate within a 'Roman' tradition.

Documents concerning the law-making process provide by far the largest source of information relating to the activities of Burgundian kings, but what little evidence there is about their other actions does nothing to contradict the picture presented above that they learnt from imperial traditions. One of the best-known scenes concerning a Burgundian king is a description of Chilperic I receiving a petition from Abbot Lupicinus on behalf of men reduced to slavery by the unjust actions of a courtier: Chilperic is depicted in a way which would be equally applicable to a high-ranking Roman official.[35] Similar portrayals are to be found in Ennodius' depiction of Epiphanius' visit to Gundobad on behalf of the Ostrogothic Theoderic the Great regarding the release of prisoners of war, and in the *Uita Eptadii*'s description of other missions in connection with prisoners.[36] The position of the king on these occasions is also similar to that of the Visigothic king, Theoderic I, when confronted by Bibianus' mission,[37] and of Galla

Placidia and Valentinian III when Germanus journeyed to Ravenna on behalf of the Alans.[38]

It was not only in their activities and administrative forms that the kings adhered to a Roman framework, because the places from which they ruled their kingdom also had Roman connotations. It is clear, for example, that Vienne, a provincial capital under the 'Roman' administration, was an important royal centre in the Burgundian kingdom,[39] in the same way as was Bordeaux, capital of Aquitanica I, in the Visigothic. Much fuller evidence survives concerning Geneva, also an important city in terms of the former administrative system: Lupicinus and Epiphanius presented, respectively, Chilperic I and Godigisel with petitions while the kings were resident at Geneva,[40] and Clovis' royal bride-to-be, Chrotechild, lived there.[41] In addition, Avitus refers to a royal residence in the city: the precise terms in which he does so are of interest, for he describes there being a church within the 'palace or *praetorium*'.[42] This would appear to indicate that the palace occupied the site of the former praetorian headquarters, if not the same buildings, a hypothesis which is strengthened by archaeological evidence which shows that the praetorian headquarters was transformed into a structure with an attached church, and remained in use until the tenth century.[43] Further material to support the contention that Geneva continued as an important administrative centre comes from the fact that, according to Fredegar (a later, but locally-informed source), Sigismund was crowned 'at the town of Geneva, in the villa of Quatruvius':[44] on the evidence of place-names, this has been identified as the modern Carouge, a site with a large Roman villa complex which continued to be occupied well into the sub-Roman period.[45] This does not mean that Geneva was the only administrative centre, or the fixed capital, of the Burgundian kingdom, for kings are known to have inhabited Lyons, a villa at Ambérieux, and Chalon-sur-Saône,[46] but it does indicate that Roman administrative centres, such as Lyons and Geneva, were still in use after the Burgundian settlement.

The kings did not, of course, legislate or rule their kingdom unaided. It is clear, for example, that they sometimes consulted their *optimates* before promulgating new laws,[47] and the leading men of the kingdom (*proceres*) and *comites* are said to have advised the king concerning the administration of justice,[48] while the Book of Constitutions was confirmed by all the king's courtiers ('comites').[49]

What, then, is known of these *comites* or 'companions' of the king? Clearly, they were involved in the making of law: they were also responsible for bringing the law to the attention of everyone in the kingdom, and for enforcing it.[50] Both Burgundians and Romans could be *comites*, and they were to give judgements in pairs.[51] *Comites* were also responsible for supplying petitioners to the king with letters of introduction.[52] It is unfortunate that *comites* are only recorded in legal material, for it means that such men are never seen in action in the way in which they might be in the chronicles or the letters of Sidonius Apollinaris. The only non-legal reference to *comites* comes from Gregory of Tours' *Life of the Fathers*, where there is a reference to a Gregory who, as *comes*, was based in Autun[53] in the same way as *comites* could be stationed in the cities of the Visigothic kingdom, and, presumably, for much the same reasons. Although it is perhaps likely that all *ciuitates* had *comites*, such a situation cannot be proved to have existed.[54] It seems clear, though, that *comites* were courtiers, and the chief agents of the king. Whether or not they could fulfil military functions, as could the late-Roman and Visigothic *comites*, is less obvious, though it is likely that, as royal agents, they could be called upon to act in any capacity the king chose.

Even less is known of other kinds of official present in the Burgundian court. This is not altogether surprising, for such officials are hardly likely to be referred to in those parts of the law which were drawn from Roman provincial law, while the nature of the new laws made by the Burgundians precludes there being a large amount of information on the topic, for most of the cases referred to the king would concern non-courtiers. Even when courtiers are referred to, it is often only their titles which are recorded: although there are references to a *domesticus* and a *spatarius*, nothing is known of their functions within the Burgundian kingdom.[55]

One type of official about whom a little is known, however, is the *wittiscalc* or *puer noster*.[56] Men who bore one of these titles were responsible for the execution of judgements and the collection of fines,[57] and, therefore, appear to have been connected with the law courts. It has been suggested that these men were treasury officials, since *witta* may be a 'translation' of the Latin *mulcta* ('fine'), and *schalk* of *puer* ('boy' or 'slave').[58] The collection of fines, however, need not be connected with the treasury rather than with the courts, and it is possible that the root of *witta* could be connected with *witi* ('wit', or 'knowledge'),[59] or with *wito* ('law'),[60] either of which would suggest a legal function. The only other thing known about *wittiscalci* is that they were subordinate to the *comites*,[61] and it is just conceivable that they could be seen as a Germanicised version of the *domestici* of the officials of the late-Roman provincial administration, though this is little more than surmise.

Another shadowy figure of the Burgundian court is the *maior domus* ('greater man of the household'): the First Constitution reveals that there could be more than one of these men in existence at any one time.[62] Those who sought to petition the king had to present their petitions to a *maior domus* or a *consiliarius* ('adviser') after they had been drafted by a *comes*. It was presumably then the duty of the *maior* or *consiliarius* to forward the petition to the king, for such men certainly had to draft the king's responses and see to their transmission to the local judges.[63] The lack of evidence is underlined by the fact that it is not apparent from the text of the law which records this whether the *maiores domus* and *consiliarii* were one and the same. What is interesting is that a Roman deacon or bishop in the Ostrogothic kingdom could employ a *maior domus*,[64] because it is another indicator that 'barbarian' kings, such as those of the Burgundians, adapted themselves to the framework of the Roman aristocratic and office-holding way of life.

8

The Franks and Gaul in the Sixth Century

The situation in the north of Gaul is considerably more confused than that in the south for almost the entire fifth century, largely owing to the poverty of source material. On the 'Roman' side, the details of Aegidius' rule are shadowy, the extent of Syagrius' power is almost impossible to assess,[1] and the *comes* Paul is little more than a name. In addition to leaders bearing Roman names, it is clear that 'barbarian' powers, in particular groups of Franks, came to form an increasingly important part of the defensive and administrative equation. Reference has already been made to a group of Chauci (a group related to the Franks) making peace with, and receiving laws from, the Empire as early as 396, and it is known that the Salian Franks had already formally been settled inside the frontiers in Toxandria (the area west of the mouths of the Rhine) long before that time. During the first half of the fifth century, other groups of Franks, in particular the Ripuarians, tried to gain entry to the Empire and established themselves higher up the Rhine, particularly in the region of Cologne and Trier. Meanwhile, the Salians began to expand their sphere of influence to the west, and around 446 are found operating under Chlodio in the vicinity of Arras and Cambrai where they were defeated by Aetius at the unidentified *uicus Helena*.[2] Later in the fifth century Tournai (to the north of the Arras region, in modern Belgium) was an important Frankish centre, for it was there that Childeric, the first Frankish king about whom much can be said, was buried *c.* 483. The confusion surrounding the events of the mid-fifth century in this area may be exemplified by the fact that some commentators have thought that Chlodio was made a federate after his defeat at *uicus Helena*,[3] while others have thought that such arrangements were made rather earlier,[4] and yet others that federation only occurred under Childeric.[5]

However that may be, it was as late as the reign of Childeric's son, Clovis, that the different groups of Franks were first brought into one 'people', by means of having their leaders (often Clovis' relatives) murdered. Clovis also brought about the expansion of Frankish dominion over large parts of Gaul, starting in the north, then moving south west and driving the Visigoths out of most of their Gallic lands into Spain. The final major expansion of the Franks in Gaul was only completed by Clovis' sons, some twenty years after his death, when the independent Burgundian kingdom was destroyed.

Until the death of Childeric almost nothing certain can be learnt of the mechanisms whereby the Franks (of whatever group) administered or exploited the areas they came to control. All that is absolutely clear is that groups of Franks had been in contact with the Empire for well over a century before Clovis' time, some of them having been settled on the fringe of the Empire by agreement with the Romans. In addition, the areas within the Empire into which the Franks expanded had a long tradition of Roman administration. It would be surprising, therefore, if the Frankish system were not seen to owe something to its Roman predecessor when it emerges from the obscurity of the fifth century into the shadows of the sixth. Before turning to the examination of that system, the sources upon which it has to be based must be examined, for without an appreciation of their chronology and nature, the quality of the data they provide cannot be evaluated.

The non-legal sources

The north of Gaul is very poorly served by the chronicles which were an important feature of the discussion of more southerly areas, and there are no local equivalents for them. Similarly, there are no northern counterparts to the letters of Sidonius Apollinaris, though there are documents in the collection known as the *Epistolae Austrasiacae*, some of which more closely parallel those of Avitus of Vienne. Many of the letters in the collection are concerned with the Church, and reveal little of secular government, but there are some diplomatic documents which furnish a certain amount of information on the way in which kings chose to represent themselves to other leaders outside the kingdom, and, while often only alluding in the most general of terms to the administrative system which produced them, do, by their very existence, demonstrate that there was a functioning governmental organisation of some sophistication. The other writings of Sidonius Apollinaris and Avitus – their poems – are also to an extent paralleled in the north, by the late-sixth-century poetical works of Venantius Fortunatus, an Italian who migrated to the Frankish kingdom in around 565, became closely associated with the court of Sigibert, and ended his days in about 610 as bishop of Poitiers: as with many of the fifth-century poems, those of Fortunatus are largely literary compositions of a personal nature which, although casting a certain amount of light on the court, only do so incidentally.

What the north does have, though, is what the southern areas lack – a large-scale narrative history, in the shape of Gregory of Tours' *Decem libri historiarum*. The document is not without its own problems: first, its earlier sections, dealing with the period before the rise of Clovis, are so brief as to be of almost no assistance for the present enquiry; second, even after it becomes a fuller source in the late fifth century, it is not strictly a primary source since it was written in the early 580s. In addition, the *Decem libri historiarum* moves in the same theological world as the chronicles and, more particularly, as the writings of Orosius and Salvian of Marseilles, championing the cause of Christianity and especially of St Martin.[6] It is a work of instruction, depicting the good deeds of the time and, more particularly, its evils;[7] it is concerned with the manipulation and evaluation of divine goodness as a way of regulating temporal authority, rather than with the administrative changes which were wrought in Gaul during the period with which it is concerned.[8] The *Decem libri historiarum* is, therefore, an extension of the overtly religious hagiographical *oeuvre* of Gregory of Tours, the purpose of which was to illustrate virtue and, in particular, the extent and ordinariness of supernatural intervention in every aspect of life.[9] On account of these features of Gregory's writings, it would be foolish to look to them for a coherent historical picture of sixth-century Gaul, and it has been widely recognised that the precise course of events portrayed in the *Decem libri historiarum* is often untrustworthy: this is not because Gregory was ignorant, or because he had fallen victim to a process of 'barbarisation', but because it was not his purpose to provide a continuous and uniform narrative.[10] Gregory's wish to portray the evils of his time inevitably leads to a concentration on violent and military affairs, and the normal functioning of the royal court and administrative system only features incidentally, though it does play a more important part than in the fifth-century chronicles. A final limitation on the usefulness of the *Decem libri historiarum* for the ensuing discussion is that the geographical area from which Gregory takes most of his examples, of both good and evil, is restricted, being to a large extent centred in the regions of Touraine and Auvergne in which he and his ancestors lived, and which, more than the north, were typical of the region with which his Gallo-Roman readership will have been familiar.[11]

Although the preceding discussion of Gregory's *Decem libri historiarum* has tended to indicate its limitations as a source for the events of the fifth and sixth centuries in Gaul, even in those areas to which most of its material relates, the importance of the document for the present study cannot be over-estimated. The great length of the work compared to many of the non-governmental documents used in earlier chapters of this book means that there is room for a large volume of material tangential to its main theological thrust. A second feature of the work is the fact that it takes the form of a series of loosely-connected vignettes in which the course of specific series of events is followed from the inception of the incidents concerned through their development to their conclusion: this provides greater detail than the terse chronicle entries on the ways in which people of all kinds behaved and were motivated. Finally, however chronologically untrustworthy Gregory is, and however much he may have manipulated the central characters in his book in order to illustrate the good or evil in their actions, the ways in which governmental officials are seen to act when engaged in official business, and particularly when they are incidental to the main action, are unlikely to be inaccurate. Since the mechanics of secular administration were not part of Gregory's concern, he will usually have left them as he found them in his sources, or, at worst, have made officials act according to his assumptions as to how the adminstrative system worked: such assumptions would almost certainly have been based in sixth-century reality (both because that was what Gregory knew, and because radical departures from it would have undermined the case he was making in the eyes of his contemporary readership) and would not, therefore, detract from the validity of his testimony for the present purpose.

Kingship and law

The first feature of Frankish kingship to emerge from the meagre sources for the fifth century is that of war leadership. Chlodio, for example, is only known as the leader of the campaign of the late 440s in the Cambrésis, and Childeric I campaigned against Aegidius, perhaps as the leader of a 'Roman' faction and federate of the eastern emperor, Marcian,[12] as well as against the Alemanni and, at Orleans, other Germanic peoples in Gaul.[13] Moving forward into the reign of Clovis, when Gregory's narrative becomes much fuller, Clovis led campaigns against Syagrius, the Alemanni, the Burgundians, the Visigoths, and leaders of other Frankish groups.[14] There can be no doubt that leading the people in war was a major aspect of Frankish kingship before, during, and after Clovis' time,[15] but is has long been recognised that Gregory of Tours may have over-emphasised it.[16] It is interesting that even in the 'barbarian' pursuit of war leadership Frankish kings behaved in a Roman way for, as K. Werner has argued, the rules governing the division of booty after the defeat of Syagrius (which led to the well-known episode concerning the Soissons vase) were identical to those practised for a long time previously within the Empire.[17]

Perhaps the single piece of evidence which can most assist in the correction of Gregory's view is the famous letter sent by Bishop Remigius of Rheims to Clovis after the death of Childeric I. In this document, the Bishop congratulates Clovis on his assumption of the 'administration' of the 'province' of Belgica II and describes the new king's tribunal as a 'praetorium'.[18] Further, the letter makes it clear that the kind of power exercised by Clovis was not new, since his ancestors had 'always' exercised it.[19] It is apparent from the precise terminology Remigius employed that the power of the kings was not simply military, an impression confirmed by another letter Remigius wrote to Clovis, on the occasion of the death of Albofled, the king's sister, in which Clovis is advised that he should not allow his sorrow to divert him from the administration and wise government of his kingdom, and is described as the 'head of the people'.[20]

The second important feature of the first of these documents is that it portrays both Clovis and his ancestors as administering a Roman province – Belgica II. It may be significant that the activities of Chlodio in the Cambrésis fall within the province, as does the burial-place of Childeric: it was suggested earlier that the Visigoths were concerned to gain control of entire provinces and dioceses, and it may be that the Franks – or at least the Salian Franks – had a similar ambition. If this is correct, then both it and the fact that Remigius referred to the 'administration of the province' could be taken as additional evidence that Childeric, at least, was a federate of one faction of imperial power. It may, additionally, be no accident that Clovis chose Rheims, the capital of Belgica II, as the place of his baptism, since that would have been the main seat of his 'legitimate' power as a federate leader: this would be particularly telling if, as has been recently argued, Clovis' baptism dates to 508, after the defeat of the Visigoths at Vouillé and the subsequent establishment of Paris as the capital of the new *Regnum Francorum*.[21] That the Roman boundaries of Belgica II did have some importance for the Franks, even after Clovis' day, may be indicated by the fact that the boundary between the Salian and Ripuarian groups was the *Silva Carbonaria*, the later division between Neustria and Austrasia and the former frontier between the provinces of Belgica II and Germania II. Further, the fifth-century divisions of Gaul into the areas occupied by the Ripuarians, Aegidian faction, Burgundians and Visigoths remained remarkably stable throughout the Merovingian period, becoming the kingdoms of Austrasia, Neustria and Frankish Burgundy, and the duchy of Aquitaine.[22]

Given this background, it is pertinent to examine what is more certainly known of the relations between Merovingian kings and the emperors at Constantinople. An interesting starting-point is that Childeric's grave-goods included a brooch (mistakenly identified in the past as a writing stylus) of a type normally worn by high-ranking imperial officials, together with a signet ring – a Roman type of object – bearing the image of the king wearing Roman-style military dress:[23] the latter may recall Olympiodorus' description of the Visigothic king, Atauulf, wearing a Roman military cloak at his marriage to Galla

Placidia, and certainly points to Childeric's seeing his power in 'Roman' terms. A similar view of Frankish kings as operating within an imperial framework comes from the reign of Childeric's son, Clovis, who received a consulate from Emperor Anastasius after the Battle of Vouillé.[24] There are several points which need to be made in relation to this event. First, it is unlikely that Anastasius would have given Clovis the added prestige of an imperial title unless it had some real significance to one or both parties. From Clovis' point of view, it secured recognition of his position in Gaul – not only in Belgica II, but in the areas subsequently conquered and annexed. On the other hand, his readiness to receive such an honour from an emperor implies that he saw himself, and was prepared to be seen by others, as in some way subordinate to the emperor. This impression is strengthened by Gregory of Tours' description of the king riding through Tours distributing largesse to the citizens on his receipt of the title: this not only sets Clovis firmly within a tradition connected with late-imperial holders of honorary offices, but can also be seen against the background of the customs surrounding the celebration of triumphs by imperial military commanders in the provinces.[25] The underlining of Clovis' subordinate position may have been precisely Anastasius' intention, but it is likely that he also sought a more concrete return for his generosity, probably in the form of assistance against the rule of the Arian Ostrogoth, Theoderic the Great, in Italy.[26]

Even after the reign of Clovis Frankish kings continued to recognise a form of imperial hegemony in Gaul. One of the most obvious expressions of this may be found in the fact that, with the one exception of Theodebert I, no king issued a gold coin with his own portrait upon it until after the reign of Emperor Justin II (died 578): until that time, coins employed imperial designs and, thereby, associated the power of the Frankish leaders with that of the emperors.[27] The exceptions to this pattern – the coins of Theodebert I – are instructive in a different way, because while in one sense he declared his independence of the emperor by placing his own portrait on the coins, in another, he still expressed his dependence upon the empire by following the changes in the types of coin produced within it.[28] A similar pattern can be seen in Theodebert's claims to power over a large number of peoples including Franks, Visigoths, Thuringians, Saxons, the Eucii, Pannonians and northern Italians: although these assertions of authority may have been made to register annoyance at imperial claims over some of the same peoples and areas, they are a direct imitation of the emperor's titles of *Francicus*, *Alamannicus*, *Gepidus* and *Langobardicus*.[29] In addition, despite his tendentiousness, Theodebert was not above referring to the emperor as 'pater', at least on occasions when diplomacy was important.[30] Finally, after Theodebert's death, his son, Theodebald, maintained cordial relations with the Empire since he was only too happy to receive gifts and messages of goodwill from the emperor on his accession to the Frankish throne.[31]

However much within imperial traditions Theodebert's claims and expressions of his ambitions lay, they can only have served to weaken the relationship between emperors and Frankish kings. A further stage in the loosening of the imperial bonds must have come with the failure of the Justinianic attempt to regain direct control of the west, since, from that time forward, it will have been clear that the old western Empire could never again be a reality. One possible indicator of the new relationship may be that in the many surviving letters of Childebert II and his mother, Brunhild, to emperors, and to officials and bishops in both Constantinople and Italy, the Empire is only twice described as an 'imperium' ('empire'), the more usual form being 'respublica' ('state' or 'commonwealth'):[32] at an earlier date, 'imperium' was more normal, and is always found in the letters in which Theodebert made his claims to quasi-imperial power.[33] Another type of symptom of post-Justinianic claims to a form of equality with the emperors may be seen in Chilperic's attempts to ape imperial traditions by having circuses built at Paris and Soissons, the main centres of his kingdom.[34] Finally, in recounting Guntram's arrival at Orleans on the Feast of St Martin on his way to the young Chlothar II's baptism, Gregory of Tours depicts the whole scene exactly as if it were an imperial *aduentus* – the citizens, singing the king's praises and carrying banners, came out of the city to greet Guntram as he approached; once within the walls, Guntram received hospitality from many of the citizens, and distributed largesse in return; he even received a formal petition from one section of the population, the Jews.[35] There is no real reason to doubt that Gregory's depiction of these events is accurate since the events of the 580s were recent enough for his readership to have been able to recognise complete fabrications of the way in which its kings behaved, but the parallel between Gregory's accounts and what is known of late-imperial *aduentus* is so close that it is legitimate to wonder whether Gregory might not have been using a Roman model.[36] Even if this were the case, however, it would indicate that Gregory's contemporaries still saw their rulers in terms of imperial traditions.

Despite the signs that some Frankish kings, especially after Justinian's reign, were keen to be seen as the equals, rather than the subordinates, of the emperors, the latter did not at once give up all hope of directly influencing the government of Gaul. For example, Tiberius II supported the usurper, Gundovald, against Guntram, and his successor, Maurice, also tried to undermine that king by making one of his courtiers an imperial patrician. In reality, it must have been clear that there was little chance of bringing Gaul back fully within the imperial fold, and it is likely that the emperors were more interested in furthering their schemes for the removal first of the Ostrogoths and then of the Lombards from Italy: certainly, throughout the sixth century, there were attempts to arrange alliances with the Franks to organise joint attacks on non-imperial forces in the Italian peninsula.[37]

Even though the type and quality of the evidence for the Frankish kings of the fifth and sixth centuries are different from those for the kings of the Visigoths and Burgundians, it has been possible to show that they operated as military leaders and in relation to the Empire in much the same way as their counterparts further south in Gaul. In order for the similarity to be complete, it remains to demonstrate that in spite of Gregory of Tours' lack of interest in the subject, the leaders of the Frankish people were also civil administrators. It has already been argued that at least the bishop of Rheims, the capital of the Roman province of Belgica II where Clovis' power was centred, thought there was a civil aspect to Frankish power, and there is other more positive evidence pointing in the same direction.

First, it is clear even from Gregory's writings that Frankish kings, at least from the time of Clovis, could be petitioned in exactly the same way as could their counterparts elsewhere in Gaul. One of the earliest examples, better known for its dramatic outcome than for the petition itself, is the request made of Clovis by a bishop for the return of a great ewer taken during the campaign against Syagrius.[38] Other petitions presented by individuals or local groups include an unsuccessful request by Avitus, abbot of S.-Mesmin de Micy, that King Chlodomer should spare the lives of the Burgundian king, Sigismund, and his immediate family;[39] a petition by Bishop Desideratus of Verdun for a loan to restore the fortunes of his city;[40] and Gregory of Tours' own intervention with Guntram on behalf of some of the supporters of the pretender Gundovald.[41] A final case, demonstrating that it was open to anyone within the *Regnum Francorum* to present a petition to the king, is that the Jews at Orleans unsuccessfully petitioned Guntram for funds to rebuild their synagogue which had been destroyed by a section of the Christian community:[42] the king was prepared to listen even to those with whom he could not be expected to have sympathy. In addition, Gregory reports a number of instances of requests being made to kings concerning the consecration of specific men as bishops – though this may be nearer to lobbying than to petitioning.[43]

Secondly, from the early sixth century there survives a Frankish law code, in the form of the *Pactus legis Salicae*. Unlike its Visigothic and Burgundian counterparts, the *Pactus legis Salicae* does not make the direct claim that it is royal law, but it is inconceivable that such a document should have been produced without its authors having the approval of the king, and unlikely that it was not in fact produced on royal initiative.[44] As with the earlier, Visigothic, code of Euric, there is no reason to suppose that the *Pactus legis Salicae* was not based, in large part, upon Roman provincial law. Against this suggestion, a number of objections could be raised. First, it could be suggested that the *Pactus legis Salicae* cannot be Roman because it contains a fairly large amount of 'Frankish' vocabulary. However, this argument can work both ways. A 'Germanic' code might very well have been written down in a fully Latinised form so that the 'Roman' population, which was unfamiliar with its provisions, could more easily understand them since they were written in their own language: by the same token, Roman provincial law, with which all the Franks might not have been familiar, could have included Frankish vocabulary in order to make it easier for the Frankish population to comprehend. Second, it might be argued that the code cannot be Roman since it was drawn up by four men – Uuisogastus, Arogastus, Salegastus and Uuidogastus – bearing apparently Frankish names.[45] Again, however, the evidence can be interpreted in more than one way. If the *Pactus legis Salicae* were indeed Frankish, it would be strange that the king should have had to resort, for an exposition of his own 'national' law, to four men who seem to be village elders (partly on account of the fact that their names are more like place names than the names of real people), rather than to his own courtiers. On the other hand, it would have been quite reasonable for the king to have summoned local judicial officials to provide him with an account of their law if he were not already familiar with it: the fact that the four individuals concerned bore 'Germanic' names is not relevant, since there had long been 'barbarians' settled in the Rhineland and northern Gaul who would have been familiar with Roman provincial law.

More positive evidence in favour of a Roman origin for the *Pactus legis Salicae* is, as with Euric's code, the similarity of content between it and the Byzantine *Farmer's Law*.[46] As suggested earlier in relation to the Burgundian and Visigothic codes, similarity between 'barbarian' laws is perhaps more likely to indicate a common Roman origin than a common 'Germanic' one. The *Pactus legis Salicae* is not, however, identical with its Visigothic or Burgundian counterparts, for it contains some elements of procedural law of a type more commonly associated with imperial than provincial provisions.[47] This does not mean that the actual procedures are the same as those found in imperial law – indeed, they are not, though this still does not prove that they are 'Germanic', since very little is known of the procedural law of the provinces under the Empire, which is what it is being suggested the *Pactus legis Salicae* incorporated.

In addition to the complete *Pactus legis Salicae*, there are other legal enactments of sixth-century Frankish kings – the Decrees of Chlothar I and Childebert II, and the Edicts of Chilperic I and Guntram.[48] These documents resemble the Novels associated with the Theodosian Code and certain of the provisions found in the Burgundian legal corpus, being collections of measures issued in response to specific cases which had been brought to the attention of the kings concerned. The process by which they were produced was probably broadly similar to that described for the Burgundian documents: it is at least clear that law was made with the consent, if not the assistance of the nobility.[49] This is especially significant since it is known that at least some of the aristocrats who assisted in the production of royal edicts and decrees had Roman names:[50] Childebert II's Decree, for example, was signed by one Asclepiodotus, known from elsewhere to have been a referendary at Childebert's court;[51] one of Sigibert I's advisers was Parthenius, who had been educated at Ravenna;[52] and Guntram employed a Roman, Celsus, who had been well educated in science and law.[53] Given that these men advised their kings, it is not unreasonable to suppose that the legal enactments in which their names appear were at least influenced by Roman legal traditions.

A second point to emerge from the legal documents is that their very existence demonstrates that the king was the ultimate source of justice and that his was the court of last resort. This is explicitly stated in Chilperic's Edict, and may indicate that the royal court operated in much the same way as had the courts of the emperors or, more particularly, their high-ranking officials in the provinces. The direct involvement of kings in the administration of the law can also occasionally be detected in the work of Gregory of Tours:[54] this reinforces the fact that the general impression Gregory conveys, of kings being little more than war leaders, is inaccurate.

The queen

Apart from the king, the most important person in the royal court was the queen.[55] The most basic function of a queen was to produce male children who would secure the continuation of the dynasty: a queen who failed to do this soon found herself cast aside, as, for example, in the case of Charibert's wife Ingoberga who, having produced only a daughter, was replaced first by Merofled and then by her sister, Marcovefa.[56] The problem a queen faced was compounded by the fact that her position was entirely dependent upon the king, there being no form of queenly inauguration to mirror the elevation of a king, and no equivalent of the position of *augusta* which had given Galla Placidia such authority as regent for the young Valentinian III.[57] In this respect, the marriage of a Frankish queen was a purely personal matter, and once a king had discarded a queen, she had no position of privilege or influence. A final source of queenly insecurity was that the Merovingian dynasty did not adhere to the system of primogeniture –

the mother of a son who did not become a king was as defenceless as an ex-wife.

One way in which queens could seek to secure their positions was for them to play an active part in the education of their children, since this meant that they retained control over them and might hope to influence them in later life. The most successful sixth-century queen in this respect was Brunhild, who was responsible for bringing up Childebert II, a fact known even to such a distant figure as Pope Gregory I:[58] her arch-enemy, Fredegund, was similarly involved with the education of her son, Chlothar II.[59] Although the control of princes could help to secure the position of a widowed queen, and some queens were at their most powerful when they acted as regents for their under-age children,[60] they did not always manage to retain influence over their offspring. Hence, for example, while his father, Sigibert I, was alive, the young Childebert was at one stage placed under the control of a 'governor' (*gubernator* or *nutritor*), Gogo,[61] and, after his death, of Wandelen.[62] These men were almost certainly not solely employed in the court as governors of the prince, but held other positions of high rank and trust.[63] Nevertheless, the enmity which could spring up between a queen and a *nutritor* is shown by the fact that although Gogo was a close adviser to Sigibert, Fredegar, writing rather later, suggests that Brunhild persuaded her husband to have him assassinated.[64] Even if Fredegar is not accurate concerning this, it is clear that it was the sort of action which could be expected of a determined queen: less drastic, but still significant, action was taken by Brunhild when Wandalen died, for Gregory explicitly states that she refused to appoint a successor to him, wishing to retain control over Childebert for herself. An alternative, and, for the queen, more devastating strategy, was for the princes to be removed from the royal palace altogether,[65] and either sent to one of the king's estates, or established with their own court in another part of the kingdom, as happened to the young Theodebert II.[66]

The control of their offspring was not the only way in which queens sought to protect themselves against the vicissitudes of their position. One of the most extreme methods queens could adopt was to have their rivals, and the sons of their rivals, banished or murdered:[67] faced with a rather similar situation, Sophia, empress of the insane Emperor Justin II, refused to allow the wife of his regent (Tiberius II) to live in the imperial palace.[68] Such a course of action, while it may have eliminated rivals, alienated many potential supporters, and a more fruitful path was for a queen to dispense patronage in order to build up a faction of supporters. Brunhild, for example, was influential in the appointment of Bishop Innocentius of Rodez[69] and, implicitly, in that of Gregory of Tours himself;[70] later in her life she became particularly involved in the appointments of Burgundian bishops.[71] It was not only churchmen who were the beneficiaries of royal patronage, for Charibert's wife, Marcovefa, promoted the interests of a courtier, Leudast.[72] This last case is particularly instructive since, at a later date, Fredegund ensured Leudast's downfall,[73] thus demonstrating that queens could dispense enmity as well as patronage, in much the same way as Empress Theodora could seek to destroy Belisarius.[74] It may not be stretching the evidence too far to find in this kind of activity echoes of the actions of Roman empresses, in particular Galla Placidia's patronage of St Germanus,[75] or her apparent promotion of the interests of Boniface:[76] were there to be more evidence concerning the western empresses of the fifth century, the parallels in this and other spheres of queenly operation might be more striking.

In order to be able to dispense patronage, queens not only had to have the ear of their husbands, but also, on occasion, access to financial resources. The care queens took to obtain treasure for themselves, particularly when their husbands died, is clear from the fact that both Theudechild (wife of Charibert) and, later, Fredegund, took the wealth of their respective husbands into their charge as soon as they heard that they had been widowed.[77] Moreover, it seems that queens themselves derived wealth from a number of sources, some of which were private, but which could include taxation.[78] One of the reasons queens may have required to have access to treasure is that they were at the head of part of the royal household when they were not with the king, and, when their husbands were at war, particularly outside the *Regnum Francorum*, they could be at the centre of court activity.[79] In addition, it is possible, though not provable from within the sixth century itself, that queens were in charge of much of the domestic administration of the palace,[80] for which access to money would also have been necessary. Certainly, queens had their own staff, for it is known that Fredegund had a *domesticus*, Leudard, under her control,[81] and that Ultrogotha, wife of Childebert I, had a referendary, Ursicinus.[82]

The court

Next to the queen, one of the members of the royal court most closely associated with the person of the king is likely to have been the *cubicularius* – an official with a title clearly indicative of a Roman ancestry. As in the late-Roman context, however, very little is known of the holders of this office: this is not unexpected since, although Gregory of Tours' *Decem libri historiarum* is a sort of narrative source, it is not primarily concerned with the functioning of the court, and the kings' servants only appear as incidentals to Gregory's main subjects. Hence, for example, little more is known than the names of Ebero and Chundo, respectively *cubicularii* of Childebert II and Guntram.[83] In addition, the actions of courtiers who operated as close to the person of the king as *cubicularii* can be expected to have done, would not necessarily be well known to a relative outsider such as Gregory. The easy access these men had to the person of the king is, perhaps, underlined by the fact that one of their number, Eberulf, was accused of being involved in the murder of Chilperic,[84] while another, Faraulf, was alleged to have plotted to murder Guntram.[85] If these allegations were true, the trust of the ruler was, in these instances, being abused. There was clearly plenty of scope for *cubicularii* to use their position for their own ends: Charegysclus, a member of Sigibert I's court, made money out of it.[86] On only one occasion can a holder of this office be seen to act on behalf of his king, when Rada, *cubicularius* of Childebert II, was sent on an embassy to Constantinople. This is a significant case because not only does it demonstrate the position of trust in which *cubicularii* were held, but it also throws into relief one of the problems inherent in the *Decem libri historiarum* as a source for the present enquiry. Although Gregory refers to the embassy, Rada is not mentioned, and it is only from an official document connected with the mission that his involvement is known:[87] that it is only illegitimate actions of *cubicularii* which are reported by Gregory underlines his moral purpose.

Although, as has been seen, the Frankish sources mention a number of *cubicularii*, nowhere is there any reference to a chief *cubicularius* whose position would be directly analogous to that of the imperial *praepositus sacri cubiculi*. It is, of course, possible that there was no such direct equivalent; alternatively, it might be that Gregory of Tours, who was not primarily interested in the details of court administration, did not distinguish between the *cubicularii* in general and their chief. There is, however, some evidence to suggest that neither of these was in fact the case, for an eighth-century saint's life describes Ebroin, a well-known and important seventh-century figure, as '*praepositus* of the palace, which is commonly called *maior domus*',[88] and also uses the title of *praepositus palatii* to describe Erchinoald, who is more commonly known as a *maior domus*.[89] Evidence from the sixth-century Ostrogothic kingdom suggests that there, at least, the titles of *praepositus sacri cubiculi* and *praepositus domus regiae* were synonymous,[90] thus making it possible to suggest that the Frankish *maior domus* was the successor to the head of the imperial bedchamber.[91]

When the spheres of activity in which they engaged are examined, it soon becomes clear that the *maiores* were leading men in the court – indeed Fortunatus says that one *maior*, Servilio, 'ruled the palace'.[92] *Maiores* did not, however, only operate within the court itself, and on almost the only occasion on which a sixth-century *maior* is seen acting legitimately on behalf of a king, Florentianus was sent by Childebert to draw up new tax lists at Poitiers[93] – though that does not mean that *maiores* were primarily financial officials. Perhaps one of the most telling passages concerning these men comes in Fredegar's Chronicle, in an account of Chrodin's election as *maior* in the Austrasian court. Apparently, Chrodin refused the office on the grounds that he was related to many of the Austrasian nobles and would not, therefore, have been able to maintain order amongst them; in addition, the aristocrats themselves would not have had confidence in him.[94] This clearly indicates that *maiores* could, at least on occasion, expect to find themselves arbitrating between the nobles or, perhaps, intervening with the king on their behalf. If the idea that the *maior* fulfilled the same sort of function as a *praepositus sacri cubiculi* is correct, then it is not difficult to see how such a situation could have arisen, since *praepositi*, at least in the eastern Empire, were the emperors' personal attendants and effectively controlled access to the rulers. The sequel to the narrative is also instructive, for Chrodin, having refused the office for himself, suggested that Gogo should be chosen.[95] This Gogo is the same as the Gogo who was placed in charge of the young Childebert II and whom Brunhild persuaded Sigibert to have murdered: Gogo also appears to have dictated a letter from Childebert to the Lombard *dux* Grasulf.[96] This again signals the importance of *maiores*, and their closeness to the heart of the court, as do two references in the poems of Fortunatus to such men as advisers to the king.[97]

Gogo is not the only *maior domus* who was personally linked with a member of the royal family other than the king himself. When a separate household was established in Austrasia for the young Theodebert, *maiores* appear on the list of officials who were sent to reside with the prince.[98] In addition, when Rigunth, Chilperic's daughter, was sent to be married in Spain, she was accompanied by a *maior domus*, Waddo.[99] It is possible that all members of the royal family who were not permanently resident in the same place as the king had a *maior domus*, but the point cannot be proved.

Another individual, though of a different kind, who must have operated close to the person of the king is Grippo. According to the *Decem libri historiarum*, Grippo was one of a number of men sent by Childebert on an embassy to Emperor Maurice: he is only mentioned on his return from the east, and is not given any title.[100] The same document which reveals the *cubicularius*, Rada's, name demonstrates that Grippo's mission was the same as that on which Rada was sent, and that Grippo was a *spatharius*. Owing to the fact that over a year elapsed between the sending of the embassy and Grippo's return, it is not at first easy to see the link between the two events, and Gregory does nothing to assist his reader to do so: the two episodes are parts of different vignettes in his work, and the link between them is as incidental to his purpose as is Grippo's office. More directly relevant to understanding the nature of the Frankish royal court, however, is the fact that it contained a *spatharius*: as was seen in Chapter 3, this was the title of imperial bodyguards: it is not surprising to find a man who occupied such a position of trust involved in an embassy. Grippo was sent again to Constantinople a year later, though on that occasion the letter connected with the mission does not accord him a title.[101] The only other reference to a *spatharius* occurs in the early part of Fredegar's Chronicle, where it is mentioned that Cariatto, a *spatharius* of Guntram, was made bishop of Geneva.[102]

Apart from a churchman (probably a bishop), there was one other man involved in the first of the two embassies to Constantinople, the *notarius*, Eusebius.[103] He is almost the only notary about whom any information survives for the sixth-century Frankish kingdoms, and his appearance in this context is of particular interest, since it marks a continuation of the imperial tradition (discussed in Chapter 3) of using *notarii* for special and delicate missions.

Also borrowed from the imperial past is the title of *domesticus*, though this time the debt may be to the provincial administration rather than to the imperial court. It was argued in Chapter 5 that *domestici* were the personal attendants of high-ranking provincial administrators, and that their position gradually became more formal, and developed into something akin to an 'office'. It does not, therefore, come as a surprise to find *domestici* on the staff of Frankish kings, especially if, as suggested earlier, those kings were the heirs to Roman governors, particularly in the province of Belgica II. The impression that these men were primarily household staff is strengthened by the fact that Fortunatus described one Attila as '*domesticus* of the royal court',[104] and Conda, perhaps while bearing the title of *domesticus*, was apparently in charge of the government of the palace.[105] The personal nature of these officials may be indicated by the fact that, as has already been seen, Queen Fredegund controlled a *domesticus*, Leunard, and, when a separate household was established for the young Theodebert II, *domestici* were among the officials appointed to it.[106] Given the nature of the sources, it is entirely predictable that some *domestici* appear as little more than names in wider dramas, and that the references to them do not provide information on their functions within the court.[107] Indeed, the only occasion on which a *domesticus* can be seen engaged in official business is when Dumnolus, *domesticus*, assisted in the transfer of the treasure of the deceased Mummolus to Chilperic's court.[108]

Although the exact functions of *domestici* are not clear, there is nothing in what has been said to cut across the view that they were the agents of the king, or of other members of the royal family: it is perfectly possible that they were personal agents who could be commissioned to carry out a wide range of tasks, as required.[109] E.

Ewig, however, has suggested that Frankish *domestici* were the successors of late-Roman *procuratores* – administrators of groups of imperial estates[110] – but, although there is some evidence that *domestici* fulfilled such a function in seventh-century Frankia,[111] there is none for the sixth century, and it seems somewhat perverse to suggest that Frankish *domestici* were descended from anything other than their imperial namesakes. Perhaps firmer evidence against Ewig's thesis comes from the case of Baudinus. This man first appears as a 'former *domesticus*' of Chlothar I, is later described as the same king's former referendary, and eventually became bishop of Tours.[112] The description of Baudinus as ex-referendary appears to relate to exactly the same period as the reference to him as an ex-*domesticus*. This could indicate that 'referendary' was the title of a specific office, the holder of which held the rank of *domesticus* or household official, perhaps in a way broadly similar to the fifth-century usage of the terms 'master of the soldiers' and '*comes*' in relation to the holders of the full title of '*comes* and master of the soldiers'. It may be significant in this context to observe that one Charigisilus, the subject of a miracle at Tours, held the titles of referendary and *domesticus* in succession,[113] and that there is evidence from the late seventh century which seems to show that one individual could hold both positions at the same time.[114]

Although the title 'referendary' itself has as many imperial overtones as all the other titles so far discussed, it is rather different in that it certainly does not relate to Roman provincial government, nor is the position attested in the western Empire: instead, the title may have come direct from Constantinople, where referendaries came into existence *c.* 427, and were responsible for processing petitions presented to the emperor and his responses to them.[115] A first indication that referendaries in sixth-century Gaul required to be educated and literate comes from the fact that a large number of them became bishops at a later stage of their lives.[116] This may also show that the satisfactory discharge of their court position demonstrated their trustworthiness, for kings did not willingly acquiesce in the appointment of their enemies to bishoprics: bishops operated at a distance from the court and could use their position to construct private factions.

The use to which referendaries' education was put can be seen on a number of occasions and from a variety of sources. Perhaps the clearest example is that of Asclepiodotus, who was instrumental in drawing up the proceedings of the 585 Council of Valence,[117] and whose name (though without title) appears at the end of Childebert II's Decree ten years later, thus indicating that he had some involvement in its production.[118] The writings of Gregory of Tours reveal that Otto, a referendary at Childebert II's court, was summoned to appear at the enquiry into a dispute between Bishop Egidius of Rheims and a former *dux*, Ennodius, so that he could testify to the authenticity of documents which were produced as evidence: having examined the signature on the deeds, Otto declared that it was not in his own script and that the documents were forgeries.[119] One way in which kings themselves sought to designate authentic documents was by placing their seals upon them, and it was referendaries, such as Siggo, who kept the seals.[120] With this information in mind, it is possible to see that two references to untitled men who were in charge of the signet rings of Chlothar I and Theodebert I must refer to referendaries; these men not only had charge of, and used, the seals, but also wrote and kept royal documents.[121]

There is one referendary, Mark, who is only known on account of his involvement in the production of new tax lists in Limoges on behalf of Chilperic, and his diversion of tax revenues for his own gain.[122] It is unlikely that referendaries were usually involved either in the collection of taxes or in drawing up assessment lists, especially as there were other officials (discussed below) whose responsibility such matters were. It is not, however, difficult to see how a man skilled in the production of documents, as Mark must have been, could be called upon to aid in the production of new tax lists, and this may be an example of the way in which, as in the Empire, governmental officials could be called upon to act outside their normal sphere of competence as required. This is particularly true if, as suggested earlier, the referendary was a special kind of *domesticus*, since, as *domestici*, referendaries could be called upon to act in almost any way the king wished.

Although referendaries and *maiores domus* could on occasion intervene in financial affairs, there were officials whose normal functions lay in the management of the royal treasury. One such type of courtier would appear to be the *camerarius*, since almost all the references to the legitimate activities of men of this kind are connected with financial administration. References to named *camerarii* are few, but perhaps the most notable case is that of Wandalmar, who was jointly responsible (with the *domesticus* Dumnolus) for seizing the treasure of the deceased Mommolus and transferring it to the palace.[123] More common are allusions to unnamed *camerarii*, such as those of Charibert's court who received a fine imposed on Bishop Leontius of Bordeaux,[124] or those who escorted Princess Rigunth on her ill-fated journey to Spain.[125] The second of these examples is particularly interesting since it suggests that *camerarii* could, in the same way as *maiores domus*, be attached to members of the royal family other than the king, and they were, perhaps, to be found wherever there was a significant quantity of treasure. Despite their undoubted association with treasure, *camerarii* could discharge other duties, as when some of their number were sent by King Theodebald to protect Bishop Cautinus of Auvergne against the supporters of a rival clergyman, Cato.[126]

The precise origins of Frankish *camerarii* are unclear: less uncertainty surrounds the antecedents of the other Merovingian official connected with the treasury, the *thesaurarius*. As was seen in Chapter 3, *thesaurarii* existed in the fifth-century Empire as the provincial officials of the *comes sacrarum largitionum*. It is not, perhaps, unexpected to find the Frankish court borrowing titles and institutions from the provincial as well as the central imperial administration, since it was at a provincial level that the Franks had the most direct experience of Roman traditions: it has already been suggested that Frankish *domestici* were the heirs of the staff of provincial governors rather than of officers of the imperial court. It is unfortunate that *thesaurarii* are rarely seen in action, but two incidents serve to underline their involvement with treasure. First, *thesaurarii* were responsible for conveying Fredegund's treasure to Childebert (the son of her rival, Brunhild) after the death of Chilperic;[127] and, second, Chilperic's short-lived son, Clovis, had a *thesaurarius* of his own.[128] These two references do nothing to elucidate the relationship between *camerarii* and *thesaurarii*, but two suggestions may, perhaps, be made. First, it is possible that *thesaurarii* were in some way subordinate to *camerarii*, and they could have been based away from the king's household either with lesser members of the royal family and/or in the main regions of the *Regnum Francorum*, perhaps in a way echoing the relationship between the *comes sacrarum largitionum* and the imperial *thesaurarii*. Second, it is conceivable that the two titles should be treated as synonymous since to Gregory of Tours, the source of almost all the available information concerning these men in the sixth century, the word *thesaurarius* could simply have designated a man involved with treasure, while *camerarius* could have been an official title: a parallel to such usage of terminology may be found in the fifth-century chroniclers' descriptions of men officially styled 'masters of the soldiers' as 'duces' – military commanders.

A title more firmly rooted in the imperial past is that of *comes stabuli*. The high rank of men of this kind is indicated by the case of Leudast, who was given the position as one of honour.[129] It is likely that the position was also one of high trust, since Fredegund sent Chuppa, probably a *comes stabuli* at the time, to rescue Rigunth when her father, Chilperic, died.[130] On the other hand, since Chuppa had already handed over a treacherous courtier responsible for the young Clovis,[131] it may be that his personal loyalty was more important to Fredegund than his actual office. A particularly interesting point concerning Frankish *comites stabuli* is that, as in the fifth-century

Empire, where the sources are similarly limited, there is evidence that they could act as military commanders.[132]

In the same way as the title of *comes stabuli* can be seen to have related to a specific office, it is likely that a similar title – that of *comes palatii* – also designated a position with a particular, though not exclusive, set of duties. It is not, however, possible, from within the sixth century itself, to establish what the special function of the *comes palatii* was, since there are only two informative incidents concerning such men: both relate to different spheres of activity – military leadership and taxation[133] – in each of which courtiers of a number of types have already been seen to have intervened on occasion. Despite this paucity of direct evidence concerning the *comites palatii* in sixth-century Gaul, two pieces of evidence, from the seventh and fifth centuries, render it possible to make a suggestion as to their specific role in the court. First, there are indications from the seventh century, particularly from the royal *diplomata*, that the *comes palatii* was the king's chief legal adviser.[134] Second, bearing that in mind, it may be significant that the fully developed title of the official responsible for placing fifth-century imperial edicts in written form was *comes et quaestor sacri palatii*,[135] for it is possible that *comes palatii* is an abbreviated form of the Roman title and, therefore, should indeed refer to some form of legal adviser.

However that may be, and it must remain somewhat tentative, a small number of men appear in the sources described simply as 'comes': these men did not hold specific offices, but were simply members of the royal court, who could be commissioned to discharge any duty the king wished. Hence, for example, Sigibert instructed the *comes* Justin to give certain relics to Bishop Euphronius of Tours;[136] Chilperic sent *'comites, duces* and other agents' to raise an army against Childebert,[137] while, after the death of Sigibert, Guntram sent *comites* to invest cities which Sigibert had seized after Charibert's death, and to exact oaths of loyalty from their inhabitants.[138] In the same way, Guntram on another occasion sent Syagrius, *comes*, on an embassy to Constantinople,[139] and Firminus, *comes*, was sent to make peace with the Emperor Justinian.[140]

Most sixth-century references to *comites*, however, are to officials based in specific areas of the *Regnum Francorum*, usually cities. *Comites* are attested at Angers,[141] Angoulême,[142] Auxerre,[143] Bordeaux,[144] Bourges,[145] Chalon-sur-Sâone,[146] Châteaudun,[147] Clermont,[148] Dax,[149] Javols,[150] Limoges,[151] Lyons,[152] Meaux,[153] Orleans,[154] Poitiers,[155] Saintes[156] and Tours.[157] That the men who held these positions were closely bound to their kings may be demonstrated by the fact that every time a king gained a city from one of his rivals, he placed a *comes* from his own court in charge of it.[158] Furthermore, although it is likely that *comites* would have had a certain amount of personal power in the areas they adminstered, it is clear that their kings sought to place restrictions upon their ability to build up private power blocs, since there is some evidence that *comites* of cities were only appointed for a limited term. The most explicit statement of this relates to Paeonius, who was *comes* of Auxerre. Paeonius wished to have his appointment renewed, and sent his son, Mummolus Euenius, bearing gifts to Guntram in order that he might achieve his end: the opportunistic son, however, availed himself of the chance to increase his own power by persuading the king to appoint him in his father's place.[159] The principle that the authority of *comites* in specific parts of the kingdom could be revoked is also clear from the case of Palladius of Javols who, after a quarrel with Bishop Parthenius, was deposed by Sigibert.[160] This case is also instructive in another way, for Palladius had inherited his position from his father, Britianus, thus indicating that although kings could, and did, depose *comites ciuitatum*, they did not seek, or were not always able, to prevent the perpetuation of family interests in areas of the kingdom. The temporary nature of these appointments is, perhaps, underlined by the fact that men known to have been *comites ciuitatum* at an earlier stage of their careers are subsequently found acting in other capacities.[161]

While a man was in power as a *comes* of a city, he was still a member of the royal court, even though he resided at a distance from it, and he must have gone to see the king fairly frequently: indeed, Gregory of Tours observes in passing that Eulalius of Clermont often went to court,[162] giving the impression that it was to be expected. Despite this maintenance of contact, there are several instances in which *comites* who operated at a distance from the court abused their power,[163] but these should not be over-emphasised, particularly since Gregory of Tours, the source for all of them, was concerned to dwell on the moral aspect of events.

There is no reason to suppose that the origins of the Frankish office of *comes ciuitatis* were very different from those in the other 'barbarian' kingdoms already discussed. Even if the Franks were not federates, it seems clear that they behaved in ways broadly similar to those of the Visigoths and Burgundians. By the sixth century, however, the functions of *comites ciuitatum* must have evolved, and, as the king's representatives in the regions, they were in charge of all aspects of civil administration. Nor is it difficult to imagine how such a state of affairs should have come about. Hence, for example, *comites ciuitatum* were responsible for the collection of taxes and for paying certain monies to the royal treasury;[164] they could find themselves quelling disturbances, as when Macco intervened in the riots at St Radegund's in Poitiers,[165] or could be placed in charge of prisoners.[166] Perhaps the main function of such *comites*, however, was the

administration of justice, a point underlined by Gregory of Tours'
description of the *comes* Armentarius as governing the city of Lyons
'with judicial power'.[167] A similar impression is created by one of the
poems Fortunatus addressed to Galactorius, *comes* of Bordeaux, in
which great stress is laid on Galactorius' position as judge.[168] On a
more practical level, the *comes* at Angoulême had the power to
authorise the execution of a criminal, for Eparchius, a local holy man,
interceded with him for the life of such a person.[169] This concern is the
one aspect of the power of local *comites* which is reflected in the legal
sources (though the Germanic term *graphio* is used rather than the
Latin *comes*[170]): such an emphasis is understandable given that legal
documents are primarily concerned with the establishment and
administration of justice. The *Pactus legis Salicae* and the royal edicts
contain a number of references to the *graphio* as a judge, in matters
ranging from squatters occupying other men's houses to investigating
crimes committed by servants.[171] The *comes* was not, however, the
judge of first instance, for the provisions of the laws make it clear that
he should only become involved if proceedings ran into difficulties;
similarly, his was not the court of last resort, since cases he was unable
to resolve could be referred to the king.[172]

It seems clear that, as the local representatives of royal authority,
the *comites* of the cities were highly important men in the civil
administration of the *Regnum Francorum*, who were responsible for
almost every aspect of the government of their regions. In this respect,
they are not very far removed from the late-Roman provincial
governors, the main difference being that they remained members of
the royal court while in office in the regions: the *Regnum Francorum*
was considerably smaller than the western Empire had been, and it
was possible both for kings to remain in closer contact with the
localities than emperors could have hoped to do, and for their regional
representatives to communicate with them more frequently. In the
same way as late-Roman provincial governors had subordinates and
local staff, so the Frankish *comites* must have had local assistance. It
is, therefore, predictable that there are a few references in the
sixth-century sources to such men as *centenarii*,[173] *tribuni*,[174] and
uicarii of the *comites*:[175] these local officials were not members of the
royal court,[176] and little is known about their precise functions since
they were rarely in a position to influence the types of event which
were of primary concern to Gregory of Tours, the main source of
information on the sixth century. Similarly, there are some references
to men as 'agents' of the king, or as 'judges', but these are almost
certainly generic terms for officials, and not the titles of specific
offices.[177]

A final sphere in which regional *comites* are known to have operated
is that of military leadership. This was probably not their prime

responsibility but, as local agents of the kings, they could sometimes find themselves involved in levying and leading militias. Hence, for example, the *comes* of Châteaudun was commanded by another of Guntram's courtiers to raise a body of three hundred men to assist in the capture of Eberulf whom Fredegund accused of having killed Chilperic,[178] and Firminus of Clermont led a force from Clermont to oppose Guntram's army at Arles during Sigibert's attempt to acquire that city.[179] That this was a recognised function of *comites ciuitatum* is clear from Fortunatus' poem on Galactorius, where his military leadership is mentioned.[180]

Even though *comites ciuitatum* were competent to lead armies and sometimes did so, the forces they controlled often seem to have been local and small. The large armies of the Franks were usually led by men described as *duces*. It is possible that not all men referred to in this way in fact fulfilled an office of 'dux', since there is some evidence that Frankish sources sometimes used the term simply to mean 'leader' in the same untechnical way (discussed in Chapter 3) as some of the fifth-century authors.[181] It is clear, therefore, that the precise position of the many men who are only reported as having led armies while being described as *duces* must be treated as uncertain.[182] Some of the individuals concerned may well have held other offices at the time they are referred to as *duces*, as in the case of Leudeghisel who appears in the *Decem libri historiarum* as a *dux*, though Fredegar, who does not use that term of him, first says he was a *comes stabuli*, and, later, that he was made patrician of Provence;[183] a similar case is that of Calumniosus Aegyla.[184] Perhaps the clearest example, though, is that of Mummolus Eunius whom Gregory of Tours states to have started as *comes* of Auxerre and subsequently to have been made patrician:[185] despite this, Gregory on more than one later occasion describes him as 'dux',[186] even though other sources, including the contemporary Chronicle of Marius of Avenches, prefer 'patrician'.[187] This would seem to be a firm indication that sixth- and seventh-century Frankish authors were as free in their use of terminology as their fifth-century counterparts.

Despite this, there was a specific office of *dux*, and it is very likely that some of the men only referred to as leaders of armies were in fact *duces* in the more technical sense. One of the reasons for being certain that there was such an office is that some *duces* were placed in charge of specific regions or cities, as were, for example, Beppolen on the Breton frontier, Berulf and Ennodius at Tours, Lupus and Wintrio in Champagne, and Nicetius in Auvergne.[188] Another indication that there was a regular position of *dux* comes from the fact that there are references to men as holding a *ducatus*,[189] while on a few occasions *duces* were removed from power and replaced by other courtiers, and *duces* who died were sometimes specifically replaced:[190] were the sources always to have employed the term in a non-technical sense, this would be very surprising.

If, then, some *duces* were based in particular regions of the *Regnum Francorum*, what were their functions, and how did they differ from those of the *comites* who were also in the provinces? On many of the occasions on which regional *duces* can be seen operating in an official capacity, they were engaged in military leadership.[191] At other times, however, these *duces* can be seen participating in the life of the kingdom in other ways, most of which are related to the military sphere. Hence, Herpo (east of the Jura) captured the troublesome Merovech,[192] and Beppolen (north-west Frankia) acted as Fredegund's escort when she went to see the dying Bishop Praetextatus after he had been attacked on her orders.[193] Not quite all references to regional *duces* related to things military, for Ennodius (*dux* of Tours) was described as the governor of the cities of Aire and Lescar,[194] and, after he ceased to be a *dux*, was ordered to prosecute Bishop Egidius of Rheims for treason:[195] this is, however, an exceptional case, as is indicated by the fact that whenever the sources refer to *duces* in general terms, it is in the context of armed forces or of some related sphere of operations.[196] The military nature of the responsibility of *duces* is perhaps underlined by the fact that most of the areas in which they are known to have been permanently, or regularly, stationed, were on the frontiers – in the Breton region, east of the Jura, in the south west near the frontier with Visigothic Spain. This does not mean that *duces* were not stationed in other regions as well, but, as G. Kurth long ago suggested, there may also have been specific, often temporary, military requirements in those internal regions.[197]

It has been argued by A.R. Lewis that, since many more *duces* than *comites* feature in the writings of Gregory of Tours, *duces* must have been more important than *comites*, particularly as they are found in areas such as Austrasia for which few *comites* are known.[198] Given that some (perhaps many) of the men described as *duces* quite clearly did not hold the 'office' of *dux*, and on the basis of the foregoing elucidation of the mainly military function of *duces* and the primarily civilian role of *comites*, an alternative explanation for the greater number of *duces* may be suggested: that it is a function of the nature of the sources, particularly of Gregory of Tours' *Decem libri historiarum*. There are two reasons why this should be so. First, and more important, *duces*, as military leaders, were more likely than *comites* to be involved in high-profile events of immediately-perceived significance from which Gregory could draw moral conclusions. Second, and related to the first point, Gregory lived in Neustria and his contacts lay in the west and centre of Gaul, not in Austrasia: in view of this, it should not be a cause for comment that most of his references to the officials who usually engaged in less spectacular business are centred outside Austrasia and, indeed, Burgundy. That the latter may have been a factor is suggested by the fact, also noted by Lewis, that more *comites* are found in Austrasia and Burgundy in the seventh century, a period for which one of the main sources, the Chronicle of Fredegar, was centred in the east of the *Regnum Francorum* rather than in Neustria.

Before leaving the subject of the sixth-century Franks, brief reference must be made to two titles which are related to that of *dux* – those of '*rector* of Provence', and 'patrician'. The royal official appointed to administer Provence (defined as 'Marseilles, Provence and the rest of the cities in that region[199]) is never described as a *comes*, though he is most likely to have been a member of the court. Instead, the generic term of '*rector* of Provence' is used.[200] On at least one occasion it describes a man whose office appears to have been that of *dux*,[201] and the position is further complicated by the fact that King Childebert sent Ratharius 'quasi dux' to intervene in the affairs of Marseilles.[202] It is quite possible that Provence, as a frontier zone and the furthest region of the *Regnum Francorum* from any of the main royal centres, usually had a *dux*, and the special position of the area is underlined by the fact that many of the men who administered it were patricians.[203] This does not mean that there was an office of 'patrician of Provence', but simply that the governors (*rectores*) of the area, many of whom engaged in military activities and may well in fact have held the office of *dux*,[204] were usually accorded the rank of patrician. This seems to be positively indicated by a poem of Fortunatus which is addressed to Jovinus, who was 'of illustrious rank, and patrician, and governor of Provence'.[205] That the patriciate was not an office may also be demonstrated by the fact that the eighth-century *Liber historiae Francorum* describes Gundovald, a *dux* of Sigibert, as 'patrician',[206] and, more tellingly, that Pope Gregory the Great, sending a letter to the referendary Asclepiodotus, addressed the Frankish courtier as 'patrician'.[207] This usage of the term 'patrician' to denote a position of honour rather than a specific office, as so much else in the Frankish administration, has its roots in late imperial practice.

9

The Vandals and Africa

There is one provincial area of the western Empire in the fifth century which lay outside the Gallic prefecture about which there is sufficient source material for meaningful discussion to be possible – namely Africa. In the second quarter of the fifth century, parts of the diocese of Africa came to be occupied by the Vandals, who were one of the peoples to have breached the Rhine frontier in *c.* 406. Between that time and their crossing of the Mediterranean in *c.* 429, the Vandals had wandered through Gaul before becoming resident in the Iberian peninsula, first in Galicia and, after *c.* 419, in Baetica. Whether they were settled in Spain as federates is still an unresolved question,[1] and the Iberian interlude as a whole forms one of the most obscure episodes in the early fifth century. What is clear, though, is that in *c.* 429 the Vandals, led by King Geiseric, crossed the Straits of Gibraltar, seeking a new homeland in Africa: it is with this event that the sources become full enough for some discussion of the form and institutions of the Vandal kingdom to be possible. Before undertaking that examination, however, a few words must be said about the sources themselves.

In addition to the brief references found in the fifth-century chronicles, there are two relatively large sources for the Vandal kingdom – the Vandalic section of Procopius' history of Justinian's wars of re-conquest, and the *Historia persecutionis Africanae prouinciae* (*History of the persecution of the African province*) by Victor of Vita. The most immediate feature of Procopius' work is that he wrote in Greek and that care must, therefore, be exercised when discussing specific titles. In fact, this is less of a problem than might at first be supposed owing to the fact that Procopius was not really interested in the Vandals or their institutions at all: the main limitation on his work for present purposes is that he was primarily a historian of Justinian's wars of re-conquest and concerned himself with the progress and politics of the Byzantine army, rather than with the relationship of the Vandals to the Empire or with their administrative institutions.[2] A problem of the same nature surrounds Victor of Vita's *History*, for, as its full title implies, it presents an account of the crimes of the Arian

Vandal authorities against the Catholic population of the regions they controlled. The first consequence of this is that the legal and administrative arrangements of the Vandals were of no direct interest to Victor, and are only seen as incidental details in the narrative framework of the document. A second feature of the work is that it is highly tendentious, deliberately stressing the cruelty and hostility of the Vandals to the 'Roman' Catholics in order to obtain support from the eastern Empire for anti-Vandal activity.[3] In the same way as the writings of Gregory of Tours, despite their moral purpose, are likely accurately to reflect the preconceptions of his age concerning its kings and the ways in which their courts and administration worked, so Victor is unlikely to have invented titles or the mechanisms by which the government worked: not only would he have gained nothing by so doing, but his readership would have found his distortions unbelievable. In fact, although Victor creates an impression of a thoroughly anti-Roman régime which set out to destroy as many features of the Roman past as possible, his *History* contains sufficient incidental fragments of non-religious material for a different reality to emerge. Elements of that less hostile picture can also be detected in a few fragmentary references in other church documents, notably the letters of Fulgentius Ferrandus, the same author's *Life of Fulgentius Bishop of Ruspe*, and Fulgentius of Ruspe's own writings.

Other sources include a number of poetical works, particularly those of poets with Roman names found in the _Codex Salmasianus_, which contain more unbiased material, though it is limited in quantity. Even when such documents do not contain directly relevant data, as is the case with the literary works of Dracontius, their very existence demonstrates not just that Latin culture survived under the Vandals, but that it flourished: indeed, P. Riché, in his discussion of education in the early middle ages, has spoken of a Vandal 'renaissance'.[4] Such works of literature can, therefore, help to counter the negative picture of the Vandal régime found in the tendentious ecclesiastical sources. More concrete evidence for the ways in which the kings operated and saw themselves comes from their few surviving legal enactments, which will be examined below, while their impact on the legal aspects of the daily lives of the majority of the population can be seen in the *Tablettes Albertini*, a series of private documents recording acts of sale.

The king

The first indication of the relationship between the Vandal kings in Africa and the Empire comes from a typically laconic entry in Prosper Tiro's Chronicle which indicates that in *c.* 435 the Vandals were settled in part of Africa as federates.[5] There can be little doubt that the legitimate imperial authorities did not want the Vandals to cross the

Mediterranean in the first place, nor that they were anxious to keep the newcomers at a distance from the provinces around Carthage, one of the major sources of grain for the Empire, and particularly for Rome: to this end, the area allotted to the Vandals appears to have lain in northern Numidia, western Proconsularis and Mauritania Sitifensis.[6] The Vandal king, Geiseric, knowing where the best land lay, was not satisfied with this and, *c.* 439, moved eastwards and conquered east Numidia, Africa Proconsularis, Byzacium and part of Tripolitania. The imperial authorities were unable to repulse the Vandal advance, and a new treaty was made, recognising the Vandal conquests.[7] The precise terms of the settlement are unclear but one feature of the treaty which is recorded is that the Vandals payed an annual 'tribute' (*dasmos*) to the Empire,[8] probably in the form of shipments of grain. Too much should not be read into the term 'tribute' since the source of the information is Procopius, an imperial writer who could deliberately have used a loaded term for what may have been little more than a guarantee that the grain trade would continue.[9] Such a trade would certainly have been desired by the Romans, and there is no reason to suppose that Geiseric would have been unwilling to supply it, since he must have known that Africa had for centuries produced more grain than its own inhabitants required, and the surplus could be exchanged for other commodities.[10] A second element in the 442 treaty would appear to be that Geiseric's son, Huneric, was taken to the imperial court as a hostage,[11] but the significance of this is unclear since hostages could be taken as sureties for many kinds of treaty.

It has been argued that the payment of tribute and taking of a hostage imply that a new federate agreement was indeed reached in *c.* 422.[12] This cannot be either proved or disproved, particularly since the tribute may not really have existed, and all that may be said with any degree of certainty is that neither the exaction of tribute nor the taking of hostages appears to have been a normal feature of fifth-century federate agreements,[13] while both have closer affinities with earlier Roman traditions concerning client kings.[14] It is possible, therefore, that after *c.* 442 the Vandals were not federates, but were fully independently established in Africa, while yet being prepared to co-operate with the Empire.

Whatever the precise 'constitutional' position of Geiseric and his successors, they saw themselves as sufficiently part of the Roman world to participate in Roman faction politics, even outside Africa itself. The most noteworthy example of this is Geiseric's raid on Rome in *c.* 455, which was apparently undertaken at the request of Valentinian III's widow, Eudoxia, in order to remove the usurper Petronius Maximus.[15] Even if Eudoxia did not invite Geiseric to Rome, the king must have calculated that he had more to gain than simply securing the release of his son, Huneric, from the imperial court, since he took care to remove from Italy Valentinian's daughter, Eudocia, to whom Huneric was already betrothed, together with her mother, Eudoxia, and sister, Placidia.[16] Geiseric's interest in imperial politics can be demonstrated to have pre-dated these events since the earlier betrothal of Huneric and Eudocia[17] may reflect a belief that a marriage alliance with the imperial dynasty would add to the king's prestige, if not to his title to rule part of the Empire. The subsequent marriage of the two royal offspring[18] may, therefore, have some similarity to Atauulf's action when, as king of the Visigoths, he had married Galla Placidia, sister of Emperor Honorius. The importance Geiseric attached to this matter is further illustrated by his subsequent support for the claim of Olybrius, the husband of Eudocia's sister, Placidia,[19] to the western imperial throne, even to the point of enduring a war with the eastern Empire.[20] The implication of these events is that, in the same way as Theoderic II of the Visigoths thought it worthwhile to control the western emperor, so too did Geiseric.

Against the view that Vandal rulers saw the emperors as in some way enhancing their title to rule, could be cited the fact that Huneric's royal documents explicitly make the claim that the king owed his power to Divine grace. Jordanes, a mid-sixth-century author, says that Geiseric had made similar claims.[21] It is not clear at precisely what date the kings began to make such an assertion, but it is not unreasonable to suppose that after the failure of Olybrius to become emperor, Geiseric might have felt less closely bound to the Empire. In any case, too much should not be read into the claims, because the documents produced by the royal court do still appear to show some respect for imperial traditions, in that they never refer to the territory ruled by the Vandals as a 'kingdom', but always as a number of 'provinces', in a way perhaps reminiscent of Bishop Remigius' letter to Clovis.[22] Firmer evidence of a desire to work within the imperial framework, even after *c.* 455, comes from the Vandal coinage, the evidence from which also has some parallels with the Frankish material. Most strikingly, Geiseric himself issued no coins in his own name,[23] and the gold coins of all his successors imitated imperial types, retaining the imperial portrait.[24] This remained the case even after the bronze and silver coins began to bear the image of the king in the reigns of Huneric and Gunthamund, respectively.[25] Even on those coins which do bear the king's portrait there are signs of considerable Roman influence, for the king is depicted wearing a diadem, a paludamentum and a cuirass – all potent symbols of authority in the imperial tradition. Further, the same coins describe the king as 'dominus noster', a further borrowing from the Roman past, and one which is paralleled in other sources by references to the king as 'clementissimus',[26] and 'gloriosissimus',[27] both of which have an imperial flavour as do other phrases.[28] Still more examples of the way in which Vandal kings operated within the canon of Roman tradition, even when claiming their independence of the Empire, are to be seen in Geiseric's use of a royal throne (in contrast to early Visigothic practice),[29] and the naming of a city, Hunericopolis, after a king.[30]

Discussion has so far concentrated on the ways in which kings seem to have seen their power, and on their intervention in imperial affairs. There is less evidence for the peaceful and administrative actions of the Vandal rulers, particularly since, unlike their counterparts in Gaul, they do not appear to have issued any form of law code. There are, however, a few individual royal legal enactments: it is significant that those which are preserved in Victor's *History* take the form of edicts,[31] not of *leges*, since this may show respect for the legislative prerogatives of the emperor, in the same way as did the Visigothic code of Euric. Furthermore, the influence of Roman law on the content of the 'Germanic' legislation produced in Gaul can be paralleled by the fact that Huneric's anti-Catholic measures were lifted out of imperial laws against heretics:[32] Roman law was turned against the Roman, Catholic, population. Similarly, the part of Geiseric's will in which the king stipulated his wishes concerning the succession, takes the precise form of a Roman *fideicommissum*, being a codicil, the execution of which was entrusted to the good faith of the heirs.[33] Not only did the form and content of the few surviving fragments of Vandal royal legal enactments conform to imperial traditions,[34] but the *Tablettes Albertini* show that the population still lived its daily life according to the formulae of classical Roman law.[35]

Alongside the evidence that kings presented their power in Roman terms and seem, at least in their legislation, to have behaved in a Roman fashion, may be set indications that they may have taken over the buildings of the Roman administration, and made them into their royal palaces. The main Vandal palace was certainly at Carthage, the capital of the Roman province of Africa proconsularis and the chief city of the African diocese, and the building itself may have been the former proconsular headquarters, in the same way as the *praetorium* at Geneva became a Burgundian palace. Since neither the late fourth-century headquarters, nor any of the public buildings of fifth- to seventh-century Carthage have yet been located on the ground,[36] this must remain conjecture. Such re-use is not unlikely, though, in view of the fact that the arrival of the Vandals in Carthage seems to have left few physical traces in the city, and that there is no evidence for major alterations to the plan of the city in the fifth century after the construction of the Theodosian wall, *c*. 425.[37] The documentary sources do not assist in resolving the question, but they do allow a glimpse of parts of the palace complex. It is clear, for example, that there was a church within the palace, since Procopius speaks of a great sanctuary as being located within it, which is probably the same as the 'palace basilica of St Mary' referred to in a poem in the *Codex Salmasianus*.[38] Elsewhere, Procopius mentions a prison room, called *Ankôna*, which must have been constructed at least partly of timber since, when a guard sought to assist prisoners to escape before the arrival of Belisarius' army, he tore a plank off the structure.[39] The palace must have been near the sea, because the guard was able to see the approach of the Byzantine fleet.[40] Finally, a palace in Carthage is also described by the poet Luxorius, who speaks of a sumptuous marble audience chamber:[41] this building could have been on a different site in the city, but the reference seems to indicate that the kings had indeed taken over some form of Roman building, since it is perhaps unlikely that they would have built such an edifice *de novo*.

Of other royal residences, nothing save the names is known in the case of three of them – *Maxula, Alicanae* and *Hermania* – and not even the location of each is known.[42] With regard to one further site, though, a little more may be learnt, since Procopius spent a night there on his way to Carthage with Belisarius' army and wrote a brief description of its location. The site is that of *Grasse* where there was a palace which was surrounded by a beautiful park with springs, trees and orchards. Procopius also states that it lay 350 *stadia* from Carthage, and was north of *Hadrumentum* (modern Sousse).[43] In his major book on the Vandals, C. Courtois has suggested that *Grasse* could be situated at the modern Hammamet, which is almost exactly the correct distance from Carthage if an allowance is made for taking the Roman road round the Lake of Tunis.[44] This, however, is a very long way round, since it was possible to cross the mouth of the Lake by a Roman road (see Map II). Even though Belisarius must have gone round the Lake on his way to Carthage,[45] there is no reason to suppose that Procopius would not have given the distance by the more direct route. Since that route renders Hammamet too near, it is, perhaps, permissible to look elsewhere for the site of *Grasse*.

In the 1860s, the traveller and antiquarian Nathaniel Davis described the site of Faradise (Firdaws, or Henchir-Fradis),[46] a small town in the hills, overlooking the sea and the surrounding territory, and believed to be the *Aphrodision* of Ptolemy and the *Grasse* of the 'late Empire'.[47] Some twenty years later, in the Tunisian part of his *Remains of the Roman Occupation of North Africa*, Alexander Graham described *Aphrodision*, set on low hills and 'surrounded by olive woods and gardens', and claimed that it was a Vandal palace until occupied by Belisarius – though he does not specifically name *Grasse*.[48] Further, traces of Roman occupation were still visible to both Graham and Davis: the former refers to a 'confused mass of stone rubble', and to the 'palace' as being 'marked by an enclosure, and constructed with huge blocks'. He also mentions triumphal arches, all except one of which were 'overthrown'.[49] The probability of the identification of Firdaws with *Grasse* was also noted by a number of nineteenth-century French authorities.[50]

A further hint that *Grasse* is Firdaws may be found in its name – *Grasse* could be related to the Gothic 'Gras' ('grass', or 'herbage'),[51] and might, therefore, mean 'place of vegetation' or 'park'. Since the Arabic name for the site is Firdaws, which is related to 'paradisus' ('park'),[52] it is not beyond the bounds of possibility that the site was once laid out as a garden or park, much as Procopius implies. Finally, it may be significant that the southern French town of Grasse is set in fertile surroundings very similar to those described for *Grasse*. The identification proposed here can only remain provisional:[53] all that may be said is that it fits Procopius' description reasonably well, is approximately 73 km south of Carthage on the direct road to Sousse, and shows signs of apparently late Roman occupation. It is, therefore, possible that at *Grasse*, as at Carthage itself, the Vandal kings took over major Roman buildings and adapted them for use as royal palaces.

The court

None of the sources for the Vandal kingdom is of a type to reveal a great deal concerning the way in which the royal court operated, but there are enough hints as to the kinds of official who participated in the administration of the kingdom for the nature of the government to be glimpsed. The paucity of evidence may be illustrated by the meagre data concerning that most basic of the court figures, the *comes*, for although it is clear that such a title existed, it is entirely typical of the sources (and of Victor of Vita in particular) that its holders are only seen in action when carrying out royal commands to persecute Catholics. Hence, for example, it was a *comes* who was sent to punish the Catholics of Tipasa for refusing to convert to Arianism,[54] and, on another occasion, it was officials of similar kind who were sent to try to convert a number of Catholics who were being exiled on account of their faith.[55] These are the only two certain references to Vandal *comites*,[56] and do nothing beyond indicating the obvious fact that the companions, or courtiers, of the king could be used to execute the royal will. There is no hint as to whether there were *comites ciuitatum* as in the Gallic kingdoms, but equally nothing to suggest that such officials did not exist in Africa.

Another kind of court title which does little more than feature in the sources is that of *domesticus*. On one occasion, it is recorded, *domestici* 'suggested' that Huneric should follow a particular course of action,[57] while, on another, bishops and *domestici* assembled to witness Sebastianus' renunciation of Catholicism after his flight to Africa from Italy and Constantinople.[58] It would appear, from these meagre indications, that *domestici* were the agents and advisers of the king, perhaps in a way similar to that found in Gaul and derived from late Roman practice.[59]

Even more obscure is the position of men described as *ministri regis*, who are only once attested by Victor of Vita, when he relates an incident in which a number of such men interrogated Catholic bishops.[60] Elsewhere, the sole reference to a *minister* is in a poem by Luxorius which describes the rapaciousness of the state: the kingdom finds personification in the person of Eutyches, *minister*, who engaged in the collection of taxes and the confiscation of goods.[61] These references are so vague that it is impossible to be certain precisely what is meant, and perhaps *minister regis* is to be understood simply as a term for an unspecified agent of the king.

The holders of all the titles so far discussed could become directly involved with the mass of the king's subjects, since it is mainly on occasions when they were engaged in some form of repression that they feature in the largely hostile sources. Of local or regional government, whose officials may not all have been members of the royal court, but are likely to have been even more closely involved with the population at large, even less is known. Thus, although, according to Victor of Vita, Victorianus was proconsul of Carthage,[62] it is not at all clear what this man's function was, and it may be doubted whether his duties were in any way similar to those of the earlier Roman bearers of the title, since Carthage was the administrative and royal centre of the Vandal kingdom. It is possible that the Vandal proconsuls were the governors of the city. The fact that the title of proconsul appears to have existed in the Vandal administration is in itself some evidence of continuity from the Roman period, and suggests that not all the existing administrative traditions were ignored, despite the hostility of the authors of most of the surviving documents from the period.

Since the local administration of the Vandal kingdom cannot be analysed in any detail, it is not surprising to find that the organisation of the king's personal staff is yet more obscure, especially given the increasing silence of imperial and Frankish sources concerning men who operated close to the person of the king. All that may be said with any degree of certainty concerning royal domestic management is that each member of the royal family seems to have had his own household, which included an official known as a *procurator domus*,[63] and that Huneric's court contained a *cellarita regis* who may have been in charge of the royal servants.[64] The sole other personal attendant of the king about whom much can be said is the *praepositus*. Although there is only one remotely helpful reference to an official of this kind in the Vandal kingdom – Obadus, who interviewed Bishop Eugenius of Carthage concerning the Catholic faith[65] – there is mention of an unnamed *maior domus*, who was responsible for presenting a document from Eugenius to King Huneric.[66] This last point is of particular significance, because it is similar to the kind of activity in which Burgundian *maiores domus* engaged, and may, therefore, serve further to strengthen the case for *maiores* having a common origin. Given that likelihood, and given what has earlier been seen of such officials in the Frankish context, it is possible that that the Vandal *praepositus* and *maior* are identical (though this cannot be demonstrated on the African evidence alone[67]), and that the origin of the position lies in the Roman world rather than in the Germanic.

A title of less uncertain Roman ancestry is that of *primiscriniarius*, which features in one of Luxorius' poems. The text of the poem demonstrates that the official was involved with the administration of justice, and that he could be present at the king's judgements ('placita').[68] The more precise functions of such a man are, however, nowhere defined, though it is probable that the title derived from that of the imperial *primiscrinius*, or head of the judicial staff.[69]

The only type of governmental official about whom any more is known is the *notarius*. This is quite clearly a Roman title. *Notarii* are better documented than other royal agents because, on account of their involvement with documents, they often came into contact with people outside the court, and especially with the Church – that is, with one of the most literate sections of the community. It is not surprising that Victor of Vita, in particular, includes a number of references to the activities of *notarii*, since they sometimes directly impinged upon his subject. In an account of the interrogation of certain Catholic bishops during the persecution, Victor records that *notarii* wrote down the bishops' answers to questions posed by *ministri regis*.[70] In addition, the Vandal *notarius*, Vitarit, was partly responsible for the proclamation of Huneric's edict of toleration,[71] and was later the bearer of a letter from Bishop Eugenius of Carthage to the king. The precise terms of the letter are of interest, since they show that Vitarit was to present Eugenius' case to Huneric:

> I [Eugenius] beseech your magnificence [Vitarit] that you should deign to bring my aforementioned suggestion [or petition] to the ears of the most clement lord and king.[72]

These last two examples move away from a concern purely with the production of documents, and into the sphere of transmitting their contents – in other words, *notarii* could act as intermediaries between the king and his subjects. This kind of activity is similar to that undertaken by referendaries, and in the western Empire (where referendaries appear to have been unknown), by imperial notaries.[73] An extension of this sort of duty may be seen in the report of a formal disputation between Catholics and Arians, which reveals that the occasion was managed by a *notarius*:[74] this is a task of a nature similar to that of the organisation of the 411 Council of Carthage by an imperial *notarius*. As was the case in 411, it is not clear exactly why a *notarius* was chosen for this task: it may be that he was the most trusted royal official available at the time, or it may be that he was an individual who had managed to secure the trust of both sides.

Similar uncertainty surrounds the exact position of Boniface, described by Procopius as 'grammateus'. Boniface was placed in charge of the royal treasure by King Gelimer, with orders to flee with it to the Visigothic King Theudis in Spain in the event of the Vandals being defeated by Belisarius.[75] Quite how a *grammateus* or *notarius* should come to be connected with the treasury is not known, though it is pertinent to observe that documents were often kept in the treasuries of other early medieval kingdoms.[76] It would be possible to erect an elaborate hypothesis that the writing office had control over the treasury, but it is perhaps more realistic to see Boniface as a royal agent chosen, in highly exceptional circumstances, to carry out the specific task simply by virtue of the fact that he was a trusted courtier, rather than on account of his exact office within the court.[77]

*

Although there are many unresolved questions concerning the Vandal court and the way in which it operated, the shadowy picture which emerges has a familiar outline. Like their counterparts in Gaul, Vandal kings worked within the framework of imperial tradition, giving symbolic precedence to the emperor, taking an active interest in the highest level of imperial politics, and adapting Roman institutions – legislative and administrative – to suit the new circumstances of their régime.[78] If a more conventional view of the Vandal kingdom emphasises its relative 'barbarity', that is largely because such a view has been conditioned by the almost universally hostile sources.

One way in which the sources have assisted in the construction of a distorted picture is that they dwell on the large number of wealthy Libyans who were dispossessed or exiled by Geiseric, or fled from him.[79] Although it is quite certain that there was an exodus of wealthy Africans, and that it was on a larger scale than anything attested for Gaul, it is inconceivable that the majority of the provincials were in a position to do anything other than remain where they had always lived. Whatever the precise number of the Vandals was, it is probable that they formed only a minority of the total population in the kingdom: in terms of daily life it is, therefore, unlikely that they could immediately (as Victor of Vita implies) have overthrown at a local level all the legal and administrative traditions with which the indigenous population would have been familiar for generations: this is particularly true since the Vandals represented a 'lower' culture than that of the provincials. By way of demonstration that not all members of the 'Roman' population did flee, and that those who remained did not witness the total destruction of their way of life, reference need only be made to the private legal acts recorded in the *Tablettes Albertini*, the parties to many of which had Roman names, and which, as already suggested, were rooted in Roman legal forms.[80] Higher up the social scale, there is some evidence to suggest that some of those who fled, or their heirs, later returned, and were even compensated for the loss of their ancestral land:[81] this is not something which the tendentious sources can be expected to stress. Equally unlikely to be deliberately noted by the authors of the sources are those 'Romans' who, as in Gaul, saw opportunities for advancement by serving 'barbarian' masters. That there were such men is quite clear since Victor of Vita records the presence of Alexander, *uir inluster*,[82] in Huneric's court; other men, already mentioned, include Victorianus, his namesake, *primiscriniarius* and *uir inluster*, the *minister regis* Eutychus, and the *grammateus* Boniface. With such people as these in royal service, and a number of other 'Romans' – such as the poets and *uiri clarissimi* Coronatus and Flavius, and *uir clarissimus et spectabilis* Luxorius[83] – known to have resided within the kingdom, it would be surprising indeed if the régime of Geiseric and his sucessors had owed nothing to the earlier history of the area they ruled.

10

Conclusion

The fifth century used to be characterised as the period in which the savage Germanic 'barbarians' invaded the western provinces of the Empire, ravaged and then seized their lands, and established themselves as the new masters of western Europe in opposition to the civilisation of the Romans. There are few researchers today who would accept such a simple or stark view, most contending that there was a greater degree of continuity in all spheres – religious, cultural and administrative – than was previously thought. It is also not new to suggest that many of the 'barbarians' did not simply acquiesce in the continuation of Roman practices, but actually promoted it. The debate is now more concerned with the varying degrees to which this happened in different areas and at different times, with the reasons for its occurrence, and with the ways in which it was achieved. What the preceding five chapters have tried to do is to examine one aspect of the problem – the administrative one – and to place the material both against the background of what is known of the central imperial administration of the period (as discussed in Part I), and in the context of an understanding of the practical effect of the nature of the source materials on the type of information which has been preserved and, therefore, on the picture of provincial administration which it is possible to recover.

That there was a major change in the fifth century is quite clear – the 'traditional' way of administering the western provinces through praetorian prefects and their subordinates, with a separate centrally-based military system, was replaced over large areas by the kingdoms of 'barbarians'. No such major change could have occurred without good cause, and the stimulus clearly lay in the problems caused by the arrival of 'barbarians' within the Empire after they had moved westwards on an unprecedented scale from both the Balkans and the Rhineland. The old system was adequate neither to repulse the 'barbarians', nor completely to subjugate them once their presence deep inside the provinces had become a permanent reality.

It was argued in Part I that the central imperial administration of the western Empire in the fifth century was not of a bureaucratic nature, and it was shown that although officials might bear certain titles which described their main functions, they could intervene in almost any sphere of imperial business if required to do so. This principle was more explicit in the 'traditional' offices of the provincial administration, since all the major officials (from the praetorian prefects down to the governors of individual provinces) had competence right across the sphere of government with the one exception of military affairs. Another feature of the system was that those at the top of the power chain were able to act in a virtually autonomous way, as is exemplified by their ability to judge in place of the emperor himself. In Gaul, the only area for which there is sufficient good evidence, it is clear that the men appointed as praetorian prefects in the fifth century were almost always local. It is only one step, though not a short one, from this to the granting of autonomous power in the same provinces to resident 'barbarian' kings: perhaps the only major difference was that the kings had military as well as civilian authority. The settlement of the Visigoths in Aquitaine certainly involved new features but can be seen as a logical development from the kind of federate agreements being made in the second half of the fourth century.

That the 'barbarians' should be seen in the context of late-Roman provincial society and government is clear from the fact that they came to participate actively in the faction politics which were as rife within the fifth-century Empire as they had been for centuries. Indeed, it was not only the 'barbarian' peoples settled as federates of the new kind who engaged in this behaviour, because the Alans, settled under an older sort of agreement,[1] had, as early as *c.* 411, supported the pretender Jovinus and even seem to have preferred Roman connections to relations with other 'barbarian' peoples.[2] It is also possible that on occasion, as in cases of the *coniuratio Marcelliniana* and the alleged treachery of Arvandus, members of the Roman aristocracy took the initiative in seeking to integrate 'barbarian' leaders into their schemes of faction politics. Viewed against a background of this kind of activity, it is interesting to note the claim made by Procopius that the Vandals were in fact invited to Africa by Boniface, *comes Africae*, in pursuit of his own factional purposes.[3] Although Procopius' testimony has to be treated with caution since it appears to be contradicted by Prosper Tiro, a nearer contemporary of the events,[4] it cannot be totally dismissed: at the very least, it reveals that an author of the Justinianic period, personally involved in anti-'barbarian' campaigns in the west, believed it possible, or even likely, that an early-fifth-century Roman aristocrat could have invited 'barbarians' to assist him and, thereby, made them part of the Roman world. Certainly, as has been seen, the Vandal kings subsequently did a great deal to link themselves to the fate of members of the highest western aristocratic circles – those in the imperial dynasty.

Involvement in the politics of the Roman Empire inevitably led 'barbarian' rulers to establish friendly relations with at least some sectors of the Roman aristocracy, both in imperial circles and in the provinces. One manifestation of such relations may be seen in the presence of members of leading families in the entourages of the 'barbarian' leaders who occupied areas of the western Empire in the fifth century. Many more courtiers, even in the reputedly hostile Vandal kingdom, bore Roman names, and some of their number may well also have been aristocrats, though not revealed as such by the often fragmentary sources.

Another feature of the 'barbarian' administrations is that they were similar in character not only to each other, but also to the Roman system they superseded. The fact that their institutions were not always identical to those of the Empire demonstrates that the process by which they became established did not simply involve the direct takeover of Roman institutions, but the creation of the new royal courts by adapting an amalgam of features from Roman imperial and provincial administration. The fact that the 'barbarians' did things differently from the Romans of the fourth and early fifth centuries does not mean that they were incompetent savages incapable of understanding Roman ways, nor that they were importing uncultured Germanic customs on a large scale. In addition, fifth-century Roman institutions were not so far removed from their successors as has often been thought.

The similarity of the administrative arrangements of the four 'barbarian' peoples calls for further comment, especially since the nature of the sources for the four kingdoms differs considerably. In such circumstances, it might be expected that the data which can be recovered for the Franks (served by a lengthy 'narrative' source relating mainly to the sixth century) would reveal a very different picture from that which can be recovered for the Visigoths (served by very fragmentary 'narrative sources', by better legal material, and by private letters): further contrasts might be expected when the Burgundians and, more especially, the Vandals, are added to the equation. It is not, of course, the case that the four kingdoms are covered equally fully, nor that the aspects of royal government revealed by each are the same. What may be said, though, is that an attempt to work with each source as the purposeful creation of an individual author provides enough points of contact between the four kingdoms for it to be possible to assert that their administrative structures were very similar, though not absolutely identical: an extension of that principle enables it to be seen that those structures were in many respects derived from the Roman system they replaced.

It is with these considerations – the nature of the sources and the *romanitas* of much of 'barbarian' administration in the western provinces – in mind that the the question of 'barbarian' rule in Italy must now be addressed.

PART III

Italy under Odoacer and the Ostrogoths

The traditional picture of the government of Italy under the rule of Odoacer and of the Ostrogoths who succeeded him is that it was well organised and bureaucratic to a much greater extent than its contemporary counterparts elsewhere in the west, and that it represented a continuation and flowering of the ordered Roman administrative system. On this model, only when the Lombards arrived, c. 568, did Italy acquire the same kind of ramshackle government as the other 'barbarian' kingdoms. The reasons for this difference between the Ostrogothic system and those of the other Germanic peoples are seldom adequately discussed, but seem to come down to the fact that Theoderic the Great had, as a child, been held hostage at Constantinople where he learnt about the Roman way of life and came to understand, respect and admire Roman culture and the Roman administrative system in a way in which no other 'barbarian' leader had the chance to do. Accordingly, when he became ruler of Italy, Theoderic worked entirely within the terms of late-Roman imperial administration, while his counterparts elsewhere in the west imported barbarous Germanic customs and turned a perfectly good Roman governmental system into something much more chaotic.

There are two reasons why this kind of interpretation must be questioned. First, unless the Ostrogoths were unlike their counterparts elsewhere in the west, their administrative system is likely to have taken the form of an adaptation of late Roman institutions. Given that imperial government, as discussed in earlier chapters, was by no means bureaucratically ordered, it is inherently unlikely that the Ostrogothic administration should have been so.

Second, since, as was argued in Part II, the 'barbarian' kings of Gaul and Africa operated very much within the framework of late Roman provincial administration, any interpretation of the differences between such leaders and the Ostrogothic kings which minimises the debt of the Visigoths, Burgundians, Franks and Vandals to the Roman past must be re-examined. It is undeniably the case that the circumstances of the post-imperial rulers of Italy were different from those of the Germanic leaders in the provinces, because the former presence of the imperial court, and of the administrative machinery of the City of Rome, meant that in Italy there was a slightly different range of institutions which could be drawn upon. However, given what has already been seen of the way in which 'barbarians' elsewhere in the west did in fact imitate certain features of the imperial court even though they did not have such a direct relationship with it as did the Ostrogoths, caution should be exercised lest the differences between the Ostrogoths and their peers be over-emphasised.

11

The Sources

A discussion of the sources upon which an examination of Ostrogothic administration must be based has to begin with reference to Cassiodorus' *Uariae*. This collection of material claims to be a set of governmental documents of a form broadly similar to that of the imperial rescripts contained in the Theodosian Code: as such, it ought to reflect the mechanics of government at least as well as do the rescripts. At first sight, the contents of the *Uariae* seem to illustrate, or at least imply, a bureaucratic system of administration such as is not found elsewhere in the 'barbarian' world. However, although, as will emerge in the discussion of Ostrogothic royal administration, careful reading of the documents contained within the *Uariae* does indeed yield much information about the way in which the system worked, the picture which emerges is not quite that which has traditionally been assumed. Once the activities of kings and their officials have been analysed, it will be necessary to return to the *Uariae* in more detail with a view to understanding both why it was written and why it has created the impression of an Ostrogothic bureaucracy: all that needs be said at the moment is that it has long been recognised that Cassiodorus was interested in welding the Gothic and Roman populations of Italy together, and that this is as clear from certain of the documents in the *Uariae* as it is from his other writings.[1]

The other surviving work of Cassiodorus which is of relevance to the present enquiry is his *Chronicle*, and this serves to illustrate the point made above. In the *Chronicle*, Cassiodorus set out the achievements of the Gothic people in the annalistic form familiar from the works of fifth-century authors. As in the earlier chronicles, the information is presented laconically and reveals very little concerning the administrative arrangements of the society in which it was produced. The *Chronicle* ends with a record of the consulate of Eutharic, *c.* 519, and his designation as the successor of Theoderic the Great:[2] that point, a landmark in the process of mutual acceptance and amalgamation of the Gothic and Roman peoples, was intended to be celebrated in a work presenting Gothic history in a thoroughly Roman literary form.

A third document of Cassiodoran authorship, the *Gothic History*, has long been lost, but has been thought to survive, in abridged form, in Jordanes' *Getica*, or *Origins and Exploits of the Getes (De origine actibusque Getarum)*.[3] More recently, though, it has been contended that while Jordanes may have borrowed material from Cassiodorus' lost history,[4] which he is known to have consulted, he used other material not employed by Cassiodorus, and his purpose was different.[5] This interpretation, which has the merit of starting with an examination of Jordanes' writings on their own terms, shows Jordanes to have been a man of Gothic descent writing at the time of Justinian and in full approval of the re-conquest: this is very different from what would have been in the lost Cassiodoran history, a work composed at the invitation of Theoderic the Great.[6] In addition, although Jordanes, in rather the same way as Gregory of Tours, has often been castigated for producing a muddled, ill-informed and badly written work, W. Goffart in particular has argued convincingly that when the *Getica* is set alongside Jordanes' other known book, the *Romana*, a coherent literary structure, executed with some competence, emerges. Also as was the case with Gregory of Tours, Jordanes wrote for religious purposes: he sought to show that it was part of the Divine plan that all 'barbarians' should be defeated, and that the history of Romano-Gothic relations contained many parallels with the history of man's Fall and Redemption. One reason for this is likely to have lain in an attempt to provide the newly re-conquered Italy with a means of coming to terms with its Gothic past, its defeat and its new situation. This aim was not achieved by means of glorifying the worldly might either of Old Rome in the past or of New Rome in the present: instead, an understanding of history should lead to a turning away from the secular world to acceptance of Divine destiny.[7] Given that the *Getica* is the larger part of this scheme, it is not surprising that the book does not contain much of relevance to the present enquiry: not only is it more akin to a work of fiction than of historical record, but even where hard facts are found, they rarely concern secular administration.

Another author who produced a narrative history covering part of the period of Gothic rule in Italy was the anonymous author of Ravenna. Although his work takes the form of a chronicle, it is fuller than almost any document of comparable type produced in the fifth or sixth century. However, its author, like the other chroniclers and like Jordanes, had a religious purpose – this time, to show that although Theoderic was a great ruler, his Arianism ultimately turned him into an enemy of God and brought about his downfall.[8] The Ravenna Chronicle therefore stands half way between the more conventional chronicles and Gregory of Tours' *Decem libri historiarum*, and is subject to some of the limitations of both.

The final work to contain a continuous narrative concerning the

Ostrogoths is the Gothic section of Procopius' *History of the Wars*. Some of the problems with Procopius' writings were touched upon in Chapter 9 in relation to the Vandal kingdom. With regard to the Gothic campaigns, it is clear that his narrative is personal and simplistic: he was not concerned with the details of Gothic administration any more than he had been of the Vandal, or was of the Constantinopolitan, but collected personal details and anecdotal information on the course of the war.[9]

There are other documents which provide varying quantities of information of significance for the present study. First, there are the writings of Bishop Ennodius of Pavia, which can be divided into letters, poems, a panegyric, a hagiographical document, and some miscellaneous pieces. Much of this material is personal and literary, and it has many similarities with the writings of Sidonius Apollinaris. Like Sidonius Apollinaris, Ennodius was a member of the aristocracy, and even where his writings lack specific reference to governmental procedures, they may reveal something of at least one strand of aristocratic opinion concerning 'barbarian' rule. A recent study has cogently argued that Ennodius was almost as partisan as Cassiodorus, seeing Theoderic the Great as having delivered Rome from the tyranny of Odoacer and as having recreated its greatness.[10]

Another member of the contemporary aristocracy – this time of the top tier of Roman senatorial society – Boethius, also produced writings which survive, including *Consolation of Philosophy*. This work contains a small amount of very valuable data though, as its title suggests, it is really a philosophical treatise. In terms of official documents other than the *Uariae*, the proceedings of the councils of the Church held at Rome during the Laurentian schism are, like those of the 411 Council of Carthage, ecclesiastical documents, but, since Theoderic was involved with the resolution of the schism, record fragments of information concerning secular administration. Similar fragments are also contained in a small number of official letters between Pope Gelasius and both Theoderic and his mother, Ereliuva.[11]

The range of material also includes a number of inscriptions, notably those connected with the restoration of the Flavian amphitheatre during Odoacer's reign.[12]

Although none of the sources, not even (as will be seen) the *Uariae*, individually provides an ideal quantity or type of information concerning Ostrogothic administration, it will be apparent from this short discussion of them that there is a greater variety of sources than for any of the kingdoms examined in Part II: this will enable the discussion of the Ostrogoths to range more widely than was possible for any other single kingdom.[13]

12

'Barbarian' Kings in Italy, 476-552

Perhaps the most striking feature of the sources for late-fifth-century Italy is that they hardly comment on the removal of Romulus Augustulus and his replacement not by an emperor, but by Odoacer: they treat the event as of no greater significance than any other usurpation. In fact, for one of the chroniclers, the later death in *c.* 480 of a former emperor, Julius Nepos, was a more noteworthy event.[1] Cassiodorus, writing in his *Chronicle*, gave Odoacer's accession a longer entry than the average in the work, but still only recorded that Odoacer became king, with the brief additional comment that he assumed neither the purple nor the imperial insignia.[2] More typical is the remark of the anonymous Ravenna chronicler, author of the fullest of the sources of its kind, that 'soon after Augustulus had been deposed from the empire, Odoacer was made king and remained in his kingdom for thirteen years'.[3] The fact that the sources do not make an issue of the replacement of an emperor by a king implies that their authors and, presumably, a large section of the Roman aristocracy, did not see the event as marking the end of an era or even as a particular calamity for Rome.[4]

Viewed from another angle – that of Odoacer's actions once he became ruler of Italy – it is clear that Odoacer was a king in exactly the same way as were the leaders of the other 'barbarians' in the west,[5] and the only two surviving royal documents from his reign refer to him simply as 'king'.[6] This does not mean, any more than in the case of the other kings, that the Empire was of no significance to Odoacer. Indeed, it can be demonstrated that such was not the case since according to Malchus, a Greek author, he sought legitimisation in the form of a patriciate from Emperor Zeno,[7] and it is probable that his defeat of the Rugians, also only known from eastern sources, was achieved in an attempt to gain respectability in the eyes of the Empire.[8] Both of these actions are closely parallel to those of the Burgundian kings who held office as patricians and Gallic masters of the soldiers: the difference is that Odoacer was unsuccessful in obtaining recognition. This may have been partly because he had no known links of kinship with prominent men in the imperial court as the Burgundians had with Ricimer, and possibly also on account of a reluctance on the part of Zeno to hand over Italy, the old heart of the Empire, to a leader whom he had not nominated, but who had taken the government of Italy for himself. This repulse did not, however, prevent Odoacer from claiming continued association with the Empire, in the same way as did the Vandal and Frankish kings, in particular by using imperial types for all his coins until at least *c.* 486, and even later for gold coins.[9]

That Odoacer's claims to power in Italy were never recognised by the eastern Empire is clear from the fact that Theoderic the Great and the Ostrogoths were sent to Italy by Emperor Zeno quite specifically to dispose of him.[10] Zeno may well have wished to remove the Ostrogoths from the Balkan peninsula where they had for some time caused problems for the east, and he may have been more concerned that at least one of the two 'barbarian' leaders should be destroyed by the other, than specifically with which one succeeded and which one lost. The pursuit of such a policy of dividing 'barbarians' against themselves was scarcely a novelty for a Roman emperor. Despite this possibility, the dice were not completely evenly weighted, because unlike Odoacer, Theoderic had held Roman offices – he had been a consul and a patrician (both honorary positions),[11] and *c.* 484 had been a master of the soldiers.[12] In *c.* 488, Theoderic may still have been *patricius*, since it is unclear whether that honorary position could be revoked, and it is possible that he undertook the invasion of Italy as a master of the soldiers of the same kind as the Burgundian kings were.[13]

Whatever the precise nature of Theoderic's Italian command (and there is no way of arriving at certainty concerning it), the Ravenna chronicler states that after he had completed the conquest of Italy, Theoderic was to rule in Odoacer's place only until such time as Zeno should arrive and re-establish full imperial authority in the west.[14] It is impossible to ascertain exactly what Zeno's intentions for the future governance of Italy were, since he died during the last stages of Theoderic's campaign, but before making the trip to the west. All that is certain is that Theoderic, on defeating Odoacer, sent Festus, leader of the Roman Senate, to Zeno in an attempt to gain legitimate royal power in the way previously denied to Odoacer.[15] Furthermore, even at the moment of Zeno's death another envoy, Faustus Niger, was on his way from Italy to Constantinople.[16] These events clearly show that Theoderic still expected to receive instructions from the emperor, and that he aspired to acquire a continuation and full legitimisation for his power in Italy.

The death of Zeno almost inevitably meant that there was a pause in imperial activity with regard to Italy. The new emperor, Anastasius, had to be chosen and installed, to secure his position in the east and to gain confidence in his own authority before he could realistically turn his thoughts to the problems of the west, or contemplate fulfilling Zeno's intention of travelling to Italy himself. The Goths, perhaps foreseeing this, and being impatient, 'themselves confirmed Theoderic as king, not waiting for the order of the new emperor'.[17] The precise implications of this statement need some consideration, since it is quite certain that Theoderic was the 'king of the Goths' (*rex gentium*) long before he went to Italy,[18] and inconceivable that he required authorisation from Constantinople to continue in that position, any more than did his contemporaries elsewhere in the west as leaders of their own peoples. The word 'rex' must, therefore, refer to the kind of royal leadership enjoyed by the kings of the federated Visigoths and Burgundians, which gave them authority to rule both Goths and Romans. Unless it is that kind of 'semi-magisterial' ('halb magistra-risch')[19] kingship which is meant, it is very difficult to see what the Ravenna chronicler was seeking to convey when he described the object of Festus' mission as being to try to get the Emperor to invest Theoderic with the royal cloak. The point is underlined by Jordanes' statement that Zeno encouraged Theoderic to lay aside the habit of a private citizen and the dress of his race, and to assume a cloak with the royal insignia, since he had become the ruler of both the Goths and the Romans.[20] Leaving aside the tendentious nature of this statement, in which Jordanes seems to have been trying to claim that Zeno had in fact authorised Theoderic's continued power in Italy, it is quite clear that the royal authority to which he alluded was different from that already held by Theoderic, was not Gothic, was something which the emperor could confer, and was related to the framework of the imperial hierarchy of public officials. The one known position which seems to fit all those conditions is that of a 'barbarian' king who had settled within the provinces under the terms of a new-style federate agreement with the Romans. That Theoderic's position could be thought of in such formal terms by his contemporaries (and the following generation) can, perhaps, be seen by a retrospective analogy, to place the 'barbarian' kings discussed in Part II in a more formally Roman context.

The last suggestion is strengthened by an examination of what can be deduced of Theoderic's attitude once he was established as king, since it is remarkably similar to that of his peers in other provinces. Even after he assumed the 'Roman' kingship without imperial sanction, Theoderic continued to treat with Anastasius and eventually made peace with him concerning his position as king, receiving the 'palace ornaments' which Odoacer had sent to Constantinople as no longer needed, thus having his position symbolically legitimised.[21] Ostrogothic coinage showed the same spirit of recognition of imperial authority: the gold and silver coins of Theoderic's reign all have imperial types on the obverse, with Theoderic's monogram (rather than portrait) on the reverse.[22] A broadly similar pattern emerges for all Theoderic's successors except Totila Baudila who reigned during the last stages of the war with Justinian, and cannot be expected to have shown the same respect for imperial claims.[23]

Another manifestation of deference to a hegemonic emperor is to be found in the fact that Athalaric, Amalasuintha and Theodahad all sought legitimisation for their power from Emperors Justin and Justinian.[24] Some gestures of this kind were reciprocated, and it is significant that Eutharic, whom Theoderic nominated as his successor, was not only consul in *c.* 519, but consul with Justin, thus perhaps demonstrating unequivocal recognition of Eutharic's position;[25] Justin also adopted Eutharic as his son at arms.[26] The point may be pressed further, since a letter from the Roman Senate to Anastasius refers to Theoderic as the 'son' ('filius') of the Emperor.[27] Finally, there is the well-known opening letter of the *Uariae*, also addressed to Anastasius, in which Theoderic is made to say:

> Our kingship is an imitation of yours, modelled on your good design, a copy of the only Empire: in as much as we follow you, so we stand before other peoples.[28]

The important point here is that although Theoderic apparently saw his kingship as imitating that of the emperor, he makes no claim to be an emperor himself, or to have parity with Anastasius. Not even an inscriptional reference to Theoderic as 'semper augustus' explicitly claims parity with the emperor, since it also calls him 'king', though it comes very close to doing so.[29] There was one Empire, of which Theoderic's kingdom was a part, and which provided his rule with a model and with legitimacy, and protected his people. One of the very few occasions on which Theoderic seems to have deviated from this slightly subservient position to the Empire was when he commissioned the great mosaic for the palace at Ravenna: there, the armed king is greeted by Rome and Ravenna as an autonomous ruler with no reference to the emperor.[30] Perhaps more significant than the apparent statement of autonomy, however, is the fact that the mosaic and the scene it depicted were entirely within the Roman tradition of artistic representations of power: in the same way as the Frankish Theoderic expressed his independence in a Roman manner, so too did his Ostrogothic namesake. Indeed, there is nothing in any of the foregoing discussion which sets Theoderic the Great apart from his contemporaries elsewhere in the west: as J.J. van den Besselaar noted in a wider context, if it were not for the documents enshrined in the *Uariae*, Theoderic would look very similar to Clovis.[31]

The same is also true of the more active side of Ostrogothic kingship. Hence, for example, Ennodius' panegyric on Theoderic dwells on the king's role as a war leader, in a way which is similar to that later carried much further by Gregory of Tours in relation to the Franks.[32] The importance of the military aspect of kingship is underlined by Theodahad's alleged statement to Justinian that he had been brought up in a wholly civilian way, as a Roman aristocrat, and was unsuitable to hold royal power since he lacked military training and experience.[33] Witigis, on the other hand, seems to have boasted of his military prowess and clearly saw it as a legitimisation for his elevation to the kingship.[34] It is, perhaps, significant that although Odoacer employed a master of the soldiers (three are known from his reign),[35] there is no evidence that Theoderic or his successors did so: this may imply that they fulfilled the role of chief military administrator themselves, in the same way as did the Burgundian kings.[36] One military campaign, waged under Theoderic, is particularly significant – that of *c.* 504 against the Gepids in the region of Sirmium. This does not seem to have been simply an anti-Gepid move, for it was also an attempt to recover for the ruler of Italy a province which had formerly belonged to the west but had come under the control of the east:[37] in this there is an interesting parallel with the possible attempt of the Visigoths to control an entire Gallic diocese noted in Chapter 6.

The civilian aspect of the power of Theoderic and his successors is also clearly documented, particularly by Cassiodorus, who refers to the king as the guardian of the art of government ('ciuilitas'):[38] an inscription commemorating Theoderic's involvement with the draining of the Pomptine marshes claims, amongst other things, that the king was 'guardian of liberty'.[39] For Cassiodorus, at least, maintaining the laws was the manifestation of *ciuilitas*,[40] a point illustrated by the fact that the king's was the ultimate court of appeal, the court to which final petitions for justice were presented.[41] A similar point emerges from other sources, as when a letter written by Pope Gelasius refers to the summoning of Bishop Serenus to Theoderic's court to account for his conduct;[42] or when a letter written by Ennodius shows its author to have petitioned a court official, Mercator, concerning the release of prisoners who were being unlawfully detained;[43] or when Ennodius' *Uita Epiphanii* recounts how Epiphanius twice sought reductions in taxation in circumstances similar to those in which Bibianus petitioned Theoderic of the Visigoths.[44]

With regard to the law which Theoderic was resposible for enforcing, it was almost certainly Roman vulgar law. One of the clues to this is that even the pro-imperial Procopius states that Theoderic observed justice and preserved the laws, while a letter from Pope Gelasius to the same king states that Theoderic was responsible for guarding the laws of the Roman *principes*.[45] That letter is of the greatest significance, for it urges the king not only to keep the Roman laws, as he was already doing, but to have due reverence for the Church, and especially for the Holy See of St Peter. The general flavour of the short document is very similar to that of Remigius to Clovis, in which the Frankish king's power is described in Roman terms, and Clovis is urged to be just and to take the advice of the Church.[46]

The parallel with the legislative activities of other kings can be taken further, because the *Edict of Theoderic*, almost certainly produced by Theoderic the Great,[47] is very similar in both form and content to the code of Euric, to the laws of the Burgundian kings, and to the *Pactus legis Salicae*. Although the Edict contained new material, it was essentially an adaptation of existing law to new circumstances, and did not interfere with imperial prerogatives.[48] It seems to be fairly generally accepted that there was only one set of laws in existence in Italy, that they applied to all who lived within the kingdom (that is, they were territorial), and that they were Roman in origin: in view of this, and of the similarities between the Edict and the other 'barbarian' codes, it is perhaps even more likely than has so far been suggested that the same set of circumstances existed in the kingdoms examined in Part II. At the very lowest level, the similarity between the various codes argues in favour of a common origin, and a Roman one seems *prima facie* more likely than a hypothetical *urgermanisch* one.

Finally, Theoderic's desire to be seen as operating within the Roman tradition can be seen in his choice of main residence – Ravenna, the seat of the last western emperors. Although Theoderic built himself a palace in the city, it has recently been suggested that he did not construct an entirely new building, but altered and enlarged an earlier complex, perhaps in some way associated with the imperial administration.[49] Ravenna was not, though, the only place where Theoderic is known to have resided and built a new palace – Verona and Pavia were similarly graced, the *praetorium* at the latter probably being converted into a royal residence:[50] this forms an obvious parallel with the activities of the Burgundians at Geneva. It is, however, perhaps a significant comment on the *ciuilitas* of Theoderic's régime that, although respectable and important Roman cities, neither of the latter sites had been the seat of an imperial residence in the recent past, and that, as B. Ward-Perkins suggested, both were probably chosen for their defensive qualities:[51] this may serve as a warning against unquestioningly taking the claims of the major source for Ostrogothic administration, the *Uariae*, at face value.

13

The Royal Court

Any examination of the composition and workings of the Ostrogothic royal court is necessarily subject to the limitations of the sources, and the problems posed by the surviving documents are no different from those already encountered in other parts of the west. Of particular significance is the fact that, yet again, no surviving material is of a nature accurately to reflect the details of court-based administration. The work of the Ravenna chronicler, for example, has much the same shortcomings in this respect as the other chronicles, and does not have the merit of being such a long document as Gregory of Tours' *Decem libri historiarum*, which to some extent makes up for its lack of primary interest in secular administration by the sheer volume of information it contains. Ennodius' writings are also largely tangential to the court, in the same way as were those of Sidonius Apollinaris and Avitus of Vienne. Even the *Uariae* of Cassiodorus poses the same problems as the imperial rescripts in that there should have been no greater need for the king to communicate with court officials by means of the written word in the Ostrogothic kingdom than there had been in the fifth-century Empire. The result of this is, once again, that the courtiers who operated nearest to the person of the king are often those about whom the least can be said.

Before the position of the court officials is examined, a few words may be said about Ostrogothic queens. Perhaps the most powerful of the royal women of Italy in the period was Theoderic's daughter, Amalasuintha, who first acted as regent for her young son, Athalaric,[1] and, after his death, shared power with her cousin, Theodahad.[2] Other queens can only by glimpsed on occasion. Theoderic's mother, Ereliuva, was petitioned by Pope Gelasius concerning the distribution of alms to the poor,[3] and, on another occasion, about two churchmen who had been found operating without a papal licence.[4] Later, Theodahad's queen, Gudeliuva, engaged in diplomacy when she participated in the efforts to bring about peace between her husband and Justinian and Theodora.[5] All these incidents have parallels in the Frankish world, and particularly in the career of Brunhild, but cannot be seen in more detail. The reason for this is not that Gothic queens behaved in a way markedly different from their Frankish counterparts, nor that the Gothic palace was organised in such a radically different way that there was no scope for queenly activity. What the Ostrogothic kingdom lacks is a source which follows specific actors and personalities, even for the moralistic and religious reasons of a Gregory of Tours.

The personal staff of the king

One of the officials closest to the person of the king, as previously to the emperors, is likely to have been the *praepositus sacri cubiculi*. Only one man is known to have borne this specific title, Triuuane: according to the Ravenna chronicler he persuaded Theoderic to assist Jews who were being persecuted by the Christian community.[6] This reveals little of the function of the *praepositus*, though it does show that such a man was in a position to petition the king either for his own purposes or on behalf of others; *praepositi* may also have been particularly able to influence the ruler's decisions. Although Triuuane is the only man known to have borne the exact title of *praepositus sacri cubiculi*, Boethius records that an individual named Triguilla was a *praepositus domus regiae*, and was in a position to commit grave injustices, though his administrative functions receive no attention.[7] Boethius' testimony has a greater significance than is at first apparent. The reason for this stems from the fact that Triuuane and Triguilla are likely to be variant forms of the same name, thus making it possible that the Ravenna chronicler's *praepositus sacri cubiculi* was the same man as Boethius' *praepositus domus regiae*. The similarity of the two titles could on its own raise the suspicion that they refer to the same office, and the fact that both references relate to the same period, *c.* 520 – *c.* 523, makes it even more likely that the two names refer to the same man, and the two titles to the same position.

If this suggestion is accepted, it becomes possible to take the argument a stage further, since the title of *maior domus (regiae)* is not very far removed from that of *praepositus domus regiae*. An equation between these two titles has already been suggested in Chapter 8, where it was seen that a later Frankish source, the *Uita Eligii*, refers to Ebroin as '*palatii praepositi* – which is commonly called *maior domus*'. It therefore seems reasonable to suggest that *praepositus sacri cubiculi*, *praepositus domus regiae* and *maior domus* are synonymous, particularly since it was seen in Chapter 9 that there are also pointers in that direction in the Vandal kingdom.

The equation of *praepositi* and *maiores* allows the activities of a small number of other men, all of whom are described as *maiores*, to be added to the discussion. Three of their number, Gudila, Bedeulf and

Arigern, were involved in transmitting messages between the king and the ecclesiastical councils held to resolve the Laurentian schism.[8] The activities of these men as the bearers of confidential messages may underline their position of trust close to the person of the king. Another *maior*, Wacca, was noted for his military leadership, and was on one occasion responsible for the provisioning of a garrison at Rome.[9] Such duties as this are, perhaps, best seen as indicators of the fact that in the Ostrogothic kingdom, as in other 'barbarian' kingdoms and in the fifth-century Empire, royal officials could be called upon to carry out any special commission the king desired. The fact that Arigern, one of the *maiores* involved with the Church councils, is sometimes described as 'comes',[10] serves as a reminder that any courtier was first a 'companion' of the king, and only second the holder of a specific office.

Despite the addition of information concerning *maiores* to that about the *praepositi*, it will be apparent that relatively little is really known of the position and function of the bearers of such titles. Even less is known of their subordinates, the *cubicularii*. One *cubicularius* is recorded on a gravestone from Ravenna but, as is normal with such inscriptions, all that is revealed is the name of the man.[11] Tuluin was a *cubicularius* in his youth, perhaps demonstrating the subordinate nature of the position, before becoming a warrior, adviser to the king, and ultimately patrician and regent for the young Athalaric.[12] With regard to what *cubicularii* actually did, there is a tantalising reference in the *Uariae* to financial reserves within the *cubiculum*, but what they were, or exactly how they were administered, it is impossible to say.[13]

It was seen in Chapter 3 that *spatharii*, or bodyguards, were associated with the *cubiculum* in imperial times, and it seems clear that such men were also present in the Ostrogothic kingdom. The only reference to an individual *spatharius* in the *Uariae* refers to Unigis, on an occasion when he was charged with the special commission of restoring to their masters slaves who had run away during the Gallic war of *c.* 508.[14] The only other mention of *spatharii* is a brief allusion to the fact that they were armed,[15] and there is nothing to suggest that they were not employed in a manner almost identical to that of their imperial predecessors.

Of the other kinds of guard associated with the court in the Empire – the palace guards, or *protectores domestici* – and of their chief, the *comes domesticorum*, virtually nothing is known: this is predictable, given that they operated within the palace, and that they are obscure even in the imperial period. One *comes domesticorum*, Pierus, held office under Odoacer and was killed in battle during Theoderic's conquest of Italy,[16] thus reinforcing the impression gained in Chapter 3 that officials of this type could be called upon to act outside the palace as military leaders, at least on occasion. The only other named *comes domesticorum* is Julius Felix Valentinian, who is commemorated on a gravestone.[17] What is known, though, is that there was an honorary position of *comes domesticorum*, which is attested in the *Uariae*. According to Cassiodorus, who apears to have preserved the formula for the appointment of such an official, *comes domesticorum* was a title which could be given simply as a way of conferring upon its holder the rank of *uir illuster*.[18] It must have been this kind of 'office' which was held by Arator, who was made *comes domesticorum* and was charged with looking after the literary health of the state.[19] It is difficult to see exactly what should be concluded from this use of the title, especially given that Cassiodorus was usually at pains to stress the *ciuilitas* and *romanitas* of the Gothic kingdom. It is possible that the Ostrogoths organised their guards differently (perhaps in some way more traditional to them), and that the title of *comes domesticorum* fell into disuse. In such circumstances it would have been reasonable for it to have been taken over and applied to a new purpose. It cannot, however, be absolutely proved that there were no 'real' *comites domesticorum* in the Ostrogothic kingdom, since the case rests on an argument from silence.[20]

The master of the offices

One of the known holders of the position of master of the offices in the Ostrogothic period is Cassiodorus himself, and his formula for the appointment of men to the position is perhaps the most important single piece of evidence concerning it. At first sight, the formula ascribes to the master of the offices an impressive set of duties – he controlled access to the court, was in charge of the public postal service (*cursus publicus*), had authority over provincial governors, and appointed the chiefs of the staffs of the praetorian and city prefects.[21] It appears, therefore, that little had changed from the imperial period in which masters of the offices were in charge of the imperial attendants and had responsibility for much of the permanent staff of the provincial administration. The lack of documents in the *Uariae* concerning the duties of the master of the offices is another example of the problems posed by officials operating close to the person of the king, and is paralleled by a lack of evidence in the earlier rescripts. It is not, therefore, possible to arrive at a full appreciation of the relationship between the position of the master under the emperors and under the later kings. Although it can be argued that the master's intra-palatine activities are unlikely to have been radically affected by the change from emperor to king, his power in the provinces must have been greatly reduced in the Ostrogothic kingdom on account of the fact that the area subject to the kings was much smaller than that formerly under the control of the western emperors. Almost the only occasion on which a master of the offices is seen in action comes from the reign of

Odoacer, when Andromachus, master of the offices (according to the Donation of Pierus[22]), was sent by the king and Pope Gelasius on an embassy to Constantinople to discuss the Henotokion question.[23] This does not, though, assist in defining the master's normal duties, as it is likely that any high-ranking and trusted official could be sent on such a mission.

Of the large body of lesser officials, or *agentes*, whom the imperial masters of the offices controlled, nothing is known in the Ostrogothic kingdom, though other agents, *saiones* or *comitiaci*, emerge and appear to have taken over some of the functions formerly associated with the master's *agentes*. Although this phenomenon has often been noted,[24] it has never adequately been explained, and it is worth pausing here to examine the issue. The first use of the term *comitiacus* seems to have been in 394, in a rescript contained in the Theodosian Code, and apparently refers to an official in the upper echelons of the praetorian prefect's staff.[25] After that time, there does not appear to be another surviving instance of the use of the word in western sources until the works of Cassiodorus, in which it is indicated that the *magistri scriniarum* and other high-ranking officials of the praetorian and city prefects were *comitiaci*.[26] In the imperial period it would have been usual for such men to be described as *agentes in rebus*, that is, as staff appointed by the central court, or *palatini*, nominated by the master of the offices: it is possible that they could also be seen in terms of an association with the retinue (*comitiua/comitatus*) of the emperor, rather than with the palace itself, in the same way as were *comites* or 'companions' of the emperor. If *agentes in rebus* and *comitiaci* can be seen as one and the same, the next question concerns the term *saio*. *Saio* is clearly a Germanic word and may mean either 'follower',[27] or, if it was derived from the Gothic *saljan* ('to dwell' or 'to abide'), someone who lived near to the person of the king.[28] Either of these derivations would fit the evidence for the Visigothic kingdom where there were *saiones*, though there they formed the retinues of members of the aristocracy rather than of the king.[29] The term can, therefore, be seen as an approximate translation of *comitiacus*.[30]

Now that it has been established that *agens in rebus*, *comitiacus* and *saio* are likely to refer to the same kind of official, the activities in which the holders of such titles engaged can be examined. At first sight it seems reasonable to conclude that very little had changed from imperial times, since the chief members of the office staffs of the praetorian and city prefects were still palace appointees and, on the evidence of Cassiodorus' formula, were still subject to the master of the offices. The point could be taken as proven when further evidence is taken into account: *saiones* and *comitiaci* were, in conjunction with the *comites* (who were of higher rank), the main royal officials who operated within the provinces. Hence, for example, they are found working under the *cancellarii* of provincial magistrates in order to ensure punctuality and fairness in the administration of taxation.[31] One Triuuilla, *comitiacus*, was responsible for bringing an unjust praetorian prefect to book.[32] This man could be the same as the *cubicularius* of the same name already discussed, though whether he was a *saio* at the same time as he was a *cubicularius* is uncertain: it is possible that *saio* could have been a designation of rank and *cubicularius* that of an office. Other similarities between the ways in which imperial *agentes* and Gothic *saiones* worked are manifold, since *saiones* are known to have performed a host of special commissions for the kings: they were assigned to officials and Senators as bodyguards;[33] they were involved in the administration of justice,[34] and of taxation and other royal revenues;[35] they played a leading role in the administration of the army,[36] and of the fleet;[37] and they participated in other, more miscellaneous, affairs.[38] In fact, there is more evidence for the operation of *saiones* than there is for their earlier counterparts.

This last point requires consideration. If the contents of the *Uariae* are of broadly similar nature to those of the Theodosian Code, it is unexpected to find them revealing so much more than do the imperial documents concerning the members of one of the lower levels of the administration. The most reasonable explanation for this is that *saiones/comitiaci* were, as Cassiodorus' documents suggest, directly controlled by the king, and not by the masters of the offices as they had been in earlier times: accordingly, they received their orders direct from him, often in written form. This marks a major change from the imperial situation, and makes the *saiones* look very similar to the *domestici* of the other 'barbarian' kingdoms and of the great Roman provincial governors. Such a change of management may well account for the alteration of name from *agentes in rebus* or *palatini* to *saiones* or *comitiaci*, both of which lay greater stress on the relationship with the king himself. Shorn of responsibility for the *agentes* or their equivalent, the position of master of the offices must have been very greatly weakened.

The writing office

In contrast to the power of the master of the offices, that of the quaestor may have been increased by the establishment of a Germanic king in Italy. According to the Cassiodoran formula for the appointment of quaestors, such men were responsible for the receipt of petitions which were to be presented to the king, and had to pronounce the law in relation to their contents.[39] The phrases Cassiodorus uses in the formula are echoed and expanded upon elsewhere in the *Uariae*, particularly in a letter notifying the Senate of the appointment of

Honoratus as quaestor.[40] If the suggestion, made in Chapter 12, that the law administered by the Ostrogothic kings was essentially Roman is correct, it is possible that the role of the courtier who informed the king concerning the content of the law was greater under a Germanic ruler than it would have been in the fifth-century Empire when Roman law was administered by Roman emperors. This would be particularly true if that courtier were a member of the Roman aristocracy, as the names of those known from the Ostrogothic kingdom suggest he usually was.[41] The statements made by Cassiodorus concerning the quaestor's position are, though, only theoretical: the rescript-like nature of the documents contained in the *Uariae* renders it unrealistic to expect its contents to reveal the way in which the system worked in practice, since the quaestor was, as in the imperial court, close enough to the person of the king not to need to receive written instructions.

One aspect of the quaestor's function is amply illustrated by some of the correspondence of Ennodius which provides concrete evidence for the presentation of petitions to the court *via* the quaestor. The reason for this is that Ennodius had connections at court and was often asked by his friends to obtain the goodwill of the quaestor, usually Festus, in presenting their petitions to the king and his courtiers, or in rendering other forms of assistance in their dealings with the court. The range of subjects upon which the court could be petitioned is well demonstrated by these documents: one letter requested Festus to take care of a certain Bassus and assist him to present his petitions to the king;[42] another asked him to help Venantius to gain justice;[43] another sought his intervention in a lengthy and intractable lawsuit between Ennodius' relation, Julian, and one Marcellinus of Milan;[44] another petitioned for help for a religious woman;[45] yet another requested assistance for one Dalmatius who was trying to re-establish his title to property in Sicily;[46] and, finally, Ennodius asked for a letter of commendation to be sent to Agnellus (either master of the offices or *comes sacrarum largitionum*) for the relations of one Opilio.[47] On one occasion, Ennodius recommended Festus as the man most likely to present an effective case in a dispute concerning the clergy at Milan,[48] while Festus' rhetorical powers are revealed by a letter which mentions an oration he had delivered on behalf of a new member of the Senate.[49]

Another stage in the petitioning process is also illustrated by the writings of Ennodius, when he records how Epiphanius requested Theoderic to declare an amnesty for those members of the Roman population who had supported Odoacer.[50] Once Epiphanius had presented his petition and it had been granted, Theoderic summoned Urbicus, *uir illuster*, and ordered him to prepare a decree putting his decision into effect. Urbicus' precise position at court is not recorded, any more than was Leo's in Euric's court, but he could have been a quaestor.[51] There are clear parallels between this procedure and that already seen at the Visigothic court, when Bibianus was the petitioner, and at the Burgundian court, when Lupicinus petitioned Chilperic.

The position of the quaestor himself is relatively well documented, owing to the unique survival of Ennodius' letters, but that source does no more than any other to cast light on the other officials of the writing office. The only source to produce any information is the *Uariae*, in which Cassiodorus included formulae for the appointment of referendaries and notaries. These documents do nothing more than make the fairly obvious points that referendaries were involved in the presentation of petitions to the king,[52] and that notaries were concerned with royal documents.[53] So uninformative are the formulae that it is not even possible to understand anything of the relationship between the referendary and the quaestor. On the sole occasion on which a notary is seen in action, the Donation of Pierus records that notaries, including a royal one, were engaged in drawing up the document.[54] The only other light which is cast on the officials of the writing office reveals that the referendaries were in a position to offer advice to the king, since it was while acting in that capacity that Cyprian denounced Albinus to Theoderic, thereby unleashing the Boethius affair.[55] This does not, however, allow any progress to be made beyond the almost self-evident fact that referendaries, like all courtiers, could obtain the ear of the king, could provide him with information and supply 'advice'.

The financial officials

There is no equivalent of the letters of Ennodius to serve the officials of the financial administration who, as high-ranking men, close to the person of the king, do not often feature in the documents of the *Uariae*, still less in the Ravenna Chronicle. The most obvious source of information is, therefore, the formulae for the appointment of courtiers to positions connected with the treasury.

The first official to be encountered is the *comes sacrarum largitionum* who, according to the formula, was responsible for the administration of the king's gifts both of money and of honours. He also had to ensure that the royal portrait was on all coins circulating within the kingdom, had jurisdiction over merchants and traders, and was responsible for the royal robes.[56] The occasions when *comites sacrarum largitionum* are seen in action are limited, but reveal that such men were ultimately responsible for the collection of the land tax (*exactio binorum et tertiorum*),[57] and of the fines payable by those who brought cases against the Church in secular courts – the fines were to be handed over to the pope for distribution as alms.[58] Almost the only other evidence directly concerning these officials relates to the existence of a *comes sacrae uestis*, who was responsible for providing the court with purple dye.[59] If Cassiodorus' formula is correct in stating that the *comes sacrarum largitionum* was in charge of the royal vestments, it seems likely that the *comes sacrae uestis* would have been subordinate to him, and may have been the successor to the *uestarius* recorded in such a position by the *Notitia Dignitatum*.[60]

One point in the formula illustrates the danger of having complete faith in the veracity of such documents when they cannot be set against other evidence. Both the formula for the position of *comes sacrarum largitionum* and that for the chief moneyer[61] imply that all coins produced within the Ostrogothic kingdom were supposed to bear the royal portrait. It is, however, known from other evidence (discussed in Chapter 12) that this was not always the case: even if 'royal' is taken to mean 'imperial' it is not so. What may have happened, therefore, is that Cassiodorus used an imperial model for the documents, and failed adequately to adjust it to fit the altered circumstances of the Ostrogothic kingdom. This would not be the first occasion on which he would have been seen to have done such a thing, since it has already been suggested that he failed to take account of the loss to the master of the offices of control over *agentes in rebus*.

Of the other main high-ranking financial official found in both the fifth-century imperial court and that of the Ostrogoths, the *comes rerum priuatarum*, equally little is known. According to the Cassiodoran formula, men of this description were in charge of the royal estates, which were administered by them through *rationales*; they were also involved with certain aspects of taxation, and had some jurisdiction within the city of Rome.[62] The only one of these roles which is attested elsewhere is that concerning the City: a *comes rerum priuatarum*, Apronianus, was in charge of an attempt to find water in the suburbs of Rome, and was responsible for drilling wells where it was found.[63] The other occasions on which *comites rerum priuatarum* are seen in action all concern one man, Senarius, who was commanded to carry out a number of tasks: once he was commissioned to reimburse grain dealers for losses they had suffered at sea;[64] on another occasion, to investigate a dispute between the *curiales* and *possessores* of Voliensis;[65] a third instruction concerned the provision of supplies to Collossaeus, who was on his way to take up the governorship of Pannonia Sirmiensis.[66] While such commissions as these all have some bearing on royal finances, they do not reflect any special concern of the *comes rerum priuatarum* with estate management. Given the kind of general financial duties allocated to such men in the fifth-century Empire, it may well be wrong to seek a rigid departmentalisation of such affairs in the Ostrogothic kingdom.

The position in the post-imperial period is further complicated by the presence of a third court official with financial competence, the *comes patrimonii.* The holder of this office, like that of the position of *comes rerum priuatarum*, is depicted in Cassiodorus' formula as being in charge of the royal estates, and was also responsible for the provisioning of the royal palace.[67] It is in connection with those spheres of activity that most of the other references to such officials occur. Bergantius, *comes patrimonii*, was ordered to make over to Theodahad, at a time before he became king, certain money and farms which had belonged to his mother, Amalfrida, Theoderic's sister;[68] on a different occasion, the same man was made responsible for overseeing the mining of gold on a royal estate in Bruttium.[69] Another *comes patrimonii*, Wilia, was commissioned to search royal lands for timber suitable for the construction of ships for the fleet;[70] an unnamed holder of the office informed the praetorian prefect, Cassiodorus himself, that stocks of wine from Venetia were needed for the palace;[71] Julian, *comes patrimonii*, was charged with assessing losses incurred by the tenant farmers (*conductores*) of Apulia on account of enemy (probably Constantinopolitan) action in the area, *c.* 508.[72] The only significant reference to a *comes patrimonii* in a source not written by Cassiodorus concerns the same Julian, and comes in a letter from Ennodius to Julian, informing him of action the author had taken in a dispute between Bauto, a tenant farmer of the king, and a *cartarius* or official subject to Julian.[73]

There are also references to *comites patrimonii* operating in capacities other than estate management, most of which are financial. In one case, an official of this kind was instructed to receive the money due from a certain man who had petitioned the king for permission to pay his father-in-law's debts and to acquire his lands.[74] On another occasion, the *comes patrimonii* was responsible for the removal of the supplementary tax (*augmentum*) due on the occasion of the appointment of a new governor to the provinces of Dalmatia and Savia.[75] When Wilia held office as *comes patrimonii*, he was commissioned to increase the pay of the *domestici* of certain *comites* in an attempt to dissuade them from exploiting the provincials for their own profit.[76] Finally, the one non-financial case concerns a *comes patrimonii* who informed Theoderic of a shortage of rowers (*dromonarii*) for the public boats.[77]

Given that the title of *comes patrimonii* does not occur in the western Empire, and that the functions of the holders of that office appear to have been very similar to those of the *comites rerum priuatarum*, it seems logical to conclude that the title of *comes patrimonii* in some way superseded that of *comes rerum priuatarum*. This development was almost certainly initiated in the eastern Empire, by Anastasius (*c.* 491 – *c.* 518),[78] and then imitated by the Ostrogothic kings in Italy. It could be objected that the old title is still found after the first attestations of the new one, and that, if the old title really was rendered obsolete by the new one, Cassiodorus would not have produced two formulae for his *Uariae*. Such arguments are weak, since it has already been observed on more than one occasion that Cassiodorus' formulae do not always reflect the precise position as it existed in the Ostrogothic kingdom, and that he may have used his historical knowledge in compiling them. In addition, since both titles were used during the reign of Theoderic, Cassiodorus would have been quite justified in including a formula for the earlier one for posterity's sake.[79]

With regard to any suggestion that the two titles could not have existed alongside each other, it can be countered that there is often a period after a change in the designation of any form of title during which both the old and new forms have currency. In the specific instance under discussion, it is possible that something of this nature can be demonstrated, since Cassiodorus refers to one of Ennodius' relatives, Senarius,[80] as 'comes rerum priuatarum',[81] while the same man's epitaph records that he had been a *comes patrimonii*:[82] it cannot be absolutely proved that the two titles relate to the same period in Senarius' life, but it is highly likely.

The case of Senarius serves to emphasise another point, since, although he is known to have been a *comes patrimonii*, he was commemorated almost solely for his influence in matters of war and peace and in the making of treaties. Commenting on this case, T.S. Burns observed that it shows that 'the government of Ostrogothic Italy was *ad hoc*':[83] it certainly was not bureaucratic, any more than was its Roman predecesssor.[84]

The *comes*

The point concerning the lack of bureaucracy is driven home by the evidence concerning the large number of men who feature in the sources simply as *comites* since, as T.S. Burns again suggests, 'the majority of references to counts are to special enterprises undertaken in [*sic*] the king's behalf'.[85] The range of activities in which the *Uariae* record *comites* as having participated is wide: such men were, for example, commissioned to erect and restore statues and monuments;[86] to deal with law suits which had been the subject of petitions to the king, or to supervise those involving Senators;[87] to protect property, or persons;[88] to organise famine relief in Gaul;[89] to find supplies of minerals for the benefit of the royal treasury, and to supervise the collection of taxes;[90] to bring offenders to court;[91] to administer oaths of allegiance to the king, even in the Senate;[92] and to assist other *comites* in carrying out the tasks assigned to them.[93] The testimony of the *Uariae* is supplemented in this matter by other sources. During the Laurentian schism, the *comes/maior domus*, Arigern, was one of a number of royal agents who carried messages between the king and the ecclesiastical synods which were convened to resolve the matter, and acted as the king's representatives on such occasions.[94] A letter of Pope Gelasius reveals that Teia, *comes*, exceeded his brief and incurred papal displeasure when he tried to intervene in an ecclesiastical trial: he received a warning that if he continued he would be reported to the king.[95] On another occasion, however, the same Pope enlisted Teia's assistance in bringing offenders to court.[96]

As in the other 'barbarian' kingdoms, some *comites* were stationed in specific provinces or cities, where they acted as the king's representatives: whether such appointments were permanent, or for a fixed term, is unclear. The *Uariae* includes a number of formulae for the nomination of such men to certain individual cities – Naples, Ravenna, Rome, Syracuse[97] – as well as one for a *comes* on the island of Krk,[98] and a more general one for the appointment of a *comes* to an unspecified province.[99] From the formulae, it is learnt that the duties of the provincial *comites* included the upholding of justice, and tax collection.[100] In addition, several other letters in Cassiodorus' work show something of the range of activity in which such locally-based *comites* engaged. Hence, for example, it is recorded that Gildila of Syracuse was responsible for at least some aspects of the administration of taxation, and for ensuring that justice was fairly dispensed in the city;[101] the same roles are outlined in a letter appointing Colossaeus to be *comes* in Pannonia Sirmiensis.[102]

It would seem likely that, as elsewhere, *comites ciuitatum* were not the heirs to a Roman position. It was suggested in Part II that the initial reason for the stationing of *comites* in the provinces may have been to place court officials of proven trustworthiness in the provinces for reasons akin to those governing the choice of imperial prefects. It was also suggested that, as regionally-based royal officials, *comites ciuitatum* could gradually have come to act as the king's representatives in a wider sphere. The Ostrogothic evidence can be interpreted in such a way as to strengthen at least the first of those propositions, though it does not permit of absolute proof of either. The key is a formula for the appointment of '*comites* of the Goths in individual cities':[103] whether this means that the *comites* only had authority over Goths, or that they were a Gothic innovation, is unclear, but either way the implication is that such officials had not existed under the imperial administration. The situation is rendered more complex by the existence of a second Cassiodoran formula, which refers to '*comites* (of various) cities', without any 'Gothic' qualification.[104] Rather than envisaging a situation in which each city might have both a *comes* of the Goths and an ordinary *comes ciuitatis* stationed within its walls, or one in which some cities might have one kind of *comes* and others the other type, it is possible that Cassiodorus is reflecting a change in the title of the same official, in the same way as it was earlier suggested he did for the *comes rerum priuatarum* and the *comes patrimonii*. If this is accepted, then it may be that the process was related to a shift in function with locally-based *comites* becoming involved in a wider sphere of government instead of with the narrower issue of the representation of the king in the cities.[105]

However that may be, and it remains partly hypothetical, it is known that the locally-based *comites* had a staff, which was, as a body, termed a *militia* (though that does not necessarily imply that it was military).[106] At the head of the staff was a *princeps*,[107] and included in its number were *domestici*.[108] In this respect, *comites ciuitatum* resemble the local administrators of the Empire, though they were fundamentally different from the latter in that they were members of the royal court. As will be seen in the next chapter, it is possible that some traditional-style local governors may have been transformed into *comites ciuitatum*, thus perhaps accounting for some of the similarity between the staffs of the two kinds of official.

One sphere of comital activity not yet discussed is that of military leadership. Involvement with the army can be illustrated from the fact that Pitzias, *comes*, was sent to capture Sirmium,[109] and Osuin, *comes*, was responsible for distributing arms to the population under his control and for supervising its military training.[110] Despite this, there is no need to see men of this kind as being heirs to the late-Roman *comites rei militaris*.[111] As was argued in Chapter 3 and throughout Part II, it is very rare to be able to prove conclusively the existence of purely military *comites*, even in the fifth-century western Empire, and it is better to view all such men (unless a specific title is given) as being the representatives and agents of the king, able to act in a variety of spheres, including the military. In other words, *comes* denotes a relationship to the king, rather than an office.

The *dux*

Any examination of the position of *duces* in the Ostrogothic kingdom is hampered by the fact that the *Uariae* is not a document of a nature to record military activity. This lack of surviving Cassiodoran evidence relating to military affairs is illustrated by the relative paucity of information concerning *duces*. It was argued in Chapter 3 that there were two potential meanings of the word *dux* in fifth-century sources, one simply being 'leader', and the other designating a military commander based in a frontier province – a *dux limitis prouinciae*. It is quite clearly to the second kind of *dux* that a formula in the *Uariae* refers, since it states that the function of *duces* in frontier provinces was to guard against external threats or invasions.[112] Given that the *Uariae* consists of 'official' documents, specifically related to the government of the kingdom, it is inherently likely that other references to *duces* within it will also refer specifically to *duces limitum prouinciarum*. In view of this, it may come as a surprise to find that the few other letters in the work which concern *duces* appear at first sight to attribute to them competence in civil affairs: Wilitancus, *dux*, was commanded to investigate a case of adultery committed by a woman while her husband was away at war;[113] *duces* in general were admonished to be just in their dealings with provincials.[114] On closer examination, though, the grounds for such an interpretation can be seen as very slight. In the case of Wilitancus, it would be perfectly normal for a military official to have investigated a matter which concerned a soldier, perhaps even one who was under his command, while in the second instance, it is clear from the fact that *duces* were active in the provinces that they must have come into contact with the provincials, and perfectly reasonable for them to have been urged not to harm the local population.

Sources other than the *Uariae* also mention *duces*, one of the best-documented of whom is Ibba. Ibba first appears in the *Getica*, where Jordanes describes him as 'comes' and depicts him leading an army against the Franks in Gaul, *c.* 508, after the death of the Visigothic king, Alaric II.[115] It might be possible to see Ibba in this context as a *comes rei militaris* but, given that Jordanes was not interested in administrative details, it is more likely that he was describing Ibba simply as a courtier, in the same way as the fifth-century narrative historians often used the term *comes*. A year later, the *Saragossa Chronicle* (*Chronica Caesaraugustana*) records that Ibba, 'dux', was responsible for driving Alaric's successor, Gisalech, out of Barcelona.[116] On the basis of this reference alone, it would be impossible to determine whether Ibba was simply the leader of an army, or whether he was a *dux prouinciae*. However, Ibba is also mentioned in the *Uariae*, where he is described as 'dux' when he was ordered to carry out a special commission relating to church property at Narbonne.[117] Since the usage of the *Uariae* is likely to be technically correct, and since it refers to the same period as the *Saragossa Chronicle*, it is probable that Ibba was indeed a *dux prouinciae*, who, on the evidence of Jordanes, was also a courtier: whether the author of the *Saragossa Chronicle* was using *dux* technically or not remains an open question, since Ibba undoubtedly did lead armies. Similar uncertainty surrounds other references to *duces* in the non-Cassiodoran sources. Jordanes mentions one Sinderith, *dux*, in connection with defending Syracuse against Belisarius,[118] and one Hunila, *dux*, who was sent by Witigis to re-take Perugia from the imperial army.[119] Marius of Avenches mentions a Gothic *dux* operating in a military context in Gaul, *c.* 509.[120] Given what has already been seen of the use of terminology by other fifth- and sixth-century writers, the exact position of such men cannot be known, but there is nothing to suggest that it was any different from that current in either the fifth-century Empire or the other 'barbarian' kingdoms. In this, as in so much else discussed in the last two chapters, there is nothing to mark the Ostrogoths out from their contemporaries in other western provinces.

14

Senators and Provincial Governors

Government personnel and the Senate

It was shown in the last chapter that many of the court-based offices of the imperial administration continued in existence after the removal of the western emperors, though often in a modified form. The essentially Roman character of the Ostrogothic court is not, however, in doubt, and can be paralleled in the courts of the kingdoms discussed in Part II. In order for such a system, based in Roman traditions, to have operated, it is clear that at least some of the men who were involved in it must either have had direct experience of the imperial administration or have been brought up within its traditions. It was earlier demonstrated that members of the Roman aristocracy in the provinces were prepared to co-operate with the new federate rulers, and even became members of their courts: the purpose of the present discussion is to examine the extent to which that situation also pertained to Italy in the post-imperial period.

The most startling statistic which can be cited concerning the governmental personnel of Italy in the period from $c.$ 476 to $c.$ 553 is that of a little over two hundred and forty named officials, approximately one hundred and ninety bore Roman names. Such a proportion is considerably higher than that which would be found in any other kingdom, but should not lead directly to the assumption that there was a vastly greater degree of continuity in Italy, still less that the Ostrogoths were more Romanophile than the other 'barbarians', because the figures are largely a product of the different types of source available for each kingdom. One of the most important distorting elements comes from the reign of Odoacer, in the form of the inscriptions found on the seats of the Flavian amphitheatre at Rome, which was restored $c.$ 490.[1] These documents provide a record of the precise social ranks, offices and names of a large number of men, all of them Romans. This cannot be taken to mean that all, or even most, of the officials Odoacer appointed to administrative positions were Roman, since the reservation of seats at the amphitheatre was a

Roman prerogative in which 'barbarians' could only very exceptionally share.[2] Another reason for exercising caution in the interpretation of the inscriptions is that at least some of the offices recorded on them were held before *c.* 476, and some may have been held after Odoacer's reign.[3] Finally, it should be borne in mind that there is no source for Odoacer's reign of a kind which might have recorded the presence of 'barbarian' personnel.

The last point is also significant for the Ostrogothic period, since the majority of documents preserved in the *Uariae* do not, of their nature, concern the officials who were closest to the king, amongst whom there may have been a higher proportion of Goths than among the holders of positions more distant from the person of the king. Many of those who received the instructions from the king which are preserved in the *Uariae* are quite simply styled 'uir illuster' or 'uir spectabilis'. These titles, strictly speaking, implied membership of the Senate,[4] and their use might be taken to indicate that their holders received commissions from the king on account of their being Senators.[5] On closer examination, however, this can be seen not to have been the case. For example, while *Uariae* III.16 and 17 record that Gemellus was made *uicarius* in Gaul, he is described simply as 'uir spectabilis' in two special commissions addressed to him shortly afterwards.[6] It is more likely that Gemellus received the later instructions on account of his position as a *uicarius* – that is, as someone in governmental service – than simply as a member of the Senate. Another example of the same kind is to be found in the case of Liuuirit, a Goth. Liuuirit is described in *Uariae* V.35 as 'comes', and in V.39 as 'uir spectabilis'. How many other *uiri illustres* and *spectabiles* held offices, even within the court, and received special commissions from the king on that account rather than because of their rank?

The case of Liuuirit raises another question concerning the Senate and continuity, since, although Liuuirit was a Goth, he ought, by virtue of the fact that he is termed a *spectabilis*, to have been a member of the Senate: he is not the only Goth to fall into this category.[7] If Goths could be Senators, then one of the most Roman and conservative institutions the Ostrogoths found in Italy, and one which was almost certainly of the greatest symbolic importance, must have been quite radically transformed. One possible explanation for this could be that the kings appointed a number of Goths to the Senate in order to gain inside sources of information on its proceedings and to attempt to ensure its corporate loyalty. It is possible that such a strategy could have been disguised as an enhancement of the Senate's position, but unlikely that the truth would not have been apparent to all involved. In addition, the way in which Theoderic's suspicions of the Senate were aroused by Cyprian's accusation against Albinus makes it unlikely that a policy of this kind was in fact pursued: had Goths been planted as informers in the Senate the king would have been able to uncover the truth of the situation with considerably less unfortunate consequences.

It is in any case hard to see why the Gothic kings should have risked alienating the Senate by altering its composition, since the Senate, as a corporate body, counted for almost nothing in their government,[8] any more than it had in the fifth-century Empire.[9] Individual Senators could be watched by other, less obvious means. Had the Ostrogoths wished to undermine the Senate in such a situation, they would have been much wiser to leave the institution alone so that it remained as a symbol of continuity: then it would gradually wither away as it became increasingly clear that it had no real power. It will be suggested later that this was precisely what happened with regard to some of the institutions of provincial government.

If many, or all, of the Gothic *spectabiles* or *illustres* are unlikely to have been Senators, an alternative explanation for their designation by such titles must be sought. Perhaps the most likely explanation is that the terms could be used as 'courtesy titles', to describe men of high rank, rather than always having the specific meaning of membership of the Senatorial *ordo*. One of the documents in the *Uariae* may demonstrate this, since it implies that an *ex-princeps* of the palatine office staff was given the rank of *comes primi ordinis* and the title of *uir spectabilis*.[10] A similar suggestion has been made by S.J.B. Barnish, who traces a 'court-type' (as opposed to a 'Roman-type') use of the titles back to the years following *c.* 432.[11] It is not difficult to see how such a state of affairs could have arisen since most of the officials of the imperial administration were traditionally *uiri illustres* or *spectabiles*,[12] and the Ostrogoths (and last emperors) could simply have been continuing to use the traditional titles associated with the government, though applying them in rather different circumstances in which by no means all officials were Senators.

Provincial governors and prefects

Given what was seen in Chapter 13 of the use of court officials, or *comites*, to govern the cities and provinces of Italy, it is perhaps unexpected to find references in the *Uariae* to provincial governors of a more traditional kind – *correctores, consulares* and *praesides* – since the need for such officials must have been greatly reduced by the presence of the *comites*, especially as the authority of *comites* came to extend beyond their suggested original function as royal agents of proven loyalty. Despite this, the Cassiodoran formulae for the appointment of governors of traditional types, together with other material from within the *Uariae*, show the main functions of such men to have lain in the fields of taxation, the administration of justice, and the carrying out of special commissions on behalf of the king[13] – in other words, in spheres very similar to those which concerned the provincial *comites*.

A second feature of the evidence concerning provincial governors is that a relatively large number of them is attested. Although only one *praeses* is known from the two Italian dioceses in the period *c.* 476 – *c.* 553, *correctores* are known from Lucania and Bruttium, Cassiodorus' homeland, while *consulares* feature in Liguria, Flaminia, Campania and Sicily. In all, there is a total of twelve different men for the whole period.[14] It is quite possible that there were more such officials, since the *Uariae*, apparently documents of similar nature to the imperial rescripts, should not contain a large proportion of instructions sent to members of the lower levels of the administration, any more than do their imperial counterparts. Many fewer – only four Italian – governors received rescripts after 394,[15] and not many more are known from other sources: fewer still are attested for other western provinces. The fact that more Ostrogothic officials are known may lead to a suspicion that they operated in a rather different way from their earlier counterparts. This suspicion is strengthened by the apparent duplication of functions between governors and *comites ciuitatum*.

That duplication of functions may be the key to understanding what was happening, since it is possible that traditional provincial governors were being replaced by *comites*, that is, by members of the royal court. In order to lessen the psychological impact of the change on the Roman aristocracy, such a change need not have been implemented everywhere at the same time, thus allowing for the two kinds of position to exist in parallel for a period. The introduction of the new office need not have involved a wholesale change of personnel, since one of the formulae in the *Uariae* states that *rectores prouinciarum* attained the position of *comites primi ordinis* after a year's service[16] – in other words, they became members of the royal court. It is also conceivable that an old-style governor, even after he had become a *comes*, could still be described loosely as some form of provincial *rector*, in the same way as a *comes patrimonii* could be referred to by the older title of *comes rerum priuatarum*. Such usage of terminology again shows Cassiodorus to have been interested in the past and to have sought to demonstrate how little had changed since the imperial period.

Against the view that the historical forms of provincial government were slowly undermined, it could be argued that there is good evidence for the continued vigorous existence of the praetorian and city prefects and their staffs. This is particularly true in the case of the praetorian prefect, where there is a large amount of material from quite late in the Ostrogothic period, pertaining to the time when Cassiodorus himself held the office. If provincial government were really to have been brought under the direct control of the royal court, the case could be made that such officials would have been redundant and, therefore, have ceased to exist. On closer examination, the evidence for the prefects, and especially for the praetorian prefects, will be seen to be much less impressive than has often been assumed.

Leaving aside the documents in the *Uariae* produced by Cassiodorus during his own tenure of the praetorian prefecture, the remainder of the *Uariae* shows that such prefects were involved in the following spheres of activity: the administration of taxation,[17] and of justice;[18] a small range of special commissions such as the construction of a fleet in the last year of Theoderic's reign;[19] the distribution of largesse[20] and supplies;[21] and the adjudication of the case of a persistent debtor.[22] It is also known that Faustus, while praetorian prefect, was able to cause the provincials of Campania sufficient hardship for a complaint to be made to the king, who sent court officials to bring him to book.[23] This range of activity is quite large, but pales into insignificance when compared to that found in the fifth-century Empire as described in Chapter 5. It cannot be argued that this is a function of the nature of the sources for the two periods, since almost all the evidence concerning imperial praetorian prefects comes from the Theodosian Code, the rescripts contained within which are of a similar kind to the documents of the *Uariae*. The other sources for the Gothic period do not cast much further light on the picture, since their authors were not concerned with the mechanics of government. Ennodius' *Uita Epiphanii* shows the involvement of Pelagius, praetorian prefect under Odoacer, in the administration of taxes in Liguria,[24] and the proceedings of the 502 synod at Rome record that Basilius, praetorian prefect and patrician, carried out a special commission on behalf of Odoacer at an earlier council.[25] Under Theoderic, Boethius' *Consolation of Philosophy* refers to the role of the praetorian prefect in organising the compulsory purchase of supplies in Campania.[26]

The last case is of particular interest, since Boethius claims that he himself argued about the level of purchases with the praetorian prefect, and that he did so in front of the king. Such a scene would have been almost inconceivable in the imperial period, because then praetorian prefects had almost unfettered freedom of action, making their appearance before the emperor over such a relatively minor matter as compulsory purchases highly unusual. What may have happened, therefore, is that the praetorian prefect's freedom was to some extent curtailed. This impression may be strengthened by the fact that many of the tasks such prefects were told to carry out in the Gothic period appear to have been initiated by the king, rather than by the prefects themselves, in a way only infrequently discernible in the Empire.

With this caution in mind, it is time to turn to the evidence produced during Cassiodorus' own tenure of the praetorian prefecture. The first striking feature concerning that material is that Cassiodorus states, in the preface to the letters he wrote as praetorian prefect, that it may be remarked upon that very few of the documents which followed concerned judicial affairs: this, he says, was because he had employed a subordinate, Felix, who had carried out most of that aspect of his duties.[27] Precisely who this Felix was is not stated, but his position would appear to be unprecedented. The need for a praetorian prefect under the Ostrogoths to have employed an assistant is not easily comprehensible since his imperial counterpart, who had administered a rather larger area than Cassiodorus (including parts of Illyricum and Africa), seems to have managed without such an official. Furthermore, Cassiodorus is quite coy about mentioning Felix, and is over-apologetic for his existence. One possible explanation for this is that Felix was in fact a court official, who had taken over the judicial side of the prefect's business.

This suggestion is not as improbable as it may at first seem, if it is seen against the background of the possible policy of bringing lower-ranking provincial governors into the court. Another important consideration is that the kings themselves, in common with those found elsewhere in fifth- and sixth-century Europe, took over most of the functions associated with the earlier praetorian prefects with regard to the administration of justice, issuing of edicts, and hearing of petitions. Furthermore, although Cassiodorus is correct in indicating that books XI and XII of the *Uariae* contain very few documents of a judicial nature[28] (the majority relate to taxation[29] and the distribution of supplies[30]), any implication that this was not the case in the rest of the work is false.[31] The absence of judicial material is not the only pattern relating to the praetorian prefect discernible in books I to V, VIII and the first part of IX, since, with two exceptions, all the documents contained in those books which concern the prefecture date from the reign of Theoderic.[32] This could be taken to indicate that, although it was retained, the position of the prefect was gradually allowed to fade away as it was seen that it no longer served any real purpose.

Against such reasoning, it could be contended that there is evidence from the Cassiodoran formula for the appointment of praetorian prefects that the position of such officials remained virtually unchanged in the Gothic period. Hence, for example, the prefect is described as 'father of the Empire' ('pater imperii'), is stated to have been in charge of the administration of justice, of taxation, and of the public postal service, to have judged *uice sacra*, and to have held power which was only able to be restricted by the master of the soldiers.[33] The validity of the document as an accurate reflection of the position of the praetorian prefect in the Ostrogothic kingdom is to some extent undermined by the lack of real evidence for the role of such officials in the administration of justice. In addition, the phrase concerning the master of the soldiers raises problems since, as argued in Chapter 12, there were almost certainly no such officials in the Ostrogothic kingdom save during royal minorities, the kings themselves having taken over their functions. The formula is therefore likely to be a further product of an antiquarian element in Cassiodorus' work. The statement concerning the master of the soldiers could simply have been based on the position in the Empire, where, in the fourth century, the offices of the master and the praetorian prefect were of equal rank,[34] or it could be an anachronistic way of stating that the prefect was subject to the king, describing the latter as a master of the soldiers, rather than as a king, in order to stress his position as part of the traditional Roman hierarchy. Given these problems, it is an open question as to how much of the remainder of the formula has validity for the Ostrogothic period.[35]

The next objection a sceptic could produce against the suggestion that the prefecture became less important under the Ostrogoths might be that there is good evidence for the continued existence of the prefect's *officium* in the period. Further, that evidence comes from the 530s, thus potentially undermining the notion that the position of the praetorian prefect may have become progressively weaker under the Ostrogoths. The weight of the testimony concerning the office staff, however, needs to be assessed very carefully, since it comes almost uniquely from the two books of the *Uariae* written by Cassiodorus during his own tenure of the prefecture. The problem with the documents is that they are of an unprecedented kind, being 'rescripts' issued by a praetorian prefect to members of his staff, giving instructions concerning their duties. The fact that there are no earlier documents of similar type does not mean that those supplied by Cassiodorus should be dismissed out of hand, but does mean that their testimony should be approached with caution, especially where it cannot be checked against other sources. This is all the more necessary when it is borne in mind that Cassiodorus used archaic material, and was concerned to show how 'Roman' Ostrogothic administration was.

One of the first things recorded concerning Cassiodorus' staff is that it was large, and that its offices were in his gift.[36] It is also revealed that there was a regular round of promotions within the service, and that each advancement brought increased remuneration.[37] The staff of the prefect included a *primicerius augustalium* and a *primicerius deputatorum*;[38] a *regerendarius*, who was in charge of the public postal service;[39] a *commentariensis*;[40] a *cornicularius* and a *primiscrinius*, both of whom became *tribuni et notarii* with access to the royal court on retirement;[41] a *primicerius excerptorum* and his subordinate (*sextus scholarius*);[42] a *scriniarius curae militaris*;[43] a *cura epistolarum canonicarum*;[44] and a *primicerius singulariorum*, who retired to the *schola* of the *protectores domestici*.[45] Despite the fact that such an impressive list can be produced, the sources do not permit any of the officials mentioned to be seen in action, any more than do those for the fifth-century Empire. It is, therefore, reasonable to concur with J.J. O'Donnell's judgement that the picture of the prefecture's office staff which emerges is largely theoretical, and is 'confined to a description of how things should run, rather than a record of actual performance', in a way which is reminiscent of the *Notitia Dignitatum*.[46] Given the element of antiquarianism in the Cassiodoran formulae, the parallel with the *Notitia Dignitatum* could be pushed rather further, especially in view of the supposed retirement of the *primicerius singulariorum* to the *protectores domestici*, for whose existence there is no positive evidence after *c.* 476. If the suggested reduction in the autonomy and spheres of jurisdiction of the praetorian prefect in the Ostrogothic kingdom is accepted, it is possible that appointments to the prefecture's staff became increasingly honorary, their distribution being more connected with the dispensation of patronage and the receipt of wealth and status, than with actual administrative functions.

Those officials of the praetorian prefect who are actually seen in action fall into two categories. First, there were *domestici* of broadly similar type to those found attached to fifth-century imperial governors, and *cancellarii*. In fact, *cancellarii* are the best-documented of the subordinates, apparently being based in the provinces and involved in the spheres of taxation; the compulsory purchase of food for the army, for the palace and for the City of Rome; the distribution of such supplies, and of other forms of largesse.[47] There are also theoretical statements concerning the need for such men to be just,[48] the retirement of *cancellarii*,[49] and the appointment of a provincial *cancellarius* to the office of the praetorian prefect himself,[50] where he seems to have controlled access to his superior.[51] As in the Empire, these appointments were presumably made by the court, the intervention of which in provincial administration is more positively demonstrated by the fact that *cancellarii* were assisted by *saiones*, the equivalent of palatine *agentes in rebus* (see Chapter 13).[52]

The second category of subordinate about whom something more than the name is known, is formed by a small number of officials of uncertain status who were connected with the major sphere of prefectural jurisdiction – taxation. There was, for example, an *arcarius*, who was responsible for paying the salaries of royal officials.[53] There was also a *canonicarius*, who on one occasion was charged with improving the supply of wine from Venetia,[54] and *censistores* were active in the administration of taxation in Sicily.[55] Finally, there were *siliquatarii*, evidently under the command of a *comes siliquatariorum*, who were concerned with the taxes levied on traders.[56] This last case is of interest, since the title of *comes siliquatariorum* implies that its bearer was a member of the royal court. It could, therefore, perhaps be one further indication of a weakening of the independence of the praetorian prefect in favour of the court.

*

The praetorian prefect of Italy is not the only such official to feature in the Ostrogothic kingdom, since Theoderic appointed a Gallic prefect to administer the parts of Gaul he acquired following the defeat of Alaric II by the Franks in *c.* 507, and his assumption of the regency for Amalaric. The man chosen for the task was Liberius, who was to hold the office for over twenty years.

Although a fair amount is known about Liberius himself,[57] unfortunately little is recorded concerning his specific functions as Gallic prefect. Letters of Avitus of Vienne and Ennodius of Pavia record that Liberius was involved with the restoration of peace with the Burgundians and the ransoming of captives after the Gothic capture of Provence,[58] and the *Uita Caesarii*, which describes him as 'patrician', shows Liberius as being personally engaged in the repulsion of a frontier raid by Visigothic forces.[59] On the occasion of the accession of Athalaric, the prefect was charged with obtaining an oath of allegiance to the new ruler from the provincials under his jurisdiction.[60] Such activities as these are of a kind in which any high-ranking official in the provinces might have engaged, and fall more into the category of special commissions than of useful indicators as to the specific spheres of competence of the prefect. Although Liberius attended, and witnessed the proceedings of, the 529 Council of Orange, that is more likely to have been for reasons connected with his own spirituality and his foundation of a church at Orange, than with his position as Gallic prefect.[61]

The only other evidence relevant to the workings of the Gallic prefecture at this date comes from what can be gleaned of the activities of Liberius' deputy (*uicarius*), Gemellus.[62] Gemellus undertook two commissions involving taxation,[63] one concerning the army,[64] and two concerning judicial cases.[65] While these commissions reflect a range of activity similar to that recorded for the Italian prefecture, little can be read into that since the body of evidence is so small. What is interesting is that there would appear to be rather better evidence for the Gallic *uicarius* than for his counterparts in the two Italian dioceses[66] – and that is despite the fact that the area of the Gallic prefecture was much smaller than it had been under the emperors. It is, perhaps, possible that the appointment of a Gallic prefect and *uicarius*, if not of their Italian counterparts, may have had more to do with a desire to appease the Roman population and to make it appear that little had changed from the imperial period, than with the strict necessities of administration in the Ostrogothic era. Cassiodorus would certainly have chosen his material to emphasise the *romanitas* of the Gothic administration.

A similar case may be made for the other great prefecture, that of the City of Rome. Although there is quite an impressive body of material concerning the city prefect in the *Uariae*, analysis of it shows the functions of this official to have been restricted to three main areas. The first sphere of activity is that of the administration of the Senate. Although Cassiodorus' formula for the city prefecture records that the holder of the office was *praesul* of the Senate, there is no direct evidence of that situation having existed in the Ostrogothic kingdom.[67] Nevertheless, it seems clear that the city prefect was in charge of the *magister census*, whose function was to supervise the Senate's archives and to record its proceedings.[68] City prefects were also responsible for admitting men to the Senate,[69] and for ensuring that candidates did not bring the *ordo* into disrepute;[70] they were also to see that it was not dishonoured in other ways.[71] Although this list of duties looks impressive, in view of the Senate's lack of corporate importance in the government, very little in the way of real power was conferred upon the city prefect by his association with it.

The second and third spheres in which city prefects played an active part are those of law enforcement within the City,[72] and taxation.[73] Although involvement in these affairs indicates a certain continuity from the imperial period, the prefect seems to have been less free to act of his own volition than had been the case under the emperors, and almost all the specific tasks assigned to city prefects in the *Uariae* were commenced upon royal initiative. As was suggested concerning the praetorian prefects, the city prefects simply had to carry out whatever specific commissions they were given, within the area subject to their jurisdiction.[74] In this context it is interesting that Ennodius on one occasion requested the city prefect, Festus, to appoint an honest *aduocatus fisci* for the province of Liguria.[75] Liguria was not a region within the area normally associated with the jurisdiction of the city prefect, nor did it even lie in the same diocese as Rome. This gives the impression that the city prefect had been commanded to see to the appointment in the same way as members of the court were given special commissions no matter what their actual offices: in other words, it may have been Festus' position as a prefect which mattered in this instance, rather than his specific office as city prefect.

As was the case with praetorian prefects, many of the duties of city prefects, especially with regard to the administration of justice, will have been taken over by the king. If this is correct, there will have been much less need for the semi-autonomous kind of prefect encountered in the fifth century when the area governed by the ruler of Italy was much larger than it was in the Gothic period. The title of city prefect could, therefore, have been retained largely in order to convey an appearance of continuity, even though the official who bore it had, effectively, become no more than another royal agent. A change of this kind was in fact noted with regard to a subordinate of the city prefect, the *praefectus annonae*, for Boethius observed that 'once, if a man had charge of the *annona*, he was believed to be great: now, what is lower than that prefecture?'[76] The circumstances surrounding the decline of the position of the *praefectus annonae* may have been slightly different from those involved in the weakening of the city and praetorian prefectures: while the internal affairs of the Ostrogothic kingdom cannot be dismissed as a factor, the *praefectus annonae* must have been affected by the loss of Africa's corn after Geiseric's raid on Rome, *c*. 455, and the decline may have begun before *c*. 476 (see Chapter 5). The important point, however, is that the Gothic kings continued to use the title – and that is not only on the evidence of the pro-Roman Boethius, or even of Cassiodorus,[77] but also of an inscription from Rome, dated *c*. 523.[78]

It is probably on account of this kind of retention of the outward appearance of the earlier imperial administration, and particularly of those features of it which related to the Senate and the extra-palatine officials of the provincial administration, that Totila was able to upbraid the Senate for not supporting the Goths against Belisarius:[79] the king claimed that under Theoderic and Athalaric the Senate had been well treated, and that its members had 'always been appointed to the chief offices throughout the kingdom'.[80] There may have been some truth in that, but his further claim that the Senators had 'thus administered the kingdom' is going too far: the palace had come to exercise increasing control over the government in the period after *c*. 476, leaving the traditional mechanisms of provincial government in place but gradually sapping them of real power. As will be seen in the next chapter, it may have been partly in an attempt to render such statements more plausible, and to assist in uniting the Roman aristocracy to the Gothic cause in face of Justinian's attack, that Cassiodorus composed his *Uariae*.

15

The *Uariae* of Cassiodorus

The largest single source for the discussion of the royal administration of Ostrogothic Italy presented in the last two chapters has been the *Uariae* of Cassiodorus. Important though the evidence supplied by that work has been, problems have been encountered in using its testimony, particularly where it cannot be checked against the writings of other authors. Those problems may be grouped under two related headings. First, there is a clear element of antiquarianism, or preservation of archaic material. Second, there is the creation of an appearance of greater continuity from the imperial period than was the case in reality. That the perception of the *romanitas* of Ostrogothic administration was heightened by Cassiodorus has been shown not only by comparing the evidence of the *Uariae* with that provided by the other sources, meagre though they often are, but also by careful reading between the lines of the *Uariae* itself. The end result has been to produce a picture of Gothic government which is less 'Roman' than that presented by many previous commentators: this does not mean that it was anti-Roman, but that it was much more similar to that which can be painted for the other 'barbarian' administrations in the west than has hitherto been argued. In order for this interpretation of Ostrogothic government to be fully acceptable, however, it is necessary to offer some explanation as to why Cassiodorus should have sought to create the illusion of 'super-romanitas'.

The first place in which to seek an understanding of Cassiodorus' reasons for composing the *Uariae* is his own preface to the work: that is where he may have stated his intentions, or at least the intentions he was prepared to acknowledge in public. The first point to emerge from the preface is that the documents contained within the *Uariae* (excluding those in books XI and XII) were written in response to petitions to the king, in order to explain specific matters concerning the administration. Within the opening sentence, it is stated that the *Uariae* were written 'pro explicanda' different affairs, while it is later recorded that everyone required a speedy response concerning his affairs: this implies that the individual documents were written in

166

response to specific requests, perhaps in much the same way as imperial rescripts were issued.[1] The largest category of letters contained in the *Uariae* is, in fact, of edict or rescript type, and closely follows the style of the documents produced by the western imperial chancery in the late fourth and fifth century.[2] This kind of material is not, however, the sole one found in the collection, since there are also formulae, letters of appointment to official positions, and letters to the Senate informing its members of such appointments, as well as a certain amount of diplomatic correspondence, none of which finds a parallel in the Theodosian Code or, for that matter, in the Justinianic collections.

The second point to emerge from the preface is that the *Uariae* was seen as a panegyric for the achievements of Theoderic the Great, of his successors, and of their officials.[3] This is the subject of an expanded statement, put into the mouths of those who are alleged to have persuaded Cassiodorus to compile the work. The documents are referred to as illustrating the king's concern with the correction of immorality, with the breaking of the audacity of transgressors, and the restoration of reverence for the law.[4] This statement is set in the context of reference to Cassiodorus' lost *History of the Goths*,[5] itself known to have been a work of propaganda written to provide the Goths with a pre-Italian history worthy of being set alongside the Roman past.

The fact that Cassiodorus himself coupled the *Uariae* and the Gothic History makes it reasonable to view his secular works as an entity. If this is done, the following pattern may be discerned. The lost *History* was concerned with the glorification of the achievements of the Gothic people, and especially the Amal dynasty.[6] The *Chronicle*, on the other hand, aimed to show something of the amalgamation of Gothic and Roman traditions in Italy. As a third element, the *Uariae*, modelled upon late Roman imperial documents – and a self-confessed work of propaganda – balanced the *History* by showing how 'Roman' – almost over-'Roman' – the Goths were. In other words, it is possible that the *History* was written primarily for a Gothic audience (though it will also have had an impact on members of the Roman aristocracy), the *Uariae* primarily for the Roman population, and the *Chronicle*, as the union of the two strands, for both.

It is significant that the contents of the *Uariae* relate to times of stress ·within the Ostrogothic kingdom – the collapse of Theoderic's diplomatic policy after the Frankish defeat of Alaric II at Vouillé in *c.* 507; the aftermath of the Boethius affair and the minority of Athalaric; the initial years of the Justinianic reconquest. It was precisely at those points that the Roman population might have needed reminding of the Romanophile nature of Ostrogothic rule. It has been suggested that Cassiodorus and, to a lesser extent, Ennodius, were not typical of

Roman aristocratic opinion in finding Gothic rule so attractive, and that this could have been because they were members of the provincial, rather than of the top flight of the Senatorial, aristocracy.[7] If this view is correct, and the highest Senators (of the level of Boethius and Arator) were not so enamoured of the Ostrogoths, it is possible that some support may be found in it for the suggestion made in Chapter 14 that the Senate and the old high-ranking institutions of provincial government were not as favoured by Gothic kings as Cassiodorus would have liked his readers to believe. Cassiodorus himself, as a person who had benefited from the new régime, would have been keen to serve his masters by trying to persuade other Romans of the good record of the Goths: in order to achieve this he would find it most advantageous to present their traditionalism in relation to times of especial difficulty for their government.

Further to this, it is interesting that the only times at which Cassiodorus himself is known to have held office are at precisely those points of tension, and that his official career is, as J.J. van den Besselaar hinted, only known from his own writings: neither Jordanes nor Ennodius mentions this aspect of Cassiodorus' life, and he does not feature at all in the pages of the Ravenna Chronicle, nor in the writings of the eastern authors, Marcellinus and Procopius.[8] It may be going too far to suggest that Cassiodorus never had an official career, but he could have fabricated a career structure for himself in order to provide a respectable set of Roman aristocratic credentials to use as a background against which to set his propaganda for the Ostrogoths. The three offices he claimed to have held could not have been better chosen to illustrate the different aspects of Roman or Gothic administration: the quaestor was, on Cassiodoran evidence, guardian of the law and *ciuilitas*; the master of the offices was, on fifth-century evidence, in charge of the palace and the court-based provincial officials; the praetorian prefect was the chief 'senatorial' or provincial administrator outside the court. The suggestion of a fabricated career structure may derive added strength from the fact that while books V, VIII, IX and X of the *Uariae* were allegedly written by Cassiodorus in the name of the king while he held the positions of master of the offices and praetorian prefect, their contents do not differ radically from those of the first four books, which were produced while he was supposedly a quaestor. There is no precedent for masters of the offices dealing with business of such a nature, still less for the praetorian prefects, who were not even members of the imperial/royal court. Even given what has been argued throughout this book concerning the flexible way in which rulers could use their officials and courtiers, it is inherently unlikely that someone styled a master of the offices should so consistently have been responsible for a function more usually associated with quaestors. Similarly, it is strange that the documents preserved in books XI and XII should be the sole examples of 'rescripts' issued by praetorian prefects for their subordinates during the whole of the period after the Diocletianic tetrarchy. The fact that not a single document of similar type exists (at least in the west) after 394, leads to the suspicion that some, at least, of Cassiodorus' documents may not be genuine governmental letters and formulae at all.[9]

It is quite possible that many, if not all, the documents found throughout the *Uariae* are not genuine, and were made up in order to present an idealised and, therefore, rather schematic illustration of the ways in which Ostrogothic administration worked and Gothic kings thought. This is most certainly the case with regard to the formulae, more of which appear to draw upon historical examples than can be accounted for by chance, and which try to demonstrate a continuance of Roman traditions. A parallel to this interpretation has already been suggested by B. Ward-Perkins, who notes that while Cassiodorus and other contemporary authors mention Gothic royal patronage of secular building works, reference to religious patronage is skilfully avoided: this is not because such patronage did not exist (since it is known from non-documentary sources that Theoderic built the splendid S. Apollinare Nuovo), but because such churches were Arian, not Catholic.[10] If sixth-century authors could 'overlook' such activity, it is not hard to see how a man such as Cassiodorus could present a distorted picture of Gothic government.

This interpretation of Cassiodorus' *Uariae* does not mean that its contents are wholly inaccurate, because when specific officials are named, even if only in the letter headings, there must have been some foundation in truth at least for the basic kinds of activity in which they engaged, in order for the work to have been credible to a contemporary readership: a lack of credibility would not have served the propagandist purpose well. On the other hand, the precise way in which the depictions are drawn may well owe more to Cassiodorus' rhetorical and literary skills, and to his knowledge of the past, than to the reality of his own day. What he did was to fashion a work which deliberately heightened the perception of the order and *ciuilitas*[11] of Ostrogothic administration in order to persuade Romans to support the Gothic cause against the Justinianic campaigns.[12] By careful reading between the lines, and by comparing the testimony of the *Uariae* with that of other sources wherever feasible, it is still possible to gain an understanding of the reality of the government of Ostrogothic Italy, though the nature of that administration is far removed from the initial impression created by Cassiodorus' work, and is more akin to that of the other western kingdoms than has often been thought.

Conclusion

The fifth century saw a major change in the way in which the western provinces of the Roman Empire were administered. At the beginning of the century, they were governed by Roman magistrates who, although virtually autonomous in the sphere of civil jurisdiction, were dependent upon the central imperial court for military power. The emperor and his court could also advise on legal matters, and, by supplying a large part of the staff of the provincial administration and publicising legal decisions right across the Empire, attempted to ensure effective and co-ordinated government. By the end of the century, the same provinces were largely under the control of the kings of 'barbarian' peoples, some of whom had been settled within the Empire by agreement with the imperial administration, but others of whom had come to occupy their territories by less legitimate means. The position of western emperor had ceased to exist.

At first sight, it may appear that the changes summarised in the last paragraph are of so radical a nature that they amount to the end of the Roman world. It has, however, been the argument of this book that, although the changes wrought during the fifth century were very great, they amounted to a transformation of the Roman Empire, rather than to its 'fall', and that the new order had its roots in Roman traditions. The basis on which the argument has been presented is an understanding of the way in which, on account of their differing natures, the sources for the Empire and for each of the various 'barbarian' kingdoms lend varying hues to the individual scenes which make up the portrayal of the fifth-century west. Close examination has shown that the variation is of shade rather than of basic colour, and is largely caused by the differing varnishes through which the parts of the picture have to be viewed.

One of the more important arguments presented earlier is that, for all their lack of perceived activity, fifth-century western emperors were not criticised for being idle, but were even fought over as being of considerable importance. It is particularly noteworthy that a large body of evidence concerning faction politics relates to Gaul, since there is some evidence (discussed in Chapter 5) to suggest that Gaul had already begun to withdraw from active participation in the Empire even before the first substantial settlement of 'barbarians' had

170

occurred within its frontiers. In addition, that evidence not only relates to the engagement of the Gallo-Roman aristocracy in imperial factionalism, but also to the involvement (often in partnership with the native aristocrats) of the kings of the newly-settled federates, and of kings (such as those of the Franks) who may have been bound to the Empire rather more loosely. There are indications that a broadly similar situation existed in Africa. Although the exploitation of factions at Rome by 'barbarians' was not in itself new (it has a long history, stretching back to the Republic), the ability of non-Romans to operate legitimately from within the frontiers was a novel element, which arose at a time when the relationship of the provinces to the heart of the Empire may already have been undergoing a change.

The integration of the 'barbarian' kings into the Roman world may be further illustrated by the fact that they almost all continued to recognise that the emperor, whether based in Italy or (after *c.* 476) Constantinople, exercised a certain *auctoritas* over them. 'Barbarians' of all kinds had for centuries wished to enjoy the perceived privileges of life within the Empire, and although those who arrived in the west during the fifth century often did so uninvited and with violence, once within the frontiers and no longer subject to the external pressures which had propelled them into the Empire, they were likely to look for militarily and economically secure places to settle, and to seek integration with the native populations.

Although, from an imperial viewpoint, allowing the 'barbarians' to settle within the Empire may have been a policy born of desperation, since the 'barbarians' were too numerous and dispersed to be driven back to the frontiers, there were more positive aspects to it. Once the Empire was their home, the new arrivals could be expected to contribute substantially to its defence. There was nothing remotely new in the use of 'barbarians' as soldiers in the 'Roman' army, and the policy was also an extension of the time-honoured Roman principle of dividing the 'barbarians' against themselves. Even the settlement of 'barbarians' within the Empire was not entirely a novelty, since the Visigoths had been permitted to dwell inside its frontiers since the late fourth century.

The new feature of the fifth-century arrangements was that the federates were more fully locked into the Roman system than their predecessors had been, since their leaders were given authority not only over their own peoples, but also over the Roman population in the areas in which they were settled.[1] They derived power over their own tribes from their position as *reges gentium*, and over the Romans from a new form of magisterial kingship: this combination of jurisdiction over both 'barbarians' and Romans gave the kings civilian as well as military authority. The disadvantages of this for the central administration were that such men were almost as difficult to control as the fourth-century praetorian prefects had been before military power had been taken from them, and that the imperial court lost some of its ability to direct (rather than simply to co-ordinate) military operations. On the other hand, the Empire gained powerful military leaders in the provinces who, because they were not Romans, could not themselves aspire to the purple.

Once the policy of establishing federates within the western provinces was widely applied, the emperor gradually became even more disengaged from routine administration, until even in Italy itself there was no need for an imperial presence. Civilian administration was in the hands of kings who were possessed of still greater autonomy than the prefects had been, and military affairs no longer called for the intervention of officials from the imperial court. Even the supplying of the army no longer required an imperial taxation system, since the federates gained their income direct from the provincials in the localities in which they were settled. This is true no matter whether the settlement involved the actual take-over of the land by the 'barbarians', as traditionally thought, or the acquisition of the tax revenues which had formerly been devoted to the support of the army, as has been recently suggested.[2] In either case, the point is graphically illustrated by the disappearance of the centrally-controlled coinage of the Empire, whose existence was almost entirely dictated by the need to provision the imperial armies.[3]

Although the settlement of the federates in the western provinces involved a withdrawal by the emperors from direct authority over the areas involved, it was not necessarily an admission of total defeat. Instead, it may be better to see the fifth-century policy as yet another attempt, in the new circumstances caused by the arrival of unprecedentedly large numbers of 'barbarians' within the frontiers, to find a suitable way of administering an area so vast as that of the later Roman Empire. The uniting of civil and military power in the hands of Roman praetorian prefects by Diocletian had caused problems, since ambitious officials had been provided with a ready-made power-base. The splitting of the two kinds of authority had worked for a time, but had involved taking military control into the hands of the court, where it was too centralised and inflexible to provide adequate defence when faced with the circumstances of the fifth century. The response to this was, therefore, to re-create military commands in the provinces, this time in the hands of men who could not aspire to higher positions – namely 'barbarians'. There are some similarities (though no close parallels) between the position of the kings thus created and that of the client kings used in the late Republic and early Principate, when the Empire was expanding into new areas. The fact that such kings were often later replaced by prefects[4] may enhance the suggestion that, although the details of the fifth-century settlements were new, the policy was drawn from within the canon of Roman tradition.

It is against the background of the kings' authority over the Roman populations of the areas they occupied, and holding of Roman 'offices' as half prefects and half masters of the soldiers,[5] that the legislative and administrative activities of such leaders have to be viewed. In addition, two further factors have to be taken into consideration when comparing the Roman and 'barbarian' administrative systems: first, the relative paucity of evidence concerning the procedures of administration within the prefectures; second, the non-bureaucratic, almost *ad hoc* nature of fifth-century Roman government. An appreciation of the personal nature of the Roman administration may make the differences between the Roman and the 'Germanic' – between the *comitatus* and the *Gefolgschaft* – appear less striking than they at first seem, and this makes it easier to understand why and how the new royal courts of the 'barbarians' were able to adopt and adapt Roman institutions. As with the policy of settlement itself, the courts were new, but their structure was drawn largely from Roman traditions.

There are many reasons why this should be so. The 'barbarians' can only ever have been a minority in the Roman world, and did not displace the local aristocracies. Indeed, many 'barbarian' kings not only made common cause with Roman aristocrats, but also employed them as courtiers, even in positions requiring officials of proven trustworthiness. In such circumstances, it is almost inconceivable that the structure of the courts should not have been influenced by the traditions of law, administrative practice and office-holding with which such men were familiar. This is particularly so in view of the pre-settlement history of the federates. Many of the 'barbarians' who came to occupy the western provinces had no recent experience of stability in one area, still less in a region in which they were in charge of cities and the other appurtenances of settled or Roman civilisation. In addition, many of the 'barbarians' had been receptive to, and influenced by, Roman culture while they were still beyond the frontiers. In view of this, it is, *prima facie*, more likely that the kings should have adopted and adapted the traditions they found in the areas they came to occupy, than that they should have cast out such traditions and started afresh to create an entirely new system of their own.

The adaptation of Roman traditions can be as well seen in the kings' legal enactments as in their administrative structures. There is positive evidence from the Vandal kingdom that imperial rescript law was understood and was applied to the new circumstances of the 'barbarian' kingdom. There is also evidence from the same region that the mass of the population continued to conduct its private affairs in accordance with Roman legal forms. The fact that the legislation of the other 'barbarian' kings does not appear familiarly 'Roman' need not, as has too often been assumed in the past, necessarily imply that it is 'Germanic', since the local laws and customs which prevailed in the provinces of the Empire are hardly recorded,[6] and might very well not seem familiar to those only acquainted with imperial law. They might also have certain elements in common with the basic regulatory codes in any 'primitive' society, whether within the frontiers of the Empire or outside them. Given that some, at least, of the kingdoms either produced versions of imperial rescript law, or enactments influenced by imperial law, it does not seem unreasonable to suppose that they might also have made collections of provincial law. The fact that the 'barbarian' law codes are not identical in their provisions does not argue for their origins in Germanic tribal codes, since it is not necessarily the case that all the provinces of the Empire enjoyed the same local edicts. In addition, in the same way as the royal courts adapted, rather than slavishly imitated, institutions from the imperial court and provincial administration, so too the compilers of the legal codes adapted their materials: this can be positively shown in the case of the 'barbarian' recensions of rescript law (see especially Chapter 6). Finally, rather than appealing to a largely hypothetical body of common 'Germanic' law to explain the similarities between the 'barbarian' codes, it is simpler to suggest that they are a product of a debt to a body of Roman law whose existence (if not whose content) is rather more certain.

It should be clear from the foregoing that the Roman Empire did not 'fall' in the fifth century, but was transformed into something new. There was no sharp break with the past, but an adjustment in the ways in which the Empire and its constituent parts were administered. There can be no doubt that the change was on a large scale, and was of considerable significance but, if the eschatological themes of much of the source material produced by churchmen are laid aside, there does not appear to have been a sense of the imminent disintegration of the Roman world amongst contemporaries. It has been noted that the removal of Romulus Augustulus, the last western emperor, provoked little comment, and it is interesting to find Rutilius Namatianus, rather earlier in the century, saying,

> For you, that which seals the destiny of other kingdoms
> means renewal;
> To be able to grow out of ill is the way of re-birth.[7]

Although the dangers of the fifth century are clearly appreciated, there is a sense of hope for the future.

To describe the fifth-century transformation of the west as a 're-birth' would be tendentious, but it was by no means necessarily the end of Rome's authority. Even after the Justinianic age, with its attempt to bring the west more directly under imperial control once more, the traditions of the Empire were felt throughout the 'barbarian' world – both in the kingdoms which were already established and in those which were born in the late sixth century. Detailed examination of that issue, however, like that of the precise character of the fourth-century base from which the developments discussed in this book sprang, lies beyond the scope of this work: such subjects must form the basis of future studies.

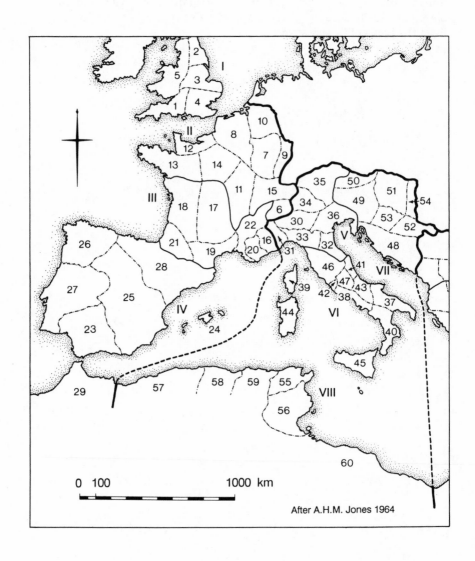

MAP I: Provinces of the Western Empire, *c.* 400

MAP I: key

The Gallic Prefecture
  I British diocese
    1 Britannia I
    2 Britannia II
    3 Flavia Caesariensis
    4 Maxima Caesariensis
    5 Valentia
  II Gallic diocese
    6 Alpes Poeninae
    7 Belgica I
    8 Belgica II
    9 Germania I
    10 Germania II
    11 Lugdunensis I
    12 Lugdunensis II
    13 Lugdunensis III
    14 Lugdunensis Senonia
    15 Maxima Sequanorum
  III Diocese of the Seven Provinces
    16 Alpes Maritimae
    17 Aquitanica I
    18 Aquitanica II
    19 Narbonensis I
    20 Narbonensis II
    21 Novempopuli
    22 Vienensis
  IV Spanish diocese
    23 Baetica
    24 Baleares
    25 Carthaginiensis
    26 Gallaecia
    27 Lusitania
    28 Tarraconensis
    29 Tingitania

The Italian Prefecture
  V Italian, or Annonarian, diocese
    30 Aemilia
    31 Alpes Cottiae
    32 Flaminia et Picenum annonarium
    33 Liguria
    34 Raetia I
    35 Raetia II
    36 Venetia et Histria
  VI Suburbicarian diocese
    37 Apulia et Calabria
    38 Campania
    39 Corsica
    40 Lucania et Bruttium
    41 Picenum suburbicarium
    42 Roma
    43 Samnium
    44 Sardinia
    45 Sicilia
    46 Tuscia et Umbria
    47 Valeria
  VII Illyrican diocese
    48 Dalmatia
    49 Noricum mediterraneum
    50 Noricum ripense
    51 Pannonia I
    52 Pannonia II
    53 Savia
    54 Valeria
  VIII African diocese
    55 Africa
    56 Byzacium
    57 Mauritania Caesariensis
    58 Mauritania Sitifensis
    59 Numidia
    60 Tripolitania

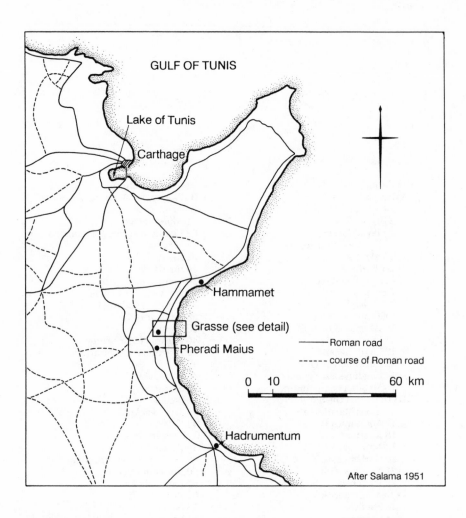

GULF OF TUNIS

Lake of Tunis

Carthage

Hammamet

Grasse (see detail)

Pheradi Maius

——— Roman road

------- course of Roman road

0   10   60 km

Hadrumentum

After Salama 1951

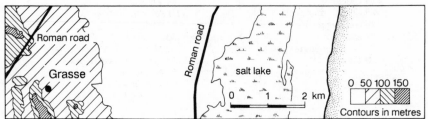

Roman road

Grasse

Roman road

salt lake

0   1   2 km

0 50 100 150

Contours in metres

MAP II: Northern Tunisia, showing the location of Grasse

Abbreviations

The list that follows does not include shortened forms of references to primary material which are sufficiently full for reference to be made straight to the list of primary sources in the Bibliography. Common abbreviations are also not included.

Acta Synhod. = *Acta Synhodorum habitarum Romae*
Add. ad Prosp. Haun. = *Auctarii Hauniensis, Continuatio Hauniensis Prosperi, additamenta codicis Hauniensis*
A.E. = *L'Année épigraphique*
Anon. Val. = *Anonymi Ualesiani pars posterior*
Anthol. Lat. = *Anthologia Latina I: carmina in codicibus scripta, fasc. I. Libri Salmasiani aliorumque carmina.* SB, followed by a number, indicates the edition by D.R. Shackleton Bailey; R, that by A. Reise.
Auct. Haun. ordo post. = *Auctarii Hauniensis, Continuatio Hauniensis Prosperi, ordo posterior*
Auct. Haun. ordo prior = *Auctarii Hauniensis, Continuatio Hauniensis Prosperi, ordo prior*
Auct. Prosp. Haun. = *Auctarium Prosperi Hauniensis*
Avitus, *Contra Arrianos* = Avitus of Vienne, *Dialogi cum Gundobado rege uel librorum contra Arrianos reliquiae*
B.G. = Procopius, *De Bello Gothico*
Boethius, *C.P.* = Boethius, *De consolatione philosophiae*
B.U. = Procopius, *De Bello Uandalico*
Cap. Mer. = *Capitularia Merowingica*
C.C.S.L. = *Corpus Christianorum series Latina*
C.E. = *Codex Eurici*
Ch.La. = *Chartae Latinae Antiquiores*
Chron. Caesaraugust. = *Chronicorum Caesaraugustanorum reliquiae*
Chron. Pasch. = *Chronicon Paschale ad exemplar Uaticanum recensuit L. Dindorf*
C.I. = *Codex Iustinianus*
C.I.L. = *Corpus Inscriptionum Latinarum*
Coll. Auell. = *Epistolae imperatorum pontificum aliorum inde ab a. CCCLXVIII ad a. DLIII date, Auellana quae dicitur collectio*
Conl. Carth. 411 = *Gesta conlationis Carthaginensis anno 411*
C.S.E.L. = *Corpus Scriptorum Ecclesiasticorum Latinorum*
C.S.H.B. = *Corpus Scriptorum Historiae Byzantinae*
C.Th. = *Codex Theodosianus*
Ep. = *Epistolae*

Ep. Arelat. = *Epistolae Arelatenses genuinae*
Ep. Austr. = *Epistolae Austrasiacae*
Ep. Theod. = *Epistolae Theodericianae uariae*
Fasti Uindob. Post. = *Fasti Uindobonenses Posteriores*
Fasti Uindob. Prior. = *Fasti Uindobonenses Priores*
Fiebiger 1944 = O. Fiebiger, *Inschriftensammlung zur Geschichte der Ostgermanen, zweite Folge*
Fiebiger and Schmidt 1917 = O. Fiebiger and L. Schmidt, *Inschriftensammlung zur Geschichte der Ostgermanen*
Fort., *Carm.* = Fortunatus, *Carmina*
Fort., *Uita Germani ep. Par.* = Fortunatus, *Uita Germani episcopi Parisiaci*
Fred. = Fredegar, *Chronicle*
Gennadius = Gennadius of Marseilles, *Liber de scriptoribus ecclesiasticis*
G.C. = Gregory of Tours, *Liber in gloria confessorum*
G.M. = Gregory of Tours, *Liber in gloria martyrum*
Greg., *Reg.* = Gregory the Great, *Register epistolarum*
H.G. = Isidore, *Historia Gothorum*
H.L. = Paul the Deacon, *Historia Langobardorum*
H.S. = Isidore, *Historia Sueborum*
Jn Bicl. = John of Biclaro, *Chronica ad a. DLXVII-DXC*
John of Ephesus, *H.E.* = John of Ephesus, *Historia ecclesiastica pars tertia*
L.H. = Gregory of Tours, *Decem libri historiarum*
L.H.F. = *Liber Historiae Francorum*
Lib. const. = *Liber constitutionum*
L.R.U. = *Lex Romana Uisigothorum*
L.U. = *Liber iudicorum siue Lex Uisigothorum edita ab Reccesuindo rege a. 654, renouit ab Eruigio rege a. 681, accedunt ... leges nouellae et extrauagantes*
Merobaudes, *Carm.* = Merobaudes, *Carmina*
M.G.H. = *Monumenta Germaniae Historica*
M.G.H., A.A. = *Monumenta Germaniae Historica, Auctores Antiquissimi*
M.G.H., Concilia I = *Monumenta Germaniae Historica, Legum sectio III, Concilia tomus I, Concilia aeui Merouingici*
M.G.H., S.R.M. = *Monumenta Germaniae Historica, Scriptores Rerum Merouingicarum*
M.I.Ö.G. = *Mitteilungen der Instituts für österreichische Geschichtsforschung*
M.Ö.I.G. = *Mitteilungen des österreichischen Instituts für Geschichtsforschung*
N.Anth. = *Nouellae Anthemii*
N.Mai. = *Nouellae Maioriani*
Not. Dig., Occ. = *Notitia Dignitatum, pars Occidentalis*
N.Seu. = *Nouellae Seueri*
N.Th. = *Nouellae Theodosii II*
N.Ual. = *Nouellae Ualentiniani III*
Oros. = Orosius, *Historia aduersus paganos libri VII*
Philostorgius, *H.E.* = Philostorgius, *Historia ecclesiastica*
P.L. = *Patrologiae cursus completus ... series Latina*, ed. J.-P. Migne (221 vols, Paris, 1844-1904)
Settimane ... = *Settimane di studio del centro italiano di studi sull'alto medioevo*
Sid. Ap., *Carm.* = Sidonius Apollinaris, *Carmina*
Sid. Ap., *Ep.* = Sidonius Apollinaris, *Epistolae*
Sirm. = *Constitutiones sirmondianes*
Sozomen, *H.E.* = Sozomen, *Historia ecclesiastica*

Sym., *Ep.* = Quintus Aurelius Symmachus, *Epistolae*

Sym., *Rel.* = Quintus Aurelius Symmachus, *Relationes*

Thiel = A. Thiel, *Epistolae Romanorum pontificorum genuinae et quae eos scriptae sunt a s. Hilaro usque ad Pelagium II*, vol. I

Uariae = Cassiodorus, *Uariarum libri XII*

U.I. = Gregory of Tours, *Liber de passione et uirtutibus sancti Iuliani martyris*

Uita Desid. ep. Biturc. = *Uita sancti Desiderati episcopi Biturcensim*

Uita Fulgentii = Ferrandus, *Uita sancti Fulgentii Ruspensis episcopi*

Uita Ioh. abb. Reom. = *Uita Iohannis abbatis Reomaensis auctore Iona*

U.M. = Gregory of Tours, *Libri I-IV de uirtutibus sancti Martini episcopi*

U.P. = Gregory of Tours, *Liber Uitae Patrum*

U.P.I. = *Uita Patrum Iurensium*

Vict. Tun. = Victor of Tunnuna, *Chronica a. CCCCXLIV-DXLVII*

Vict. Vit. = Victor of Vita, *Historia persecutionis Africanae prouinciae*

Z.R.G., g.A. = *Zeitschrift der Savigny-Stiftung für Rechtsgeschichte, germanistische Abteilung*

Notes

Introduction

1. Goffart 1988b, pp.117-18 draws attention to the lack of fifth- and sixth-century Latin historians.
2. Goffart 1988b, p.161.
3. Eunapius, frg. 66.2.
4. Matthews 1970, p.91.
5. *L.H.* II.8.
6. Philostorgius, *H.E.* XII.14.
7. Avitus, *Ep.* 49.

Introduction to Part I

1. This point is discussed in more detail at the start of Part II.
2. For a summary of the position of the Senate in the later Empire, see A.H.M. Jones 1964, pp.329-33, and see also Matthews 1975, e.g. pp.302-3, 305, 358-60; for a recent discussion of the Senate and the senatorial *ordo* in the fifth century, see Barnish 1988.

Chapter 1

1. See Wood 1987, p.254, on the problem in general; ibid, pp.255-6, discusses the *Chronicle of 452* in greater detail; Greek chroniclers and historians also arranged their material thematically rather than strictly chronologically, at times – see M.E. Jones and Casey 1988, pp.384-5 on Zosimus and Sozomen. Courtois 1951 contains an important discussion of the chronological problems encountered in Hydatius' Chronicle. See also Muhlberger 1990.
2. Laistner 1957, p.9.
3. M.E. Jones and Casey 1988, p.367.
4. Markus 1986, pp.40-1.
5. Markus 1986, p.40, with specific reference to Prosper.
6. For the evidence concerning imperial rescripts in the period up to 337, see Millar 1977, pp.252-9; see also A.H.M. Jones 1964, pp.347-8, Wal 1981, p.280, and Harries 1988, p.149.
7. Salway 1981, p.336; Musset 1975, p.22.
8. *C.I.L.* VI.1725: 'Flauio Olbio Auxentio Drauco uiro clarissimo et inlustri, patriciae familiae uiro, senatus muniis prompta deuotione perfuncto; comiti ordinis primi et uicario urbis Romae; comiti sacri consistoris; prefecto urbis Romae ...'

Chapter 2

1. Sid. Ap., *Carm.* VII.312-13.
2. Sid. Ap., *Carm.* II.382-86:

> ... modo principe nobis
> est opus armato, ueterum qui more parentum
> non mandat sed bella gerat, quem signa mouentum
> terra uel unda tremant, ut tandem iure recepto
> Romulo desuetas moderentur classica classes.

3. Sid. Ap., *Carm.* V.511-52; Hydatius, 200, p.31; *Chron. Caesaraug., s.a.* 460, p.222.
4. Prosper, 1259, p.468; *Chronicle of 452*, 77, p.654; Marcellinus, *s.a.* 424.1, p.76.
5. Hydatius, 84, pp.20-1; Cassiodorus, *Chronicle*, 1209, p.155.
6. Marcellinus, *s.a.* 437, p.79.
7. Hydatius, 162, p.27; Prosper, 1375, pp.483-4; the same may be seen in *Chron. Pasch.* I.594, where it is reported that Olybrius married the younger Placidia.
8. Marcellinus, *s.a.* 434, p.79; Cassiodorus, *Chronicle*, 1205, p.155.
9. *Chronicle of 452*, 109, p.658; Marcellinus, *s.a.* 432.2, p.78.
10. Marcellinus, *s.a.* 455.3, p.86; see also *B.U.* I.4.38-5.5
11. *Chronicle of 511*, 599, p.661: 'Eudoxia Rauenna regnum accepit.'
12. Constantius, *Uita Germani* VII.35.
13. On the imperial women of Constantinople at this date, see Holum 1982.
14. Hydatius, 234, p.34.
15. Prosper, 1286, p.470, and 1289, p.471; Hydatius, 84, pp.20-1.
16. The best recent account of the complex events of the early fifth century in northern Gaul is Wightman 1985, esp. at pp.300ff; see also Matthews 1975, p.320.
17. Marius, *s.a.* 456, p.232; Marcellinus, *s.a.* 457, p.87, must be mistaken in believing that Majorian became emperor by the wish of Leo.
18. *Fasti Uindob. Prior.*, p.305; Hydatius, 210 and 211, p.32; Marcellinus, *s.a.* 461.2, p.88; Cassiodorus, *Chronicle*, 1274, p.157; Vict. Tun., *s.a.* 463.2, p.187; Marius, *s.a.* 461, p.232.
19. *Fasti Uindob. Prior.*, p.305, and Marcellinus, *s.a.* 465.2, p.88, simply record that Severus died; Cassiodorus, *Chronicle*, 1280, p.158, says that he was murdered by Ricimer.
20. Marcellinus, *s.a.* 467.1, p.89, Cassiodorus, *Chronicle*, 1283, p.158, and Hydatius, 234, p.34, record that Anthemius was sent by Leo; *Fasti Uindob. Prior.*, p.305, Vict. Tun., *s.a.* 467.2, p.187, and Marius, *s.a.* 467, p.233, simply state that Anthemius became emperor. For the ensuing rebellions, see various passages in *Fasti Uindob. Prior.*, pp.306-10; Marcellinus, pp.90-1; Cassiodorus, *Chronicle*, p.158; Vict. Tun., p.188; Marius, p.233.
21. Mathisen 1979, pp.598-603.
22. Ibid., pp.605-7.
23. See, most explicitly, Priscus, frg. 39.1.
24. See Van Dam 1985, p.53; ibid., p.41, also suggests that many of the cases of revolt in the fifth century in which there was no apparent attempt to establish an alternative emperor are also indicative of a desire to maintain the existing social order of the Empire. On the difference between 'revolution' and 'rebellion' in general, see Gluckman 1966, pp.27-53.

25. *Chronicle of 511*, 628, p.664; immediately before he was created emperor by Ricimer he was made *magister militum* – *Fasti Uindob. Prior.*, p.305. See also Sid. Ap., *Carm.* V.305-8, 378.

26. Sid. Ap., *Carm.* II.205-7.

27. *C.I.* VI.61.5.

28. MacCormack 1981, p.173.

29. Reydellet 1981, pp.52-3, 60-4.

30. MacCormack 1981, pp.214, 220.

31. A.H.M. Jones 1964, pp.170-1.

32. Prosper, 1339, p.477; as the last of the rescripts date to 429, it is more likely to have been the advent of the Vandals than the rebellion of Boniface which caused their cessation.

33. Marcellinus, *s.a.* 455.3. p.86; Hydatius, 216, p.32; *B.U.* I.4.38-5.5; cf. John of Antioch, frg. 204, pp.119-20.

34. Hydatius, 57, p.18; Marcellinus, *s.a.* 410, p.70.

35. *U.P.I.* 92-5.

36. See Stevens 1933, pp.28-9, citing Sid. Ap., *Carm.* VII, the panegyric on Avitus.

37. Mathisen 1979, pp.609-10.

38. Cassiodorus, *Chronicle*, 1295, p.158; see also Vict. Tun., *s.a.* 473.6 and 473.7, p.188.

39. Only *C.Th.* XII.1.171, and *Sirm.* 6.

40. The most explicit reference is Claudian, *In Eutropium*, I.377-83, but see also *De consulatu Stilichonis*, I.188-245 and II.64-5; cf. *De IV consulatu Honorii* 439-59, *Carmina minora* 46, *De bello Gothico* I.371-4, 423-9; see also Sym., *Ep.* IV.28. For modern comments, see Wallace-Hadrill 1962, p.151, and Matthews 1975, pp.270-2.

41. Sid. Ap., *Carm.* V.474-8.

42. MacCormack 1981, pp.59-60, where the Arch of Constantine and the column of Arcadius are given as specific examples.

Chapter 3

1. *C.Th.* VI.8.1.

2. Heraclius was later murdered at the same time as Valentinian III; for that incident, see Marcellinus, *s.a.* 455.1, p.86, where Heraclius is referred to as 'spado', and Vict. Tun., *s.a.* 455, p.186, where he is 'praepositus'; Prosper, 1373-5, pp.483-4, the only contemporary source, recounts the whole narrative, and describes Heraclius as 'spado'.

3. Constantius, *Uita Germani* VII.39, 44: 'praepositus regalis cubiculi'.

4. *Not. Dig., Occ.* XIV.

5. *C.I.L.* VI.9297, *a.* 471: 'Hic quiescit in pace Anthemius cubicui [*sic*] qui uixit annos LX. Depositus IIII Nonas Octobr. cons. Probiani.'

6. With regard to *curae palatii*, we know from *L.H.* II.8 that Aetius had held the position under the usurper John, and that Aetius later appointed Consentius, former *tribunus et notarius*, to the position (Sid. Ap., *Carm.* XXIII), but neither source tells us anything of the function of such an official. The position of *castrensis sacri palatii* is recorded in *Not. Dig., Occ.* XV, where he is described as the superior of the *curae palatii*, but there is no real information on his duties. The *decuriones palatii* were exempted from certain taxes (*C.Th.* VI.23.2, 23.3, and, in the east, 23.4), but the nearest we get to seeing anything of such an official in action is when Aphthonius, *decurio sacri palatii*, carried a letter from Honorius to the younger Symmachus when the latter was city prefect (*Coll. Auell.* 19).

7. A.H.M. Jones 1964, p.567, though this concerns the eastern Empire.

8. Hydatius, 160, p.27.

9. *L.H.* II.9.

10. Augustine, *Ep.* CCXX.7: 'domesticorum et Africae comes.'

11. *Dux* – Prosper, 1278, p.469; *magister militum* – Prosper, 1282, p.470, and Hydatius, 77, p.20.

12. Prosper, 1310, pp.473-4.

13. *Comes domesticorum* – *Chronicle of 511*, 628, p.664; *magister militum* – *Fasti Uindob. Prior.*, p.305.

14. *C.Th.* XV.11.1: 'comes domesticorum et uices agens magistri militum.'

15. *Not. Dig., Occ.* XIII.

16. *C.Th.* VI.25.1.

17. Ibid.

18. *C.Th.* VI.24.8-11.

19. For a different view, based on the fourth century, see Cosenza 1905, p.93, who suggests that the *domestici* were young nobles of senatorial rank, while the *protectores*, also bodyguards, were retired legionaries. A.H.M. Jones 1964, pp.638-40, believed that in the fifth century these *protectores domestici* ceased to be young men in training, arguing that they remained in service until they retired, and that they then received senatorial rank (see above). This, however, need not be the case, as 'retirement' could simply mean leaving the service, so that those who 'retired' could move on as fully-fledged military commanders who would then have senatorial rank.

20. *Conl. Carth. 411* I.1, p.53.

21. *C.Th.* XVI.5.42, forbidding heretics from being employed in imperial service, and XV.11.1, concerning lion-hunting in Africa.

22. *C.Th.* XI.17.3.

23. *Chronicle of 511*, 649, p.664; it is not clear how many *comites stabuli* were involved, though Stroheker 1937, pp.33-4, believed that there were three. The point will be further discussed in the section of this Chapter concerning *duces*.

24. *C.Th.* I.9.1.

25. *C.Th.* I.9.2, 9.3.

26. *C.Th.* VI.27.18.

27. *C.Th.* VI.27.11.

28. *Not. Dig., Occ.* IX on *curiosi* for the *cursus publicus*; see also *C.Th.* VI.29.1, 29.5, 29.7, 29.8 from the fourth century.

29. Giardina 1977, pp.13-72. This fact, incidentally, accounts for the loss of importance in the position of the master of the offices which will be seen reflected in the Ostrogothic kingdom where the provincial administration was on a much smaller scale owing to the loss of much of the western Empire: see Chapter 13, below.

30. *C.Th.* XVI.5.42.

31. *C.Th.* VI.26.11.

32. *C.Th.* IX.38.11.

33. Namatianus, *De reditu suo*, I.563-4:

> officiis regerem cum regia tecta magister
> armigerasque pii principis excubias.

34. Leontius carried a letter for Quintus Aurelius Symmachus concerning the arrangements for the games to celebrate his son's praetorship (Sym., *Ep.* IX.16, *a.* 399); Nectarius carried a letter from Pope Leo I to Bishop Anatolius of Constantinople (Leo I, *Ep.* 135, *a.* 454); and *agentes* carried further letters from Pope Leo to Emperor Leo and to Bishop Gennadius of Constantinople, *c.* 460 (*Coll. Auell.* 51, 52).

35. Eutyches, Iulianus and Maximus, *Sirm.* 12.

36. *C.Th.* I.8.2.

37. *Not. Dig., Occ.* X.

38. Sid. Ap., *Carm.* I.23-8. 1.

39. Sid. Ap., *Carm.* I.26: '[Uictor] aut Phoebe uestro [Anthemio] qui solet ore loqui'; Namatianus, *De reditu suo*, I.171-2. The same may be inferred from a letter of Quintus Aurelius Symmachus which appears to comment on the position of a quaestor, though this is not stated in so many words: Sym., *Ep.* V.54, of Felix – 'quaeso te, cogites quid de augusto adyto, cuius loqueris oracula, deceat impetrari'; cf. Zosimus V.32.6. There are several other references to quaestors in the sources, but they are mostly in inscriptions and do nothing save record that the men commemorated were *quaestores candidati* – e.g. *C.I.L.* VI.1761, 1783, 32037; XII.1542; XIV.2165; *A.E.* 1928.80. It is far from clear whether there were still senatorial quaestors at this date who were nominated by the emperor, which is what the latter term really means (see Wesner 1936, cols 801-27; Millar 1977, pp.303-4), or whether this is an abuse of the term, meaning simply 'imperial quaestors' or 'quaestors of the emperor'. See also Harries 1988 on the development of the position of the quaestor in the fourth century.

40. Sid. Ap., *Ep.* III.7.

41. Sid. Ap., *Ep.* V.16.

42. Harries 1988, pp.155-6, discusses other, fourth-century, examples of the use of quaestors as ambassadors.

43. Patricius, Sym., *Ep.* VII.60; Petrus, Sid. Ap., *Ep.* IX.13 and *Carm.* V.564-7.

44. Cl. Lepidis, *C.I.L.* XII.1524; Zenobius, Augustine, *Ep.* CXVII.

45. John, the usurper of *c.* 423, *Chronicle of 452* 92, p.658; Agroecius, *L.H.* II.9.

46. Harries 1988 discusses the mainly fourth-century evidence for lesser officials.

47. *Not. Dig., Occ.* XVI and XVII.

48. A.H.M. Jones 1964, p.575.

49. Teitler 1985, pp.19-20, 54-7.

50. *C.I.L.* VI.1749.

51. Sid. Ap., *Ep.* I.3; on *uicarii*, see Chapter 5, below.

52. Sid. Ap., *Carm.* XXIII.210-16.

53. *Conl. Carth. 411 passim.*

54. Nampius and Rufinianus, scribes, *Conl. Carth. 411*, I.1, p.53.

55. Oros. VII.42.

56. Sinnigen 1959a, pp.240-1; see also Teitler 1985, p.36, and A.H.M. Jones 1964, pp.127, 572-3.

57. *Coll. Auell.* 15.

58. Hydatius, 177, p.29.

59. *Coll. Auell.* 14 and 16.

60. Sid. Ap., *Ep.* VII.11 (10).

61. Augustine, *Ep.* CCIIII.
62. Prosper, 1292, p.471.
63. Constantius, *Uita Germani*, III.15: 'uir tribuniciae potestatis.'
64. Salway 1981, pp.466-7.
65. *Not. Dig., Occ.* XI.
66. *C.Th.* I.10.7.
67. *C.Th.* VII.6.5.
68. *N.Th.* 17.2.
69. *C.Th.* XV.1.32; V.14.35.
70. *N.Ual.* 24.1.
71. *C.Th.* XII.8.1.
72. *C.Th.* VI.26.18.
73. *C.Th.* VI.30.16, 30.17.
74. *N.Ual.* 7.1, 7.2.
75. *C.Th.* I.10.5.
76. A.H.M. Jones 1964, pp.428-9.
77. *Not. Dig., Occ.* XI lists *rationales summarum* in Africa; Britain; Dalmatia and Savia; The Gauls; Italy; Noricum mediterraneum and ripensis; Numidia; Pannonia I and II; Quinque prouinciae; Rome; Sardinia and Corsica; Sicily; The Spains; Valeria. *Praepositi thesaurorum* were also widely spread, being found in Aquileia, Arles, Augsburg, London, Lyons, Milan, Rheims, Rome, Sabaria, Salona, Sisak (nr Zagreb) and Trier. For a map of the known distribution of the officers of the *comes sacrarum largitionum* (and of the *comes rerum priuatarum*) see A.H.M. Jones 1964, Map III.
78. *C.Th.* I.5.12; see also I.5.13.
79. *C.Th.* I.5.13. The punishment was to be carried out by a *comes sacri aurarii* – was he the same as the *comes largitionum per Africam*, or was he a *praepositus thesauri*?
80. *C.Th.* XV.14.12.
81. *N.Ual.* 7.3.
82. Sid. Ap., *Ep.* I.7.
83. Cosenza 1905, p.87.
84. *C.Th.* X.2.1.
85. *C.Th.* V.15.20 (*a.* 366); V.16.29 (*a.* 399); V.16.30 (*a.* 405).
86. *N.Th.* 17.1; for other instances in which a *comes sacrarum largitionum* was involved with imperial lands, see *C.I.* XI.62.11, 71.4.
87. *C.Th.* V.16.31, 16.32.
88. *C.Th.* X.1.14.
89. *C.Th.* X.2.2., where the *comes rerum priuatarum*, Firminus, is mistakenly referred to as *comes sacrarum largitionum*, perhaps underlining the perceived similarity between these two positions, which will be discussed below.
90. *Not. Dig., Occ.* XII.
91. *C.Th.* VI.30.16.
92. *C.Th.* VI.30.24.
93. *C.Th.* I.11.1 (*a.* 399).
94. *C.Th.* I.5.13.
95. *N.Ual.* 7.1, 7.2.
96. *N.Th.* 17.2.
97. Millar 1977, pp.189-201, esp. at pp.199-200.
98. *C.Th.* XI.1.27.

99. *C.Th.* VII.13.20.
100. *C.Th.* XIII.11.14.
101. *C.Th.* X.3.7; XI.28.13.
102. *C.Th.* XVI.2.47, 5.64.
103. *C.Th.* VI.2.24; XIII.6.9, 11.15-17.
104. *N.Ual.* 6.3; *C.I.L.* VI.1725.
105. Cosenza 1905, p.4.
106. A.H.M. Jones 1964, pp.336, 339.
107. Arce 1986, p.65; Nesselhauf 1938, p.59; A.H.M. Jones 1964, pp.124-5, 609-10.
108. *C.Th.* VII.1.18.
109. *C.Th.* I.7.3; on the position of master of the soldiers, see below.
110. *C.Th.* VI.14.2.
111. *Not. Dig., Occ.* XXIV, XXVI, XXVII.
112. *C.Th.* XI.17.3.
113. Hydatius, 74, p.20.
114. Augustine, *Ep.* CCXX; Boniface has already been mentioned as *comes domesticorum*; he later became master of the soldiers – Prosper, 1310, pp.473-4.
115. Marcellinus, *s.a.* 413, p.71.
116. Oros. VII.42.10; *Chronicle of 452*, 75, p.654.
117. *Chronicle of 452*, 59, p.652.
118. Augustine, *De ciuitate Dei,* 21.4.
119. Hydatius, 155, p.27.
120. *C.Th.* IX.42.18.
121. *C.Th.* XVI.5.51 = 56.
122. The same questions concerning permanence are raised by the notice in *Not. Dig., Occ.* XI of a *comes Gildoniaci patrimonii,* almost certainly a temporary appointment; see Warmington 1954, p.62.
123. Sid. Ap., *Ep.* VII.2, dated to 471 in Loyen's edition.
124. E.g. Sánchez-Albornoz y Menduiña 1971, p.28; Ewig 1976a, pp.410-11; Wightman 1985, p.304; Anton 1986, p.8.
125. *Ep. Austr.* 23.
126. Declareuil 1910, pp.805-7.
127. Sid. Ap., *Ep.* V.18.
128. Declareuil 1910, pp.807-9.
129. Claude 1964, pp.5-6; Anton 1986, p.5, disagrees, but his arguments are inconclusive. Gregory of Tours' grandfather, Gregory, is described as 'comes' of Autun (*U.P.* VII.1), but is even more likely to have held such a position under the Burgundians.
130. Sánchez-Albornoz y Menduiña 1971, p.28, states that the *comites ciuitatum* at Trier, Marseilles and Autun 'Eran oficiales, miembros de la comitiva imperial, que por razonas militares tomaron el mundo de la *urbs* y del *territorium* de las ciudades, cuya defesa les estaba encomendada', and that they took over all the functions of the *curiae* and the civil magistracies: this is to read later evidence back into the fifth-century Empire, and is unconvincing. Even less convincing is C.E. Stevens' suggestion (Stevens 1933, p.52 n.1) that Sidonius Apollinaris was a 'comes ciuitatis Aruenorum'. The sole evidence for this is that Majorian is supposed to have referred to Sidonius as his *comes* while dining with him at Arles (Sid. Ap., *Ep.* I.11): there is absolutely no indication, however, that the word here means anything other than

'companion' in an informal sense – there is not even anything to suggest that Sidonius was a member of the imperial court.

131. Declareuil 1910, p.802.

132. Claude 1964 p.6, suggested that it was inherently unlikely that there was a permanent 'Roman' *comes ciuitatis* at Marseilles as he at that time thought that no such official was found in the city under Ostrogothic or Frankish rule. His argument is not, however, valid, for, as he himself later recognised (Claude 1966, p.280), there was an Ostrogothic *comes* at Marseilles at least for a time – *Uariae* III.4.

133. *Chronicle of 452*, 100, p.658.

134. *N.Ual.* 6.3.

135. Hydatius, 151, p.26; 217, p.33; see also *U.P.I.*, 96, which may use Hydatius as a source.

136. *Uita Aniani*, 3; Mathisen 1979, pp.614-17.

137. Hydatius, 197, p.31, and 201, pp.31-2.

138. Marcellinus, *s.a.* 408.1, p.69.

139. *C.I.L.* VI.1731 and 31913 (all one), dating to *c.* 405; see also *C.I.L.* VI.1188-90 and 3157 (all one), from *c.* 401.

140. *C.Th.* VII.22.12, 5.1, 13.18, 20.13.

141. *C.Th.* I.7.3; VII.1.18; also VII.20.12 (*a.* 400), where he is styled 'magister militum'.

142. *C.I.L.* XIII.10032.2.

143. Hydatius, 143, p.25, and Sid. Ap., *Ep.* VIII.6, refer to him as 'consul'; Hydatius, 125, p.24, as 'dux utriusque militum'; and Hydatius, 128, p.24, as 'magister utriusque militum'. There are other cases in which officials are described as 'comites' and it is impossible to tell what is meant: Bubuculus *C.Th.* XI.1.34; Gerontius, a *comes* of the usurper Constans, Prosper, 1243, p.466, and Oros. VII.42.4; Palladius, *N.Ual.* 13. In these cases there is no direct military involvement, and it is, therefore, more likely that the references are to court officials or 'companions' of the emperors concerned. Other cases show military involvement, but cannot be absolutely proved to refer to *comites rei militaris*: Aetius, Prosper, 1298, p.472, and Hydatius, 92, p.21; Alla, *Chronicle of 511*, 653, p.665; Censorius, Hydatius, 98, p.22 and 121, p.23; Fronto, Hydatius 155, p.27 and 170, p.28; Litorius, Prosper, 1234, p.465; Maximus, Marcellinus, *s.a.* 413, p.71, and Oros. VII.41.14; Ricimer, Hydatius, 176, p.29; Segisvult, Prosper, 1294, pp.471-2. See also Hydatius, 234, p.34, which refers to unnamed 'comites' accompanying Anthemius when Leo sent him to take up the western throne.

144. *Coll. Auell.* 30, 32; John Malalas, *Chronographia* bk XIII, p.350, where the word used is *komês*, a direct transcription of the Latin.

145. Oros. VII.42.

146. Prosper, 1243, p.466; Hydatius, 50, p.18.

147. *Not. Dig., Occ.* XXXII-XXXVI, XXXVIII.

148. A.H.M. Jones 1964, pp.44, 101; Nesselhauf 1938, p.59.

149. *C.Th.* XV.11.2.

150. *N.Ual.* 13.1.

151. *C.Th.* VII.1.18.

152. *C.Th.* VI.4.28.

153. *Chronicle of 511*, 649, p.664: Antimiolus a patre Anthemio imperatore cum Thorisario, Euerdingo et Hermiano com. [*sic*] stabuli directus est: quibus rex Euricus trans Rhodanum occurrit occisisque ducibus omnia uastauit.

154. Sprandel 1957, p.52 recognised this possibility, but did not follow through its implications for the fifth century, as that was not his purpose.

155. Prosper, 1294, pp.471-2: 'ducibus Mauortio et Gallione et Sanoece.'

156. Prosper, 1243, p.466: 'per Honorii duces Constantium et Ulphulam.'

157. Hydatius, 50, p.18: 'Honorii dux.'

158. Hydatius, 54, p.18.

159. Vict. Tun., *s.a.* 449, p.185; Cassiodorus, *Chronicle*, 1253, p.157.

160. *N.Ual.* 17.

161. Prosper, 1300, p.472.

162. Claudian, *Carmina minora* 50.

163. Prosper, 1364, pp.481-2; *Chronicle of 511*, 615, p.663; see also John Malalas, *Chronographia*, bk XIV, p.358, which describes Aetius as 'the first senator of the Romans' (*ho prôtos sunklêptikos Rhômês*) at the battle, and later, p.459, as 'patrician' (*patrikios*).

164. E.g. *Add. ad Prosp. Haun., ad a. 396 in margine*, p.299; Prosper, 1218, p.464, and 1240, p.466; *Chronicle of 452*, 67, p.654; Cassiodorus, *Chronicle*, 1185, p.155.

165. Prosper, 1218, p.464.

166. *Chronicle of 452*, 50, p.650; *Add. ad Prosp. Haun., ad a. 405 in margine*, p.299.

167. Constantius, *Uita Germani*, III.13, 17.

168. For a discussion of this, and of former interpretations of the text, see Evans 1965, pp.180-1.

169. See, in addition to the examples already given, Prosper, 1278, p.469, on Castinus; Hydatius, 116, p.23, and Cassiodorus, *Chronicle*, 1232, p.156, on Litorius; Hydatius, 125, p.24, which refers to Asterius as 'dux utriusque militiae'; and, on unnamed *duces*, Hydatius, 84, pp.20-1. Arce 1986, p.65, comes to the conclusion that, 'Los *comites* y los *duces* mandan las tropas fronterizas y provinciales en general', when discussing the fourth century, but because he does not deal with the fifth century he does not touch upon the specific usage of the word *dux* discussed here.

170. Hydatius, 77, p.20.

171. Hydatius, 134, p.24.

172. *Chronicle of 452*, 38, p.650.

173. Hydatius, 110, p.23.

174. For the Gothic expedition, see Hydatius, 218, p.33, where he is described as a master; cf. Marius *s.a.* 463, p.232, *G.C.* 22, and *U.M.* I.2, where he is not. Other references to Aegidius as master of the soldiers include *U.P.I.* 96, and *L.H.* II.11, 12; for other military campaigns before Aegidius' secession to the north of Gaul after Majorian's murder, see Hydatius, 218 and 228, p.33.

175. *Not. Dig., Occ.* V, VI; see also XLII, where it is clear that the *magister peditum* also controlled both the foreigners serving in the Roman army (*laeti*), and the fleets. For the Gallic master, see A.H.M. Jones 1964, pp.125, 191-2.

176. *C.Th.* I.7.3; see also Arce 1986, p.65.

177. *C.Th.* VII.20.12, 13.8; *N.Ual.* 6.1.

178. *C.Th.* VII.20.12, 18.17.

179. *C.Th.* VII.5.1.

180. *C.Th.* VII.22.12.

181. *C.Th.* II.23.1.

182. *C.Th.* VII.1.18.

183. *C.Th.* VII.4.34.

184. *C.Th.* I.7.3; see also *Not. Dig., Occ.* IV.

185. *N.Ual.* 9.

186. Hydatius, 197, p.31.

187. Sid. Ap., *Carm.* VII.375-8, 392-4, 399-402, 425-36, and 464-8.

188. Cosenza 1905, p.50, notes that in 413 civil jurisdiction was given to masters of the soldiers in judicial cases in which soldiers were involved: this still only really involves soldiers, however. The rescripts cited as evidence are *C.I.* III.13.6 and XII.36.18, both of which belong to the eastern Empire: even there, the powers were strictly limited – see *C.I.* I.46.2 and *C.Th.* II.1.9.

189. *N.Ual.* 17; *N.Mai.* 11.

190. Prosper, 1247, p.466.

191. Prosper, 1292, p.471.

192. Prosper, 1282, p.470: Castinus 'qui exercitui magister militum praeerat'.

193. Hydatius, 218, p.33, for the title *comes utriusque militiae*, and the later *U.P.I.* 96, for the title *magister militum*; on his later career, see *L.H.* II.11, 12; *L.H.F.* 7, 8; and Fred. III.11; See also Wightman 1985, pp.303-4.

194. *Fasti Uindob. Prior.*, p.304; *Auct. Prosp. Haun.*, *s.a.* 456.2; p.304; Vict. Tun., *s.a.* 456, p.186.

195. *Fasti Uindob. Prior.*, p.305; *Chronicle of 511*, 635, p.664.

196. *Fasti Uindob. Prior.*, p.305; Marcellinus, *s.a.* 465.2, p.88; Cassiodorus, *Chronicle*, 1280, p.158.

197. *Fasti Uindob. Prior.*, p.306.

198. Binding 1868, pp.54-6.

199. On Ricimer's kin, see Castritius 1972, pp.233-43. and idem 1984, pp.1-33.

200. On the importance of factionalism in the period up to *c.* 425, see Matthews 1975. Later in the century, factionalism may be illustrated by the charges of writing malicious verse levelled by Paeonius against Sidonius Apollinaris (Sid. Ap., *Ep.* I.11) and, in a different way, perhaps, by Anthemius' creation of Sidonius Apollinaris as city prefect – if Stroheker 1948, p.79, is right in seeing this as an attempt to buy the support (or create a faction in Rome) of Gallic aristocrats against Ricimer. The events surrounding Stilicho's ascendancy can also be seen in terms of faction politics rather than as a direct result of his holding the office of master of the soldiers: while it is usually argued that Stilicho tried to place the military firmly and irrevocably in the ascendant over civilian government (e.g. Sirago 1961, pp.43-72, and, implicitly, Demandt 1980, esp. at pp.623-33), it is possible that his bad reputation is due to hostile sources, and that Stilicho in fact never did anything other than what he genuinely believed to be in the best interests of the Empire, rather than of himself (Alan Cameron 1969, pp.247-80).

201. See *Auct. Haun. ordo post.*, pp.307-9; *Auct. Haun. ordo prior*, pp.309-11; *Fasti Uindob. Prior.*, pp.306-10; Anon. Val., VII.36, VIII.36; Ennodius, 80 (= *Op.* 3) *Uita Epiphanii*, 95-100. On *patricii*, see the next section of this Chapter.

202. On Odoacer, see *Fasti Uindob. Prior.*, p.308; *Auct. Haun. ordo prior*, p.309; Cassiodorus, *Chronicle*, 1301, p.158; Marcellinus, *s.a.* 475, p.91; Anon. Val., VII.36.7; Jordanes, *Getica*, 241.

203. Ensslin 1931b, p.497: '... in Verlauf des 5. Jahrh. im Westreich patricius schlechthin mit der obersten Reichsfeldherrn, dem erster magister utriusque praesentalis, geworden.'

204. Barnes 1975, pp.168-9; Demandt 1970, col. 631, where the position is well summarised: 'Der Patriciat ist keine *archê*, sodern eine *axia*, eine Würde';

see also Meyer 1969, p.7, and Mathisen 1986.

205. O'Flynn 1983, p.86.

206. Hydatius, 103, p.22. Marcellinus, *s.a.* 432.2, p.78, refers to Aetius as 'patricius' in relation to an earlier incident, the conflict between Aetius and Boniface; either Marcellinus, a later and eastern (though Latin) source, was mistakenly reading back Aetius' patriciate, or else, as Barnes 1975, p.157, suggests, he may have been using the term in an 'unofficial' sense, perhaps simply to mean 'aristocrat'.

207. Hydatius, 150, p.26; Prosper, 1364, pp.481-2; *Chronicle of 511*, 615, p.663.

208. Hydatius, 160, p.27; *Fasti Uindob. Post.*, p.303; Prosper, 1373, p.483; Cassiodorus, *Chronicle*, 1260, p.157; Vict. Tun., *s.a.* 454, p.155.

209. *N.Ual.* 19.

210. Prosper, 1375, pp.483-4; Marcellinus, *s.a.* 455.1, p.86; Vict. Tun., *s.a.* 455, p.186.

211. *Fasti Uindob. Prior.*, pp.305-6; Vict. Tun., *s.a.* 456, p.186, *s.a.* 473.6, p.188; *Chronicle of 511*, 635, p.664; Cassiodorus, *Chronicle*, 1278 and 1293, p.158; see also *N.Mai.* 11. Hydatius, 247, p.35, must be mistaken in believing that Ricimer was only made patrician *c.* 468, because *N.Mai.* 11 (of 459), an official document (likely to be correct), refers to him as 'patricius'. On the other hand, the later Vict. Tun., *s.a.* 456, p.186, is equally likely to be mistaken in believing that Ricimer was *patricius* at the time of the overthrow of Avitus – this is a parallel case to that of Marcellinus, *s.a.* 432.2, discussed in note 206 above.

212. *N.Ual.* 19.

213. *N.Ual.* 33.

214. *C.Th.* XV.14.14, addressed to Constantius.

215. *N.Ual.* 17, to Aetius, and *N.Mai.* 11, to Ricimer.

216. *N.Ual.* 21.1, 21.2, 22, 23, 25, 26, to Albinus; *N.Ual.* 31, 32, 34, 35, 36, and *N.Seu.* 1, to Firminus.

217. The masters of the soldiers who are also referred to as patricians are: Aetius; Anthemius; Boniface; Constantius; Felix; Ricimer; Segisvult. Masters of the soldiers not referred to in this way include Agrippinus; Arborius; Asterius; Avitus; Castinus; Majorian; Merobaudes; Nepotinaus; Sebastian; Stilicho; Valentius; Vincentius; Vitus. Patricians who are not known to have been masters of the soldiers or former masters of the soldiers are: Sidonius Apollinaris (otherwise city prefect); Ecdicius; Gundobad, King of the Burgundians; Hosius (also *comes*); Jovius – on the evidence of Zosimus V.47.1 (also praetorian prefect); Litorius, implicitly (also *comes* and *dux*); Marcellinus; Petronius Maximus (also *tribunus et notarius*, *comes sacrarum largitionum*, and city prefect); Messianus; Nepos; Opilio (also master of the offices and city prefect); Orestes; Remistus; Romanus; Severus (also city prefect).

218. This is shown by the following cases (the dates are the minimum period for which the title can have been held): Aetius, *c.* 434 – *c.* 454 (Hydatius, 103, p.22, and 160, p.27; Prosper, 1364, pp.481-82, 1373, p.483; Cassiodorus, *Chronicle*, 1260, p.157; Vict. Tun., *s.a.* 454, p.185; *Fasti Uindob. Post.*, p.303; *N.Ual.* 17, 33); Albinus, 446-8 (*N.Ual.* 21-3, 25, 26); Firminus, 451-63 (*N.Ual.* 31, 32, 34-6; *N.Seu.* 1); Messianus, *c.* 456 (*Fasti Uindob. Prior.*, p.304; *Auct. Prosp. Haun.*, *s.a.* 456, p.304); Remistus *c.* 456 (*Fasti Uindob. Prior.*, p.304; *Auct. Prosp. Haun.*, *s.a.* 456, p.304); Ricimer, *c.* 457-473 (Hydatius, 247, p.35;

Cassiodorus, *Chronicle*, 1278 and 1293, p.158; *Fasti Uindob. Prior.*, *s.a.* 457 and *s.a.* 461, p.305, and *s.a.* 472, p.306; *Chronicle of 511*, 635, p.664; Vict. Tun., *s.a.* 456, p.186, and *s.a.* 473.6, p.188; *N.Mai.* 11).

219. Prosper, 1300, p.472, and 1375, pp.483-4.

220. Sid. Ap., *Ep.* II.3.

221. Sid. Ap., *Ep.* V.16

222. Sid. Ap., *Ep.* V.16.

223. *Coll. Auell.* 30, cited in O'Flynn 1983, p.86.

224. *C.I.L.* VI.8406: 'Hic quiescit in pace Fl. Celerinus uir deuotus scriniarius inlustris patriciae sedis dep. D. IIII id. Nouemb. Qui uixit ann. xxxiii plm Dn Pl Ualentiniano VII et Auieno vcs'; see also Picotti 1928, pp.48-9.

225. Constantius, *Uita Germani*, VII.38

226. Mathisen 1986 has collected the evidence relating to the use of patricians as ambassadors.

227. Hydatius, 84, pp.20-1.

228. Sid. Ap., *Carm.* II.205-207:

hinc [Anthemius] reduci datur omnis honos, et utrique magister
militiae consulque micat, coniuncta potestas
patricii ...

229. Prosper, 1335, p.476.

230. Litorius is described as 'comes' (Prosper, 1324, p.475) and 'dux' (Hydatius, 116, p.23; Cassiodorus, *Chronicle*, 1232, p.156); Anthemius is described as 'magister utriusque militum' and 'consul' (Sid. Ap., *Carm.* II.205-7), and, elsewhere in the same text (lines 199-201), as 'comes'.

231. Mathisen 1986.

Introduction to Part II

1. For example, Cesa 1982, Barnish 1986 and Wolfram 1983.

2. Goffart 1980.

3. See Wolfram 1988, esp. pp.222-5, and the papers collected in Wolfram and Schwarcz 1988.

4. Durliat 1988.

Chapter 5

1. *C.I.L.* XII.1524, *c.* 409.

2. *C.I.L.* XIV.2165.

3. *A.E.* 1928.80.

4. *Comes rerum priuatarum*, *C.Th.* X.10.31; praetorian prefect, *C.Th.* XIII.6.10.

5. *Comes rerum priuatarum*, *C.Th.* XI.28.13; praetorian prefect, *C.Th.* VI.23.2. The years concerned are 422 and 423, the same as for Proculus, but the significance of this is unclear.

6. *Comes sacrarum largitionum*, *C.Th.* V.14.35 (*a.* 395); *magister officiorum*, *C.Th.* VI.26.11 (*a.* 397), VI.27.11 (*a.* 399); praetorian prefect, *C.Th.* I.10.6, VIII.2.5, XV.1.41, XI.7.16 (all *a.* 401); VII.13.21, 18.11, VI.27.13, VII.18.12-14 (all *a.* 403); VIII.5.65, VII.5.2, XVI.8.17, XIII.5.13 (all *a.* 404); XVI.2.35 (= *Sirm.* 2). II.8.24, XVI.6.4, 6.5, 5.37, XV.1.43, XI.20.3 (all *a.* 405); XV.14.13 (*a.* 413); VI.29.11, VII.4.33, 8.12 (all *a.* 414); *C.I.* XI.59.11 (*a.* 400).

7. In addition to the examples already cited of court officials becoming praetorian, or city, prefects, see also: Basilius, *comes sacrarum largitionum, c.* 383 (*C.Th.* IV.20.1, XII.1.101, XI.30.40), and city prefect, *a.* 395 (*C.Th.* VII.24.1, see also Sym., *Rel.* X.34); Bassus, *comes rerum priuatarum, c.* 425 (*C.Th.* XVI.2.46, 5.64), and praetorian prefect, *a.* 426 (*C.Th.* X.26.1, IV.10.3, XVI.7.7, 8.28) and *a.* 428 (*C.Th.* IV.6.7); Draucus, *comes primi ordinis*, vicar of Rome, and then city prefect (*C.I.L.* VI.1725); Eusebius, *comes sacrarum largitionum, a.* 395 (*C.Th.* XV.14.12, 1.32), then, later in 395, praetorian prefect (*C.Th.* I.15.14), and praetorian prefect still in 396 (*C.Th.* XIII.11.8, XIV.3.19, XIII.5.26); Felix, ?quaestor *a.* 396-397 (Sym., *Ep.* V.54), and city prefect *a.* 398 (*C.Th.* XVI.5.53, VI.2.21); Flavianus, who started as *consular* (governor) of Sicily, became vicar of Africa, then entered the court as quaestor in the eastern court of Theodosius II, before becoming praetorian prefect in Italy, Illyricum and Africa (*C.I.L.* VI.1783 – he also received *C.Th.* XI.1.36 and VI.23.3 [*a.* 431-432], and *C.I.* II.15.1 [*a.* 408], IV.61.13 [*a.* 431] as praetorian prefect; and *C.Th.* XIV.10.1, XIII.5.29, III.31.3, XI.30.61, XV.2.9 as city prefect [*a.* 400]); Florentinus, *comes sacrarum largitionum, a.* 385 (*C.Th.* I.10.3, XI.30.46, 36.30, V.17.3), and city prefect, *a.* 395-397 (*C.Th.* VI.2.26, VIII.18.7, 5.55, VII.21.3, XI.14.2, XIV.4.7, 2.3, VI.14.2, VIII.7.19, XII.1.153-6, VI.2.20, *C.I.* XI.17.2); Iohannes, *primicerius notariorum* (according to Zosimus, V.40), and Sozomen (*H.E.* IX.8.3, referring to *c.* 409), master of the offices, then, *a.* 412-413 and 422, praetorian prefect (*C.Th.* XI.28.7, XIII.11.13, III.8.3, II.8.26 = VIII.8.8 = XVI.8.20, I.2.12, II.19.6, VIII.17.14, VI.30.20, VIII.8.10, II.13.1, 28.1, 30.2, 31.2, 32.1, VIII.8.10, *C.I.* VI.23.19); Limenius, *comes sacrarum largitionum, a.* 401 (*C.Th.* I.10.7, 40.10), and then, according to Zosimus (V.32), praetorian prefect of Gaul, *a.* 408; Longinianus, *comes sacrarum largitionum, a.* 399 (*C.Th.* VI.30.17), city prefect, *a.* 399-400 (Sym., *Ep.* VII.96, 100, and *C.I.L.* VI.1188-1190+31257 [all one]), and praetorian prefect, *a.* 406 (*C.Th.* XIII.7.2, 11.11, VII.18.15); the future emperor, Petronius Maximus, was earlier *comes sacrarum remunerationum* (= *comes sacrarum largitionum*), and city prefect (see *C.I.L.* VI.1749 [*c.* 421], and *C.Th.* V.1.16 [*a.* 420]), and then praetorian prefect (*N.Ual.* 3, 4, 7.1, 1.2, 10); Namatianus, master of the offices, *a.* 412 (*C.Th.* VI.27.15, and his own *De reditu suo*, I.563-4), and then city prefect (Namatianus, *De reditu suo*, I.415-28); Namatianus' father was *comes sacrarum largitionum* and quaestor before becoming city prefect (Namatianus, *De reditu suo*, I.578-86), he then apparently 'retired' to become a governor in Tuscany and Umbria (ibid.); Rusticus, ex-master of the offices, and then 'praefectus' of Constantine III or Jovinus (*L.H.* II.9 – according to Zosimus [VI.13.1] he was praetorian prefect of Gaul *a.* 410); Theodorus – see next note; Trygetius, *comes rerum priuatarum, a.* 423 (*C.Th.* XI.20.4), and 'uir praefectus', *c.* 452 (Prosper, 1367, p.482); Volusianus, quaestor before *c.* 412 (Namatianus, *De reditu suo*, I.171-2), city prefect (ibid., I.415-28), and then praetorian prefect, *a.* 428-429 (*C.Th.* VII.13.22, I.10.8, XI.1.35, XII.6.32, *C.I.* I.14.4).

8. Flavius Manlius Theodorus was an advocate (perhaps in the office of the praetorian prefect), then provincial governor in Libya and, later, Macedonia; he then went to Rome, probably as *magister epistularum* under Gratian, and subsequently became *comes sacrarum largitionum*; finally, 'sic cum clara diu mentis documenta dedisses', he became praetorian prefect of Gaul – Claudian, *Panegyricus dictus Manlio Theodoro consuli*, lines 21-57.

9. *C.Th.* XI.14.2, XIII.5.38.

10. *C.Th.* XV.2.9.
11. *C.Th.* XV.1.48; *N.Mai.* 4.
12. *C.Th.* II.12.6, VII.12.3, VIII.8.7, VI.18.1.
13. *C.Th.* VII.21.3, VI.14.2, VIII.7.19, XII.1.153-6, XIV.1.6.
14. *C.Th.* VI.26.14, 24.7; *N.Ual.* 11.
15. *C.Th.* XIV.4.7, 2.3, 4.8, 2.4; *N.Ual.* 20.
16. *C.Th.* XIII.5.29, 5.38, III.31.1; *N.Ual.* 29.
17. *C.Th.* VII.13.15.
18. *C.Th.* XIV.10.3.
19. *C.Th.* XV.14.9, 14.11, XVI.5.53; *N.Ual.* 8.1, 8.2.
20. *C.Th.* XVI.5.40, 5.62.
21. *C.Th.* VIII.5.55.
22. *C.Th.* VII.24.1; VI.2.26, 2.20, 2.21.
23. *C.Th.* VIII.18.7, V.1.6, 1.7.
24. *C.Th.* XI.30.54, 30.61.
25. Sym., *Rel.* 18, 35.
26. Sym., *Rel.* 25, 26.
27. Sym., *Rel.* 17, 22, 27, 42.
28. Sym., *Rel.* 14, 29, 44.
29. Sym., *Rel.* 13, 15, 23, 30, 32, 36, 37, 40, 46.
30. Sym., *Rel.* 16.
31. Sym., *Rel.* 19, 21, 28, 31, 33, 38, 39, 41.
32. Sym., *Rel.* 5, 8, 11, 12, 24, 43, 45.
33. Sym., *Rel.* 6, 7.
34. Sid. Ap., *Ep.* I.10.
35. *C.I.L.* VI.9920.
36. *C.I.L.* VI.1659 and 1703, referring to Albinus, *c.* 414; *C.I.L.* VI.1663, referring to Audax, *post* 455; *C.I.L.* VI.1669 and 31993, referring to Auxentius, 415x450; *C.I.L.* VI.37114, plus 31419 and *A.E.* 1941.62, referring to Bellicus, 408x423; *C.I.L.* VI.1718, referring to Epiphanius, *c.* 412; *C.I.L.* VI.1662 and 31888, referring to Epitynancius, *c.* 450; *C.I.L.* VI.1763, referring to Lampadius, 425x450; *C.I.L.* VI.1188-1190 = 31257 (all one), referring to Longinianus, *c.* 401; *A.E.* 1948.98, referring to Paulus, n.d.; *C.I.L.* VI.1750, referring to Quadratianus, n.d.; *C.I.L.* VI.32091, 32092, 32188, 32189, referring to Severus, *c.* 470.
37. *N.Ual.* 5.1.
38. *C.Th., Gesta senatus,* 1.5; *N.Ual.* 1.3.
39. Chastagnol 1960, pp.70-1.
40. *N.Ual.* 13.1, *a.* 455.
41. For the loss of the province of Africa, *c.* 442, see Chapter 9, below.
42. *C.Th.* I.4.3. On the same subject, see *C.Th.* I.4.1, 4.2, dating from the reign of Constantine.
43. *C.Th.* I.6.11.
44. *C.I.L.* VI.1663, 1718, 37114; *A.E.* 1941.62.
45. See especially *Coll. Auell.* 14, 16, 29 and 32.
46. *Not. Dig., Occ.* IV.
47. *Coll. Auell.* 32.
48. *Coll. Auell.* 16.
48. Sym., *Rel.* 38; see A.H.M. Jones 1964, p.518, for a discussion of the case.
50. *Not. Dig., Occ.* IV lists one of each of the following: *praefecti annonae,* and *uigilum; comites formarum, riparum et aluei Tiberis et cloacarum,* and *portus;*

magister census; *tribuni fori suarii*, and *rerum nitentium*; *consularis aquarum*; *curatores operum maximorum, operum publicanorum, statuarum, horreorum Galbanorum*; *centenarius portus*.

51. See Chapter 14, below.

52. *C.Th.* I.12.7, 15.17, XI.7.15, XIV.5.6, 23.1; all date from 400, and it is these five which are jointly addressed to the *praefectus annonae* and the city prefect.

53. *C.Th.* XIV.3.21.

54. *C.Th.* XIII.5.38.

55. *C.Th.* XIII.9.5.

56. Sym., *Ep.* IX.29 (food), and III.36 (oil).

57. Sid. Ap., *Ep.* I.10.

58. See *Not. Dig., Occ.,* II and III.

59. A.H.M. Jones 1964, p.1134 n.27.

60. The full title occurs in Prosper, 1373, p.483, and Cassiodorus, *Chronicle,* 1260, p.157; Vict. Tun., *s.a.* 454, p.185, and *Fasti Uindob. Post.*, p.303, record that he was 'praefectus', the latter giving his name as 'Ueaetius'.

61. *C.Th.* VI.27.12.

62. *C.Th.* XV.1.37.

63. *C.Th.* XI.16.21, 16.22 (these two are the same as XVI.2.30), XVI.2.35 (= *Sirm.* 2), II.4.7, XVI.5.47, 2.40 (= *Sirm.* 11), 2.41 (= *Sirm.* 15).

64. *C.Th.* XVI.2.39 (= *Sirm.* 9), 5.45, IX.25.3, XVI.2.44 (= *Sirm.* 10), *N.Ual.* 3. See also *N.Ual.* 35, addressed to a 'praefectus praetorio et patricius'.

65. *C.Th.* V.18.1. See also *N.Ual.* 31, addressed to a 'praefectus praetorio et patricius'.

66. *C.Th.* II.1.11.

67. *C.Th.* VIII.4.25, XIV.7.2. See also *N.Ual.* 35, addressed to a 'praefectus praetorio et patricius', and *C.I.* III.23.1.

68. *C.Th.* VIII.5.53, 5.54, 5.59, 5.65.

69. *C.Th.* II.13.1, 28.1, 30.2, 31.1, 32.3, VIII.8.10.

70. *C.Th.* XII.1.146, III.1.8, IX.35.6, XII.1.161, XIV.1.15, IX.31.1, XII.1.170, 1.178, 1.147; *N.Ual.* 3; *N.Mai.* 7.

71. *C.Th.* VII.18.11-14.

72. *C.Th.* X.26.1.

73. *C.Th.* IV.10.3; See also *N.Ual.* 25, addressed to a 'praefectus praetorio et patricius'.

74. *C.Th.* X.3.5, XV.1.41, 1.43, IV.15.1, IX.42.23, X.10.29, 10.30. See also *C.I.* II.15.1.

75. *C.Th.* II.8.24, 8.25.

76. *C.Th.* II.19.6, VIII.17.4, IV.4.6, II.27.1; *N.Ual.* 14. See also *N.Ual.* 21.1, 21.2, 35.1, addressed to a 'praefectus praetorio et patricius'. See also *C.I.* VI.23.19.

77. *C.Th.* XII.1.157, 1.158, XVI.8.14, 8.16, 8.17, II.8.26, VIII.8.8, XVI.8.20, 8.24.

78. *C.Th.* XI.30.58, 30.55, II.7.3, IX.35.6, XII.1.161, IX.36.2, 39.13, 3.7, 37.4, V.18.1; *N.Ual.* 27. See also *N.Ual.* 26, 35.1, addressed to a 'praefectus praetorio et patricius', and *C.I.* III.13.5, I.54.6, 14.4.

79. *C.Th.* III.10.1, 8.3, 16.2, 5.12, 13.3; *N.Anth.* 1. See also *N.Ual.* 35.1, addressed to a 'praefectus praetorio et patricius', and *C.I.* V.4.20.

80. *C.Th.* IX.23.2.

81. *C.Th.* XII.1.140, VI.26.15, VIII.4.22, IX.26.4; *N.Ual.* 22. See also *C.I.* I.51.3, 51.5.

82. *C.Th.* XVI.6.4, 6.5, 5.37, 5.43 (= *Sirm.* 12), 10.19, 2.31, 5.46 (= *Sirm.* 14), 8.19, 5.52, 7.7, 8.28; *N.Ual*.18.

83. *C.Th.* VI.30.16, 30.20; *N.Ual.* 7.1.

84. *Sirm.* 16; *C.Th.* V.7.2.

85. *C.Th.* IX.2.5, 2.6.

86. *C.Th.* VII.8.6.

87. *C.Th.* VI.1.19, 26,16.

88. *C.Th.* VII.4.23.

89. *C.Th.* VII.19.1, IX.42.20, 42.21, VII.21.4, IX.40.20, 40.22, XV.14.13.

90. *C.Th.* VII.13.13, 13.21, 13.22.

91. *C.Th.* XV.3.4.

92. *C.Th.* I.15.14, XIV.15.4, XI.28.2, XIV.15.6, 23.1; XIII.5.34, XIV.3.22, 4.9, XII.6.33. See also *C.I.* IV.40.4.

93. *C.Th.* XIV.3.19, 3.20, 4.10.

94. *C.Th.* XIII.5.26, 5.28, 6.8, 5.31, 7.2, 5.34, 5.35, XI.28.8, XIII.6.10.

95. *C.Th.* XI.28.2, VIII.8.5, VI.4.27, XIII.11.7, 11.8, VII.4.22, VI.1.19, I.5.12, 15.17, XI.7.15, XIV.15.6, XI.7.16, 20.3, XIII.11.11, XI.28.4, 8.3, 16.23, 18.1, 28.7, XIII.11.13, XI.28.8, 5.2, VIII.8.9, I.10.8, XI.1.36, XII.6.32, XI.1.36; *N.Ual.* 1.1, 4, 1.2, 10, 13; *N.Mai.* 1. See also *C.I.* X.19.6, IV.2.16, 63.3, 61.13.

96. *C.Th.* XI.30.16, dated to 331.

97. See A.H.M. Jones 1964, p.473, and Cosenza 1905, pp.12-13, both citing *C.I.* I.26.2, dating from 235: 'Formam a praefecto praetorio datam et si generalis sit, minime legibus uel constitutionibus contrariam, si nihil postea ex auctoritate mea innouatum est, seruari aequum est.' On the civil jurisdiction of the praetorian prefects in the fourth century, see also Piganiol 1947, pp.325, 326. On the different types of law in the empire after the third century, see Wieacker 1964, pp.47-64.

98. Sid. Ap., *Carm.* VII.312-13.

99. A.H.M. Jones 1964, p.371.

100. A.H.M. Jones 1964, p.371; see also Boak and Dunlap 1924, pp.29-31.

101. *C.Th.* VI.7.1, dated to 372.

102. Constantius, *Uita Germani*, IV.24; see also *C.I.L.* XII.5494.

103. Prosper, 1285, p.470; *Chronicle of 452*, 97, p.658; he also features in Namatianus, *De reditu suo*, I.213-16, but without a title.

104. Sid. Ap., *Ep.* II.3.

105. *C.I.L.* XII.5336, recording a donation, most likely out of private wealth, for the rebuilding of a church at Narbonne, *c.* 460.

106. Sid. Ap., *Ep.* I.11; he spread malicious rumours about Sidonius Apollinaris.

107. *L.H.* II.9.

108. Sid. Ap., *Ep.* I.7, VII.12; *Carm.* XXIV.35.

109. Sid. Ap., *Carm.* VII.312-23.

110. *Ep. Arelat.* 8.

111. Mercator, col.392.

112. *C.I.* XI.48.13.

113. *C.Th.* IV.23.1, XII.19.1-3.

114. *C.Th.* VIII.5.61.

115. *C.Th.* VII.18.10.

116. *C.Th.* I.5.11, XI.1.26, I.15.15.

117. *C.Th.* XI.28.3.

118. *C.Th.* XII.1.171.

119. *Sirm.* 6.
120. *C.Th.* VII.14.1.
121. *C.Th.* XII.15.1, VII.8.6.
122. *C.Th.* XII.1.171; *Sirm.* 6.
123. For the *conuentus*, see *Ep. Arelat.* 8, and Sid. Ap, *Ep.* I.6. Chastagnol 1973, pp.29-33, suggests that it was established as early as *c.* 407, the date at which the seat of the prefect was moved from Trier to Arles, and that of the vicar of Gaul from Bordeaux to Arles.
124. Rusticus in *c.* 410 (Sid. Ap., *Ep.* V.9; *L.H.* II.9); Dardanus in 412-413 (*C.Th.* XII.1.171; *C.I.L.* XII.1524; Sid. Ap., *Ep.* V.9); Agricola in *c.* 418 (*Ep. Arelat.* 8; Mercator, col.392); Exuperantius in *c.* 424/425 (Prosper 1285, p.470; *Chronicle of 452*, 97, p.658); Ferreolus in *c.* 451 (Sid. Ap., *Ep.* I.7, II.9, VII.12, and *Carm.* XXIV.35); Valerianus in *c.* 455/456 (Sid. Ap., *Carm.* VIII, *Ep.* V.10); Magnus in 458/459 (Sid. Ap., *Carm.* XV.154-7); Arvandus in 464x469 (Sid. Ap., *Ep.* I.7); Felix in *c.* 469 (Sid. Ap. *Ep.* II.3); Polemius in 471/472 (Sid. Ap., *Ep.* IV.4); Aurelianus, *c.* 473 (see Stroheker 1948, p.150 no.48).
125. Stroheker 1948, p.48; Matthews 1975, p.333.
126. *Not. Dig., Occ.* XIX.
127. Sinnigen 1959b, pp.98-100.
128. *Coll. Auell.* 29 and 32.
129. *C.Th.* XIII.9.5.
130. *C.Th.* XI.1.25.
131. *C.I.L.* XIV.4720, *a.* 408x423; he is also mentioned on *C.I.L.* X.6425.
132. *C.Th.*, *Gesta senatus*.
133. *C.Th.* IX.30.5, XII.1.162, 6.26.
134. See *Not. Dig., Occ.* XX for the vicar of Africa, XXI for Spain, XXII for the seven provinces (Gaul), and XXIII for Britain.
135. *Not. Dig., Occ.* p.104.
136. *C.I.L.* VI.1715, referring to Cronius Eusebius.
137. Sid. Ap. *Ep.* I.3.
138. Namatianus, *De reditu suo,* I.500-1.
139. *C.I.L.* VI.1783.
140. *Not. Dig., Occ.* XII, XX, XXII and XXIII.
141. The subjects covered include: ceremonial dress (*C.Th.* I.15.16); the Church (*C.Th.* XVI.2.29, 2.34); illegitimacy (*C.Th.* IV.6.5); inheritance (*C.Th.* IV.21.1); office and other staff (*C.Th.* I.12.6, IX.26.3; see also *C.I.* I.51.4); pagans and heretics (*C.Th.* XVI.5.35, 10.15); taxation (*C.Th.* XI.1.30); title to property (*C.Th.* IV.22.5); traitors and their property (*C.Th.* VII.8.9). In addition, *C.Th.* I.15.15, 15.17, addressed to praetorian prefects, indicate that vicars were involved in the collection of taxes in the provinces.
142. See Cosenza 1905, pp.7-8; on the *comites*, see Chapter 3, above.
143. *C.Th.* VII.15.1.
144. Hydatius, 74, p.20.
145. *Conl. Carth. 411,* I.1 p.53.
146. *C.I.L.* VIII.23878, 25377 and 25837, all relating to the fifth century.
147. The topics covered include: the Church (*C.Th.* XVI.2.38, 2.46); the *cursus publicus*, or public postal service (*C.Th.* VIII.5.64, VI.29.9); decurions and those in imperial service (*C.Th.* XI.30.53, XII.1.141-5, XI.1.24, XII.1.149, XIII.5.25, XII.5.3, VIII.4.23, XII.6.31, 1.174, 1.176, 1.185, 1.186); grants of land (*C.Th.* X.9.3, 10.27, 10.28); imperial property and estates (*C.Th.* X.1.16, XI.7.21); the officials of the proconsul (*C.Th.* XI.26.2); pagans and heretics

(*C.Th.* XVI.10.17, 10.18, 11.1, 11.2, 5.39, 5.41, 5.44, 5.54, 5.55, 5.63); the rank of those in imperial service (*C.Th.* VI.28.7); ships and shipping (*C.Th.* XIII.5.30); taxation (*C.Th.* XI.8.2, XIII.1.18, VIII.10.3, XI.1.28, XII.6.27, XI.17.2, XII.6.28, XI.5.1, XIII.1.18, XVI.2.36, XII.6.29, XIII.1.19, XI.28.6, 1.32, 7.19, 7.20, VIII.10.4, XI.1.34); traitors (*C.Th.* VII.8.7, IX.40.19, 38.12); trials and appeals (*C.Th.* IX.39.3, XI.30.60, I.12.8, XI.30.62, 30.65).

148. Sym., *Ep.* IX.14.

149. *C.I.L.* VIII.25377 and 25837.

150. Augustine, *Ep.* XCVII, C, CXXXIII, CLI; *Conl. Carth. 411,* I.1, p.53. The existence of an office staff is attested by *Not. Dig., Occ.* XVIII.

151. *Not. Dig., Occ.* XLIII-XLV.

152. *C.I.L.* VI.1738, XII.1524.

153. Claudian, *In Eutropium*, I.196-209.

154. *C.Th.* XI.30.59.

155. *C.Th.* XIV.7.1.

156. *N.Mai.* 9.

157. *C.Th.* IV.22.4.

158. *C.Th.* XIII.1.17.

159. *C.Th.* I.10.8.

160. *C.Th.* VII.10.1.

161. See Chapter 3, above.

162. Sinnigen 1957, pp.83-4; A.H.M. Jones 1964, pp.602-3.

163. Sym., *Ep.* II.71.

164. *C.Th.* VI.24.8: 'domestici ... qui nobis, ut indicio nominis apparet, familiarius militarent.'

165. *C.I.L.* VIII.2272 and p.950; XI.1731.

166. *C.I.* I.51.3.

167. *C.Th.* I.51.4.

168. *C.Th.* I.34.3.

168. Boak and Dunlap 1924, p.102, discusses the changing role of *domestici*.

170. For comments on the poverty of evidence for northern Gaul, see Wood 1987, pp.256-7.

171. Gildas, *De excidio,* 15-20.

172. E.A. Thompson's interpretation of the position of the Sueves as non-federates is here followed – see Thompson 1982, pp.152-5.

173. Oros. VII.40.6.

174. Hydatius, 141-2, p.25.

175. Hydatius, 201, pp.31-2.

176. Hydatius, 246, p.35; *H.S.* 90.

177. *Chron. Caesaraug., s.a.* 506, p.222.

178. Felix III, *Ep.* 5.

179. Sid. Ap., *Ep.* VIII.5; IX.12 may also have been sent to a Spaniard – see Thompson 1982, 3, citing Stevens 1933, p.65 n.1.

180. Thompson 1982, pp.172-4; on Majorian's expedition, see also Chapter 2, above.

181. Thompson 1982, pp.169-70.

182. Aegidius was made master of the soldiers by Majorian, *c.* 457 (*L.H.* II.11; he is also described as holding the office in *U.P.I.* 96, and Hydatius, 218, p.33); on the title of 'king' of the Franks, see *L.H.* II.12.

183. *L.H.* II.18, 27.

184. For a good summary discussion of Aegidius and Syagrius which is cautious concerning the extent and significance of their 'kingdom', see James 1988a, cf. James 1988b, pp.67-71; see also Wallace-Hadrill 1962, pp.159-60, where it is suggested that Syagrius may have seen himself as a 'Roman', but was also as independent of imperial authority as the federate Alaric I of the Visigoths.

185. *L.H.* II.18.

186. Namatianus, *De reditu suo,* I.213-16; for recent discussions of the incident, see Van Dam 1985, pp.41-2, and Wightman 1985, pp.301-2.

Chapter 6

1. Oros. VII.43.

2. Claude 1972, p.2.

3. Olympiodorus, frg. 24.

4. Olympiodorus, frg. 35, see Wolfram 1988, p.205.

5. Wolfram 1988, pp.204-5.

6. Sid. Ap., *Ep.* I.2.

7. Reydellet 1981, pp.74-7.

8. Staubach 1983, pp.12-15.

9. Dio Cassius, LXXVI.17.1-3; more generally, see Millar 1977, pp.208-10.

10. Ennodius, 80 (= *Op.* 3) *Uita Epiphanii,* 85ff. The 'Roman' nature of the description is so forceful that Cook 1942, p.142, suggests that Leo was in fact a quaestor.

11. *Uita Bibiani,* 4; Krusch, in his edition of the text, believed it to be an eighth- or ninth-century forgery, but Lot 1929 and Griffe 1964-1966, vol. 2 pp.70-1 have rehabilitated it.

12. *H.G.* 51.

13. Jahn 1874, vol. II p.213; Claude 1970, p.50; Wolfram 1988, p.205.

14. Wolfram 1988, pp.183, 233.

15. See Chastagnol 1973, p.35, citing *Ep. Arelat.* 8.

16. Collins 1983a, pp.27-30.

17. D'Ors 1960, pp.6-7, cf. his earlier work, D'Ors 1956, pp.393-97; see also Gibert 1968, p.14, though he cites no supporting evidence. As long ago as the 1930s, this possibility was hinted at, for Stevens 1933, pp.118-19, showed that Roman vulgar law and 'Germanic' law were very similar in at least some respects.

18. Collins 1983a, pp.27-30.

19. Wood 1986, pp.14-19.

20. Sánchez-Albornoz y Menduiña 1962, pp.146-60 esp. at p.151.

21. For *comites ciuitatum,* see *C.E.* 322, and for *saiones,* 311. The lack of evidence for *comites ciuitatum* in the 'Roman' areas is discussed in Chapter 3, above, while their existence in the early Burgundian kingdom is referred to in Chapter 7, below.

22. García-Gallo 1974, p.430, observed that the agreement of the Visigoths to accept federate status must have involved some acceptance of things Roman, one of which will have been elements of Roman law.

23. Gaudemet 1965, p.24.

24. *C.Th.* II.1.3 – *L.R.U.* II.1.3: 'qui etiam praesentiae nostrae [regis] dignitas comitantur'.

25. Wood 1980, p.175 and, more recently, Wood 1985, p.258; see also D'Ors 1956, p.403. Both Wood and D'Ors take issue with the more traditional

interpretation that the *L.R.U.* was produced in order to gain the co-operation of the Roman population against Clovis: for an expression of that view, see Bruck 1953, and, for a related interpretation, Wolfram 1988, pp.194-7.

26. See, for example, Hydatius, 97, p.22; 134, p.24; 170-81, pp.28-9; 186, p.30; 193, p.31; 197, p.31; 201, pp.31-2; 220, p.33; 230-3, p.33-4; 237-51, pp.34-5; See also *H.G.* and *H.S., passim.*

27. Hydatius, 77, p.20; 158, p.27.

28. Jordanes, *Getica,* 173.

29. Wolfram 1988, p.182.

30. *Chronicle of 511,* 615, p.663; Prosper, 1364, pp.481-2; *Add. ad Prosp. Haun., ad a. 451 in textu,* pp.301-2; see also Hydatius, 150, p.26.

31. Wolfram 1988, p.175.

32. Prosper, 1290, p.471; *Chronicle of 452,* 102, p.658; Hydatius, 92, p.21.

33. Prosper, 1324, p.475, 1333 and 1335, p.476, 1338, p.477; see also Hydatius, 110, p.23.

34. See, most conveniently, Stevens 1933, pp.130-60.

35. For Gothic expansion under Euric, see Stroheker 1937, and, for its significance, see Wolfram 1988, p.204. For the later expansion from Spain into Africa, see *H.G.,* 42; for the position of Tingitania in the Spanish diocese, see Arce 1986, pp.46-8, and, on the significance of dioceses to later political units in Europe more generally, see Piganiol 1947, p.321.

36. See Werner 1988, p.5, and Wolfram 1988, pp.180-1, for discussions of this event, and the references there.

37. Stevens 1933, pp.28-9, citing Sid. Ap., *Carm.* VII, the panegyric on Avitus; see also Hydatius, 163, p.27; the later Vict. Tun., *s.a.* 455, p.186, records that Avitus was made emperor in Gaul, but does not mention the part played by the Goths.

38. Mathisen 1979, pp.598-603; Wolfram 1988, p.175.

39. Musset 1975, p.127.

40. On Leo, see Sid. Ap., *Ep.* IV.22, VIII.3, and *Carm.* XXIII; on Namatius, see Sid. Ap., *Ep.* VIII.6; and on Vincentius, see Hilarus, *Ep.* XIV, and *Chronicle of 511,* 652-3, p.665. See also Thompson 1982, pp.174-6; Claude 1972, p.8; more generally, Stroheker 1948, *passim,* and Wolfram 1988, pp.232-4.

41. *L.H.* II.37. On the possible meanings of 'senator' in the writings of Gregory of Tours, see Stroheker 1948, pp.200-1; see also Stroheker 1965b.

42. Sid. Ap., *Ep.* VIII.6.

43. Sid. Ap., *Ep.* VII.17; *L.H.* II.20; *U.P.I.* III.1. The dates of his involvement with the area are likely to be *c.* 471 – *c.* 480 – see Wolfram 1988, p.451 n.28.

44. *L.H.* II.20; *U.P.* III.1; *G.C.* 32; *G.M.* 44; Sid. Ap., *Ep.* VII.17.

45. *Chronicle of 511,* 652-3, p.665.

46. Hilarus, *Ep.* XIV; see also the later *G.M.,* 44, where he is simply 'dux'.

47. Stroheker 1937, p.92, believed that the title of *dux prouinciae* implied civil as well as military jurisdiction, but did not cite any positive evidence for it.

48. *H.G.* 41.

49. Hydatius, 193, 197 and 201, pp.31-2.

50. *Chronicle of 511,* 651, p.664.

51. *Chron. Caesaraugust., a.* 511, p.223.

52. *L.R.U.* p.2.: 'In hoc corpore continentur leges siue species iuris de Theodosio et diuersis libris electae et, sicut praeceptum est, explanatae anno xxii regnante domino Alarico rege, ordinante uiro illustri Goarico comite. Commonitorium Timotheo, u.s. comiti.' Goar could be the same as the man

killed at Barcelona by Gesalic in *c.* 510 – see *Chron. Caesaraug., a.* 510, p.223 – though the latter is not accorded a title.

53. *C.E.* 322
54. Sánchez-Albornoz y Menduiña 1959, p.374; the distinction is presumably that *comes* refers to a rank, and *iudex* to a function.
55. Sid. Ap., *Ep.* I.2.
56. *Spatharii* in the fifth-century western imperial court, see Chapter 3, above.
57. *L.R.U., commonitorium* and *subscriptio*, pp.2-4.
58. See Chapter 3, above. Although Gallic *praepositi thesaurorum* were, according to *Not. Dig., Occ.* XI, situated at Trier, Rheims, Lyons and Arles, and not within the area initially settled by the Visigoths, there is no reason why they, as the nearest examples of imperial treasuries, should not have served as the model for the Visigothic kings who were, after all, in the provinces.
59. For a discussion of the period from 569 to 711, see Barnwell 1987, pp.189-227.

Chapter 7

1. *Chronicle of 452*, 118, p.660; see also Fred. II.46; Marius, *s.a.* 456, p.232; and the comments in Wood 1980, p.3.
2. Prosper, 1250, p.467; Cassiodorus, *Chronicle, s.a.* 413, p.155; for a discussion of the area of the settlement, see Jahn 1874, vol. I, p.329.
3. *Ep. Arelat.* 19 = Hilarus, *Ep.* IX.
4. Sid. Ap., *Ep.* VI.6; *U.P.I.* 93, 95.
5. *Fasti Uindob. Prior.*, p.306; it is possible that he was also a master of the soldiers, for John Malalas, *Chronographia,* bk XV, pp.374-5, describes him as 'stratêlatês'.
6. Avitus, *Ep.* 84.
7. *Uita s. abbatum Acaunensium,* 3; Avitus, *Ep.* 8.
8. See A.H.M. Jones 1964, pp.241-2.
9. *Fasti Uindob. Prior.*, p.306.
10. Cassiodorus, *Chronicle,* 1295, p.158; John of Antioch, frg. 209.9.
11. See Sid. Ap., *Ep.* V.6.
12. *U.P.I.* 92.
13. Jordanes, *Getica* 231-2; Hydatius, 173, 174, pp.28-9; see also Binding 1868, pp.54-7, and Jahn 1874, vol. I pp.419-23.
14. Jordanes, *Getica* 191.
15. For the Burgundian expansion and the connivance of Gallic aristocrats, see Marius, *s.a.* 456, p.232 and *Add. ad Prosp. Haun.,* p.305; for a clear exposition of the complex events, see Wood 1980, pp.3-4.
16. Wolfram 1988, p.183.
17. Sid Ap., *Ep.,* V.7: 'tetrarcha noster'.
18. Binding 1868, p.72, believed in the four-fold division between Gundioc's sons; this was questioned by Jahn 1874, vol. I pp.534-6, and, more recently, has been dismissed by Reydellet 1981, pp.92-3. For the suggestion that it may be Chilperic I, rather than Chilperic II to whom reference is made, if a division of the kingdom is not to be envisaged – see Saitta 1977, pp.47-8. On the lack of evidence that the Burgundian kingdom was ever split between the members of one generation of the Gibuching family, see Wood 1977, pp.21-2. The only evidence that there was ever more than one *rex* at a time concerns Sigismund,

who was made king at a time when his father, Gundobad, was still alive (see Marius, *s.a.* 516, p.234, and Fred. III.33). It is significant that this was a father-son relationship, as that is very different from a division of the kingdom between members of the same generation: Avitus, *Ep.* 77, describes Sigismund as 'caesar', perhaps indicating that he was 'ruler elect', as in the early fourth-century imperial tradition. Even in this case, though, there is no evidence to suggest that Gundobad relinquished control over part of the kingdom – see Wood 1977, pp.21-22 and Wood 1980, pp.212-13.

19. See *Oxford Latin Dictionary*, p.1934; from 40 BC Judaea was ruled by a pair of tetrarchs, Herod the Great and his brother Phasael – see Smallwood 1976, pp.50-1. It may be significant that Herod, usually described as tetrarch (Luke III.19, IX.7; Acts XIII.1) appears in Matthew II.1, 3 as king, while the same Gospel (XIV.1) later refers to him as tetrarch.

20. Avitus, *Ep.* 93: 'uester quidem est populus meus, et plus me seruire uobis quam illi praesse delectat'; 'patria noster uestra orbis est'; 'cumque gentem nostram uideamur regere, non aliud nos quam milites uestros credimus'.

21. Avitus *Ep.* 94: 'igitur post obitum deuotissimi fidelissimique uobis patris mei, proceris uestri, cui ad felicissimos integra prosperitate successus id quoque contigit diuino fauore uotiuum, ut laetam florentemque rempublicam uobis orbem regentibus sciret uosque dominos nationum placido receptus fine derelinqueret: ad haec intimanda uobisque commendanda quin etiam meae militiae rudimenta, quae genitore quidem meo superstite nutristis, sed magis magisque post eum cumulo sacrae dignationis augebitis, sicut debebam uel optare par fuerat, unum de consiliariis meis, qui, quantum ad ignorantiam Gallicanam, ceteros praeire litteris aestimatur, uenerandi comitatus uestri auribus offerebam, specialius securitate concepta, quod rector Italiae de pace uestra publice plauderet et rumore disperso redditam sibi orientis gratiam coloraret.'

22. Wood 1980, pp.8-9; Wood 1977, p.25.

23. Engel and Serrure 1964, pp.37-9; Jahn 1874, vol. I pp.161-2.

24. On the dating of the laws, see Wood 1980, pp.221-2.

25. Sid. Ap., *Ep.* V.5; see Wormald 1977, pp.125-6. There were many Gallo-Romans active in the Burgundian kingdom – see Stroheker 1948, pp.98-9.

26. Respectively, *Lib. const.* XLII.1 and 2; XLV; LXXVI; LXXIX.

27. *Lib. const.* LXII.

28. *Lib. const.* XLVII.1.

29. *Lib. const.* LI.1.

30. *Lib. const., prima constitutio* 10; see also *Lib. const.* L.1; LXXX.1.

31. *Lib. const., const extrau.* XX.

32. *Lib. const.* LII.1: 'specialis causa generalem teneat aequitatem.'

33. *Lib. const.* XLVIIII.1: 'Ad utilitatem et quietam constat omnium pertinere, ut de singulis quibusque causis generalis definitio proferatur, sicque fiat ut locorum comites atque praepositi competenter instructi euidentius iudicanda cognoscant.'

34. Wormald 1977, p.125, suggested that royal law had an 'ideological' purpose as much as a practical one, representing the aspirations of the rulers to have their will enforced, rather than the realities of their power. While it is certainly true that the making of law will have greatly enhanced the prestige of the king, and have given him a 'visible' function, Wormald carries the argument a stage further than I believe to be warranted.

35. *U.P.I.* 92; *U.P.* I.5.

36. Ennodius, 80 (= *Op.* 3) *Uita Epiphanii,* 136-73; *Uita Eptadii,* 11-13.

37. *Uita Bibiani,* 4.

38. Constantius, *Uita Germani,* VII.35.

39. Jahn 1874, vol. II, pp.476ff., 489-90.

40. *U.P.* I.5; Ennodius, 80 (= *Op.* 3) *Uita Epiphanii,* 174.

41. Fred. III.18.

42. Avitus, *Contra Arrianos,* XXX.

43. Blondel 1940b, esp. pp.72-4, 83-5.

44. Fred. III.33.

45. Blondel 1940a, pp.54-68.

46. Wood 1977, p.22.

47. *Lib. const.* LIII.1: '... postmodum cum obtimatibus populi nostri inpensimus de causas tractantur aduertimus ...'; see also *prima constitutio* 2. Other laws were made 'in conuentu' – *Lib. const., const. extrau.* XXI; see also *Lib. const.* LIII.1, LXXIV.1, and *const extrau.* XVIII.

48. *Lib. const., prima constitutio,* 2.

49. *Lib. const., prima constitutio,* 14.

50. *Lib. const.* LXXIX.4; *const. extrau.,* XIX and XXI.11.

51. *Lib. const., prima constitutio,* 13.

52. *Lib., const., const. extrau.,* XXI.14.

53. *U.P.* VII.1.

54. This was thought by Jahn 1874, vol. II pp.419-29, who tried to find *ciuitates* for all the *comites* who subscribed to the *prima constitutio.* See also Saitta 1977, pp.101-5, where it is suggested that *comites* were the normal governmental officers in the *pagi,* with some other type of *comes* set over them: this is unwarranted by the sources.

55. See *Lib. const., prima constitutio,* 5, and *Lib. const.* LII.

56. *Lib. const.* LXXVI, 'de wittiscalcis', refers to *wittiscalci* and *pueri nostri* interchangeably.

57. *Lib. const.* LXVI, XLVIII.4.

58. Drew 1949, p.57 n.2.

59. Skeat 1868, col. 273.

60. Skeat 1868, col. 273; Feist 1939, p.570.

61. *Lib. const.* LXXVI.

62. *Lib. const., prima constitutio,* 5.

63. *Lib. const., const. extrau.,* XXI.14.

64. Avitus, *Ep.* 38.

Chapter 8

1. See James 1988a, and Werner 1988.

2. Sid. Ap., *Ep.* V.210-54, cf. *L.H.* II.9; Wightman 1985, p.303.

3. Wightman 1985, p.303.

4. Werner 1984a, p.5.

5. James 1988b, p.75.

6. Wallace-Hadrill, 1962, pp.49-70.

7. Goffart 1988b, Chapter 3, esp. pp.152-74.

8. Van Dam 1985, pp.182, 194.

9. Goffart 1988b, Chapter 3, esp. pp.132-4.

10. See, for example, Wood 1985 and, most recently and fully, Goffart 1988b, Chapter 3.

11. Goffart 1988b, pp.138-40; see also Van Dam 1985, pp.183-4.

12. On Childeric, see Fred. III.11, and the comments in Wallace-Hadrill 1962, pp.161-2.

13. *L.H.* II.18, 19.

14. Syagrius: *L.H.* II.27, *L.H.F.* 9; Alemanni: *L.H.* II.30, *L.H.F.* 14, 15; the Burgundians: *L.H.* II.32, *L.H.F.* 16; the Visigoths: *L.H.* II.37; Ragnachar: *L.H.* II.43, *L.H.F.* 18.

15. Kings are in order of year of death, campaigns in chronological order for each king. Chlodomer: *L.H.* III.6, cf. *L.H.F.* 20. Theuderic I: *L.H.F.* 17; *L.H.* III.4, cf. *L.H.F.* 22; *L.H.* III.6, cf. *L.H.F.* 20; *L.H.* III.7, cf. *L.H.F.* 22; *L.H.* III.12, 13; *G.M.* 51; *U.I.* 13; *U.P.* V.2. Theudebert I: *L.H.* III.7, cf. *L.H.F.* 22; *L.H.* III.21, 22; *L.H.* III.32, cf. *L.H.F.* 26; *L.H.F.* 19; *L.H.* III.28, cf. *L.H.F.* 25. Childebert I: *L.H.* III.6, cf. *L.H.F.* 20; *L.H.* III.9, 11; *L.H.F.* 23; *L.H.* III.28; *L.H.* III.29, cf. *L.H.F.* 26; *L.H.* IV.17. Chlothar I: *L.H.* III.6, cf. *L.H.F.* 20; *L.H.* III.7, cf. *L.H.F.* 22; *L.H.* III.11; *L.H.* III.28, cf. *L.H.F.* 25; *L.H.* III.29, cf. *L.H.F.* 26; *L.H.* IV.10, cf. *L.H.F.* 27; *L.H.* IV.16; *L.H.* IV.20, cf. *L.H.F.* 28. Sigibert I: *L.H.* IV.23, cf. *L.H.F.* 30; *L.H.* IV.29, cf. Fort., Carm. VI.1a; Fred. III.71; *L.H.* IV.49, cf. *U.M.* 7; *L.H.* IV.50, cf. *L.H.F.* 32, and *L.H.* IV.51. Chilperic I: *L.H.* IV.23, cf. *L.H.F.* 30; *L.H.F.* 31; *L.H.* IV.45; Fred. III.71; *L.H.* IV.49, cf. *U.M.* 7; *L.H.* IV.50, 51, cf. *L.H.F.* 32; *L.H.* V.2, cf. *L.H.F.* 33; *L.H.* V.26. Guntram: Fred. III.71; *L.H.* V.17. Childebert II: *L.H.* V.17; *L.H.* VI.42, cf. *L.H.F.* 35.

16. Wallace-Hadrill 1962, pp.162-84; *idem* 1975, pp.96-103.

17. Werner 1984a, p.9.

18. *Ep. Austr.* 2.

19. James 1988b, p.65.

20. *Ep. Austr.* 1.

21. For this chronology, see Wood 1985, esp. pp.268-72.

22. Werner 1985, pp.31, 32.

23. The primary source for Childeric's tomb is Chifflet 1655, a book rendered all the more important by the loss, in the nineteenth century, of almost all the objects themselves. There have been many subsequent discussions of the burial and its significance, one of the best recent summary views being Kazanski and Périn 1988 (see esp. p.21). The most recent discoveries at Tournai (those of the 1983 excavations) are discussed in Brulet, Ghenne-Dubois and Coulon 1986, and Brulet, Coulon, Ghenne-Dubois and Vilvorder 1988.

24. *L.H.* II.38; see also Avitus, *Ep.* 38.

25. McCormick 1986, pp.335-7.

26. Wood 1985, pp.268-9.

27. Prou 1892, p.xxix; Fischer 1925, pp.550-1. The only other king known to have issued a gold coin – though without his own portrait – before 578 is Childebert II – see Prou 1892, p.xxxv.

28. Collins 1983b, pp.27-30.

29. *Ep. Austr.* 20; see Wallace-Hadrill 1962, pp.190-1, and Collins 1983b, pp.11-12.

30. *Ep. Austr.* 19, 20.

31. *Ep. Austr.* 18.

32. *Ep. Austr.* 29, 30, 31-9, 45-7 all used 'respublica'; 'imperium' only appears in 37 and 43. It is interesting that both terms are used in a letter from Emperor Maurice to Childebert (no.42).

33. See *Ep. Austr.* 19, 20.

34. *L.H.* V.17.

35. *L.H.* VIII.1.

36. For a full discussion of the elements of Roman *aduentus*, see MacCormack 1981, pp.15-89; for other Frankish manifestations of *aduentus*, see McCormick 1986, pp.332-3.

37. For a full and clear exposition of the practical relations between the Empire and the Franks, see Ewig 1983.

38. *L.H.* II.27.

39. *L.H.* III.5.

40. *L.H.* III.33.

41. *L.H.* VIII.6.

42. *L.H.* VIII.1.

43. See, for example, *L.H.* III.2; IV.14, 35.

44. Wallace-Hadrill 1955, p.441.

45. *Pactus legis Salicae*, shorter prologue, 2; *L.H.F.* 4.

46. For the latter, see Ashburner 1910 and Ashburner 1912.

47. E.g. *Pactus legis Salicae*, 39, 40, 45, 46, 50, 56, 57.

48. *Decretio Chlotharii primi, Cap. Mer.* pp.5-7; *Childeberti II decretio, Cap. Mer.* pp.15-17; *Chilperici edictus, Cap. Mer.* pp.8-10; *Guntchramni regis edictum, Cap. Mer.* pp.10-12.

49. *Chilperici edictus, Cap. Mer.*, 1; *Childeberti II decretio, Cap. Mer.*, 1-4, 8.

50. Werner 1979, p.143; Wormald 1976, p.224.

51. *Childeberti II decretio, Cap. Mer.* p.17; see also the proceedings of the 585 Council of Valence, *M.G.H. Concilia I*, pp.162-3.

52. *L.H.* IV.46.

53. *L.H.* IV.24; see also Riché 1965, p.7, and Wormald 1976, p.224.

54. E.g. *L.H.* IV.39, 43, 46; V.25; VI.10; VII.23; VIII.20; IX.10, 33.

55. The basic works on queens are Nelson 1978, Stafford 1983 and Merta 1988: much of what follows is indebted to them.

56. *L.H.* IV.26.

57. Nelson 1978, p.35; Stafford 1983, p.137.

58. Greg., *Reg.* VI.5; cf. *L.H.* VIII.22.

59. *L.H.* VIII.31.

60. The zenith of Brunhild's power probably came when she was regent for the young Childebert II – see Greg., *Reg.* VI.5, and *L.H.* VIII.22. – and for her grandchildren, Theudebert II and Theuderic II – see Nelson 1978, p.43; Stafford 1983, p.154.

61. *L.H.* V.46, cf. VI.1; later, in the 620s, Chlothar II's son, Charibert, was also in the care of a 'gubernator' – Fred. IV.55.

62. *L.H.* VI.1, VIII.22.

63. This is discussed further below.

64. For Gogo as adviser to Sigibert, see Fort., *Carm.* VII.1-4, esp. at VII.1.35-6; for his death, see Fred. III.59.

65. This at one stage happened to Chlothar II – *L.H.* VI.41.

66. *L.H.* VI.36.

67. E.g. Fredegund, wife of Chilperic I, persuaded her husband to murder another of his wives, the Visigothic princess Galswintha, and had Chilperic's son by Audovera, Clovis, murdered – *L.H.* IV.28, V.39.

68. John of Ephesus, *H.E.* III.7

69. *L.H.* VI.38.

70. Fort., *Carm.* V.3.11-15.
71. Fred. IV.19, 24.
72. *L.H.* V.48.
73. *L.H.* VI.32.
74. Procopius, *Secret History*, IV.4-6, 13-17, 20-1, 28-31, 37, 38, perhaps partly confirmed by Marcellinus, *Chronicle*, *s.a.* 545.3, p.107; see Cameron 1985, pp.161-2.
75. Constantius, *Uita Germani*, VII.35.
76. See, for example, *Chronicle of 452*, 109, p.658; Marcellinus, *s.a.* 432.2, p.78.
77. *L.H.* IV.26, VIII.4.
78. Under the terms of the Treaty of Andelot, Brunhild was given the tax revenue from Cahors – *L.H.* IX.20; Fredegund said that the treasure she added to Rigunth's dowry was private, not that received from taxes – *L.H.* VI.45 – though the precise significance of this is unclear, given that there appears to have been little distinction between 'private' and 'public' wealth – see Doehaerd 1949.
79. Brunhild, for example, 'held the kingdom' for Sigibert while he was on campaign – *L.H.* VI.4.
80. See Stafford 1983, p.106.
81. *L.H.* VII.15.
82. *L.H.* V.42.
83. *L.H.* VII.13, X.10.
84. *L.H.* VII.21, 22, 29.
85. *L.H.* VII.18.
86. *L.H.* IV.51.
87. *L.H.* IX.25; *Ep. Austr.* 25.
88. *Uita Eligii*, II.56.
89. *Uita Eligii*, II.20, 27.
90. See Chapter 13, below.
91. The origins of the office of *maior domus* have been much discussed, notably in Schöne 1856. Schöne (p.3) suggested that *maior domus* was a Latinised version of *siniscalc*, but it has subsequently been suggested that *maiores* may have been the heirs of Roman officials, probably either the *curae palatii* or the *praepositi sacri cubiculi* (Fustel de Coulanges 1930, p.169; Dill 1926, p.140), but the evidence of the *Uita Eligii* has not before been brought to bear on the subject, nor has that, discussed in Part III of this book, for the Ostrogothic kingdom: without this material the evidence is very slender, and led Tardif (1881, pp.53-4) to believe that the Frankish *maior* was a completely new creation.
92. Fort., *Carm.* IV.13.5-6
93. *L.H.* IX.30, cf. *U.M.* IV.6.
94. Fred. III.58.
95. Fred. III.59.
96. *Ep. Austr.* 48.
97. Fort., *Carm.* VII.1, and the same author's *Uita Germani ep. Par.*, 20.
98. *L.H.* IX.36.
99. *L.H.* VI.45, cf. VII.27, 43, where he is described as former *maior* of Rigunth.
100. *L.H.* X.2-4.
101. *Ep. Austr.* 43.

102. Fred. III.89; Cariatto signed the proceedings of the 585 councils of Valence and Mâcon as bishop of Geneva – see *M.G.H. Concilia I*, pp.163, 173.

103. *Ep. Austr.* 25.

104. Fort., *Uita Germani ep. Par.*, 60.

105. Fort., *Carm.* VII.16.23-32: the poem is entitiled 'De Condane domestico', but the specific titles are not always given in the text of the poem, and it is just conceivable that the passage cited does not refer to a period when Conda was a *domesticus*.

106. *L.H.* IX.39.

107. Such are the references to Flavian (*L.H.* IX.19, X.15), Gundulf (*U.P.* VIII.1), and Leonardus (*L.H.* VII.15).

108. Fred. IV.4; Gregory of Tours is, predictably, more concerned with the moral aspects of the torture and death of Mummolus than with his treasure, which is merely said to have been taken over – *L.H.* IV.35.

109. This was suggested over a century ago by Jules Tardif: 'Il est difficile d'indiquer d'une manière précise la nature de leurs fonctions et de faire connaître exactement l'étendue de leurs attributions; elles variaient sans doute au gré du prince et sous l'influence des circonstances' – Tardif 1881, p.59.

110. Ewig 1976a, p.412.

111. Barnwell 1987, pp.248-50.

112. *L.H.* IV.3, X.31, and *U.M.* I.1, respectively.

113. *U.M.* I.25.

114. See Barnwell 1987, p.243.

115. On the lack of western referendaries, see Chapter 3, above. For the situation in the east, see A.H.M. Jones 1964, p.575, and Bury 1910, pp.23-39; see also Procopius, *Secret History*, XIV.11.

116. Baudinus, referendary and *domesticus* of Chlothar I (*L.H.* IV.3, X.31), later became bishop of Tours (*L.H.* IV.3, cf. *U.M.* 1); Charimeris, referendary of Childebert II (*G.C.* 93) became bishop of Verdun (*L.H.* IX.23); Flavius, referendary of Guntram, became bishop of Chalon-sur-Saône (*L.H.* V.45, cf. X.28); Licerius, referendary of Guntram, became bishop of Arles (*L.H.* VIII.39, cf. IX.23); Ursicinus, referendary of Ultrogotha, became bishop of Cahors (*L.H.* V.42, cf. VI.38, VIII.20). In addition to these cases, the referendary Faramod (Fort., *Carm.* IX.12), was an unsuccessful candidate for the see of Paris (*L.H.* X.26); the referendary Theutharius (of Sigibert) became a priest (*L.H.* IX.33, cf. IX.43, X.16); and Bishop Desideratus of Bourges was almost certainly a referendary, though the title itself is not applied to him (*Uita Desid. ep. Biturc.*, 2).

117. *M.G.H., Concilia I*, pp.162-3.

118. *Childeberti II Decretio, Cap. Mer.* p.14.

119. *L.H.* X.19.

120. *L.H.* V.3, cf. *U.M.* III.17.

121. *Uita Desid. ep. Biturc.*, 2, referring to Desideratus himself; *Uita Mauri*, 50, referring to Ansebald.

122. *L.H.* V.28, 34; VI.28.

123. Fred. IV.4.

124. *L.H.* IV.26.

125. *L.H.* IV.45.

126. *L.H.* IV.7.

127. *L.H.* VII.4.

128. *L.H.* V.39.

129. *L.H.* V.48.

130. *L.H.* VII.39; he is not accorded any title there, but is described as 'comes stabuli' at V.39, and, rather later, as having formerly held the office – X.5.

131. *L.H.* V.39; later he was to act against Childebert II, son of Fredegund's rival, Brunhild – X.5.

132. Leudeghisclus was a military commander and *comes stabuli* – *L.H.* VII.37, cf. Fred. IV.2; he is later known as a *dux* (*L.H.* VIII.30), and a *patricius* (Fred. IV.5). On imperial *comites stabuli*, see Chapter 3, above.

133. Trudulf, *comes palatii*, led an army (*L.H.* IX.12), and Romulf assisted the *maior domus*, Florentianus, to compile tax lists for Childebert II at Poitiers (*L.H.* IX.30, cf. *U.M.* IV.6).

134. Barnwell 1987, pp.240-1.

135. Harries 1988, pp.154-5, discusses most of the evidence relevant to this.

136. *Uita s. Radegundis* II.16; *U.M.* I.40 also refers to Justin.

137. *L.H.* VI.19.

138. *L.H.* VII.12.

139. Fred. IV.6.

140. Fred. III.64. *L.H.* IV.40 also mentions the embassy, but does not accord Firminus a title – he came from Clermont, where he was later a regional *comes*, cf. *L.H.* IV.30.

141. *L.H.* VIII.18.

142. *L.H.* V.36.

143. *L.H.* IV.42.

144. *L.H.* VIII.6; Fort., *Carm.* X.19.

145. *L.H.* VII.38, 42.

146. *G.M.* 53.

147. *L.H.* VII.29.

148. *L.H.* IV.13, 30, 35, 39, VIII.18, X.6, 8; *G.C.* 34; *U.P.* IV.3.

149. *L.H.* VII.31.

150. *L.H.* IV.39, VI.37, 38.

151. *L.H.* VI.22, VIII.30.

152. *U.P.* VIII.3.

153. *L.H.* VIII.18.

154. *L.H.* VII.13.

155. *L.H.* V.24, X.15, 21.

156. *L.H.* VI.45, VIII.22.

157. *L.H.* V.14, 47, 49, VII.23, VIII.26, 38; *U.M.* I.24, II.58.

158. Kurth 1919a, pp.219-20.

159. *L.H.* IV.42; Kurth 1919a pp.220-1 drew attention to this strange case.

160. *L.H.* IV.39.

161. For example, Ennodius of Poiters was later a *dux* (*L.H.* V.24, VIII.26, IX.7, X.19), as was Nicetius of Clermont (*L.H.* VIII.18); Waddo, Rigunth's *maior domus*, was a former *comes* of Saintes (*L.H.* VI.45); Gundegisclus of Saintes (*L.H.* VIII.22, cf. IX.41, 43, X.15), Marachius of Angoulême (*L.H.* V.36), and Nicetius of Dax (*L.H.* VIII.20, cf., VII.31), all became bishops.

162. *L.H.* X.8.

163. E.g. Firminus of Clermont tried to influence an episcopal election (*L.H.* IV.35); Gaiso of Tours attempted to tax the property of St Martin, which had earlier been exempted in perpetuity (*L.H.* IX.30); Innocentius of Javols accused Abbot Lupicinus of St Privatus of treason, and executed him (*L.H.* VI.37); Leudast of Tours was responsible for many crimes during his tenure of

office (*L.H.* V.47); Ollo of Bourges tried to render monks liable for military service (*L.H.* VIII.42 with VII.38).

164. *L.H.* VII.23, IX.21.

165. *L.H.* X.15-17, 21; see also IX.39-43.

166. *L.H.* X.6.

167. *U.P.* VIII.3: Armentarius 'Lugdunensis urbem his diebus iudicaria gubernabat'.

168. Fort., *Carm.* X.19.

169. *L.H.* VI.8; *G.C.* 99.

170. On the synonymity of the two terms, see Fustel de Coulanges 1930, p.203 and, more recently, Murray 1986, who convincingly argues against the suggestion (made in Claude 1964) that in some parts of the *Regnum Francorum* the words had different meanings until the seventh century.

171. E.g. *Pactus legis Salicae* 32.5, 45.2, 50.3, 50.4, 51.1-3, 53.2, 53.4, 53.6, 53.8; *Chilperici I edictus, Cap. Mer.*, 8.

172. The fullest expression of this principle is to be found in *Chilperici I edictus*.

173. *Pactus Childeberti I et Chlotharii I, Cap. Mer*, 16; *Childeberti II decretio, Cap. Mer.*, 7; *Pactus legis Salicae*, 44.1, 46.1, 46.4, 60.1, where it appears that *thungius* was the Germanic word for *centenarius*. For a full discussion of *centenarii*, see Murray 1988.

174. Fort., *Uita Germani ep. par.*, 61, 66; *L.H.* VII.23; *U.M.* II.11; *G.C.* 40.

175. *L.H.* VII.23, X.5; *Guntchramni regis edictum, Cap. Mer.*, p.12.

176. Fustel de Coulanges 1930, pp.222-3.

177. E.g. *agentes* appear in *L.H.* VI.19, and *iudices* in *L.H.* VII.15, Fort, *Carm.*, VII.10 and *Guntchramni regis edictum, Cap Mer.*, p.11.

178. *L.H.* VII.29.

179. *L.H.* IV.30; for other examples of military involvement, see *L.H.* VII.13 and X.9, both relating to Willachar of Orleans.

180. Fort., *Carm.* X.19.

181. Sprandel 1957, p.52; on fifth-century *duces*, see Chapter 3, above.

182. Men who fall into this category include: Amingus (*H.L.* II.2); Audovald (*L.H.* X.3; *H.L.* III.31); Bladastes (*L.H.* VI.12, VII.34, cf. VI.31, VII.37, VIII.6); Bobo (*L.H.* V.39); Boso (Fred. III.89, IV.10; Jn Bicl. *s.a.* 589.2, p.218; cf. *L.H.* VII.38, Fred. IV.2.); Buccolenus (*Uita Ioh. abb. Reom.*, 15; Marius. *s.a.* 555.4, p.237); Calomnosius Aegyla (*L.H.* VIII.30, cf. Fred. IV.2); Chedinus (*L.H.* X.3; *H.L.* III.31; *Ep. Austr.* 40); Chramnichus (*H.L.* III.9); Desiderius (Fred. III.87; *L.H.* V.13, 39, VI.12, VII.10, 27, 34, VIII.27 – he is also recorded elsewhere, though without this title); Gararicus (*L.H.* VII.13, 25); Godigisil (*L.H.* IV.50, IX.12, *L.H.F.* 32); Guntrum Boso (*L.H.* V.4, 14, VIII.21; *L.H.F.* 32; he is also recorded elsewhere, though without this title); Helpingus (*U.P.* IV.2); Lanthacarius (Marius, *s.a.* 548.2, p.236); Leudeghisel (recorded as 'dux' in *L.H.* VII.40, VIII.20, 30); Leutharius (*H.L.* II.2); Mummolenus (*Uita Ioh. abb. Reom.*, 15); Eunius Mummolus (described as 'dux' in *L.H.* VI.24, VII.34); Olfigandus (*Ep. Austr.* 40); Olo (*L.H.* X.3; *H.L.* III.31); Rauching (*L.H.* VIII.26, cf. 29 – he is also recorded elsewhere, though without this title); Raudingus (*Ep. Austr.* 40); Roccolenus (Fred. III.74 – he is also recorded elsewhere, though without this title); Sigulf (Fred. III.69, 70 – he is also recorded elsewhere, though without this title); Wiolicus (Fred. III.68, cf. 56).

183. *L.H.* VII.37, 39 have no title; VII.40 and VIII.30 use the term *dux*; Fred. IV.2 says he was *comes stabuli*, and IV.5 reports his elevation to the patriciate.

184. *L.H.* VIII.30 describes him as 'dux', and Fred. IV.2 and 21 as 'patrician'.
185. *L.H.* IV.42.
186. *L.H.* VI.24, 26, VII.34; at V.13 Gregory uses *patricius*, and at VI.1, 26, VII.10, 38, 39, no title.
187. Marius, *s.a.* 581.2 p.239; Fred. III.67, 78, 85 (III.68 uses no title); *H.L.* III.4, 5, 8.
188. Beppolen, *L.H.* VIII.42 with V.29, X.9 and Fred, IV.12; Berulf and Ennodius, *L.H.* VIII.26; Lupus, *L.H.* VI.4, Fred. III.86; Wintrio, *L.H.* VIII.18, Fred. IV.14; Nicetius, *L.H.* VIII.18, cf. VIII.30. For other, similar cases, see *L.H.* VIII.18, 42; Fred. IV.8, 13, 43 (with *L.H.* V.14).
189. *L.H.* VIII.18; Fort., *Carm.* II.8.
190. *L.H.* VIII.26, IX.9; Fred. IV.8; Marius, *s.a.* 573.2, p.238; see also *L.H.* V.14.
191. See *L.H.* III.13; V.49 with VI.12, 31; VIII.30; X.9 with VIII.42, cf. V.29; *Ep. Austr.* 40 with Fred. IV.8; Fred. III.68 with Marius, *s.a.* 573.2, p.238, and Fred. IV.13; Fred. IV.14, cf. *L.H.* X.3 with VIII.18 and Fred. IV.18.
192. *L.H.* V.14 – Merovech subsequently escaped, and Herpo was fined and removed from office ('ab honorem').
193. *L.H.* VIII.31 with VIII.42.
194. *L.H.* IX.7.
195. *L.H.* X.19.
196. *L.H.* VI.19, 31, 45; X.3.
197. Kurth 1919c, p.188; Kurth 1919a, p.222.
198. Lewis 1976, pp.386-9.
199. *L.H.* VIII.43: '... Massiliensis Prouinciae uel reliquiam urbium, quae in illis partibus ad regnum ... pertinebat.'
200. *L.H.* IV.43; VI.7, 11; VIII.43. See also Fort., *Carm.* VII.11.
201. Bodegisilus is described in *L.H.* VIII.22 as 'dux', as he is also in Fort., *Carm.* VII.5, 6, in the former of which the word 'rector' is also applied to him.
202. *L.H.* VIII.12.
203. Aegyla, Fred. IV.2. Amatus, *H.L.* III.3, cf. *L.H.* IV.42. Jovinus, Fort., *Carm.* VII.11. Leudegisil, Fred. IV.5 (he was earlier a *comes stabuli* and is also described as a *dux* in a military context – see Fred. IV.2; *L.H.* VII.40, VIII.30). Eunius Mummolus, described as 'patrician' in *L.H.* IV.42, V.13; Fred., III.67, 75, 85; Marius, *s.a.* 581.2, p.239; *H.L.* III.4.
204. See Fred. IV.2 on Aegyla; *L.H.* IV.42, 45, and *H.L.* III.3 on Amatus; *L.H.* IV.42, V.13, VI.24, VII.10, 34, with Fred. III.67, 68, 75, 85, and Marius, *s.a.* 581.2, p.239, and the later *H.L.* III.4, 5, 8, on Eunius Mummulus.
205. Fort., *Carm.* VII.11: 'inluster et patricius et rector Prouinciae.'
206. *L.H.F.* 36; for other references to Gundovald, all as *dux*, see *L.H.* IV.47, V.1, and *L.H.F.* 32.
207. Greg., *Reg.* XI.43.

Chapter 9

1. Collins 1983a, pp.17-20 summarises the case for federate status, and Thompson 1982, pp.154-7 that against.
2. The modern study of Procopius and his writings is Averil Cameron 1985, of which Chapter 10 discusses the Vandal wars in particular.
3. Courtois 1954, pp.16-22.
4. Riché 1962, pp.76-78, 94-5.

5. Prosper, 1321, p.474: 'pax facta cum Uandalis data eis ad habitandum Africae portione [per Tingetium in loco Hippone III idus Fbr.].' This phrase is strikingly similar to the same author's comment on the Visigothic occupation of Aquitanica II as federates, *c*. 418: 'Constantius patricius pacem firmat cum Wallia data ei ad inhabitandum secunda Aquitanica et quibusdam ciuitatibus confinum prouinciarum,' Prosper, 1271, p.469.

6. Courtois 1955, pp.170-2; Musset 1975, p.57.

7. Prosper 1347, p.479; Courtois 1955, p.479.

8. *B.U.* I.4.13.

9. Clover 1971, p.53.

10. Humphrey 1980, pp.116-17.

11. *B.U.* I.4.3; Clover 1971, pp.52-4.

12. Loyen 1972, p.163.

13. Neither appears on the list of normal terms in Cesa 1984, pp.312-13.

14. Braund 1984, pp.9-17, 63-6.

15. See especially Marcellinus, *s.a.* 455, p.86; *B.U.* I.4.38-5.5.

16. Prosper, 1375, p.484; Hydatius, 107, p.28; Vict. Tun., *s.a.*455, p.186.

17. Merobaudes, Panegyric II.27-9; see Clover 1971 p.54, and pp.23-4 where he comments on Merobaudes, *Carm.* I, though Barnes 1974, pp.314-19 thinks the latter refers to Tibatto rather than to Huneric.

18. Hydatius, 216, p.32; Vict. Tun., *s.a.* 464, p.187; *B.U.* I.5.6. See also *Chron. Pasch., s.a.* 455, p.592, and John Malalas, *Chronographia*, bk XIV, p.368. On the date of the marriage, see Courtois 1955, pp.396-7.

19. Clover 1971, pp.25-6.

20. *B.U.* I.5.22-6.27. On the reasons for the war, and its course, see Courtois 1955, pp.200-5; See also Clover 1978.

21. Vict. Vit. II.39, III.14; Jordanes, *Getica*, 169.

22. Vict. Vit. II.39, III.14; on Remigius' letter, see Chapter 8, above.

23. Wroth 1911, pp.xv-xvii.

24. Wroth 1911, Geiseric nos 1-5; Thrasamund nos 1-9; of silver coins, Geiseric nos 6-9, Huneric nos 1 and 2, and Hilderic nos 1 and 2 are of the same type.

25. The bronze coins with the king's portrait are Wroth 1911, Huneric nos 12-14, Hilderic nos 9 and 10, Gelimer nos 4-6; Geiseric nos 10-13 depict a male figure which could conceivably be that of the king, but that is not certain. The silver coins are Gunthamund nos 1-8, Thrasamund nos 10-15, Hilderic nos 3-8 and Gelimer nos 1-3.

26. Vict. Vit. II.42; Fulgentius, *Ad Trasamundum* I.2.2.

27. *Synodus Carthaginensis*, col.636.

28. 'Uestra celsitudo' (Fulgentius, *Ad Trasamundum* I.1.1); 'benigna mansuetudo' (ibid. I.2.2); 'regalis prouidentia' (Vict. Vit. III.42); 'clementia nostra' (Vict. Vit. III.3), and 'pietas nostra' (Vict. Vit. III.12), the last two of which occur in one of Huneric's edicts.

29. Vict. Vit. II.8, cf. *B.U.* I.20.21, which shows that Gelimer also used a throne; on the lack of a royal throne in the Visigothic kingdoms before 568, see Chapter 6, above.

30. Courtois 1955, p.243. For further examples, see McCormick 1986, pp.261-6.

31. Vict. Vit. II.39, III.3-14.

32. Vismara 1972-1973, esp. pp.857, 863-4, 867-72.

33. Martroye 1911, pp.235-6.

34. Claude 1974, p.347.
35. Courtois, Leschi, Perrat and Saumagne 1952, p.97.
36. Humphrey 1980, p.86.
37. Wells 1984, pp.55-63.
38. *B.U.* II.14.37; *Anthol. Lat.* SB375 (= R380): 'basilica palatii sanctae Mariae.'
39. *B.U.* I.20.4, 20.9.
40. *B.U.* I.20.7.
41. *Anthol. Lat.* SB194 (= R203), cf. SB206 (= R215); on the location, see Rosenblum 1961, p.250.
42. *Maxula* (modern Radès): Vict. Vit. I.17. *Alicanae: Anthol. Lat.* SB371 (= R376); Vict. Vit. II.19ff. *Hermania: B.U.* I.14.10.
43. *B.U.* I.17.8-10.
44. Courtois 1955, p.250 n.6. One *stadium* is approximately 210 metres.
45. Bury 1958. vol. 2 pp.131-5.
46. The orthography was unstable at least until the late nineteenth century. In vol. 3 of *La grande Encyclopédie* (1886-1887), it is given as 'Faradise' (p. 313, *s.v.* Aphrodisium); but in Larousse 1878-1890, vol. 3 p.99, it is 'Faradès' (*s.v.* Faradès). Both these works underestimate the distance from Tunis to Firdaws, the former giving 48 km, and the latter 57 km: the correct distance is about 72 km, which compares favourably with Procopius' 73.5 km.
47. Ptolemy, *Geographia*, vol. I.2 p.621; Davis 1862, pp.339-40 (he calls the site 'Elfaradees').
48. Graham 1886, pp.10-11.
49. Graham 1886, pp.10-11; Davis 1862, pp.339-40.
50. It is suggested in Babelon, Cagnat and Reinach 1892-1913, where earlier references are conveniently gathered together.
51. Feist 1939, p.220.
52. I am grateful to Dr B.S.J. Isserlin for this information.
53. Despois 1955, pp.126-7 tentatively suggests the identification without giving detailed reasons; see also the map on p.116.
54. Vict. Vit. III.30, which well illustrates the circumstances in which Victor's work mentions royal officials: 'Quae cum regi innotuisset, comitem quendam cum iuracundia dirigens praecepit ut in medio foro, congregata illuc omni prouincia, linguas et manus dextras radicitus abscidisset.'
55. Vict. Vit. II.18.
56. According to Vict. Vit. I.19, Sebastianus was a *comes*, but this almost certainly refers to his former status in the imperial government, and not to a position in Geiseric's court. Fulgentius Ferrandus wrote a letter 'ad Reginum comitem' (*Ep.* VII), going on to refer to Reginus as a *dux*, but here again the reference is likely to be to a status held within the Empire (see Diesner 1968, col. 1207, and Diesner 1966, pp.174-5). It is, further, possible that in both these cases the word *comes* may mean 'companion in faith' – that they were fellow Catholics; in any case, African authors could use the term in a completely untechnical sense – Vict. Vit. I.46, cf. *Anthol. Lat.* SB3 (not in R), SB189 (= R198), 191 (= R200).
57. Vict. Vit. II.24.
58. Vict. Vit. I.19.
59. A state of some confusion has existed concerning Vandal *domestici* since Schmidt 1942, p.177, suggested that they were *fideles*, bound to the king by an oath. Schmidt may be correct, but there does not appear to be any firm

evidence concerning the matter. Courtois 1955, p.254, finds two cases to support Schmidt's contention: (a) Vict. Vit. I.19, the passage concerning Sebastianus' expected conversion; (b) Prosper, 1329, pp.475-6, concerning the arrival of four Spaniards (Arcadius, Paschasius, Probus and Eutycianus) in Africa. In Victor, the only mention of fidelity is in the sentence, ' "Sebastiane," inquit [Geisericus], "scio quia fideliter nobis adhaesisse iurasti" ': this clearly only refers to Sebastianus who, *pace* Diesner 1966, p.174, is not known to have been a *domesticus*, only being described as a *comes*. In Prosper, Geiseric made the four Spaniards swear fidelity, but there is no indication that they were *domestici*: the oaths demanded were probably concerned with the men's position as foreigners (and Romans) in the Vandal kingdom.

60. Vict. Vit. III.19.

61. *Anthol. Lat.* SB336 = (R341):
> Bella die noctuque suis fecit Eutychus armis,
>> diuitias cunctis e domibus rapiens,
> huic si forte aliquis nolit dare siue repugnet,
>> uim facit et clamat 'regis habenda' nimis.
> quid grauius hostis, fur aut latrunculus implet,
>> talia si dominus atque minister agit?

See also SB337 (= R342).

62. Vict. Vit. II.39.

63. Vict. Vit. I.45, 48; see Diesner 1967, p.349. Other great landowners also had *procuratores* (*Uita Fulgentii* 14).

64. Vict. Vit. III.33; Courtois 1955, p.252.

65. Vict. Vit. II.43-4; II.15 mentions a *praepositus regni*, but gives no hint as to his functions.

66. Gennadius, XCVII.

67. Heuberger 1929, p.89, suggested that the two positions were the same, but did not cite any supporting evidence: Schmidt 1942, p.176, dismissed the idea; for further supporting material from outside Africa, see Chapter 13, below, where the situation in the Ostrogothic kingdom is discussed. Courtois 1955, p.252, and Diesner 1967, p.349, see the Vandal *maiores* as being in charge of the royal estates and treasury, but there is no firm evidence for this.

68. *Anthol. Lat.* SB248 (= R254).

69. A.H.M. Jones 1964, pp.587, 590.

70. Vict. Vit. III.19.

71. Vict. Vit. II.3.

72. Vict. Vit. II.41-42: 'peto magnificentiam tuam ut ad domni et clementissimi regis aures memoratam suggestionem mecum preferre digneris.'

73. On the lack of referendaries in the western Empire, see Chapter 3, above; on eastern referendaries' functions, see Bury 1910. *Anthol. Lat.* SB375 (= R380), written in Africa, claims to have been composed by Peter, referendary, but cannot be taken to indicate the presence of referendaries in the Vandal kingdom, since the titles of the poems in the *Codex Salmasianus* are not original (Rosenblum 1961, pp.65-8); it is the only mention of referendaries in the Vandal area.

74. Vict. Vit. II.52-5.

75. *B.U.* I.4.33-41.

76. E.g., *L.R.U.*, p.2; *L.H.* X.19; *Gesta Dagoberti*, 39.

77. It has been suggested that Boniface was the same person as the *minister*,

Eutychus, who features in two of Luxorius' poems. The grounds for this are that 'Eutychus' is a Greek 'translation' of 'Boniface' (see Rosenblum 1961, p.219, followed by Diesner 1966, p.176) and, presumably, that both men were involved with royal finances. However, there is no evidence that Eutychus was a scribe, or that Boniface was *regularly* involved with the treasury. More damaging to Rosenblum's case, however, is that fact that the Greek name appears in the Latin source, and the Latin name in the Greek document, for there would have been little point in either Luxorius or Boniface translating the name *out of* the language in which he was writing: even if there was a reason for one of them doing so, it would be a rare coincidence for both to have found it necessary.

78. Courtois 1955, pp.253-4 recognised this, but still laid undue emphasis on the 'rudimentary' (i.e. un-'Roman') aspects of the Vandal administration.

79. Vict. Vit. I.15; *B.U.* I.5.11-13; *Uita Fulgentii*, I.

80. Courtois, Leschi, Perrat and Saumagne 1952, p.206 n.7, pp.13, 97.

81. *Uita Fulgentii*, I: Fulgentius' father fled, but his children returned and were given compensation for the loss of their land.

82. Vict. Vit. II.3.

83. Coronatus: *Anthol. Lat.* SB214, 218 and 220 (= R223, 226 and 228); Fl. Felix: *Anthol. Lat.* SB201-5 and 248 (= R210-14 and 254); Luxorius: *Anthol. Lat.* SB194 and 282-370 (= R203 and 287-375).

Chapter 10

1. Claude 1988b.

2. Bachrach 1967, esp. pp.482-3.

3. *B.U.* III.3.14-30.

4. Prosper, *Chronicle*, 1294, pp.471-2.

Chapter 11

1. Krautschick 1983, pp.41-9, 107-17; Goffart 1988b, p.28.

2. Momigliano 1955, p.217.

3. Wes 1967, pp.185-93; Momigliano 1956; Luiselli 1980; Krautschick 1983, pp.21-40.

4. Heather 1989.

5. O'Donnell 1982, pp.235-8.

6. Goffart 1988b, Chapter 2, provides the fullest discussion; see also Reydellet 1981, pp.262-3, Baldwin 1979, and O'Donnell 1982.

7. Goffart 1988b, Chapter 2; O'Donnell 1982 (esp. pp.224-5 for the last point).

8. Barnish 1983, pp.595-6; see also Chadwick 1981, p.63.

9. Averil Cameron 1985, esp. pp.205, 222.

10. Näff 1990.

11. *Ep. Theod.* 1-6.

12. Chastagnol 1966.

13. One document which has not been used is a list, of governmental officials, perhaps more familiar as of seventh-century date and Frankish provenance, but for which an Ostrogothic context has been suggested. The text, a summary of the conflicting views concerning it, and a fresh suggestion as to its origin are to be found in Barnwell 1991.

Chapter 12

1. *Auct. Haun. ordo prior.*, *s.a.* 476.2, p.309; *Auct Haun. ordo post.*, *s.a.* 476.1, p.309. For a discussion of the perception of Odoacer's accession by contemporaries, see Wes 1967, esp. at pp.62-3.

2. Cassiodorus, *Chronicle*, 1303, pp.158-9.

3. Anon. Val. X.45: 'Odoacer ... mox deposito Augustulo de imperio, factus est rex mansitque in regno annos XIII.'

4. Wes 1967; Momigliano 1973.

5. A.H.M. Jones 1962, pp.126-7.

6. *Ch.La.* XX.703; *Acta Synhod.* II, *a*. DII, 4.

7. Malchus, frg. 14.

8. McCormick 1977.

9. Kraus 1928, pp.46, 52-8; Wroth 1911 only notes one example of a silver coin with Odoacer's portrait (no.8, p.44), and observes on p.xxxii that even on that he is not depicted wearing a crown.

10. Anon. Val. XI.49.

11. Marcellinus, *s.a.* 481, p.92; *B.G.* I.1.9, II.6.16; Jordanes, *Romana*, 348; Ennodius, 263 (= *Op.* 1) *Panegyric* IV.16; see also the later *H.G.* 39.

12. Marcellinus, *s.a.* 483, p.92; Jordanes, *Romana*, 348.

13. See Chapter 7.

14. Anon. Val. XI.49.

15. Anon. Val. XI.53.

16. Anon. Val. XII.57.

17. Anon. Val. XII.57: 'Gothi sibi confirmauerunt Theodericum regem, non exspectantes iussionem noui principis.'

18. Wolfram 1988, pp.269-70.

19. Wolfram 1967, pp.49-50.

20. Jordanes, *Getica*, 295: '... Zenonemque imperatorem consultu priuatum abitum suaeque gentis uestitum seponens insigne regio amictu, quasi iam Gothorum Romanorumque regnator, adsumit ...'

21. Anon. Val. XII.64.

22. Kraus 1928, pp.82-99, lists all issues of Theoderic's reign; only two bronze types (nos 98 and 99) have no imperial models.

23. Kraus 1928, pp.110-24, describes the coinage of Athalaric; pp.141-8 that of Theodahad; pp.157-60 that of Witigis; pp.185-99 that of Totila; pp.205-9 that of Teia.

24. *Uariae* VIII.1, XII.1, 2.

25. Cassiodorus, *Chronicle*, 1362-3, pp.160-1; Anon. Val. XIV.80; see Ensslin 1947, pp.306-7.

26. *Uariae* VIII.1; Theoderic had also been the son at arms of the emperor (Zeno) at an earlier date – Jordanes, *Getica*, 289.

27. *Coll. Auell.* 114.

28. *Uariae* I.1: 'Regnum nostrum imitatio uestra est, forma boni propositi, unici exemplar imperii: qui quantum uos sequimur, tantum gentes alias antiemus'; see Reydellet 1981, p.209, and Staubach 1983, p.42.

29. *C.I.L.* X.6850-2: the text is given at note 40, below. See A.H.M. Jones 1962, p.128, Ensslin 1947, p.155, and McCormick 1986, pp.278-9.

30. Ward-Perkins 1984, pp.162, 164-5.

31. Besselaar 1945, p.69.

32. Ennodius, 263 (= *Op.* 1) *Panegyric*; see Reydellet 1981, pp.180-1, who

suggests that the Panegyric had a religious purpose, though not, of course, the same one as Gregory's *Decem libri historiarum*.

33. *B.G.* I.6.15-21.

34. *Uariae* X.31. As with much of Cassiodorus' work, the account is undoubtedly embellished for rhetorical effect, but it is likely to have a basis in truth.

35. Leuila was *magister militum c.* 491 (Anon. Val. XI.54); Tufa in *c.* 489 x *c.* 493 (Anon. Val. XI.51; *Fasti Uindob. Prior.*, p.320; *Auct. Prosp. Haun., s.a.* 493.2, p.321); Aemilianus, probably (Gelasius, *Ep.*, frg. 3, *c.* 492 x *c.* 496).

36. Tuluin was created *patricius praesentalis* during Athalaric's minority (*Uariae* VIII.9). The letter announcing his appointment to the Senate (*Uariae* VIII.10) lays stress on his military achievement, and another document in the *Uariae* (VIII.12) records that his appointment provided for the military affairs of the state. There is no real evidence to suggest that his position should be assimilated to that of a master of the soldiers. The patriciate in the Ostrogothic kingdom was, as in the fifth-century Empire, purely honorary (see Chapter 3, above; for the Gothic period, see *Uariae* VI.2, Cassiodorus' formula for the position, and I.3, 20; II.6, 14, 22; III.10; IV.30). In addition, Athalaric, as a minor, could not have been expected to lead armies himself. Finally, the addition of the word *praesentalis* to Tuluin's title may simply reflect that he was to be resident at court and act as regent for the king in matters in which Amalasuintha was unable to participate, rather than being connected with the old Roman title of *magister militum praesentalis*.

37. Wolfram 1988, p.321; Näff 1990, pp.108-11.

38. *Uariae* X.14.

39. *C.I.L.* X.6850-2, reading, 'd.n. gloriosissimus adque inclitus rex, uictor ac triumphator, semper Augustus, bono reipublicae natus, custos libertatis et propugnator Romani nominis, dominator gentium.'

40. *Uariae* IV.33: 'custodia legum ciuilitas est indicium.'

41. Esp. *Uariae* I.7; III.37, 46; IV.46, IX.20.

42. *Ep. Theod.* 7.

43. Ennodius, 444 (= *Ep.* IX.20).

44. Ennodius, 80 (= *Op.* 3) *Uita Epiphanii*, 95-100, 182-9; on Bibianus, see Chapter 6.

45. *B.G.* I.1.28; *Ep. Theod.* 6.

46. See Chapter 8.

47. In 1967, G. Vismara made a valiant attempt (Vismara 1967, developing ideas first expressed in Vismara 1956) to show that the Edict is the lost code of the Visigothic Theoderic II, but his arguments are not wholly convincing. If the Edict was Roman vulgar law, it could have been re-issued without prejudicing Procopius' claim (*B.G.* I.1.28) that Theoderic issued no laws of his own. The fact that some of the contents of the *Uariae* appear to contradict the Edict (pp.36-43) is not relevant, since praetorian law only remained in force as long as it was not contradicted by imperial law (see above, Chapters 5, 6). The fact that the Edict is not mentioned by any other source cannot be taken as proof that Theoderic did not issue it because, despite Vismara's belief to the contrary (pp.28-34), there is not enough source material of a kind to have reported it for the significance of the silence to be assessed properly: no source for sixth-century Gaul mentions the initial issuing of the *Pactus legis Salicae*, or its re-issuings, or the other surviving legal enactments. Equally unfounded is Vismara's argument (pp.80-3) that the Edict was written for an armed and

violent society and therefore cannot have applied to Italy which is known to have been peaceful. To come to this conclusion when making a comparison with the other kingdoms is to fail to take adequate account of the nature of the sources, and to be hoodwinked by Cassiodorus' propaganda (see Chapter 15, below), though even in Cassiodorus' writings there are examples of violence.

48. Wolfram 1988, p.289.
49. Ward-Perkins 1984, p.162.
50. Ibid., pp.159-62.
51. Ibid., pp.165-6.

Chapter 13

1. Jordanes, *Getica*, 304-5; *B.U.* I.14.5-6, II.5.18; *B.G.* I.2.3ff., I.4.4.
2. *Uariae* X.3, 4; *B.G.* I.4.8-10; Jordanes, *Getica*, 306.
3. *Ep. Theod.* 4.
4. *Ep. Theod.* 5.
5. *Uariae* X.21, 24.
6. Anon. Val. XIV.82.
7. Boethius, *C.P.* I.4.
8. *Acta Synhod.* II, *a.* DI, 7, 8, 20, cf. 14.
9. *Uariae* X.18.
10. *Acta Synhod.* II, *a.* DI, 7, 20.
11. *C.I.L.* XI.310.
12. *Uariae* VIII.10.
13. *Uariae* IV.51.
14. *Uariae* III.43.
15. Cassiodorus, *Orationum reliquae,* p.476, lines 10ff; Ensslin 1947, pp.174-5, comments on this.
16. Anon. Val. XI.53.
17. *C.I.L.* VI.32003.
18. *Uariae* VI.11, cf. II.15.
19. *Uariae* VIII.12.
20. A.H.M. Jones 1964, p.256.
21. *Uariae* VI.6.
22. *Ch.La.* XX.703.
23. Gelasius, *Ep.* 10.
24. A.H.M. Jones 1964, pp.254-5; Sinnigen 1965, pp.464-5; Zimmermann 1944, p.245.
25. *C.Th.* VIII.4.18.
26. E.g., *Uariae* VI.13; Bury 1910, p.27.
27. A.H.M. Jones 1964, p.255.
28. Skeat 1868, col. 193. Schade 1872-1882 is alone is suggesting a derivation from *saga*, 'to say', and in believing that *saio* referred to an official of a judicial court; this argument is implicitly rejected in Thompson 1969, pp.142-3.
29. *C.E.* 311; *L.U.* V.3.2. See Thompson 1969, pp.142-3.
30. Wolfram 1988, p.294. More generally, see Morosi 1981, esp. at p.163.
31. *Uariae* XII.3.
32. *Uariae* III.20.
33. *Uariae* IV.27; VII.42.
34. *Uariae* II.13; IV.39; VIII.27.

35. *Uariae* II.4; IV.14, 32, 34; IX.10.
36. *Uariae* I.24; III.48; V.23, 27.
37. *Uariae* V.19, 20.
38. *Uariae* II.20; V.10.
39. *Uariae* VI.5.
40. *Uariae* V.4; cf. VIII.13, 18 and X,6.
41. See the references in n. 40, above.
42. Ennodius 25 (= *Ep.* I.20).
43. Ennodius 137 (= *Ep.* IV.9).
44. Ennodius 90 (= *Ep.* III.20).
45. Ennodius 115 (= *Ep.* III.33).
46. Ennodius 121 (= *Ep.* IV.5).
47. Ennodius 150 (= *Ep.* IV.18).
48. Ennodius 91 (= *Ep.* III.21).
49. Ennodius 71 (= *Ep.* III.4).
50. Ennodius 80 (= *Op.* 3) *Uita Epiphanii*, 135.
51. Cook 1942, p.214.
52. *Uariae* VI.17.
53. *Uariae* VI.16.
54. *Ch.La.* XX.703.
55. Anon. Val. XIV.85; see also *Uariae* V.41.
56. *Uariae* VI.7; on the coinage see Hendy 1972, p.135.
57. *Uariae* III.8; see also the formulae concerning the tax, VII.20, 21. A.H.M. Jones 1964, p.254, and Thibault 1901-1902, pp.715-25, see this as a land tax; Zimmermann 1944, p.222, suggests that it was the tax from which the army was supplied with clothing, though does he does not produce enough evidence to substantiate the idea.
58. *Uariae* VIII.24.
59. *Uariae* I.2.
60. *Not. Dig., Occ.* XI.
61. *Uariae* VI.7, VII.32.
62. *Uariae* VI.8.
63. *Uariae* III.53.
64. *Uariae* IV.7.
65. *Uariae* IV.11.
66. *Uariae* IV.13.
67. *Uariae* VI.9.
68. *Uariae* VIII.23.
69. *Uariae* IX.3.
70. *Uariae* V.18.
71. *Uariae* XII.4.
72. *Uariae* I.16.
73. Ennodius 306 (= *Ep.* VII.1); for *c(h)artarii* as subordinates of the *comes patrimonii*, see *Uariae* VIII.23 and IX.3; cf. VII.43, and *Uita Caesarii*, 11.
74. *Uariae* V.7.
75. *Uariae* IX.9.
76. *Uariae* IX.13.
77. *Uariae* IV.15.
78. Mommsen 1910, pp.401-2; see also Ensslin 1947, p.171, and Zimmermann 1944, p.210. Wolfram 1988, p.193, suggests the reverse process – an Ostrogothic origin followed by imitation in the east: while not impossible, it

would form a virtually unique case. Mommsen's point, based on the evidence of the Donation of Pierus (*Ch.La.* XX.703), that under Odoacer the *comes rerum priuatarum/patrimonii* was known as *comes et uicedominus*, is unfounded: there is no evidence that even in the eastern Empire the shift away from the title of *comes rerum priuatarum* had begun by that time, and the *uicedominus* is more likely to have been a lesser official, perhaps the overseer of an individual estate or group of estates.

79. *Uariae*, preface 9.

80. Ennodius 18 (= *Ep.* I.23), 241 (= *Ep.* V.15).

81. *Uariae* IV.3, 7, 11, 13.

82. Fiebiger 1944, no. 8.

83. Burns 1980, pp.113-14.

84. This is a point which Burns does not follow up in his more recent work, Burns 1984.

85. Burns 1980, p.116.

86. *Uariae* II.7; *C.I.L.* XI.268.

87. *Uariae* IV.12, 22; cf. III.36, 45.

88. *Uariae* II.29, IV.9.

89. *Uariae* IV.5.

90. *Uariae* III.25.

91. *Uariae* IV.18, 28; V.35.

92. *Uariae* VIII.2, 5.

93. *Uariae* III.26.

94. See notes 8 and 10, above.

95. *Ep. Theod.* 2.

96. Gelasius, *Ep.* 24.

97. Naples, *Uariae* VI.23, 25; Ravenna, VII.14; Rome, VII.13; Syracuse, VI.22.

98. *Uariae* VII.16.

99. *Uariae* VII.1.

100. *Uariae* VI.23; VII.1; cf. VII.14.

101. *Uariae* IX.11, 14.

102. *Uariae* III.23, cf. 24.

103. *Uariae* VII.3: 'comites Gothorum per singulas ciuitatum.'

104. *Uariae* VII.26: 'comites (diuersarum) ciuitatum.'

105. For an alternative view, see Wolfram 1988, pp.290-1.

106. *Uariae* VI.22, VII.28.

107. *Uariae* VII.24, 25, 28.

108. *Uariae* V.14, IX.13.

109. Jordanes, *Getica*, 300.

110. *Uariae* I.40.

111. Mommsen 1910, p.441, believed Ostrogothic *comites prouinciarum* to be the successors of the Roman *comites rei militaris*, on the simple grounds that 'Comites rei militaris finde ich freilich in gothischen Quellen nicht, aber dafür *comes prouinciae*' (n. 6). Schmidt 1925, p.130, seemed to believe that the Gothic *comites* in the towns of Arles, Marseilles and Avignon were the equivalent of Roman *comites rei militaris*, though with civil jurisdiction added to their other functions. Ensslin 1947, p.198, suggested that Gothic *comites prouinciarum* were subordinate to a *comes rei militaris*, whose very existence is hypothetical. Wolfram 1988, p.213, sees Gothic *comites rei militaris* as the main military leaders in the field, ranking above the *duces* who only led local militias.

112. *Uariae* VII.4.
113. *Uariae* V.33.
114. *Uariae* I.11, V.30.
115. Jordanes, *Getica*, 302.
116. *Chron. Caesaraugust., s.a.* 510, p.223; cf. *H.G.* 38.
117. *Uariae* IV.17.
118. Jordanes, *Getica*, 308.
119. Jordanes, *Getica*, 311.
120. Marius, *s.a.* 509, p.234.

Chapter 14

1. The inscriptions are published in Chastagnol 1966.
2. Barnish 1988, pp.126-7.
3. Alan Cameron and Schauer 1982, esp. at pp.144-5, argue this point, which can be illustrated by the fact that eighteen city prefects are recorded whose tenure of office could have fallen in the period *c.* 476 – *c.* 490: unless it is assumed that there was a highly unusual number of years in which for some reason there was more than one prefect, some of the men must have held office rather earlier (or, just possibly, later).
4. Sinnigen 1963, p.159, but see Barnish 1988, pp.126-7 for a refinement of this.
5. See *Uariae* I.19, 21, 25, 27; II.35; IV.15, 20; V.14, 29, 35, 39; VIII.28, 30-3.
6. *Uariae* III.32, 41; see also IV.12, 19.
7. E.g. *Uariae* II.35 (Tancila); IV.20 (Geberic); V.29 (Neudis); VIII.28 (Cunigast). Ennodius 60 (= *Ep.* II.23) described Tancila as 'comes', though it could refer to a slightly earlier period.
8. Almost all the documents addressed to the Senate which are preserved in the *Uariae* are merely notifications of appointments, which it is unlikely that the Senate could realistically have done anything other than accept (*Uariae* I.4, 13, 30, 43, 44; II.3, 16; III.6, 12; IV.4, 16; V.4, 22; VIII.10, 14, 17, 19, 22; IX.23, 25). Virtually the only occasions on which the Senate as a body was asked to do anything are *Uariae* III.31, when it was asked to pay for the repair of public buildings in Rome, and IV.43, when it was commanded to investigate an arson attack on a synagogue – the latter is in fact a special commission of the normal kind, with the sole difference that the Senate was allowed to nominate the officials to carry it out rather than the king doing so.
9. A.H.M. Jones 1964, pp.329-30.
10. *Uariae* II.28.
11. Barnish 1988, pp.126-7.
12. Chastagnol 1966, pp.46-8, lists all the fifth-century officials and their titles. See also A.H.M. Jones, 1964, pp.528-30, on the eastern Empire, though it is not possible to say whether the precise decline in the *spectabiles* he describes was paralleled in the west. Even if the *spectabiles* were to be removed from the discussion, though, the problem would still remain for the Gothic *illustres*, Neudis (*Uariae* V.29) and Cunigast (*Uariae* VIII.28).
13. The formulae are *Uariae* VI.20, 21; VII.2. See also *Uariae* III.8, 52; IV.10, 49; V.8, 24.
14. For the details, see Chastagnol 1963.
15. *C.Th.* IV.22.4, XIV.7.1, XI.30.59; *N.Mai.* 9.
16. *Uariae* VI.12.

17. *Uariae* II.16, 26, 30, 38; IV.36, 38, 50; VIII.20.
18. *Uariae* III.7.
19. *Uariae* V.16, 17.
20. *Uariae* II.37; III.51.
21. *Uariae* V.23.
22. *Uariae* V.34, cf. IX.4.
23. *Uariae* III.20, 27.
24. Ennodius 80 (= *Op.* 3) *Uita Epiphanii*, 107.
25. *Acta Synhod.* III *a.* DII, 4.
26. Boethius, *C.P.* I.4.
27. *Uariae, praefatio chartarum praefecturae*, 4, 5.
28. Only *Uariae* XI.8, 9; XII.6, 9, really reflect this sphere of activity.
29. *Uariae* XI.7, 11, 12, 14-16; XII.2, 5, 7, 8, 10, 16, 20, 22, 23, 26, 28; see also X.26.
30. *Uariae* XI.5; XII.4, 11, 24, 27; see also X.27, 28. There are also a few special commissions – XII.18, 19.
31. See nn. 17-22, above.
32. The exceptions are *Uariae* VIII.20; IX.4.
33. *Uariae* VI.3; cf. preface, 6.
34. *C.Th.* VI.7.1.
35. Ennodius 48 (= *Ep.* II.13) states that the 'gubernacula reipublicae' was entrusted to the praetorian prefect, Olybrius. This does not constitute good evidence for the continued importance of the office after the early years of Theoderic's kingdom, since it relates to *c.* 503. In any case, it may be a reflection of Ennodius' rhetorical style, more than of reality.
36. *Uariae* XI.17.
37. *Uariae* XI.22, 33, 35; Morosi 1977, pp.118-19, attempts to put the offices into a rigid hierarchy.
38. *Uariae* XI.30.
39. *Uariae* XI.29.
40. *Uariae* XI.28
41. *Uariae* XI.18, 20, 21.
42. *Uariae* XI.25, 26.
43. *Uariae* XI.24.
44. *Uariae* XI.23.
45. *Uariae* XI.31, 32.
46. O'Donnell 1979, pp.64-5.
47. *Uariae* XI.27, 37, 39; XII.3, 12-14.
48. *Uariae* XII.1.
49. *Uariae* XI.36.
50. *Uariae* XI.27.
51. *Uariae* XI.6.
52. *Uariae* XII.3.
53. *Uariae* I.10; cf. XII.7, 8, 10, 23, 27.
54. *Uariae* XII.4.
55. *Uariae* IX.12.
56. *Uariae* II.12, 26; XII.17. A.H.M. Jones 1964, p.432, is uncertain whether they were subordinate to the praetorian prefects or to the *comites sacrarum largitionum*, but the evidence of Cassiodorus favours the latter, at least for the Ostrogothic period.
57. O'Donnell 1981.

58. Avitus, *Ep.* 35; Ennodius 457 (= *Ep.* IX.29).

59. *Uita Caesarii* II.10; that Liberius was a patrician is also attested by Anon. Val. XII.67, 68.

60. *Uariae* VIII.6; cf. VIII.7, 8.

61. Council of Orange, a. 529, *M.G.H. Concilia I*, pp.46, 53-4.

62. *Uariae* III.16, 17 concern his appointment as *uicarius*: the references cited in the following notes do not specifically record his office, but are unlikely to refer to another period in his career.

63. *Uariae* III.32; IV.19.

64. *Uariae* III.41.

65. *Uariae* III.18; IV.12.

66. For the Italian *uicarii*, see *Uariae* I.37, concerning a criminal case; II.24, concerning taxation; XII.19, concerning the preparations for a visit to Rome by Theodahad; and VI.15, the formula for the appointment of the *uicarius urbis Romae*. The references in Chastagnol 1963, p.354, most of which are uninformative about the functions of the *uicarius urbis Romae*, complete the evidence.

67. *Uariae* VI.4; Chastagnol 1960, pp.70-1, and, on the position of the city prefect as head of the Senate, Chastagnol 1966, p.54.

68. *Uariae* V.21, 22.

69. *Uariae* IV.25.

70. *Uariae* I.41.

71. *Uariae* IV.29, cf. IV.22.

72. *Uariae* I.30-32, 44; III.11; IV.42; IX.16, 17, 19.

73. *Uariae* I.6; II.34; III.29, 30; VII.15; X.30; see also *C.I.L.* VI.1716[6] = 32094[6].

74. E.g. *Uariae* II.34, III.29, III.30 and X.30, concerning public works; IV.42, X.17 and X.19 concerning law enforcement. Before *c.* 476, it is unlikely that the specific cases covered in those documents would have reached the imperial/royal court, since the city prefect would have had the power to take the initiative himself – see Chapter 5.

75. Ennodius 33 (= *Ep.* I.26).

76. Boethius, *C.P.* III.4.

77. *Uariae* VI.18 (the formula for the position), and XII.9, 11.

78. Fiebiger and Schmidt 1917, no. 190.

79. On the degree to which the Senate failed to support the Goths, see Moorhead 1983a.

80. *B.G.* III.21.12.

Chapter 15

1. *Uariae*, preface, 1, 3, 7.

2. Fridh 1956, pp.95, 174-83, 194.

3. *Uariae*, preface, 9; O'Donnell 1979, pp.76-85, believes the work to be propaganda for the reconciliation of Goths and Romans during the war with Justinian's forces.

4. *Uariae*, preface, 10.

5. *Uariae*, preface, 11.

6. Barnish 1984; Heather 1989.

7. Moorhead 1987, pp.164-8.

8. Besselaar 1945, p.45: 'Want het is zeer opvallend, dat tijdgenooten ons niets over den politicus Cassiodorus weten mede te deelen. Noch Procopius, noch de Anonymus Valesianus, noch Macellinus Comes of eenig ander kroniekschrijver, noch zelfs Ennodius of Boethius, vermelden het ooit of ergens. Zelfs Jordanes die zijn "Historia Gothica" geëxcerpeerd heeft, wijdt geen enkel woord aan de positie van Cassiodorus Senator te Ravenna. Al is een "argumentum ex silentio" vaak misleidend, toch kan man uit dit eenparige zwijgen met zekerheid aflieiden, dat hij voor het bewustzijn van zijn tijdgenooten geen leidende rol de politiek gespeeld heeft.'

9. Krautschick 1983, p.57, comes nearer than most commentators to a similar suggestion, but stops short of such a charge of wholesale fabrication.

10. Ward-Perkins 1984, p.69.

11. Wickham 1981, p.23, notes that the term occurs more than forty times in the *Uariae*; cf. Reydellet 1981, pp.221-31.

12. O'Donnell 1979, pp.76-85.

Conclusion

1. Wolfram 1988, pp.133-4, 222-4.
2. Durliat 1988.
3. Hendy 1988.
4. Braund 1988, p.6.
5. Wolfram 1967, p.44.
6. Harries 1988, p.149.
7. Namatianus, *De reditu suo,* I.139-40:

> Illud te reparat quod cetera regna resoluit,
> Ordo renascendi est crescere posse malis.

Bibliography

Primary sources

The following list includes selected editions of primary sources; translations are not generally cited.

Acta Synhodorum habitarum Romae, ed. T. Mommsen, *M.G.H.*, *A.A.* XII, Berlin 1894

Anecdoton Holderi, ed. T. Mommsen, *M.G.H.*, *A.A.* XII, Berlin 1894

L'Année épigraphique, 1888-

Anonymi Ualesiani pars posterior, ed. T. Mommsen, *M.G.H.*, *A.A.* IX, Berlin 1892

Anthologia Latina I: carmina in codicibus scripta, fasc. I, Libri Salmasiani aliorumque carmina, ed. D.R. Shackleton Bailey, Stuttgart 1982; see also the older edition by A. Riese, Leipzig 1894

Auctarii Hauniensis, Continuatio Hauniensis Prosperi, additamenta codicis Hauniensis, ed. T. Mommsen, *M.G.H.*, *A.A.* IX, Berlin 1892

Auctarii Hauniensis, Continuatio Hauniensis Prosperi, ordo posterior, ed. T. Mommsen, *M.G.H.*, *A.A.* IX, Berlin 1892

Auctarii Hauniensis, Continuatio Hauniensis Prosperi, ordo prior, ed. T. Mommsen, *M.G.H.*, *A.A.* IX, Berlin 1892

Augustine, *De ciuitate Dei*, ed. B. Dombart and A. Kalb, 2 vols Leipzig 1928-1929

Augustine, *Epistolae*, ed. A. Goldbacher, 5 vols Vienna 1895-1923 (*C.S.E.L.* 34.i; 34.ii; 44; 57; 58)

Auspicius (Bishop of Toul), *Epistolae*, in *P.L.* LXI, Paris 1861

Avitus of Vienne (Alcimus Ecdicius), *Dialogi cum Gundobado rege uel librorum contra Arrianos reliquiae*, ed. R. Peiper, *M.G.H.*, *A.A.* VI.ii, Berlin 1883

Avitus of Vienne (Alcimus Ecdicius), *Epistolae*, ed R. Peiper, *M.G.H.*, *A.A.* VI.ii, Berlin 1883

Boethius (Anicius Manlius Torquatus Severinus), *De consolatione philosophiae*, ed. L. Bieler, Turnholt 1957 (*C.C.S.L.* XCIV)

Capitularia Merowingica, ed. A. Boretius, *M.G.H.*, *Leges, sectio II tomus I*, Hanover 1883

Cassiodorus (Flavius Magnus Aurelius, *Senator*), *Orationum reliquiae*, ed. L. Traube, *M.G.H.*, *A.A.* XII, Berlin 1894

Cassiodorus (Flavius Magnus Aurelius, *Senator*), *Chronicle*, ed. T. Mommsen, *M.G.H.*, *A.A.* XI, Berlin 1894

Cassiodorus (Flavius Magnus Aurelius, *Senator*), *Uariarum libri XII*, ed. T. Mommsen, *M.G.H.*, *A.A.* XII, Berlin 1894; see also the edition by Å. Fridh, *Magni Aurelii Cassiodori Senatoris Opera, pars I: Uariarum libri XII*, Turnholt 1973 (*C.C.S.L.* XCVI)

Chartae Latinae Antiquiores, 1954-

A. Chastagnol, *Le Sénat romain sous le règne d'Odoacre: recherches sur l'épigraphie du Colisée au Vᵉ siècle*, Bonn 1966

Chronica rerum Uisigothorum, ed. K. Zeumer, *M.G.H., Leges, sectio I tomus I*, Hanover and Leipzig 1902

Chronicle of 452 (Chronica Gallica a. CCCCLII), ed. T. Mommsen, *M.G.H., A.A.* IX, Berlin 1892

Chronicle of 511 (Chronica Gallica a. DXI), ed. T. Mommsen, *M.G.H., A.A.* IX, Berlin 1892

Chronicon Paschale ad examplar Uaticanum recensuit L. Dindorf, 2 vols Bonn 1832 *(C.S.H.B.)*

Chronicorum Caesaraugustanorum reliquiae, ed. T. Mommsen, *M.G.H., A.A.* XI, Berlin 1894

Claudian (Claudius), *Carmina*, ed. T. Birt, *M.G.H., A.A.* X, Berlin 1892; see also the edition by J.B. Hall, *Claudianus Carmina*, Leizpig 1985. The works actually cited are: *Carmina minora, De bello Gothico, De consulatu Stilicho-nis, De IV consulatu Honorii, In Eutropium*, and *Panegyricus dictus Manlio Theodoro consuli*.

Codex Eurici, ed. K. Zeumer, *M.G.H., Leges, sectio I tomus I*, Hanover and Leipzig 1902; see also the edition by A. D'Ors, *El código de Eurico: edición, palingensia, indices*, Rome and Madrid 1960

Codex Iustinianus, ed. P. Kreuger, Berlin 1900

Codex Theodosianus, ed. T. Mommsen, *Theodosiani libri XVI cum consti-tutiones sirmondianes*, Berlin 1905; see also the translation by C. Pharr *et al.*, *The Theodosian Code and Novels and the Sirmondian constitutions*, Princeton 1952

Constantius, *Uita Germani episcopi Autissiodorensis*, ed. R. Borius, *Constance de Lyon, Vie de S. Germain d'Auxerre*, Paris 1965 (Sources chrétiennes 112)

Constitutiones sirmondianes, see under *Codex Theodosianus*

Corpus Inscriptionum Latinarum, Berlin 1863-

Dio Cassius, *Historia Romana*, ed. L. Dindorf and I. Melber, 3 vols Leipzig 1890-1928; see also the edition and translation in E. Cary, *Dio's Roman History*, 9 vols London 1914-1927 (Loeb)

Dracontius (Blosius Aemilius), *Romulea carmina*, ed. F. Vollmer, *M.G.H., A.A.* XIV, Berlin 1905

Dracontius (Blosius Aemilius), *Satisfactio*, ed. F. Vollmer, *M.G.H., A.A.* XIV, Berlin 1905

Edictum Theoderici regis, ed. F. Bluhme, *M.G.H., Leges (in folio)* V, Hanover 1875-1889

Ennodius (Magnus Felix), *Opera*, ed. F. Vogel, *M.G.H., A.A.* VII, Berlin 1885; see also the edition by G. Hartel, *Ennodius: omnia opera*, Vienna 1882 *(C.S.E.L.* 6), where the works are divided into *Ep(istolae), Op(uscula), Dictiones* and *Carmina*.

Epistolae Arelatenses Genuinae, ed. W. Gundlach, *M.G.H., Epistolae* III, Berlin 1892

Epistolae Austrasiacae, ed. W. Gundlach, *M.G.H., Epistolae* III, Berlin 1892; see also the edition by M. Rochais, Turnholt 1957 *(C.C.S.L.* CXVIIa)

Epistolae imperatorum pontificum aliorum inde ab a. CCCLXVII ad a. DLIII, Auellana quae dicitur collectio, ed. O. Guenther, 2 vols Vienna 1895 *(C.S.E.L.* 35.i; 35.ii)

Epistolae Theodericianae uariae, ed. T. Mommsen, *M.G.H., A.A.* XII, Berlin 1894

Eugipius, *Uita sancti Seuerini*, ed. H. Sauppe, *M.G.H., A.A.* I.ii, Berlin 1877

Eunapius, fragments, ed. R.C. Blockley, *The Fragmentary Classicising Historians of the Later Roman Empire*, 2 vols Liverpool 1981-1983

Farmer's Law, ed. W. Ashburner, in *Journal of Hellenic Studies*, XXX (1910), pp.85-108; see also Ashburner's translation in *J.H.S.* XXXII (1912), pp.68-95

Fasti Uindobonenses Posteriores, ed. T. Mommsen, *M.G.H., A.A.* IX, Berlin 1892

Fasti Uindobonenses Priores, ed. T. Mommsen, *M.G.H., A.A.* IX, Berlin 1892

Felix III, *Epistolae*, in Thiel

Ferrandus (Fulgentius), *Epistolae*, in *P.L.* LXVII, Paris 1865

Ferrandus (Fulgentius), *Uita sancti Fulgentii Ruspensis episcopi, Acta Sanctorum, Ianuarii I*, Brussels 1863

O. Fiebiger, *Inschriftensammlung zur Geschichte der Ostgermanen, neue Folge, Akademie der Wissenschaften in Wien, philosophisch-historische Klasse*, Denkschriften 70 Band 3, Vienna 1939

O. Fiebiger, *Inschriftensammlung zur Geschichte der Ostgermanen, zweite Folge, Akademie der Wissenschaften in Wien, philosophisch-historische Klasse*, Denkschriften 72 Band 2, Vienna 1944

O. Fiebiger and L. Schmidt, *Inschriftensammlung zur Geschichte der Ostgermanen, Kaiserliche Akademie der Wissenschaften in Wien, philosophisch-historische Klasse*, Denkschriften 60 Band 3, Vienna 1917

Fortunatus (Venantius Honorus Clementianus), *Carmina*, ed. F. Leo, *M.G.H., A.A.* IV.i, Berlin 1881

Fortunatus (Venantius Honorus Clementianus), *Uita Germani episcopi Parisiaci*, ed. B. Krusch, *M.G.H. S.R.M.* VII, Hanover and Leipzig, 1920

Fredegar, *Chronicle*, ed. B. Krusch, *M.G.H., S.R.M.* II, Hanover 1888; for Book IV and the Continuations, see also J.M. Wallace-Hadrill, *The Fourth Book of the Chronicle of Fredegar with its Continuations*, London 1960

Fulgentius (Bishop of Ruspe), *Ad Trasamundum libri III*, ed. J. Fraipont, *Fulgentii Ruspensis episcopi: opera*, 2 vols Turnholt 1968 (*C.C.S.L.* XCI, XCIa)

Galasius, *Epistolae*, in Thiel

Gennadius of Marseilles, *Liber de scriptoribus ecclesiasticis*, in *P.L.* LVIII, Paris 1862

Gesta conlationis Carthaginensis anno 411, ed. S. Lancel, Turnholt 1974 (*C.C.S.L.* CXLIXa)

Gesta Dagoberti I regis Francorum, ed. B. Krusch, *M.G.H., S.R.M.* II, Hanover 1888

Gildas, *De excidio et conquestu Britanniae ac flebili castigatione in reges principes et sacerdotes*, ed. T. Mommsen, *M.G.H., A.A.* XIII, Berlin 1898

Gregory of Tours, *Decem libri historiarum*, ed. B. Krusch and W. Arndt, *M.G.H., S.R.M.* I.i, Hanover 1937-1951

Gregory of Tours, *Liber de passione et uirtutibus sancti Iuliani martyris*, ed. B. Krusch, *M.G.H., S.R.M.* I, Hanover 1885

Gregory of Tours, *Liber in gloria confessorum*, ed. B. Krusch, *M.G.H., S.R.M.* I, Hanover 1885

Gregory of Tours, *Liber in gloria martyrum*, ed. B. Krusch, *M.G.H., S.R.M.* I, Hanover 1885

Gregory of Tours, *Liber Uitae Patrum*, ed. B. Krusch, *M.G.H., S.R.M.* I, Hanover 1885

Gregory of Tours, *Libri I-IV de uirtutibus sancti Martini episcopi*, ed. B. Krusch, *M.G.H., S.R.M.* I, Hanover 1885

Gregory the Great, *Dialogues*, ed. A. de Vogüé, 3 vols Paris 1978-1980 (Sources chrétiennes 251; 260; 265)

Gregory the Great, *Register epistolarum*, ed. P. Ewald and L.M. Hartmann, *M.G.H., Epistolae* I and II, Berlin 1891-1899

Hilarus, *Epistolae*, in Thiel

Hydatius of Lemica, *Chronicle*, ed. T. Mommsen, *M.G.H., A.A.* XI, Berlin 1894; see also the edition by A. Tranoy, *Hydace: Chronique*, 2 vols Paris 1974 (Sources chrétiennes 218; 219)

Isidore, *Chronica maiora*, ed. T. Mommsen, *M.G.H., A.A.* XI, Berlin 1894

Isidore, *Etymologiarum siue origines libri XX*, ed. W.M. Lindsey, 2 vols Oxford 1911

Isidore, *Historia Gothorum*, ed. T. Mommsen, *M.G.H., A.A.* XI, Berlin 1894

Isidore, *Historia Sueborum*, ed. T. Mommsen, *M.G.H., A.A.* XI, Berlin 1894

Isidore, *Historia Uandalorum*, ed. T. Mommsen, *M.G.H., A.A.* XI, Berlin 1894

John of Antioch, fragments, ed. C. Müller, *Fragmenta Historicarum Graecorum* IV, Paris 1851

John of Biclaro, *Chronica ad a. DLXVII-DXC*, ed. T. Mommsen, *M.G.H., A.A.* XI, Berlin 1894

John of Ephesus, *Historia ecclesiastica pars tertia*, ed. E.W. Brooks, 2 vols Paris 1935-1936 (*Corpus Scriptorum Christianorum Orientalium* CV; CVI)

Jordanes, *Getica*, ed. T. Mommsen, *M.G.H., A.A.* V.i, Berlin 1882

Jordanes, *Romana*, ed. T. Mommsen, *M.G.H., A.A.* V.i, Berlin 1882

Justinian, *Digest*, ed. T. Mommsen and P. Kreuger, with a translation by A. Watson, *The Digest of Justinian*, 4 vols Philadelphia 1985

Leo I, *Epistolae*, in *P.L.* LIV, Paris 1881

Lex Ribuaria, ed. F. Beyerle and R. Buchner, *M.G.H., Leges, sectio I tomus III.ii*, Hanover 1954

Lex Romana Burgundionum, ed. L.R. de Salis, *M.G.H., Leges, sectio I tomus II.i*, Hanover 1892

Lex Romana Uisigothorum, ed. G. Haenel, Berlin 1849

Liber constitutionum, ed. L.R. de Salis, *M.G.H., Leges, sectio I tomus II.i*, Hanover 1892

Liber Historiae Francorum, ed. B. Krusch, *M.G.H., S.R.M.* II, Hanover 1888

Liber iudicorum siue Lex Uisigothorum edita ab Reccesuindo rege a. 654 renouata ab Eruigio rege a. 681 accedunt ... leges nouellae et extrauagantes, ed. K. Zeumer, *M.G.H., Leges, sectio I tomus I*, Hanover and Leipzig 1902

Liber Pontificalis, ed. L. Duchesne, 3 vols Paris 1955-1957

Malalas (John), *Chronographia*, ed. L. Dindorf, Bonn 1831 (*C.S.H.B.*)

Malchus, fragments, ed. R.C. Blockley, *The Fragmentary Classicising Historians of the Later Roman Empire*, 2 vols Liverpool 1981-1893

Marcellinus (*comes*), *Chronicle*, ed. T. Mommsen, *M.G.H., A.A.* XI, Berlin 1894

G. Marini, *I papiri diplomatici raccolti ed illustrati dall'abate Gaetano Marini ...*, Rome 1805

Marius of Avenches, *Chronicle*, ed. T. Mommsen, *M.G.H., A.A.* XI, Berlin 1894

Mercator (Marius), *Monumenta ad haeresim Pelagianam spectantia*, in *P.L.* XLVIII, Paris 1892

Merobaudes, *Carmina*, ed. F. Vollmer, *M.G.H., A.A.* XIV, Berlin 1905

Merobaudes, *Panegyrics*, ed. F. Vollmer, *M.G.H., A.A.* XIV, Berlin 1905

Monumenta Germaniae Historica, Legum sectio III, Concilia tomus I:

Conciliae aeui Merouingici, ed. F. Maassen, Hanover 1883; for the councils which are cited, see also C. de Clerq, *Conciliae Gallicae a. 511 – a. 695*, Turnholt 1963 (*C.C.S.L.* CXLVIIIa)

Namatianus (Rutilius Claudius), *De reditu suo siue iter Gallicum*, ed. E. Doblhofer, 2 vols Heidelberg 1972-1977

Notitia Dignitatum, pars Occidentalis, ed. O. Seeck, *Notitia Dignitatum accedunt Notitia urbis Constantinopolitanae et Latercula prouinciarum*, 1876 repr. Frankfurt a.M. 1962

Notitia Galliarum, as *Notitia Dignitatum*

Notitia prouinciarum et ciuitatum Africae, ed. C. Halm, *M.G.H.*, *A.A.* III.i, Berlin 1879

Nouellae Anthemii, ed. P.M. Meyer, *Leges nouellae ad theodosianum pertinentes*, Berlin 1905; see also the translation by C. Pharr *et. al.*, *The Theodosian Code and Novels and the Sirmondian Constitutions*, Princeton 1952

Nouellae Maioriani, as *Nouellae Anthemii*

Nouellae Marciani, as *Nouellae Anthemii*

Nouellae Seueri, as *Nouellae Anthemii*

Nouellae Theodosii II, as *Nouellae Anthemii*

Nouellae Ualentiniani III, as *Nouellae Anthemii*

Olympiodorus, fragments, ed. R. C. Blockley, *The Fragmentary Classicising Historians of the Later Roman Empire*, 2 vols Liverpool 1981-1983

Orosius (Paul), *Historiarum aduersum paganos libri VII*, ed. C. Zangemeister, Leipzig 1889

Pactus Legis Salicae, ed. K.A. Eckhardt, *M.G.H.*, *Leges, sectio I tomus IV.i*, Hanover 1962

J. M. Pardessus, ed. *Diplomata, chartae, epistolae, leges ...*, 2 vols Paris 1843-1848 repr. 1969

Passio beatissimorum martyrum qui apud Carthaginem passi sunt sub rege Hunerico VII Nonas Iulias, ed. C. Halm, *M.G.H.*, *A.A.* III.i, Berlin 1879

Passio sancti Uincenti, ed. B. de Gaiffier, 'La Passion de S.-Vincent d'Agen', *Analecta Bollandiana* LXX (1952), pp.160-81

Paul the Deacon, *Historia Langobardorum*, ed. G. Waitz, *M.G.H.*, *Scriptores Rerum Germanicarum in usum scholarum separatim editi*, Hanover 1878

Paulinus of Pella, *Eucharisticos*, ed. W. Brandes, Vienna 1888 (*C.S.E.L.* 16)

Philostorgius, *Historia ecclesiastica*, ed. J. Bidez, *Philostorgius Kirchengeschichte*, Leipzig 1913

Priscus, fragments, ed. R.C. Blockley, *The Fragmentary Classicising Historians of the Later Roman Empire*, 2 vols Liverpool 1981-1983

Procopius, *De Bello Gothico*, ed. J. Haury, *Procopius, opera omnia*, 3 vols Leipzig 1905-1913

Procopius, *De Bello Persico*, as Procopius, *De Bello Gothico*

Procopius, *Be Bello Uandalico*, as Procopius, *De Bello Gothico*

Procopius, *Secret History*, as Procopius, *De Bello Gothico*

Prosper Tiro, *Chronicle*, ed. T. Mommsen, *M.G.H.*, *A.A.* IX, Berlin 1892

Ptolemy, *Geographia*, ed. C Müller and C.T. Fischer, 2 vols Paris 1901 (Books I-III only)

Salvian, *De gubernatione Dei libri VIII*, ed. C. Halm, *M.G.H.*, *A.A.* I.i, Berlin 1877

Sidonius Apollinaris (Gaius Sollius), *Carmina*, ed. A. Loyen, Paris 1960

Sidonius Apollinaris (Gaius Sollius), *Epistolae*, ed. A. Loyen, 2 vols Paris 1970

Sozomen, *Historia ecclesiastica*, ed. J. Bidez and G.C. Hansen, *Sozomenus Kirchengeschichte*, Berlin 1960

Symmachus (Quintus Aurelius), *Epistolae*, ed. O. Seeck, *M.G.H., A.A.* VI.i, Berlin 1883; the *Relationes* form Book X of this collection, for which see also R.H. Barrow, *Prefect and Emperor: the 'relationes' of Symmachus, A.D. 384*, Oxford 1973

Synodus Carthaginensis, A.D. 525, in G.D. Mansi, *Sacrorum conciliorum noua et amplissima collectio*, vol. 8, Florence 1762 repr. Berlin 1901

Tablettes Albertini, in C. Courtois, L. Leschi, C. Perrat and C. Saumagne, *Tablettes Albertini: actes privés de l'époque vandale (fin du Ve siècle)*, 2 vols Paris 1952

A. Thiel, *Epistolae Romanorum pontificorum genuinae et quae ad eos scriptae sunt a s. Hilaro usque ad Pelagium II*, vol. I, Brunswick 1867

J.-O. Tjäder, *Die nichtliterarischen lateinischen Papyri Italiens aus der Zeit 445-700*, 3 vols Lund and Stockholm 1954-1982

Victor of Tununna *Chronica a. CCCCXLIV-DLXVII*, ed. T. Mommsen, *M.G.H., A.A.* XI, Berlin 1894

Victor of Vita, *Historia persecutionis africanae prouinciae*, ed. C. Halm, *M.G.H., A.A.* III.i, Berlin 1879

Uita Aniani episcopi Aurelianensis, ed. B. Krusch, *M.G.H., S.R.M.* III, Hanover 1896

Uita Bibiani uel Uiuiani episcopi Santonensis, ed. B. Krusch, *M.G.H., S.R.M.* III, Hanover 1896

Uita Caesarii episcopi Arelatensis libri duo auctoribus Cypriano, Firmino, Ueuentio episcopis, Messiano presbytero, Stephano diacono, ed. B. Krusch, *M.G.H., S.R.M.* III, Hanover 1896

Uita Eligii episcopi Nouiomagensis, ed. B. Krusch, *M.G.H., S.R.M.* IV, Hanover and Leipzig 1902

Uita Eptadii presbyteri Ceruidunensis, ed. B. Krusch, *M.G.H., S.R.M.* III, Hanover 1896

Uita Iohannes abbatis Reomaensis auctore Iona, ed. B. Krusch, *M.G.H., S.R.M.* III, Hanover 1896

Uita Memorii presbyteri et martyris, ed. B. Krusch, *M.G.H., S.R.M.* III, Hanover 1896

Uita Patrum Iurensium, ed. F. Martine, *Vie des Pères de Jura*, Paris 1968 (Sources chrétiennes 142)

Uita sanctae Radegundis, ed. B. Krusch, *M.G.H., S.R.M.* II, Hanover 1888

Uita sancti Desiderati episcopi Biturcensim, Acta Sanctorum, Maii II, Paris and Rome 1866

Uita sancti Marcelli Diensis episcopi et confessoris, ed. F. Dolbeau, 'La Vie en prose de saint Marcel évêque de Die: histoire du texte et édition critique', *Francia*, 11 (1983), pp.97-130

Uita sancti Mauri abbati Glannafolensi in Gallia, Acta Sanctorum, Ianuarii II, Brussels 1863

Uita sanctorum abbatum Accaunensium, ed. B. Krusch, *M.G.H., S.R.M.* III, Hanover 1896

J. Vives, *Inscripciones cristianas de la España romana y visigoda*, Barcelona 1942

Zosimus, *Historia noua*, ed. L. Mendelssohn, Leipzig 1887; see also the edition by I. Bekker, Bonn 1837 (*C.S.H.B.*)

Secondary works

ANDERSSON, T.M., 1963. 'Cassiodorus and the Gothic legend of Ermanaric', *Euphorion: Zeitschrift für Literaturgeschichte*, 57 pp.28-43

ANTON, H.H., 1986. 'Verfassungsgeschichtliche Kontinuität und Wandlungen von der Spätantike zum hohen Mittelalter: das Beispiel Treir', *Francia*, 14 pp.1-25

ARCE, J., 1986. *El último siglo de la España romana: 284- 409*, 2nd ed., Madrid

ASHBURNER, W., 1910. 'The Farmer's Law I', *Journal of Hellenic Studies* XXX pp.85-108

ASHBURNER, W., 1912. 'The Farmer's Law II', *Journal of Hellenic Studies* XXXII pp.68-95

BABELON, E., CAGNAT, R., & REINACH, S., 1892-1913. *Atlas archéologique de la Tunisie: édition spéciale des cartes topographiques publiées par le ministère de la guerre, accompagnée d'un text explicatif*, Paris

BACH, E., 1935-1937. 'Théodoric: romain ou barbare?' *Byzantion* XXV-XXVII pp.413-20

BACHRACH, B.S., 1967. 'The Alans in Gaul', *Traditio* XXIII pp.476-89

BACHRACH, B.S., 1969. 'Another look at the barbarian settlement in southern Gaul', *Traditio* XXV pp.354-8

BACHRACH, B.S., 1972. *Merovingian Military Organization, 481-751*, Minneapolis

BALDWIN, B., 1979. 'The Purpose of the *Getica*', *Hermes* 107 pp.489-92

BALIL, A., 1965. 'Aspectos sociales del Bajo Imperio (s. IV – s. VI): los senadores hispánicos', *Latomus* XXIV pp.886-904

BARNES, T.D., 1974. 'Merobaudes on the imperial family', *Phoenix* XXVIII pp.314-19

BARNES, T.D., 1975. '*Patricii* under Valentinian III', *Phoenix* XXIX pp.155-70

BARNISH, S.J.B., 1983. 'The *Anonymous Valesianus* II as a source for the last years of Theoderic', *Latomus* XLII pp.572-96

BARNISH, S.J.B., 1984. 'The Genesis and Compilation of Cassiodorus' *Gothic History*', *Latomus*, XLIII pp.336-61

BARNISH, S.J.B., 1986. 'Taxation, land and barbarian settlement in the Western Empire', *Papers of the British School at Rome* LIV pp.170-95

BARNISH, S.J.B., 1988. 'Transformation and survival in the western senatorial aristocracy, c. AD 400-700', *Papers of the British School at Rome* LVI pp.120-55

BARNWELL, P.S., 1987. 'Kings, courts and the late Roman past, AD 395-c. 725', unpublished Ph.D. thesis, University of Leeds

BARNWELL, P.S., 1991. '*Epistula Hieronimi de gradus Romanorum*: an English School Book', *Historical Research* 64 pp.77-86

BESSELAAR, J.J. VAN DEN, 1945. *Cassiodorus Senator en zijn Variae: de hoveling, de diplomatieke oorkonden der Variae, de rhetor*, Nijmegen and Utrecht

BESSELAAR, J.J. VAN DEN, 1950. *Cassiodorus Senator: leven en werken van een staatsman en monnik uit de zesde eeuw*, Haarlem and Antwerp

BEYERLE, F., 1950. 'Zur Frühgeschichte der westgotisches Gesetzgebung', *Z.R.G., g.A.*, 67 pp.1-33

BEYERLE, F., 1954. 'Zur Textgestalt und Textgeschichte der Lex Burgundionum', *Z.R.G., g.A.*, 71 pp.22-54

BEYERLE, F., 1961. 'Das legislative Werk Chilperichs I', *Z.R.G., g.A.*, 78 pp.1-38

BIERBRAUER, V., 1973. 'Zur ostgotischen Geschichte in Italien', *Studi medievali*,

3rd ser. XIV pp.1-37

BINDING, K., 1868. *Das burgundisch-romanische Königreich (von 443-532 n. Chr.): eine reichs- und rechtsgeschichtliche Untersuchungen, einziger Band: Geschichte der burgundisch-romanischen Königreich*, Leipzig. Reprinted 1969.

BLOCH, M., 1927. 'Observations sur la conquête de la Gaule romaine par les rois francs', *Revue historique* 154 pp.161-78

BLONDEL, L., 1940a. 'Carouge, villa romaine et burgonde', *Genava* 18 pp.54-68

BLONDEL, L., 1940b. 'Praetorium, palais burgonde et château comtal', *Genava* 18 pp.69-87

BOAK, A.E.R., & DUNLAP, A.E., 1924. *Two Studies in Later Roman and Byzantine Administration*, New York (= *University of Michigan Studies*, Humanistic series, XIV)

BRADLEY, D.R., 1966. 'The composition of the Getica', *Eranos* LXIV pp.67-79

BRAUND, D.C., 1984. *Rome and the Friendly King: the character of client kingship*, London and Canberra

BRAUND, D.C., 1988. 'Introduction: the growth of the Roman Empire (241 BC – AD 193)', in D.C. Braund, ed., *The Administration of the Roman Empire (241 BC – AD 193)*, Exeter, pp.1-13

BRENNAN, B., 1985. 'Senators and social mobility in sixth-century Gaul', *Journal of Medieval History* 11 pp.145-61

BRUCK, E.F., 1953. 'Caesarius of Arles and the Lex Romana Visigothorum', *Studi in onore de Vincenzio Arangio-Ruiz nel XLV anno del suo insegnamento*, Naples, pp.201-17

BRULET, R., COULON, G., GHENNE-DUBOIS, M.-J., & VILVORDER, F., 1988. 'Nouvelles recherches à Tournai autour de la sépulture de Childéric', *Revue archéologique de Picardie* 3-4 pp.39-43 (= *Actes des VIIIᵉ journées internationales d'archéologie mérovingienne de Soissons, 19-22 juin 1986*)

BRULET, R., GHENNE-DUBOIS, M.-J., & COULON, G., 1986. 'Le Quartier Saint-Brice de Tournai à l'époque mérovingienne', *Revue du Nord* LXIX pp.361-9

BUCKLAND, W.W., 1932. *A Text-Book of Roman Law from Augustus to Justinian*, 2nd. ed., Cambridge

BURNS, T.A., 1978. 'Ennodius and the Ostrogothic settlement', *Classical Folia* 32 pp.153-68

BURNS, T.S., 1980. *The Ostrogoths, Kingship and Society*, Wiesbaden (= *Historia Einzelschriften* 36)

BURNS, T.S., 1984. *A History of the Ostrogoths*, Bloomington

BURY, J.B., 1910. '*Magistri scriniorum, antigraphês*, and *rhepherendarioi*', *Harvard Studies in Classical Philology* XXI pp.23-9

BURY, J.B., 1958. *History of the Later Roman Empire: from the death of Theodosius I to the death of Justinian*, 2 vols, New York (reprint edition)

CAMERON, ALAN, 1969. 'Theodosius the Great and the regency of Stilicho', *Harvard Studies in Classical Philology* LXXIII, pp.247-80

CAMERON, ALAN, 1970. *Claudian: poetry and propaganda at the court of Honorius*, Oxford

CAMERON, ALAN, & CAMERON, AVERIL, 1964. 'Christianity and tradition in the historiography of the Late Empire', *Classical Quarterly* n.s. 14 pp.316-28

CAMERON, ALAN, & SCHAUER, D., 1982. 'The last consul: Basilius and his Diptych', *Journal of Roman Studies* LXXII pp.126-45

CAMERON, AVERIL, 1968. 'Agathius on the early Merovingians', *Annali della scuola normale superiore di Pisa: lettere, storia e filosofia* XXXVII pp.95-140

CAMERON, AVERIL, 1985. *Procopius and the Sixth Century*, London

CARLOT, A., 1903. 'Étude sur le domesticus franc', Liège (= *Bibliothèque de la faculté de philosophie et lettres de l'Université de Liège*, fasc. XIII)

CASTRITIUS, H., 1972. 'Zur Sozialgeschichte der Heermeister des Westreichs nach der Mitte des 5. Jahrhunderts: Flavius Valila qui et Theodosius', *Ancient Society* 3 pp.233-43

CASTRITIUS, H., 1984. 'Zur Sozialgeschichte der Heermeister des Westreichs', *M.I.Ö.G.* 91 pp.1-33

CESA, M., 1982. 'Hospitalitas o altre "techniques of accommodation"? A proposito di un libro recente', *Archivio storico italiano* CXL pp.537-52

CESA, M., 1984. 'Überlegungen zur Föderatenfrage', *M.I.Ö.G.* 92 pp.307-16

CHADWICK, H., 1981. *Boethius: the consolations of music, logic, theology and philosophy*, Oxford

CHASTAGNOL, A., 1960. *La Préfecture urbaine à Rome sous le bas-empire*, Paris (=Publications de la faculté des lettres et sciences humaines d'Alger XXXIV)

CHASTAGNOL, A., 1963. 'L'Administration du diocèse italien au bas-empire', *Historia* XII pp.348-79

CHASTAGNOL, A., 1965. 'Les Espagnols dans l'aristocratie gouvernmentale à l'époque de Théodose', *Actes du colloque international sur les Empereurs romains d'Espagne, organisé à Madrid du 31 mars au 6 avril 1964*, pp.268-92

CHASTAGNOL, A., 1966. *Le Sénat romain sous le règne d'Odoacre: recherches sur l'épigraphie du Colisée au Ve siècle*, Bonn (= *Antiquitas* Reihe 3: Abhandlungen zur Vor- und Frühgeschichte, zur classischen und provinzial-römischen Archäologie)

CHASTAGNOL, A., 1970. 'La Prosopographie, méthode de recherche sur l'histoire du Bas-Empire', *Annales, économies, sociétés, civilisations* 25 pp.1229-35

CHASTAGNOL, A., 1973. 'Le Repli sur Arles des services administratifs gaulois en l'an 407 de notre ère', *Revue historique* 249 pp.23-40

CHEVRIER, G., & PIERI, G., 1969. *La Loi romaine des Burgondes*, Milan (= *Ius Romanum Medii Aevi* pars I, 2b *aa* δ)

CHIANEA, G., 1969. 'Les Idées politiques de Sidoine Apollinaire', *Revue historique du droit français et étranger*, 4th ser. XLVII pp.351-89

CHIFFLET, J.J., 1655. *Anastasis Childerici I Francorum regis, sive thesaurus sepulchralis Tornaci Nerviorum effossus et commentario illustratus*, Paris

CHRYSOS, E.K., 1981. 'Die Amaler-Herrschaft in Italien und das Imperium Romanum: der Vertragsentwurf des Jahres 535', *Byzantion* LI pp.430-74

CLAUDE, D., 1964. 'Untersuchungen zum frühfränkischen Comitat', *Z.R.G., g.A.*, 81 pp.1-79

CLAUDE, D., 1966. 'Zu Fragen frühfränkischer Verfassungsgeschichte', *Z.R.G., g.A.*, 83 pp.273-80

CLAUDE, D., 1971a. *Adel, Kirche und Königtum im Westgotenreich*, Sigmaringen (= *Vorträge und Forschungen*, Sonderband 8)

CLAUDE, D., 1971b. 'Millenarius und thiuphadus', *Z.R.G., g.A.* 88 pp.181-90

CLAUDE, D., 1972. 'Gentile und territoriale Staatsideen im Westgotenreich', *Frühmittelalterliche Studien* 6 pp.1-38

CLAUDE, D., 1973. 'Beiträge zur Geschichte der frühmittelalterlichen Königsschätze', *Early Medieval Studies* 7 (= Antikvariskt arkiv 54), Stockholm, pp.5-24

CLAUDE, D., 1974. 'Probleme der vandalischen Herrschaftsnachfolge', *Deutsches Archiv für Erforschung des Mittelalters*, 30 pp.329-55

CLAUDE, D., 1978a. 'Prosopographie des spanischen Suebenreichs', Francia, 6 pp.647-76

CLAUDE, D., 1978b. 'Universale und partikulare Züge in der Politik Theoderichs', Francia, 6 pp.19-58

CLAUDE, D., 1978c. 'Zur Königserhebung Theoderichs des Grossen', in K. Hauck and H. Mordek, ed., Geschichtsschreibung und geistiges Leben im Mittelalter: Festschrift für Heinz Löwe zum 65. Geburtstag, Cologne and Vienna, pp.1-13

CLAUDE, D., 1980. 'Die ostgotischen Königserhebungen', in H. Wolfram and F. Daim, ed., Die Völker an der mittleren und unteren Donau im fünften und sechsten Jahrhundert. Berichte des Symposions der Kommission für Frühmittelalterforschung 24 bis 27 Oktober 1978. Stift Zwettl, Niederöster-reich, Vienna, pp.149-86 (= Österreichische Akademie der Wissenschaften, philosophisch- historische Klasse, Denkschriften 145)

CLAUDE, D., 1988a. 'Der millenarius', in Wolfram and Schwarcz 1988, pp.17-20

CLAUDE, D., 1988b. 'Zur Ansiedlung barbarischer Föderaten in der ersten Hälfte des 5. Jahrhunderts', in Wolfram and Schwarcz 1988, pp.13-16

CLAUSS, M., 1980. Der magister officiorum in der Spätantike (4.-6. Jahrhundert): das Amt und sein Einfluss auf die kaiserliche Politik, Munich (= Vestigia: Beiträge zur alten Geschichte, Band 32)

CLEMENTE, G., 1968. La 'Notitia Dignitatum', Cagliari

CLOVER, F.M., 1971. Flavius Merobaudes: a translation and historical commentary, Transactions of the American Philosophical Society 61.1

CLOVER, F.M., 1978. 'The family and early career of Anicius Olybrius', Historia XXVII pp.169-96

CLOVER, F.M., 1989. 'Felix Carthago', in F.M. Clover and R.S Humphreys, ed., Tradition and Innovation in Late Antiquity, Madison, pp.129-69

COLLINS, R., 1983a. Early Medieval Spain: unity and diversity, 400-1000, London

COLLINS, R., 1983b. 'Theodebert I, "Rex Magnus Francorum" ', in P. Wormald, D. Bullough and R. Collins, ed., Ideal and Reality in Frankish and Anglo-Saxon Society: studies presented to J.M. Wallace-Hadrill, Oxford, pp.7-33

COOK, G.M., 1942. The Life of St Epiphanius by Ennodius: a translation with an introduction and commentary, Washington D.C.

COSENZA, M.E., 1905. Official Positions after the Time of Constantine, Lancaster Pa.

COURTOIS, C., 1951. 'Auteurs et scribes: remarques sur la chronique d'Hydace', Byzantion XXI pp.23-54

COURTOIS, C., 1954. Victor de Vita et son oeuvre: étude critique, Algiers

COURTOIS, C., 1955. Les Vandales et l'Afrique, Paris

COURTOIS, C., LESCHI, L., PERRAT, C., & SAUMAGNE, C., 1952. Tablettes Albertini: actes privés de l'époque vandale (fin du Vᵉ siècle), 2 vols, Paris

CROKE, B., 1983. 'The origins of the Christian World Chronicle', in Croke and Emmett 1983b, pp.116-31

CROKE, B., & EMMETT, A.M., 1983a. 'Historiography in Late Antiquity: an overview', in Croke and Emmett 1983b, pp.1-12

CROKE, B., & EMMETT, A.M., 1983b. History and Historians in Late Antiquity, Sydney

DAVIS, N., 1862. Ruined Cities within Numidian and Carthaginian Territories, London

DECLAREUIL, J., 1910. 'Des Comtes de cité à la fin du Ve siècle', *Revue historique du droit* 34 pp.794-836

DEMANDT, A., 1970. 'Magister Militum', in *Paulys Realencyclopädie der classischen Altertumswissenschaft*, Supplementband XII, Stuttgart, cols 553-790

DEMANDT, A., 1980. 'Der spätrömische Militäradel', *Chiron* 10 pp.609-36

DEMOUGEOT, E., 1978. 'Bedeutet das Jahr 476 das Ende des römischen Reichs in Okzident?' *Klio* 60 pp.371-81

DEMOUGEOT, E., 1981. 'La Carrière politique de Boèce', *Congresso internazionale di studi Boeziani: Atti*, Rome, pp.97-108

DESPOIS, J., 1955. *La Tunisie orientale, Sahel et basse steppe: étude géographique*, Paris

DIESNER, H.-J., 1966. 'Comes, domesticus, minister(ialis) im Vandalenreich', *Forschungen und Fortschritte*, 40 pp.174-6

DIESNER, H.-J., 1967. 'Mobilität und Differenzierung des Grundbesitzes im nordafrikanischen Vandalenreich', *Acta antiqua academiae scientiarum Hungaricae* 15 pp.347-58

DIESNER, H.-J., 1968. 'Reginus', in *Paulys Realencyclopädie der classischen Altertumswissenschaft*, Supplementband XI, Stuttgart, col. 1207

DIESNER, H.-J., 1971. 'Fragen der Sozialgeschichte und des frühen Feudalismus bei Gregor von Tours', *Philologus* 115 pp.52-7

DIESNER, H.-J., 1972. 'Das Buccellariertum von Stilicho und Sarus bis auf Aetius (454/455)', *Klio* 54 pp.321-50

DILL, S., 1926. *Roman Society in Gaul in the Merovingian Age*, London. Reprinted New York 1966.

DOEHAERD, R., 1949. 'La Richesse des mérovingiens', *Studi in onore de Gino Luzzatto*, 4 vols, Milan, vol. I pp.30-46

DOI, M., 1989. 'Bagaudes movement and German invasion', *Klio* 71 pp.344-52

D'ORS, A., 1956. 'La territorialidad del derecho de los visigodos', *Settimane ... III. I Goti in occidente: problemi*, Spoleto, pp.363-408

D'ORS, A., 1960. *El Codigo de Eurico: edición, palingensia, indices*, Rome and Madrid

DREW, K.F., 1949. *The Burgundian Code*, Philadelphia (reprinted 1972)

DREW, K.F., 1967. 'The barbarian kings as lawgivers and judges', in R.S. Hoyt, ed., *Life and Thought in the Early Middle Ages*, Minneapolis, pp.7-29

DUMOULIN, H., 1902. 'Le Gouvernement de Théodoric et la domination des Ostrogoths en Italie d'après les oeuvres d'Ennodius', *Revue historique* 78 pp.1-7, 241-65; 79 pp.1-22

DURLIAT, J., 1988. 'Le Salaire de la paix sociale dans les royaumes barbares (V^e-VIe siècles)', in Wolfram and Schwarcz 1988, pp.21-72

ENGEL, A., & SERRURE, R., 1964. *Traité numismatique du moyen âge*, 3 vols, Bologna (all references are to vol. I: *Depuis la Chute de l'empire romain d'occident jusqu'à la fin de l'époque carolingienne*)

ENSSLIN, W., 1930. 'Zum Heermeisteramt des spätrömischen Reichs I: Die Titulatur der magistri militum bis auf Theodosius I', *Klio* 23 pp.306-25

ENSSLIN, W., 1931a. 'Zum Heermeisteramt des spätrömischen Reiches II: Die magistri militum des 4. Jahrhunderts', *Klio* 24 pp.102-47

ENSSLIN, W., 1931b. 'Zum Heermeisteramt des spätrömischen Reiches III: Der magister utriusque militiae et patricius des 5. Jahrhunderts', *Klio* 24 pp.467-502

ENSSLIN, W., 1936a. 'Nochmals zu der Ehrung Chlodowechs durch Kaiser

Anastasius', *Historisches Jahrbuch* 56 pp.499-507

ENSSLIN, W., 1936b. 'Der Patricius Praesentalis im Ostgotenreich', *Klio* 29 pp.243-9

ENSSLIN, W., 1940. 'Zu den Grundlagen von Odoakers Herrschaft', *Hoffillerou zbornik. Naučni posvećni Viktorou Hoffilero o 60 godišnjici njegova života 19 veljače 1937. godine (Serta Hoffilleriana)*, 2 vols, Zagreb, vol. I pp.381-8

ENSSLIN, W., 1947. *Theoderich der Grosse*, Munich

ENSSLIN, W., 1954. 'Der Kaiser in der Spätantike', *Historische Zeitschrift* 177 pp.449-68

EVANS, J., 1965. 'St Germanus in Britain', *Archaeologia Cantiana* LXXX pp.175-85

EWIG, E., 1976a. 'Das Fortleben römischer Institutionen in Gallien und Germanien', in *idem, Spätantikes und fränkisches Gallien: gesammelte Schriften (1952-1973)*, 2 vols, Munich, vol. I pp.409-34

EWIG, E., 1976b. 'Die fränkischen Teilungen und Teilreiche (511-613)', in *idem, Spätantikes und fränkisches Gallien: gesammelte Schriften (1952-1973)*, 2 vols, Munich, vol. I pp.114-71

EWIG, E., 1983. *Die Merowinger und das Imperium*, Opladen (= Rheinisch-Westfälische Akademie der Wissenschaften, *Vorträge* G261)

FEIST, S., 1939. *Vergleichendes Wörterbuch der gotischen Sprache*, 3rd ed., Leiden.

FERRILL, A., 1986. *The Fall of the Roman Empire: the military explanation*, London

FISCHER, H., 1925. 'The belief in the continuity of the Roman Empire among the Franks of the fifth and sixth centuries', *Catholic Historical Review* 4 pp.536-53

FRANCISCI, P. DE, 1946. 'Per la storia del senato romano e della curia nei secoli V e VI', *Rendiconti della pontifica accademia d'archeologia* XXII pp.275-317

FRIDH, Å.J., 1956. *Terminologie et formules dans les 'Variae' de Cassiodore: études sur le développement du style administratif aux derniers siècles de l'antiquité*, Stockholm (= *Studia Graeca et Latina Gotheburgensia*, 2)

FUSTEL DE COULANGES, 1930. *Histoire des institutions politiques de l'ancienne France*, vol. 3, *La Monarchie franque*, 6th ed., Paris

GARCIA-GALLO, A., 1936-1941. 'Nacionalidad y territorialidad del derecho en la época visigoda', *Anuario de historia del derecho español* XIII pp.168-264

GARCIA-GALLO, A., 1940. 'Notas sobre el reparto de tierras entre visigodos y romanos', *Hispania: Revista española de historia* 18 pp.40-63

GARCIA-GALLO, A., 1974. 'Consideración crítica de los estudios sobre la legislación y la costumbre visigodas', *Anuario de historia del derecho español* XLIV pp.343-464

GAUDEMET, J., 1955. 'Survivances romaines dans le droit de la monarchie franque du Vᵉ siècle au Xᵉ siècle', *Tijdschrift voor Rechtsgeschiedenis* (= *Revue d'histoire du droit*) XXIII pp.149-206

GAUDEMET, J., 1965. *Le Bréviaire d'Alaric et les épitomes*, Milan (= *Ius Romanum Medii Aevi* pars I, 2b *aa* β)

GAUDIANZI, A., 1887. 'Die Entstehungszeit des Edictum Theoderici', *Z.R.G., g.A.*, 7 pp.29-52

GAUTIER, E.-F., 1932. *Genséric, roi des Vandales*, Paris

GEARY, P.J., 1988. *Before France and Germany: the creation and transformation of the Merovingian world*, New York and Oxford

GIARDINA, A., 1977. *Aspetti della burocrazia nel basso impero*, Rome

GIBERT, R., 1956. 'El reino visigodo y el particularismo español', *Settimane* ... *III. I Goti in occidente: problemi*, Spoleto, pp.537-83

GIBERT, R., 1968. 'La fundación del reino visigótico: una perspective histórica-jurídica', *Album J. Balon*, Namur, pp.1-25

GILLIARD, F.D., 1979. 'The senators of sixth-century Gaul', *Speculum* LIV pp.685-97

GLUCKMAN, M., 1966. *Custom and Conflict in Africa*, Oxford

GOFFART, W., 1963. 'The Fredegar problem reconsidered', *Speculum* XXXVIII pp.206-41

GOFFART, W., 1980. *Barbarians and Romans AD 418-584: the techniques of accommodation*, Princeton

GOFFART, W., 1982. 'Old and new in Merovingian taxation', *Past and Present* 96 pp.3-21

GOFFART, W., 1988a. 'After the Zwettl Conference: comments on the "Techniques of Accommodation" ', in Wolfram and Schwarcz 1988, pp.72-85

GOFFART, W., 1988b. *The Narrators of Barbarian History (AD 550-800): Jordanes, Gregory of Tours, Bede and Paul the Deacon*, Princeton

GRAHAM, A., 1886. *Remains of the Roman Occupation of North Africa with Special Reference to Tunisia*, extracted from the *Transactions of the Royal Institute of British Architects*, n.s. 2, London

GRAHN-HOEK, H., 1976. *Die fränkische Oberschicht im 6. Jahrhundert: Studien zu ihrer rechtlichen und politischen Stellung*, Sigmaringen (= *Vorträge und Forschungen*, Sonderband 21)

La Grande Encyclopédie, 31 vols, Paris 1886-1902

GRIFFE, É., 1964-1966. *La Gaule chrétienne à l'époque romaine*, 3 vols, Paris

HARRIES, J., 1986. 'Sozomen and Eusebius: the lawyer as church historian in the fifth century', in C. Holdsworth and T.P. Wiseman, ed., *The Inheritance of Historiography, 350-900*, Exeter, pp.45-52

HARRIES, J., 1988. 'The Roman imperial quaestor from Constantine to Theodosius II', *Journal of Roman Studies* LXXXVIII pp.148-72

HEATHER, P., 1989. 'Cassiodorus and the rise of the Amals: genealogy and the Goths under Hun domination', *Journal of Roman Studies* LXXIX pp.103-28

HENDY, M.F., 1972. 'Aspects of coin production and fiscal administration in the late Roman and early Byzantine period', *Numismatic Chronicle* 7/12 pp.117-35

HENDY, M.F., 1988. 'From public to private: the western barbarian coinages as a mirror of the disintegration of late Roman state structures', *Viator* 19 pp.29-78

HEUBERGER, R., 1929. 'Vandalische Reichskanzlei und Königsurkunden. Mit Ausblicken auf die Gesamtentwicklung der frühgermanischen Herrscherurkunde', *M.Ö.I.G.*, Ergänzungsband XI pp.76-113

HODGKIN, T., 1880-1899. *Italy and Her Invaders*, 8 vols, Oxford

HOLUM, K., 1982. *Theodosian Empresses: women and imperial domination in Late Antiquity*, Berkeley

HUMPHREY, J.H., 1980. 'Vandal and Byzantine Carthage: some new archaeological evidence', in J.G. Pedley, ed., *New Light on Ancient Carthage: papers of a symposium sponsored by the Kelsey Museum of Archaeology, the University of Michigan, marking the 50th anniversary of the Museum*, Michigan, pp.85-120

JAHN, A., 1874. *Die Geschichte der Burgundionen und Burgundiens bis zum Ende der I. Dynastie, in prüfing der Quellen und der Ansichten älteres und neuerer*

Historiker, 2 vols, Halle

JAMES, E., 1983. ' "Beati pacifici": bishops and the law in sixth-century Gaul', in J. Bossy, ed., *Disputes and Settlements: law and human relations in the West*, Cambridge, pp.25-46

JAMES, E., 1988a. 'Childéric, Syagrius et la disparition du royaume de Soissons', *Revue archéologique de Picardie* 3-4 pp.9-12 (*Actes des VIIIᵉ journées internationales d'archéologie mérovingienne de Soissons, 19-22 juin 1986*)

JAMES, E., 1988b. *The Franks*, Oxford

JONES, A.H.M., 1949. 'The Roman civil service (clerical and subclerical grades)', *Journal of Roman Studies* XXXIX pp.38-55

JONES, A.H.M., 1962. 'The constitutional position of Odoacer and Theoderic', *Journal of Roman Studies* LII pp.126-30

JONES, A.H.M., 1964. *The Later Roman Empire, 284-602: a social, economic and administrative survey*, 3 vols, Oxford 1964

JONES, A.H.M., MARTINDALE, J.R., & MORRIS, J., 1971. *The Prosopography of the Later Roman Empire: vol. I, AD 260-395*, Cambridge

JONES, M.E., & CASEY, P.J., 1988. 'The Gallic Chronicle restored: a chronology for the Anglo-Saxon invasions and the end of Roman Britain', *Britannia* XIX pp.367-98

KAZANSKI, M., AND PÉRIN, P., 1988. 'Le Mobilier funéraire de la tombe de Childéric Iᵉʳ: état de la question et perspectives', *Revue archéologique de Picardie* 3-4 pp.13-38 (= *Actes des VIIIᵉ journées internationales d'archéologie mérovingienne de Soissons, 19-22 juin 1986*)

KENT, J.P.C., 1966. 'Julius Nepos and the fall of the Western Empire', in *Corolla Memoriae Erich Swoboda dedicata*, Graz and Cologne, pp.146-50 (= *Römische Forschung in Niederösterreich* Band V)

KING, P.D., 1972. *Law and Society in the Visigothic Kingdom*, Cambridge

KRAUS, F.F., 1928. *Die Münzen Odovakars und des Ostgotenreiches in Italien*, Halle

KRAUTSCHIK, S., 1983. *Cassiodor und die Politik seiner Zeit*, Bonn

KURTH, G., 1893. *Histoire poétique des mérovingiens*, Paris

KURTH, G., 1919a. 'Les Comtes et les ducs de Tours au VIᵉ siècle', *idem*, *Études franques*, 2 vols, Paris, vol. I pp.205-25

KURTH, G., 1919b. 'De la Nationalité des comtes francs au VIᵉ siècle', *idem*, *Études franques*, 2 vols, Paris, vol. I pp.169-81

KURTH, G., 1919c. 'Les Ducs et les comtes d'Auvergne au VIᵉ siècle', *idem*, *Études franques*, 2 vols, Paris, vol. I pp.183-203

KURTH, G., 1919d. 'La Reine Brunehaut', *idem*, *Études franques*, 2 vols, Paris, vol. I pp.265-356

KURTH, G., 1919e. 'Les Sénateurs en Gaule au VIᵉ siècle', *idem*, *Études franques*, 2 vols, Paris, vol. II pp.97-115

LAISTNER, M.L.W., 1957. 'Some reflections on Latin historical writing in the fifth century', in C.G. Starr, ed., *The Intellectual Heritage of the Early Middle Ages: selected essays by M.L.W. Laistner*, Ithaca, pp.3-22. Reprinted New York 1966 and 1983

LAMMA, P., 1951. 'Recenti studi su Teoderico', *Convivium*, pp.296-311

LAPORTE, J., 1953. 'Le Royaume de Paris dans l'oeuvre hagiographique de Fortunat', *Études mérovingiennes: actes des journées de Poitiers 1ᵉʳ-3 mai 1952*, pp.169-76

LAROUSSE, 1878-1890. *Grand Dictionnaire universel du XIXᵉ siècle*, 17 vols, Paris

LEVEEL, P., 1953. 'Le Consulat de Clovis à Tours', *Études mérovingiennes: actes des journées de Poitiers, 1ᵉʳ-3 mai 1952*, pp.187-90

LEVILLAIN, L., 1933. 'La Crise des années 507-508 et les rivalités d'influence en Gaule de 508 à 514', *Mélanges offerts à M. Nicholas Iorga par ses amis de France et des pays de langue française*, Paris, pp.537-67

LEVY, E., 1942. 'Reflections on the first "reception" of Roman law in Germanic states', *American Historical Review* 48 pp.20-9

LEVY, E., 1951. *West Roman Vulgar Law: the law of property*, Philadelphia (= *Memoirs of the American Philosophical Society* XXIX)

LEVY, E., 1956. *Weströmische Vulgarrecht: das Obligationenrecht*, Weimar (= M. Kaser *et al.*, *Forschungen zum römischen Recht* VII)

LEWIS, A.R., 1976. 'The Dukes in the *Regnum Francorum*, AD 550-751', *Speculum* LI pp.381-410

LOT, F., 1928. 'Du Régime de l'hospitalité', *Revue belge de philologie et d'histoire* 7 pp.975-1011

LOT, F., 1929. 'La *Vita Viviani* et la domination visigothique en Aquitaine', in *Mélanges Paul Fournier*, Paris, pp.467-77

LOYEN, A., 1942. *Recherches historiques sur les panégyrics de Sidoine Apollinaire*, Paris (= *Bibliothèque de l'École des Hautes Études*, 285)

LOYEN, A., 1963. 'Résistants et collaborateurs en Gaule à l'époque des Grandes Invasions', *Bulletin de l'Association Guillaume Budé* XXIII pp.437-50

LOYEN, A., 1972. 'L'Oeuvre de Flavius Merobaudes et l'histoire de l'occident de 430 à 450', *Revue des études anciennes* 74 pp.153-74

LUISELLI, B., 1980. 'Cassiodoro e la storia dei Goti', *Atti dei convegni Lincei, 45: Passaggio dal mondo antico al medio evo da Teodosio a san Gregorio Magno, Roma 25-28 maggio 1977*, Rome, pp.225-53

MacCORMACK, S.G., 1981. *Art and Ceremony in Late Antiquity*, Berkeley and Los Angeles

McCORMICK, M., 1977. 'Odoacer, the Emperor Zeno, and the Rugian victory legation', *Byzantion* XLVII pp.212-22

McCORMICK, M., 1986. *Eternal Victory: triumphal rulership in late antiquity, Byzantium and the early medieval west*, Cambridge. Reprinted 1990.

MAGNOU-NORTIER, É., 1976. *Foi et fidélité: recherches sur l'évolution des liens personnels chez les Francs du VIIᵉ au IXᵉ siècle*, Toulouse (= Publications de l'Université de Toulouse-le Mirail, ser. A 28)

MARKUS, R.A., 1982. 'The End of the Roman Empire: a note on Eugippius, *Vita Sancti Severini*, 20', *Nottingham Medieval Studies* 26 pp.1-7

MARKUS, R.A., 1986. 'Chronicle and Theology: Prosper of Aquitaine', in C. Holdsworth and T.P. Wiseman, ed., *The Inheritance of Historiography, 350-900*, Exeter, pp.31-44

MARTINDALE, J.R., 1980. *The Prosopography of the Later Roman Empire: vol. 2, AD 395-527*, Cambridge

MARTROYE, M.F., 1911. 'Testament de Genséric', *Bulletin de la Société nationale des Antiquaires de France*, pp.232-6

MATHISEN, R.W., 1979. 'Resistance and Reconciliation: Majorian and the Gallic aristocracy after the fall of Avitus', *Francia*, 7 pp.597-627

MATHISEN, R.W., 1986. 'Patricians as diplomats in late antiquity', *Byzantinische Zeitschrift* LXXIX pp.35-49

MATTHEWS, J.F., 1970. 'Olympiodorus of Thebes and the history of the West (AD 407-425)', *Journal of Roman Studies*, LX pp.79-97

MATTHEWS, J.F., 1975. *Western Aristocracies and Imperial Court, AD 364-425*,

Oxford. Reprinted 1990.

MAYER, E., 1909. *Italienische Verfassungsgeschichte von der Gothenzeit bis zur Zunftherrschaft*, 2 vols, Leipzig

MAYER, E., 1925-1926. *Historia de las instituciones sociales y políticas de España y Portugal durante los siglos V al XIV*, 2 vols, Madrid

MERTA, B., 1988. 'Helenae conparanda regina – secuda Isebel. Darstellung von Frauen des merowingischen Hauses in frühmittelalterlichen Quellen', *M.I.Ö.G.* XCVI pp.1-32

MEYER, H., 1969. 'Der Regierrungsantritt Kaiser Majorians', *Byzantinische Zeitschrift* LXII pp.5-11

MILLAR, F., 1977. *The Emperor in the Roman World (31 BC – AD 337)*, London

MOMIGLANO, A., 1955. 'Cassiodorus and the Italian culture of his time', *Proceedings of the British Academy* XLI pp.207-45

MOMIGLIANO, A., 1956. 'Gli Anicii e la storiographia latina del VI° secolo d.C.', *Entretiens de la fondation G. Hardt* IV pp.249-76

MOMIGLIANO, A., 1973. 'La caduta senza rumore di un impero nel 476 d.C.', *Annali della Scuola Normale Superiore di Pisa, classe di lettere e filosofia*, 3rd. ser III pp.397-418

MOMMSEN, T., 1910. 'Ostgothische Studien', in *idem, Gesammelte Schriften* (8 vols, 1905-1913) Berlin, vol. VI pp.362-84

MOORHEAD, J., 1978. 'Boethius and Romans in Ostrogothic service', *Historia* XXVII pp.604-12

MOORHEAD, J., 1983a. 'Italian loyalties during Justinian's Gothic war', *Byzantion* LII pp.575-96

MOORHEAD, J., 1983b. 'The last years of Theoderic', *Historia* XXXII pp.106-20

MOORHEAD, J., 1984a. 'The Decii under Theoderic', *Historia* XXXIII pp.107-15

MOORHEAD, J., 1984b. 'Theoderic, Zeno and Odoacer', *Byzantinische Zeitschrift* LXXVII pp.261-6

MOORHEAD, J., 1986. 'Culture and power among the Ostrogoths' *Klio* 68 pp.112-23

MOORHEAD, J., 1987. 'Libertas and the Nomen Romanum in Ostrogothic Italy', *Latomus* XLVI pp.161-8

MOROSI, R., 1977. 'L'Officium dal prefetto del praetorio nel VI secolo', *Romanobarbarica: contributi allo studio dei rapporti culturali tra mondo latino e mondo barbarico* 2 pp.104-48

MOROSI, R., 1981. 'I *saiones*, speciale agenti di polizia presso i Goti', *Athenaeum*, n.s. 59 pp.150-65

MUHLBERGER, S., 1983. 'The Gallic Chronicle of 452 and its authority for British events', *Britannia* XIV pp.23-34

MUHLBERGER, S., 1990. *The Fifth-Century Chronicles: Prosper, Hydatius and the Gallic Chronicler of 452*, Leeds

MURRAY, A.C., 1986. 'The position of the "Graphio" in the constitutional history of Merovingian Gaul', *Speculum* LXI pp.787-805

MURRAY, A.C., 1988. 'From Roman to Frankish Gaul: "Centenarii" and "Centenae" in the administration of the Merovingian kingdom', *Traditio* XLIV pp.59-100

MUSSET, L., 1975. *The Germanic Invasions: the making of Europe AD 400-600*, London

NÄFF, B., 1990. 'Das Zeitbewusstein des Ennodius und der Untergang Roms', *Historia* XXXIX pp.100-23

NELSON, J.L., 1978. 'Queens as Jezebels: the careers of Brunhild and Balthild in

Merovingian history', in D. Baker, ed., *Medieval Women*, Oxford, pp.31-77 (= *Studies in Church history*, Subsidia 1)

NESSELHAUF, H., 1938. *Die spätrömische Verwaltung der gallish-germanischen Länder,* Berlin (= *Abhandlungen der preussischen Akademie der Wissenschaften, philosophisch-historische Klasse*, 1938.2)

O'DONNELL, J.J., 1979. *Cassiodorus*, Berkeley, Los Angeles & London

O'DONNELL, J.J., 1981. 'Liberius the Patrician', *Traditio* XXXVII pp.31-72

O'DONNELL, J.J., 1982. 'The Aims of Jordanes', *Historia* XXXI pp.223-40

O'FLYNN, J.M., 1983. *Generalissimos of the Western Roman Empire*, Edmonton

OOST, S.I., 1968. *Galla Placidia Augusta: a biographical essay*, Chicago and London

O'SULLIVAN, T.D., 1978. *The 'De Excidio' of Gildas: its authenticity and date*, Leiden

The Oxford Latin Dictionary, Oxford 1968

PALLU DE LESSERT, A.C., 1892. *Vicaires et comtes d'Afrique de Dioclétian à l'invasion vandale*, Constantine (Extracted from *Recueil des notices et mémoires de la Société archéologique de Constantine* XXVI 1890-91)

PEDERSEN, F.S., 1976. *Late Roman Public Professionalism*, Odense

PICOTTI, G.B., 1928. 'Il "Patricius" nell'ultima età imperiale e nei primi regni barbarici', *Archivio storico italiano* LXXXVI pp.3-80

PICOTTI, G.B., 1939. 'Sulle relazioni fra re Odoacre e il senato e la chiesa de Roma', *Rivista storica italiana*, 5th ser., 4 pp.363-86

PIETRI, C., 1966. 'Le Sénat, le peuple chrétien et les partis du cirque à Rome sous le pape Symmaque (498-514)', *Mélanges d'archéologie et d'histoire de l'École française à Rome* 78 pp.123-39

PIGANIOL, A., 1947. *L'Empire chrétien (325-395)*, Paris (G. Glotz, ed., *Histoire générale: histoire romaine IV.2*)

PIRENNE, H., 1933. 'Le Trésor des rois mérovingiens', in *Festskrift til Halvdan Koht på sekstiårsdagen 7 de Juli 1933*, Oslo pp.71-8

PIRENNE, H., 1934. 'De l'État de l'instruction des laïques à l'époque mérovingienne', *Revue bénédictine* XLIV pp.164-77

PROU, M., 1892. *Les Monnaies mérovingiennes*, Paris

REINHART, W., 1951. 'Über die Territorialität der westgotischen Gesetzbücher', *Z.R.G., g.A.*, 69 pp.348-54

REINHART, W., 1952. *Historia general del reino hispanico de los Suevos*, Madrid (=Publicaciones del seminario de historia primitiva del hombre: monografías, 1)

REYDELLET, M., 1981. *La Royauté dans la littérature latine de Sidoine Apollinaire à Isidore de Séville*, Rome

RICHÉ, P., 1962. *Éducation et culture dans l'occident barbare, VIᵉ-VIIIᵉ siècles*, 3rd ed., Paris

RICHÉ, P., 1965. *Enseignement du droit en Gaule du VIᵉ au IXᵉ siècle*, Milan (= *Ius Romanum Medii Aevi* pars 1, 5b, bb)

ROSENBLUM, M., 1961. *Luxorius: a Latin poet among the Vandals*, New York and London

SAITTA, B., 1977. *I Burgundi (413-534)*, Catania

SALAMA, P., 1951. *Les Voies romaines de l'Afrique du nord*, Algiers

SALWAY, P., 1981. *Roman Britain*, Oxford

SANCHEZ-ALBORNOZ Y MENDUIÑA, C., 1959. 'El gobierno de las ciudades en España del siglo V al X', *Settimane ... VI. La città nell'alto medioevo*, Spoleto, pp.359-91

SANCHEZ-ALBORNOZ Y MENDUIÑA, C., 1962. 'Pervivencia y crisis de la tradición jurídica romana en la España Goda', *Settimane* ... *IX. Il passaggio dall'antichità al medioevo in occidente*, Spoleto, pp.128-99

SANCHEZ-ALBORNOZ Y MENDUIÑA, C., 1971. 'Ruina y extinción del municipio romana en España e instituciones que le reemplazan', in *idem, Estudios Visigodos*, Rome pp.9-147

SANTIFALLER, L., 1952. 'Die Urkunde des Königs Odovakar von Jahre 489 (mit Faksimile)', *M.I.Ö.G.* 60 pp.1-30

SCHADE, O., 1872-1882. *Altdeutsches Wörterbuch*, 2 vols, Halle

SCHLESINGER, W., 1956. 'Über germanischen Heerkönigtum', in T. Mayer, ed., *Das Königtum, seine geistigen und rechtlichen Grundlagen*, Lindau and Constance, pp.105-41 (= *Vorträge und Forschungen*, III)

SCHMIDT, L., 1925. 'Die *comites Gothorum*. Ein Kapitel zur ostgotischen Verfassungsgeschichte', *M.Ö.I.G.* 40 pp.127-34

SCHMIDT, L., 1934. *Geschichte der deutschen Stämme bis zur Ausgang der Völkerwanderung*, 2nd ed., 2 vols, Munich

SCHMIDT, L., 1942. *Geschichte der Wandalen*, 2nd ed., Munich

SCHÖNE, G., 1856. *Die Amstgewalt der fränkischen maiores domus*, Brunswick

SCHRAMM, P.E., 1954-1956. *Herrschaftszeichen und Staatssymbolik*, 3 vols, Stuttgart

SCHUBERT, W., 1969. 'Die rechtliche Sonderstellung der Dekurionen (Kurialen) in der Kaisergesetzgebung des 4.-6. Jahrhunderts', *Zeitschrift der Savigny-Stiftung für Rechtsgeschichte, romanistische Abteilung* 86 pp.287-333

SEECK, O., 1897-1920. *Geschichte des Untergangs der antiken Welt*, 6 vols, Berlin

SEECK, O., 1905. 'Domesticus', in *Paulys Realencyclopädie der classischen Altertumswissenschaft*, vol. V, Stuttgart, cols 1296-9

SEECK, O., 1919. *Regesten der Kaiser und Päpste für die Jahre 311 bis 476 n. Chr.: Vorarbeit zu einer Prosopographie der christlichen Kaiserzeit*, Stuttgart. Reprinted Frankfurt a.M. 1964

SELLE-HOSBACH, F., 1974. *Prosopographie merowingischer Amtsträger in der Zeit von 511-613*, Bonn

SINNIGEN, W.G., 1957. *The Officium of the Urban Prefect during the Later Roman Empire*, Rome (= Papers and Monographs of the American Academy in Rome 17)

SINNIGEN, W.G., 1959a. 'Two branches of the late Roman secret service', *American Journal of Philology* LXXX pp.238-54

SINNIGEN, W.G., 1959b. 'The Vicarius Urbis Romae and the Urban Prefecture', *Historia* VIII pp.97-112

SINNIGEN, W.G., 1963. '*Comites consistoriani* in Ostrogothic Italy', *Classica et medievalia* XXIV pp.158-65

SINNIGEN, W.G., 1965. 'Administrative shifts of competence under Theoderic', *Traditio* XXI pp.456-67

SIRAGO, V.A., 1961. *Galla Placidia e la transformazione politica dell'occidente*, Louvain (= Université de Louvain, *Recueil de travaux d'histoire et de philologie*, 4th ser., 25)

SKEAT, W.W., 1868. *A Moeso-Gothic Glossary*, London

SMALLWOOD, E.M., 1976. *The Jews under Roman rule: from Pompey to Diocletian*, Leiden

SPRANDEL, R., 1957. 'Dux und Comes in der Merovingerzeit', *Z.R.G., g.A.*, 74 pp.41-84

SPRANDEL, R., 1965. 'Bemerkungen zum frühfränkischen Comitat', *Z.R.G., g.A.*,

82 pp.288-91

STAFFORD, P.A., 1983. *Queens, Concubines and Dowagers: the king's wife in the early middle ages*, London

STAUBACH, N., 1983. 'Germanisches Königtum und lateinischen Literatur vom fünften bis zum siebten Jahrhundert. Bemerkungen zum Buch von Marc Reydellet, La Royauté dans la littérature latine de Sidoine Apollinaire à Isidore de Séville', *Frühmittelalterliche Studien* 17 pp.1-54

STEIN, E., 1949-1959. *Histoire du bas-empire*, 2 vols, Paris

STEVENS, C.E., 1933. *Sidonius Apollinaris and His Age*, Oxford

STROHEKER, K.F., 1937. *Eurich, König der Westgoten*, Stuttgart

STROHEKER, K.F., 1948. *Die senatorische Adel im spätantiken Gallien*, Tübingen

STROHEKER, K.F., 1965a. 'Die politische Zerfall des römischen Westens', in *idem*, *Germanentum und Spätantike*, Zurich and Stuttgart, pp.88-100

STROHEKER, K.F., 1965b. 'Die Senatoren bei Gregor von Tours', in *idem*, *Germanentum und Spätantike*, Zurich and Stuttgart, pp.192-206

STROHEKER, K.F., 1965c. 'Spanische Senatoren der spätrömischen und westgotischen Zeit', im *idem*, *Germanentum und Spätantike*, Zurich and Stuttgart, pp.54-87

SUNDWALL, J., 1919. *Abhandlungen zur Geschichte des ausgehenden Römertums*, Helsingfors (= *Öfersigt af Finska Vetenskaps – Societatens Förhandlinger* Bd LX 1917-1918, Afd. B. N:O 2)

TARDI, D., 1927. *Fortunat: étude sur un dernier représentant de la poésie latine dans la Gaule mérovingienne*, Paris

TARDIF, J., 1881. *Études sur les institutions politiques et administratives de la France: période mérovingienne*, Paris

TARRADELL, M., 1978. 'El govern de la pre-Catalunya soto l'imperi Romà i el regne visigòtic', *Cuadernos de historia economica de Cataluna* 18 pp.9-21

TEITLER, H.C., 1985. *Notarii and Exceptores: an inquiry into role and significance of shorthand writers in the imperial and ecclesiastical bureaucracy of the Roman Empire (from the early Principate to c. 450 AD)*, Amsterdam

THIBAULT, F., 1901-1902. 'L'Impôt direct dans les royaumes des Ostrogoths, des Wisigoths et des Burgondes', *Nouvelle Revue historique de droit français et étranger* 25 pp.698-728, 26 pp.32-48

THOMPSON, E.A., 1969. *The Goths in Spain*, Oxford

THOMPSON, E.A., 1982. *Romans and Barbarians: the decline of the Western Empire*, Madison and London

THOMPSON, E.A., 1984. *St Germanus of Auxerre and the end of Roman Britain*, Woodbridge

TWYMAN, B.L., 1970. 'Aetius and the aristocracy', *Historia* XIX pp.480-503

VAN DAM, R., 1985. *Leadership and Community in late Antique Gaul*, Berkeley and Los Angeles

VASSILI, L., 1938. 'Il "dux" Vincenzo e l'incursione gotica in Italia nell'anno 473', *Rivista di filologia* LXVI pp.56-9

VERCAUTEREN F., 1978. 'Étude critique d'un diplôme attribué à Chilpéric I', *Études d'histoire médiévale: recueil d'articles du Professeur Vercauteren publiés par le Crédit Communal de Belgique*, Brussels, pp.629-59

VISMARA, G., 1956. 'Romani e Goti di fronte al diritto nel regno ostrogoto', *Settimane … III. I Goti in occidente: problemi*, Spoleto, pp.409-63

VISMARA, G., 1967. *Edictum Theoderici*, Milan (= *Ius Romanum Medii Aevi* pars 1, 2b *aa* α)

VISMARA, G., 1972-1973. 'Gli editti dei re Vandali', in *Studi in onore di Gaetano Scherillo*, 3 vols, Milan, pp.849-78

VYVER, A. VAN DE, 1931. 'Cassiodore et son oeuvre', *Speculum*, VI pp.244-92

WAITZ, G., 1860-1878. *Deutsche Verfassungsgeschichte*, 8 vols, Kiel. Reprinted Graz 1953-1955

WAITZ, G., 1896. *Abhandlungen zur Deutsches Verfassungs- und Rechtsgeschichte*, Göttingen

WAL, N. VAN DER, 1981. '*Edictum* und *lex edictalis*: Form und Inhalt der Kaisergesetze im spätrömischen Reich', *Revue internationale des droits de l'antiquité*, 3rd ser. 28 pp.277-313

WALLACE-HADRILL, J.M., 1955. Review of *M.G.H., Legum sectio I. Legum nationum Germanicarum, tomi III pars II: Lex Ribuaria*, ed. F. Beyerle and R. Buchner (1954), in *English Historical Review* LXX pp.440-3

WALLACE-HADRILL, J.M., 1962. *The Long-Haired Kings*, London

WALLACE-HADRILL, J.M., 1971. *Early Germanic Kingship in England and on the Continent*, Oxford

WALLACE-HADRILL, J.M., 1975. 'Gregory of Tours and Bede: their views on the personal qualities of kings', in *idem, Early Medieval History*, Oxford, pp.96-114

WARD-PERKINS, B., 1984. *From Classical Antiquity to the Middle Ages: urban public buildings in northern and central Italy* AD *300-850*, Oxford

WARMINGTON, B.H., 1954. *The North African Provinces from Diocletian to the Vandal Conquest*, Cambridge

WELLS, C.M., 1984. 'Quelques remarques sur Carthage à la veille des invasions arabes', *Actes du Iᵉʳ colloque international sur l'histoire et l'archéologie de l'Afrique du nord: réuni dans le cadre du 106ᵉ congrès national des sociétés savants (Perpignan 14-18 avril 1981)*, pp.55-63 (= *Bulletin archéologique du C.T.H.S.*, n.s. 17 fasc. B)

WERNER, K.F., 1979. 'Important noble families in the kingdom of Charlemagne – a prosopographical study of the relationship between king and nobility in the early middle ages', in T. Reuter, ed., *The Medieval Nobility – studies on the ruling classes of France and Germany from the sixth to the twelfth centuries*, Amsterdam, pp.137-202

WERNER, K.F., 1984a. 'Conquête franque de la Gaule ou changement de régime?' in *idem, Vom Frankenreich zur Entfaltung Deutschlands und Frankreichs, Ursprünge-Strukturen-Beziehungen. Ausgewählte Beiträge. Festgabe zu seinem sechzigsten Geburtstag*, Sigmaringen, pp.1-11

WERNER, K.F., 1984b. *Les Origines (avant l'an mil)*, Paris (= J. Favier, ed., *Histoire de France* I)

WERNER, K.F., 1985. 'Qu'est-ce que la Neustrie?' in P. Périn and L.-C. Feffer, ed., *La Neustrie: les pays au nord de la Loire de Dagobert à Charles le Chauve (VIIᵉ – IXᵉ siècles)*, Rouen, pp.29-38

WERNER, K.F., 1988. 'De Childéric à Clovis: antécédants et conséquences de la bataille de Soissons en 486', *Revue archéologique de Picardie* 3-4 pp.3-7 (= *Actes des VIIIᵉ journées internationales d'archéologie mérovingienne de Soissons (19-22 juin 1986)*

WES, M.A., 1967. *Das Ende des Kaisertums im Westen des römischen Reichs*, The Hague

WESNER, G., 1936. 'Quaestor', in *Paulys Realencyclopädie der classischen Altertumswissenschaft* XXIV, Stuttgart, cols 801-28

WICKHAM, C.J., 1981. *Early Medieval Italy: central power and local society*,

400-1000, London

WIEACKER, F., 1964. *Recht und Gesellschaft in der Spätantike*, Stuttgart

WIGHTMAN, E.M., 1985. *Gallia Belgica*, London

WOLFRAM, H., 1967. *Intitulatio I: lateinische Königs- und Fürstentitel bis zum Ende des 8. Jahrhunderts*, Graz, Vienna and Cologne (*M.I.Ö.G.* Ergänzungsband XXI)

WOLFRAM, H., 1979. 'Gotisches Königtum und römisches Kaisertum von Theodosius dem Grossen bis Justinian I', *Frühmittelalterliche Studien*, 13 pp.1-28

WOLFRAM, H., 1983. 'Zur Ansiedlung reichsangehöriger Föderaten: Erklärungsversuche und Forschungsziele', *M.I.Ö.G.*, 91 pp.5-36

WOLFRAM, H., 1988. *History of the Goths*, Berkeley

WOLFRAM, H., & SCHWARCZ, A., 1988. *Anerkennung und Integration. Zu den wirtschaftlichen Grundlagen der Völkerwanderungszeit 400-600. Berichte des Symposions der Kommission für Frühmittelalterforschung 7. bis 9. Mai 1986 Stift Zwettl, Niederösterreich* (= *Österreichische Akademie der Wissenschaften, philosophisch-historische Klasse*, Denkschriften 193)

WOOD, I.N., 1977. 'Kings, kingdoms and consent', in P.H. Sawyer and I.N. Wood, ed., *Early Medieval Kingship*, Leeds, pp.6-29

WOOD, I.N., 1980. 'Avitus of Vienne: religion and culture in the Auvergne and the Rhône valley, 470-530', unpublished D.Phil. thesis, Corpus Christi College, University of Oxford

WOOD, I.N., 1984. 'The end of Roman Britain: Continental evidence and parallels', in M. Lapidge and D. Dumville, ed., *Gildas: new approaches*, Woodbridge, pp.1-23

WOOD, I.N., 1985. 'Gregory of Tours and Clovis', *Revue belge de philologie et d'histoire* 63 pp.249-72

WOOD, I.N., 1986. 'Disputes in late fifth- and sixth-century Gaul: some problems', in W. Davies and P. Fouracre, ed., *The Settlement of Disputes in Early Medieval Europe*, Cambridge, pp.7-22

WOOD. I.N., 1987. 'The fall of the Western Empire and the end of Roman Britain', *Britannia* XVIII pp.251-62

WORMALD, P., 1976. 'The decline of the Western Empire and the survival of its aristocracy', *Journal of Roman Studies* LXVI pp.217-26

WORMALD, P., 1977. '*Lex scripta* and *verbum regis*: legislation and Germanic kingship from Euric to Cnut', in P.H. Sawyer and I.N. Wood, ed., *Early Medieval Kingship*, Leeds, pp.105-38

WROTH, W., 1911. *Catalogue of the Coins of the Vandals, Ostrogoths and Lombards, and of the Empires of Thessalonica, Nicaea and Trebizond, in the British Museum*, London

ZECCHINI, G., 1981. 'La politica degli Anicii nel V secolo', *Congresso internazionali de studi Boeziana: Atti*, Rome, pp.123-38

ZIMMERMANN, O.J., 1944. *The Late Latin Vocabulary of the Variae of Cassiodorus, with special advertance to the technical terminology of administration: a dissertation*, Washington D.C.

Index

In view of the large amount of material included in the book merely by way of illustration, this index is simply a selective guide to significant discussions of the main sources and principal themes.